Invest In Company Evolution

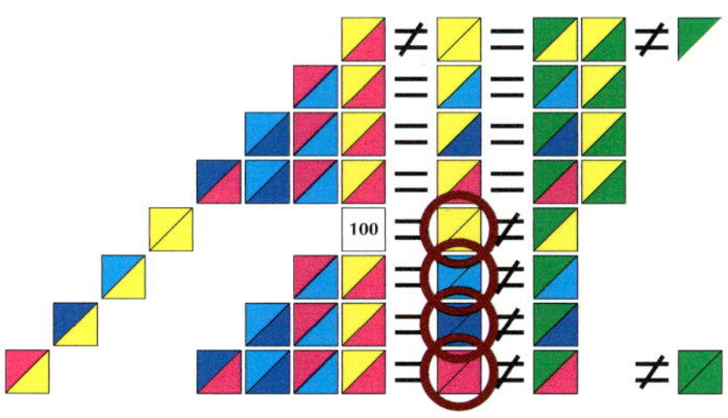

GAAP Structure

MICROSOFT (MSFT)

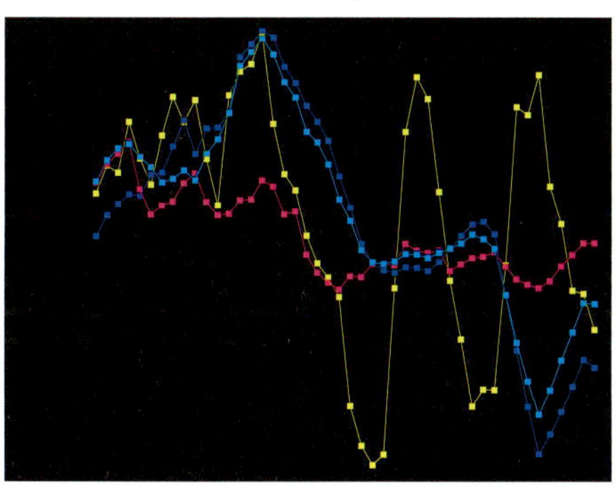

Income Growth
Equity Growth
Revenue Growth
Assets Growth

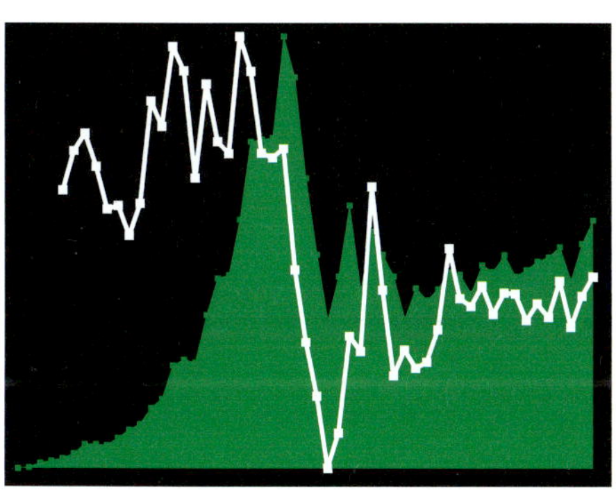

Share Price Growth (white)—Share Price

> Great investment opportunities come around when excellent companies are surrounded by unusual circumstances that cause the stock to be misappraised.
>
> Warren E. Buffett—*Fortune*, December 19, 1988

Invest In Company Evolution pictures company finances. The *front cover* of this book charts the shapes of great investment opportunities, excellent companies, unusual circumstances, and misappraised stocks. The rest of the book explains its *front cover* tools by expanding on one structure, one table, and one chart. Don't gather data or make charts. Just take a few hours to read and think.

Evaluating company performance is scattered and complex. We use *Generally Accepted Accounting Principles (GAAP)* to derive a structure of *Securities and Exchange Commission (SEC)* data. *GAAP Structure* unites accounting measures to form evaluation measures. Its colored buttons relate these measures to form equations. Equations enable you to systematically explore the health and progress of a company.

We reduce equations to four growth curves circled in *GAAP Structure*. Then, we compare them in a four-growth chart. Wall Street's current habit is to pay for evolution. As you see in the early phase, when company growth accelerated, *Share Price Growth (white)* accelerated. *Share Price (green)* was an unexpected great investment opportunity.

Use this *GAAP Structure* to define, chart, and understand company performance: track companies, talk with advisors, and make better informed investment decisions. Use it to understand limits to factors of growth, a growth hierarchy, criteria you enter in stock screening tools, rankings from stock ranking tools, and meanings of advice.

This book is for people who enjoy thinking their way to true answers. It solves investment riddles, so you can now apply the measures in shelves of investment strategy books. An e-book version enables quick reference, printing, and electronic education—*www.seroia.com*

You can cause an investment revolution by asking companies to begin *Quarterly* and *Annual Reports* with a downloadable *Quarterly Data Summary* back to 1993 in *XBRL* (useful) format. Read the first page of every chapter to unfold a story of evolution. Then, snap into place concepts that help us recognize great investment opportunities.

Contents

Simple design, intense content.

Edward R. Tufte—*Scientific American, April, 2005*

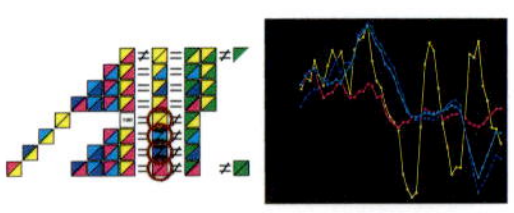

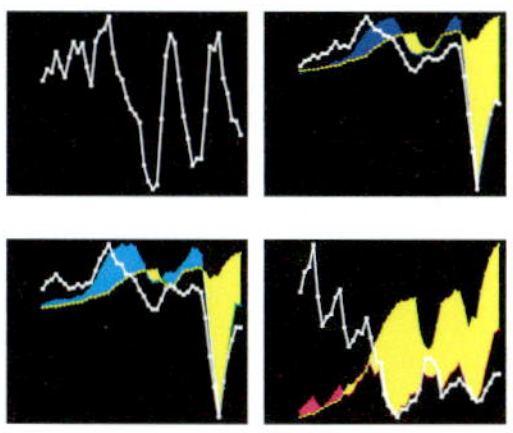

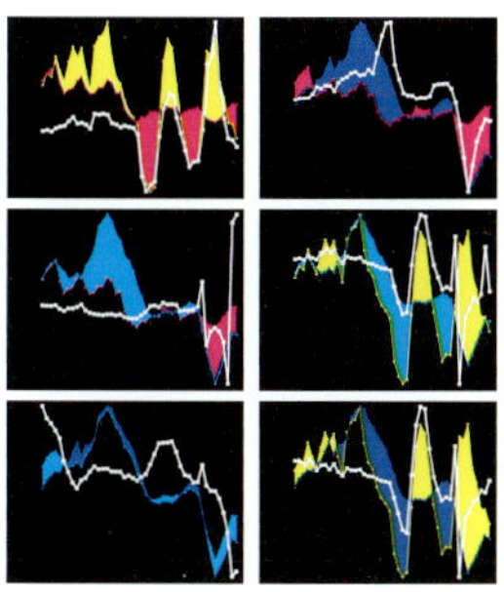

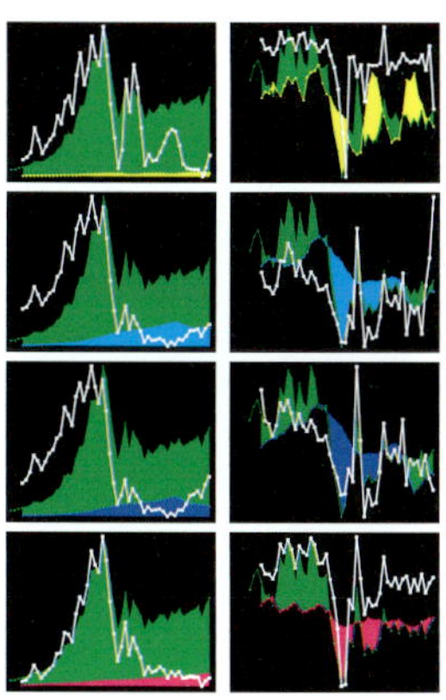

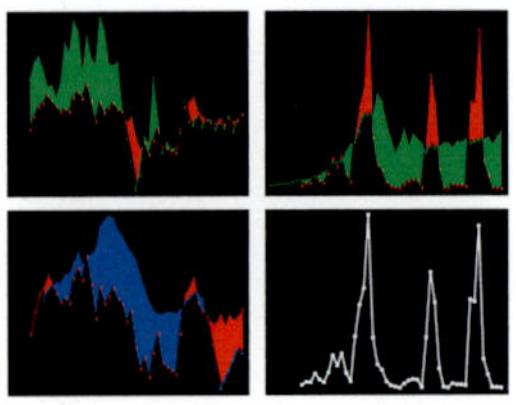

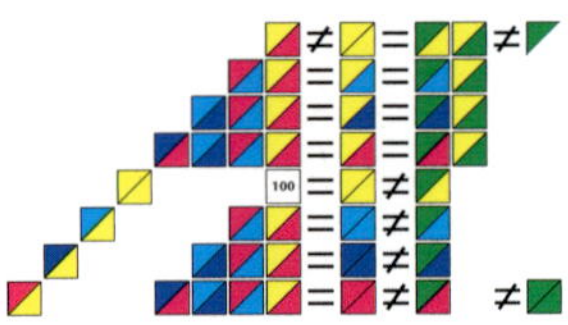

AGAINST THE GODS
BENJAMIN GRAHAM
THE INTELLIGENT INVESTOR
INVESTMENT BIKER
PRACTICAL SPECULATION
A Random Walk Down Wall Street
FOOLED BY RANDOMNESS
THE FIVE RULES FOR SUCCESSFUL STOCK INVESTING
Gold
Marc Faber

GAAP Structure—Fundamental Trends Datastreams

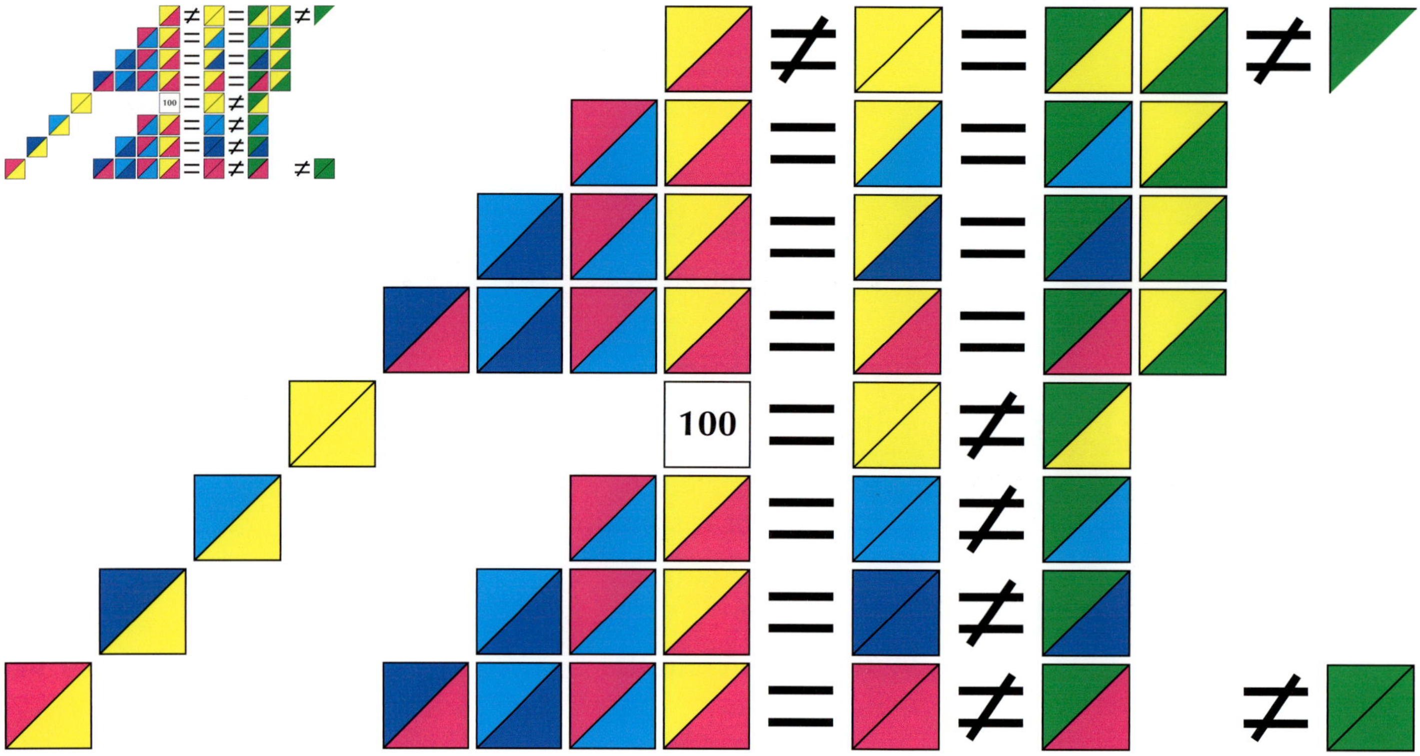

1 Fundamental Trends

DATASTREAMS *MICROSOFT*

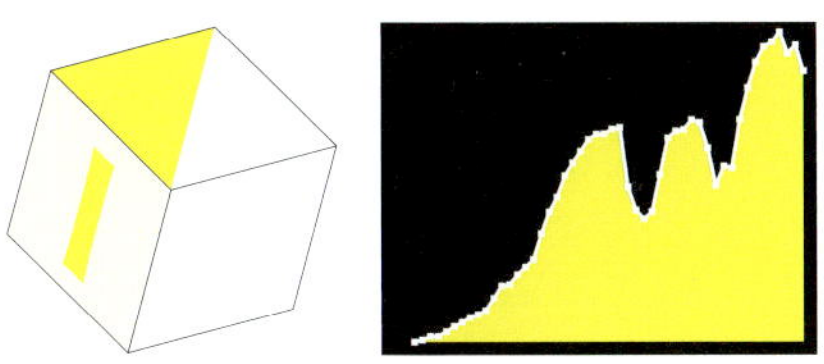

Income

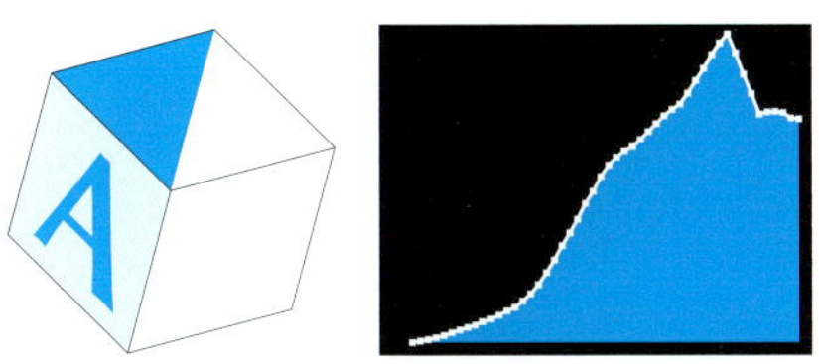

Assets

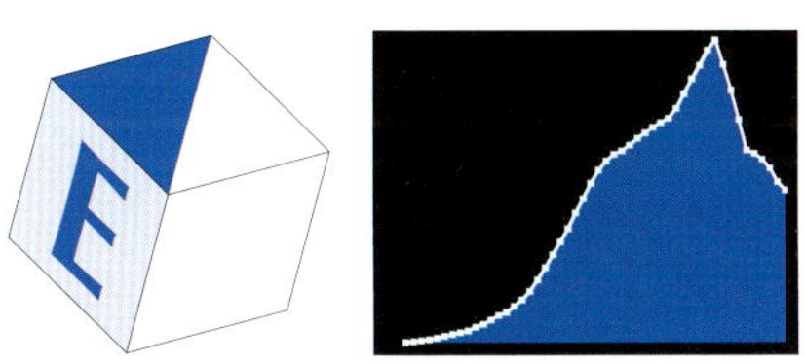

Equity

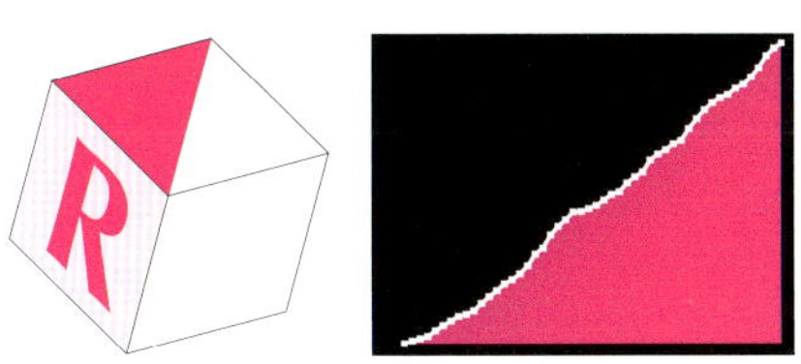

Revenue

Nature cannot be reduced to fundamental entities.... It has to be understood entirely through its self-consistency, with its components being consistent both with one another and with themselves.

Fritjof Capra—*Physicist—The Tao of Physics*

We begin simplifying the financial puzzle by mathematically relating the four fundamental datastreams—income, assets, equity, revenue, and price for public companies—to derive *GAAP Structure* on the facing page, explained on page 87. We need only five colors.

These fundamentals define the datastreams for our *inside front cover Quarterly Data Summary*. We use those datastreams to calculate and chart each measure that supports informed investment decisions.

In this chapter we study the fundamentals. In each of four sections we show how to use original datastreams as elements to build related trend charts. We then show how events do or don't affect each trend. Picturing fundamental datastreams reveals a company's basic characteristics. Data become Buffett's "aid to business thinking".

We need these fundamentals to apply a strategy Robert G. Hagstrom describes in *The Warren Buffett Way*: "The best business to own is one that over time can employ large amounts of capital at very high rates of return." Assets and equity on the left measure "capital". The three income *Ratio Trends* on page 21 measure "rates of return". †

If you define fundamentals as revenue and income (that summarize their contributors on an *income statement*), and assets and equity (that summarize their contributors on a *balance sheet*), then these four are the only fundamentals reported by public companies to the United States *Securities and Exchange Commission (SEC)*, complying with United States *Generally Accepted Accounting Principles (GAAP)*.

Fundamentals are elements of *front cover* charts. You'll need only those few charts—systematically related by the *GAAP Structure* of *SEC* data—to reveal much of a company's story: its evolution, its unique personality, and its "great investment opportunities".

† Trend charts and tables work with any money: gourdes, yuan, yen, dollars, digital.

Income

MICROSOFT

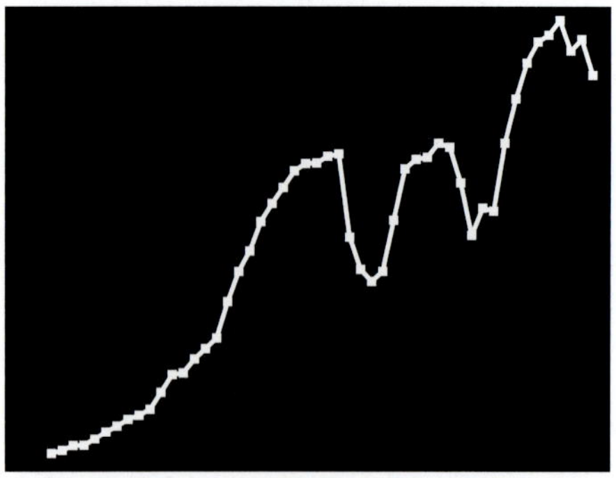

Income

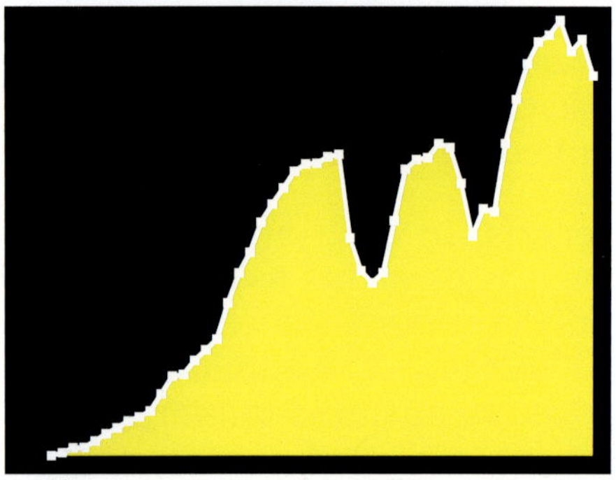

Income

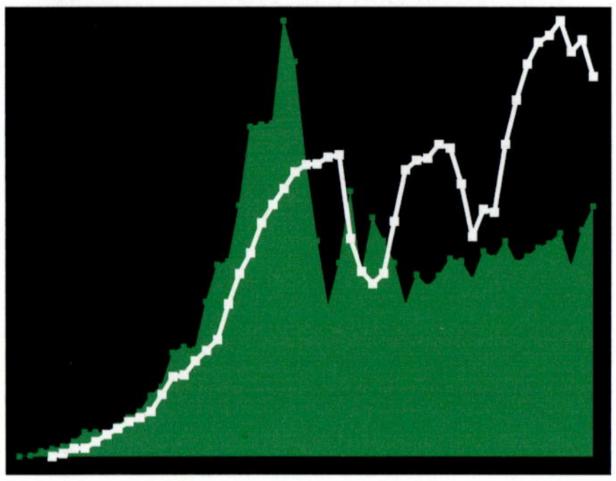

Income—Share Price

> Notwithstanding these arguments, earnings (income) forecasts remain the focal point of equity research on Wall Street and elsewhere. For many companies, the other components of cash flow—depreciation typically being the largest—are highly predictable over the near term. By accurately forecasting (income)—the more variable component—an investor can best hope to identify a misvaluation.
>
> Martin S. Fridson—*Financial Statement Analysis*

Income is the portion of revenue remaining after costs. Income and income growth are both factors in calculating your *Fair Price Estimate—Intrinsic Value* on page 85. Contrast *Share and Fair Price Trends* on page 77 to see if a company is undervalued or overvalued.

Income, also known as earnings or profits, is revenue minus costs (*income = revenue – costs*). Income is an amount of money. The charts on the left show the sum of four quarters income updated each quarter—as in *The Annual Report Every Quarter Riddle* on page 101. Income is not per share—we want to see total money.

We contrast by scaling the white overlay independent of color fill. Income and income are the same. Income and price are different.

Income is employed by analysts in at least three approaches to calculating *Fair Price Estimate—Intrinsic Value* on page 85:

- Income—This is the approach we use for simple illustration;
- Cash flow from operations—Martin S. Fridson in *Financial Statement Analysis* offers a thorough discussion of income and cash flow, from which we quote in the margin note on the *facing page*.
- Owner Earnings—Warren E. Buffett in his *Letter to Berkshire Shareholders, Appendix, 1986*, describes owner earnings, which we prefer and we include in *The Definitions Riddle* on page 111.

The *Income—Share Price* chart overlays income on quarterly price. Investors want income strong and trending upward, and share price increasing the same or faster than income. When the company doesn't reinvest some income, *Net Profit Margin—Income to Revenue* on page 22 may be lower, then price increases slower than income.

You have now seen that income is what you have left over after different versions of costs are subtracted from revenue. On first consideration you might conclude there are always two paths to better profits: decrease costs, and increase revenue. That conclusion is partially not correct, due to the causal relation between costs and revenue. If your company reduces its costs too far, it will eventually decrease revenue and thus income it reinvests to make more income.

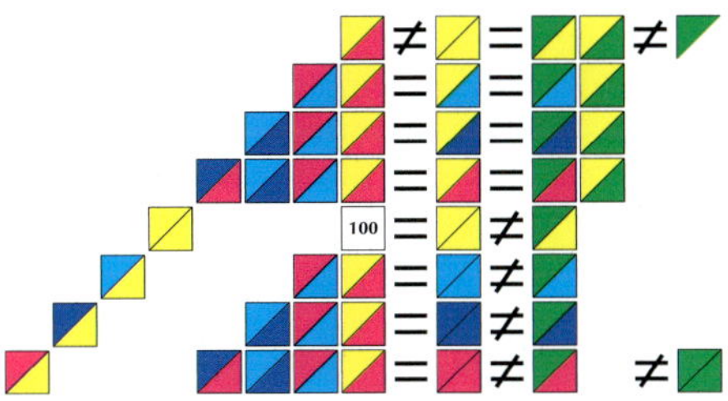

GAAP Structure

Equity Change to Income on page 40 shows the change in equity that may be due to income flowing in, debt payoff, share buyback, or dividend payout.

Martin S. Fridson in *Financial Statement Analysis* says, "Anyone with a sense of history will surely conclude that the introduction of the cash flow statement must have been premised by expectations of great new analytical insights. Such an inference is in fact well founded. The advantages of a cash flow statement correspond to the shortcomings of the income statement, and more specifically, of the concept of profit (income). Over time, profit has proven so malleable a quantity, so easily enlarged or reduced to suit management's needs, as to make it useless, in many instances, as the basis of a fair comparison among companies."

"One example of the erroneous comparisons that can arise involves the contrasting objectives that public and private companies have in preparing their income statements."

"For financial-reporting (as opposed to tax-accounting) purposes, a publicly owned company generally seeks to maximize its reported net income, which investors use as a basis for valuing its shares. Therefore, its incentive in any situation where the accounting rules permit discretion is to minimize (costs)."

Income Events

Income (yellow) events affect net profit margin, return on assets, return on equity, income change to income, assets change to income, equity change to income, revenue change to income, income growth, price to income, price growth to income growth, and income to price. Leave the details of *GAAP Structure* on the left until page 87.

As an investor, you see that income's role in net profit margin (yellow over magenta) influences seven of eight rows in *GAAP Structure*. When we consider income growth, income events influence all rows in *GAAP Structure*.

As an investor, you want to know that big income events are infrequent and reasonably explained, and the trend of income continues to increase, even if temporarily interrupted. For example, the first dip below is Microsoft's "one-time write-off of WebTV in-process R&D".

Microsoft's evolution has led to clean reporting as one exchange for the benefits of monopoly. Hold companies to this standard. You want to see, "We lost on WebTV. Now we're back on our income trend." To get this picture, you don't have to be "finance person".

MICROSOFT

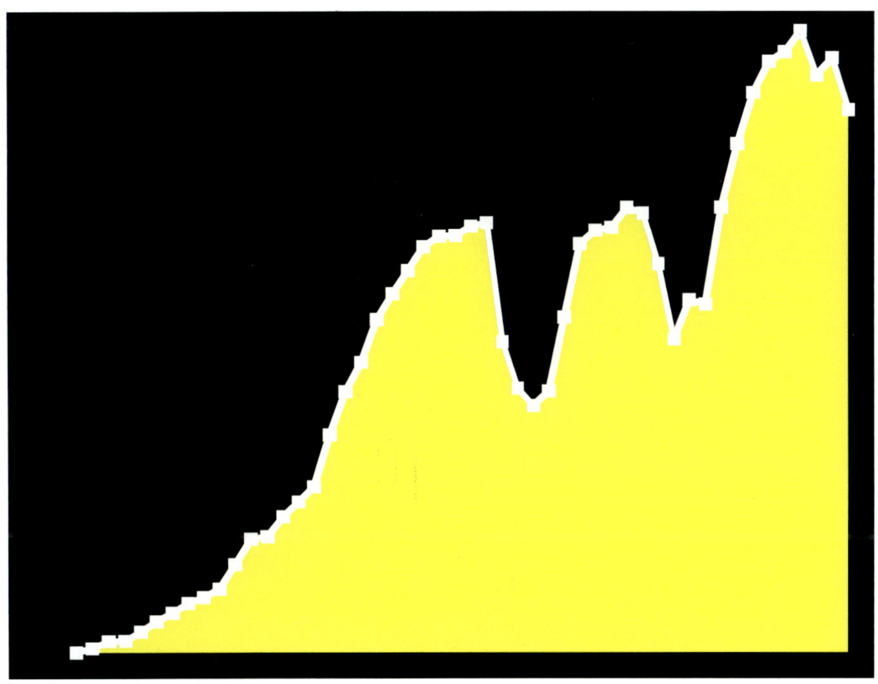

Income

Assets

MICROSOFT

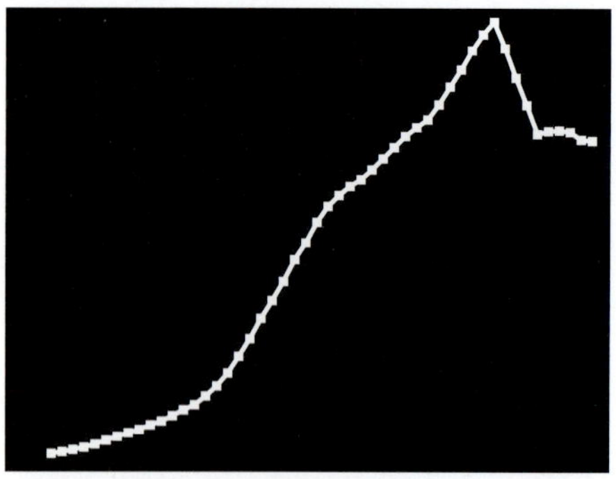

Assets

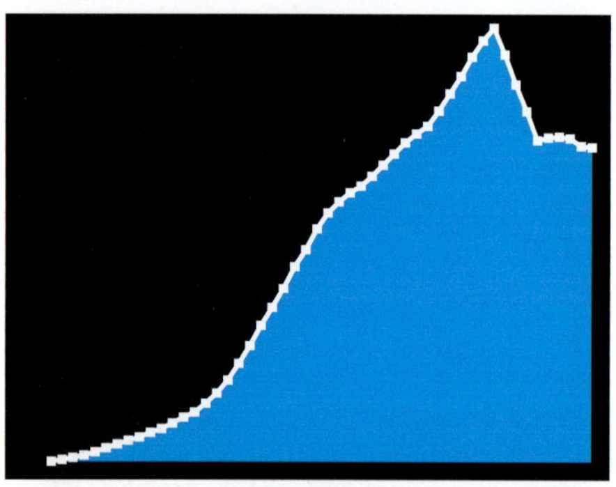

Assets

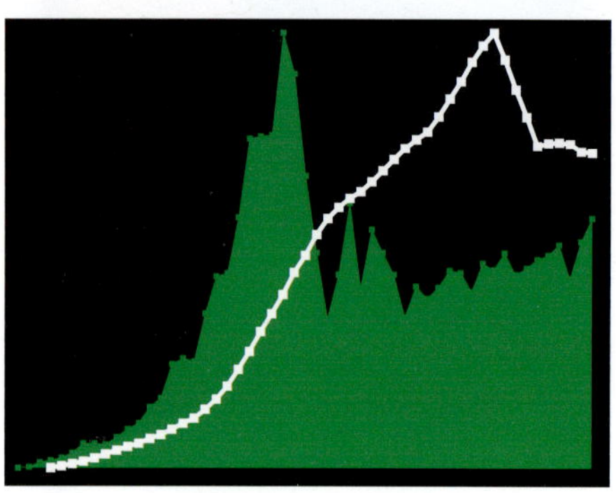

Assets—Share Price

> Some newcomers to finance believe assets are a good thing: the more the better. The reality is just the opposite: Unless a company is about to go out of business, its value is in the income stream it generates, and its assets are simply a necessary means to this end. Indeed, the ideal company would be one that produced income without any assets; then no investment would be required, and returns would be infinite.
>
> Robert C. Higgins—*Analysis for Financial Management*

Assets are probable future economic benefits obtained or controlled by a particular entity as a result of past transactions or events.†

Assets, also known as assets capital, are liabilities plus equity (*assets* = *liabilities* + *equity*). Assets are an amount of money. The assets chart shows the average of four quarters updated each quarter—as in *The Assets and Equity Riddle* on page 103. Assets are not per share—we want to see total money.

We contrast by scaling the white overlay independent of color fill. Assets and assets are the same. Assets and price are different.

One characteristic of an excellent company is that not all of the income stream flowing to assets is spent on current operations. This leaves money to grow the business or otherwise benefit shareholders. You could look for current operations money on the *balance sheet* as *property and equipment*, and other accounts. The *Assets—Share Price* chart, however, may show you a shortcut in some cases.

Consider this reasoning. Informed investors know that Microsoft operations assets earn more than cash assets. When the company increases assets beyond what it needs to maintain operations, investors know those assets are cash or short-term equivalents. Informed investors expect to pay a lower share price for cash assets, causing share price to fall away from assets. The December 2004 dividend is cash suggested by the black fill between share price and assets.

The company is growing without capital infusions—as you see on the left by the December 2004 dividend paid from cash assets, explained in *The Split-Adjusted Close Price Riddle* on page 108. *Leverage—Assets to Equity* on page 26 shows a decreasing portion of assets are purchased with borrowed money. *The Per Share Growth Riddle* on page 107 shows the company is buying back shares.

---

† United States *Generally Accepted Accounting Principles (US GAAP)*
Financial Accounting Standards Board (FASB) at **http://www.fasb.org/st/**
View FASB Pronouncements, Concepts Statement No. 6, Definition of Elements, Assets

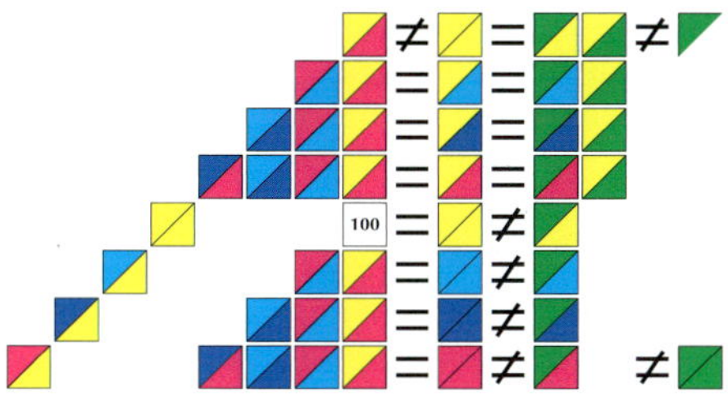

GAAP Structure

Robert Solow won his 1987 Nobel Prize showing that advanced economies grow mostly on the strength of research and development. The *Financial Accounting Standards Board (FASB)* issues *Statements* that affect many of us.

We use *FASB* formal definitions of assets and equity to cover vague territory better than popular definitions.

Companies issue stock options to employees as an incentive for taking the risks of inventing our future. Initially, more shares cause an appropriately lower per share price. Shareholders expect employee's inventions to produce profits that influence price to go up even more than it was lowered.

One *FASB Statement* has sent society, companies, shareholders, and employees scrambling for ways to share risks of invention and rewards of success. *View FASB Pronouncements, Summary of Statement No.* 123 (*revised* 2004), *Key Provisions of This Statement*: "This Statement requires a public entity to measure the cost of employee services received in exchange for an award of equity instruments based on the grant-date fair value of the award (with limited exceptions). That cost will be recognized over the period during which an employee is required to provide service in exchange for the award—the requisite service period (usually the vesting period)."

Assets Events

Assets (cyan) events affect efficiency, leverage, assets change to income, return on assets, assets growth, price to assets, and price growth to assets growth. Leave the details of *GAAP Structure* on the left until page 87.

As an investor, you see conceptually that the role of assets in efficiency (magenta over cyan) influences six of eight rows in *GAAP Structure*, while leverage (cyan over blue) influences four of those six rows, and assets change to income influences one of those six.

Assets' biggest event is caused by the December 2004 dividend payout of 30 billion dollars. In the *Assets Quarterly* chart in *GAAP Original Data* on page 91, you see the full drop occurs in one quarter.

However, in the chart below you see the drop spread over several quarters. The reason is that each assets datapoint in the chart below is an average of four quarters, as explained in *The Assets and Equity Riddle* on page 103. We chose the average so it matches the sum of four quarters in *The Revenue and Income Riddle* on page 102. The drop in assets does not mean that less income is flowing into assets—but in this case it is the result of the large dividend payout.

MICROSOFT

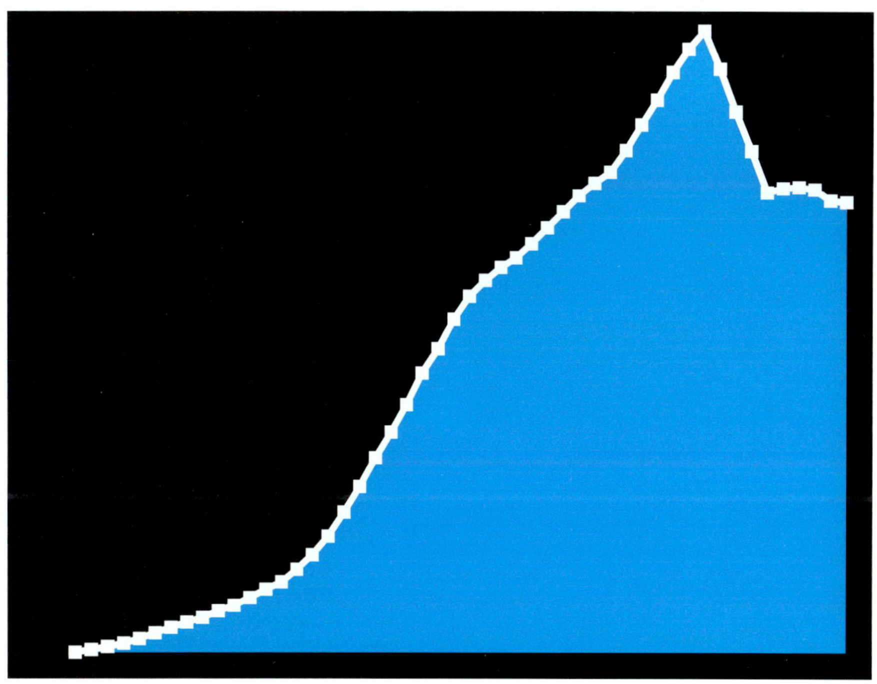

Assets

Equity

MICROSOFT

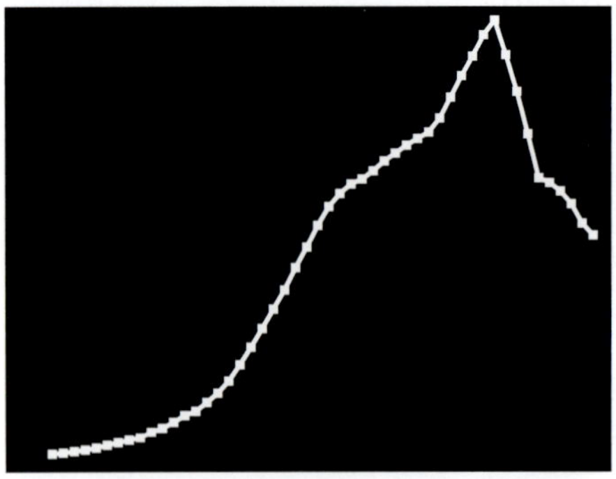

Equity

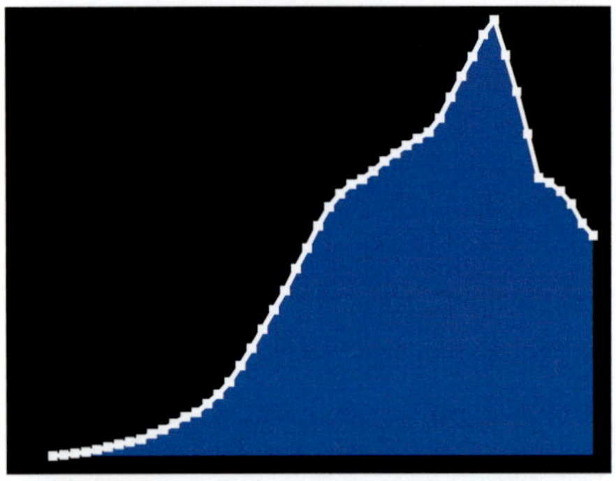

Equity

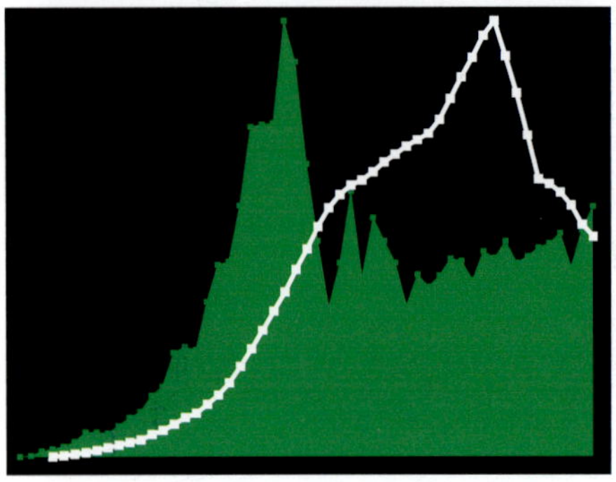

Equity—Share Price

> In the end, "true" equity remains an elusive number and the analyst must use judgment to arrive at correct conclusions about a company's well-being.
>
> Martin S. Fridson—*Financial Statement Analysis*

Equity or net assets is the residual interest in the assets of an entity that remains after deducting its liabilities.†

Equity, also known as net assets or equity capital or owners' equity or total stockholders' equity or net worth or book value or an unlabeled number (not liabilities and stockholders' equity), is assets minus liabilities (*equity* = *assets* – *liabilities*). Equity is an amount of money. The equity chart shows the average of four quarters updated each quarter—as in *The Assets and Equity Riddle* on page 103.

We contrast by scaling the white overlay independent of color fill. Equity and equity are the same. Equity and price are different.

The *Equity—Share Price* chart shows the *equity white line* increasing beyond where it produces a similar or greater increase in income. As with assets, share price reflects the lower income earned on cash.

We have encouraged "judgment to arrive at correct conclusions about a company's well-being." Microsoft decreased equity with its December 2004 dividend, as you see in the charts on the left. No informed investor judges Microsoft's dividend to result in well-being less than that of Warren Buffett's Berkshire which paid no dividend.

However, we want to find "excellent companies" that are also "great investment opportunities" because they are "misappraised". On one hand, we search with uncommon insights for uncommon opportunities because we expect uncommon profit. On the other hand, we expect no searching through financial rubble and obscurities—we expect to find rare, obvious, and consistent financial excellence.

We follow Buffett by using equity growth as a proxy for fair price growth and share price growth. Microsoft fits Buffett's model ***only on the average***—as you see on the page facing *Share and Fair Price Trends* on page 77. There, average equity growth is close to average share price growth. Thus, Microsoft's equity—not equity growth—on this page is very close to what informed investors believe is "true".

---

† United States *Generally Accepted Accounting Principles (US GAAP)*
Financial Accounting Standards Board (FASB) at **http://www.fasb.org/st/**
View FASB Pronouncements, Concepts Statement No. 6, Definition of Elements, Equity

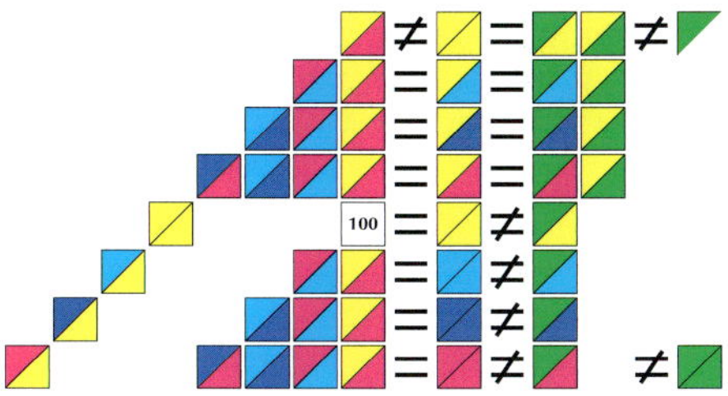

GAAP Structure

Martin S. Fridson in *Financial Statement Analysis* guides you toward equity numbers you should believe are "true" enough to use in calculations of your several investment criteria—including equity growth: "By closely examining the underlying values reflected in the balance sheet, this chapter emphasizes the need for a critical, rather than a passive, approach to financial statement analysis. The discussion of goodwill underscores the chapter's dominant theme, the elusiveness of *true* value. While the case studies in the chapter expose the weaknesses of historical cost accounting, the intricacies of goodwill accounting demonstrate that mere tinkering with historical cost does not necessarily improve the picture. Market capitalization may be a better approach in this instance, yet as shown in another case study, questions can be raised about the validity of a company's stock price as a standard of value. In the final analysis, users of financial statements cannot retreat behind the numbers derived by any one method, but must exercise judgment to draw sound conclusions."

Equity Events

Equity (blue) events affect leverage, equity to revenue, equity change to income, return on equity, equity growth, price to equity, and price growth to equity growth. Leave the details of *GAAP Structure* on the left until page 87.

As an investor, you see conceptually that the role of equity in leverage (cyan over blue) influences four of eight rows in *GAAP Structure*, while equity to revenue (blue over magenta) influences two of those four rows, and equity change to income influences one of those four.

Equity's biggest event is caused by the December 2004 dividend payout of 30 billion dollars. In the *Equity Quarterly* chart in *GAAP Original Data* on page 91, you see the full drop occurs in one quarter.

However, in the chart below—as with assets—you see the drop spread over several quarters. The reason is that each equity datapoint is the average of four quarters, as explained in *The Assets and Equity Riddle* on page 103. We chose the average so it matches the sum of four quarters in *The Revenue and Income Riddle* on page 102. The drop in equity does not mean that less income is flowing into equity—but in this case it is the result of the large dividend payout.

MICROSOFT

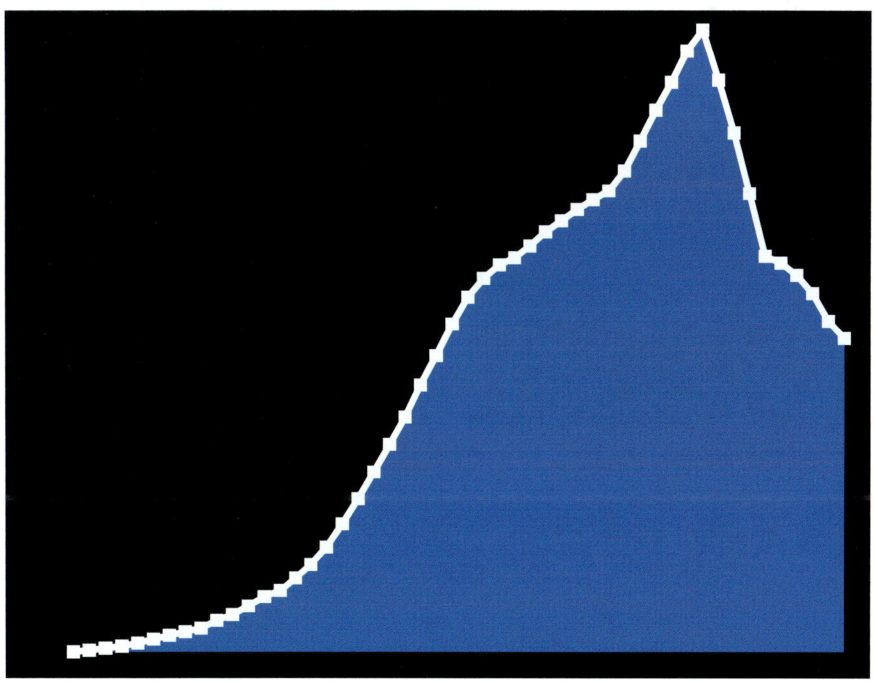

Equity

Revenue

According to the *accrual principle* of accounting, revenue is recognized as soon as "the effort to generate the sale is substantially complete and there is a reasonable certainty that payment will be received".

Robert C. Higgins—*Analysis for Financial Management*

MICROSOFT

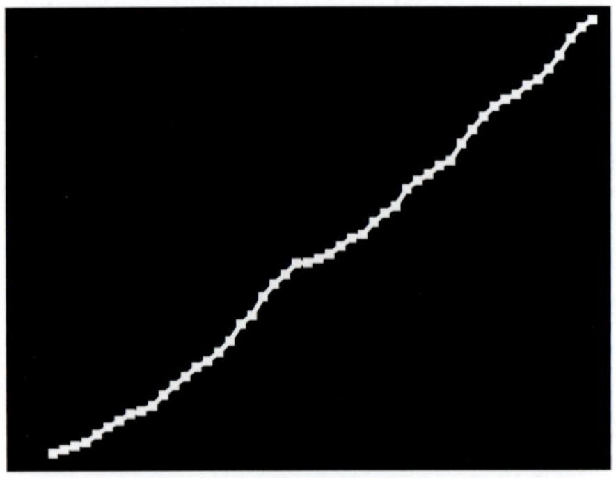

Revenue

Revenue

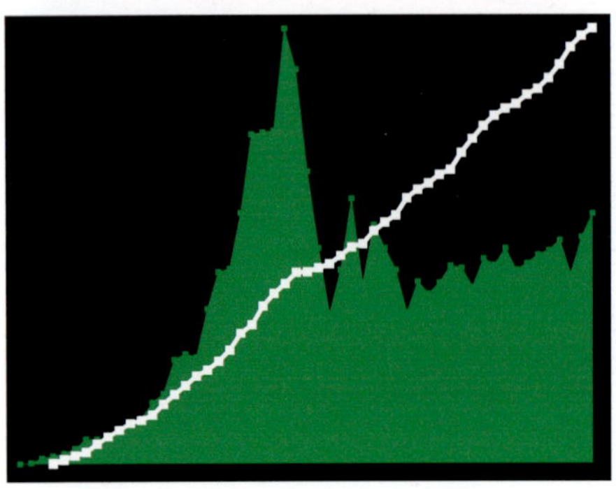

Revenue—Share Price

Revenue is the inflow of money from the sale of products or from other activities central to the operations of a company.

Revenue, also known as sales, is reasonably certain payment for sale of products—recognized either conservatively on shipment to a customer, or aggressively on shipment to a distributor with the option to return. Revenue is costs plus income (*revenue* = *costs* + *income*). Revenue is an amount of money.

We contrast by scaling the white overlay independent of color fill. Revenue and revenue are the same. Revenue and price are different.

One characteristic of an excellent company is increasing revenue. In the early period of the bottom chart, management may be increasing revenue, income, and costs at the same rate. Investors may be responding to the increases by increasing share price at the same rate. Of course, we expect increasing revenue to be sustainable as discussed in *Equity Growth to Revenue Growth* on page 52, otherwise the company will, as Professor Higgins says, "grow broke".

A great investment opportunity may occur when share price increases faster than revenue—seen as the spike in the bottom chart. Here, *Revenue—Share Price* overlays revenue on quarterly price from *The Split-Adjusted Close Price Riddle* on page 108. This chart suggests that during the *dot-com boom*, the income portion of revenue increased faster than revenue—enticing investor prices. We confirm this in *Net Profit Margin—Income to Revenue* on page 22.

The revenue trend in charts on the left shows the sum of four quarters updated each quarter—as in *The Annual Report Every Quarter Riddle* on page 101 and *The Revenue and Income Riddle* on page 102. These charts show all the revenue data available since 1993, free from the *SEC* website as demonstrated in the *The Get Data Riddle* on page 113. Revenue is not per share—we want to see total money.

Avoid companies with long-term decreasing revenue, even if they boast a high *Return on Assets—Income to Assets* on page 30 and high *Return on Equity—Income to Equity* on page 32. Decreasing revenue must ultimately result in decreasing income. This will lower the company's *Fair Price Estimate—Intrinsic Value* on page 85. Informed investors may then lower the company's share price.

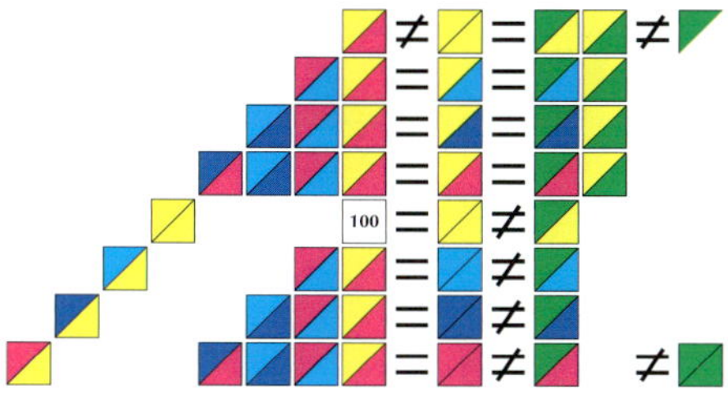

GAAP Structure

GAAP Structure is a navigational tool that shows how the fundamentals relate conceptually and mathematically to create measures in a matrix. A box divided by a line shows that a measure is part of a ratio. Multiply boxes on a row as factors in equations.

The *GAAP Structure* matrix above pictures the numerous roles of revenue (magenta) described in *GAAP Structure* on page 87, derived from United States *Securities and Exchange Commission (SEC)* data, complying with United States *Generally Accepted Accounting Principles (GAAP)*.

GAAP Structure is implied in the data as you see in *GAAP Structure Verified by SEC Data* on page 93. We use the well-known factors of return on assets and return on equity, the four growth measures, and income yield, to derive *GAAP Structure* (expandable to detailed tiers), and to develop our visual matrix.

In the matrix, revenue is the magenta color described in *The Color Codes Riddle* on page 112. When you see the magenta color, you know that some form of the revenue datastream is used in the computation. In this chapter, the revenue datastream is used to calculate the rolling sum of four quarters of revenue for every datapoint as described in *The Annual Report Every Quarter Riddle* on page 101, and the *The Revenue and Income Riddle* on page 102.

Revenue Events

Revenue (magenta) events affect net profit margin, efficiency, equity to revenue, revenue change to income, revenue growth, price to revenue, and price growth to revenue growth. Leave the details of *GAAP Structure* on the left until page 87.

We show conceptually that revenue's role in net profit margin (yellow over magenta) influences seven of eight rows in *GAAP Structure*. Since income is the portion of revenue remaining after costs, you'll see that revenue events influence all of the rows in *GAAP Structure* that include revenue or income.

Revenue increases through big events: decreasing equity growth; early 2000 *Federal Communications Commission's* triggering the burst of the *dot-com bubble*; leveling income; September 11, 2001 terrorism; anti-trust court battles; amassing equity; the December 2004 dividend payout; and achieving a temporary consumer monopoly through the Windows operating system dominating 90 percent of the world's personal computers. Look at *Revenue Growth* on page 18. What do you believe about share price when revenue is going up and growth is going down, versus when both revenue and growth are going up? Other investors may draw similar conclusions.

MICROSOFT

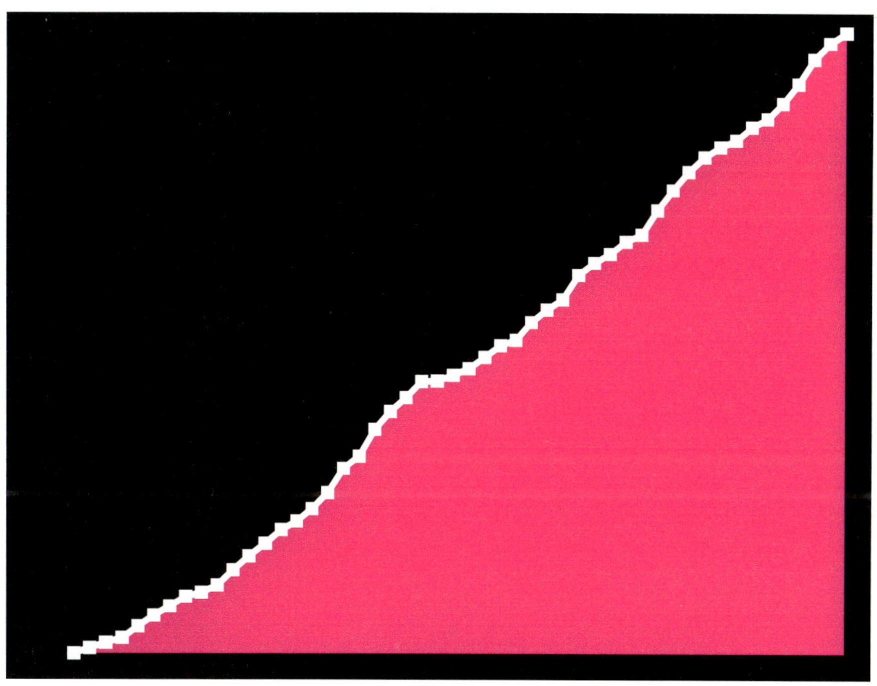

Revenue

GAAP Structure—Growth Trends Datastreams

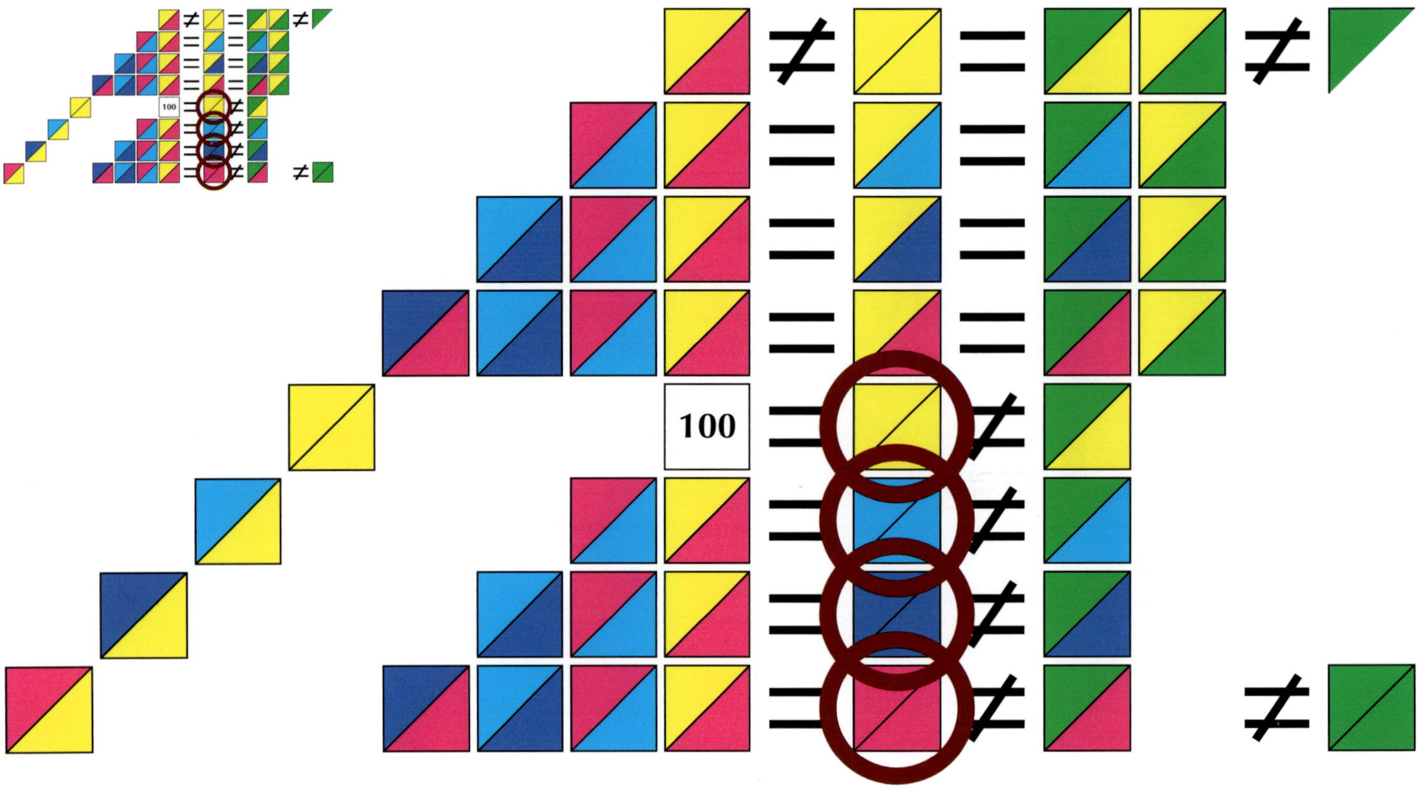

2 Growth Trends

DATASTREAMS MICROSOFT

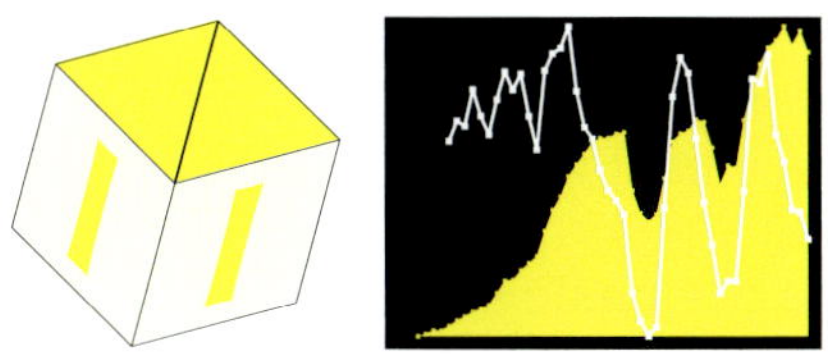

Income Growth

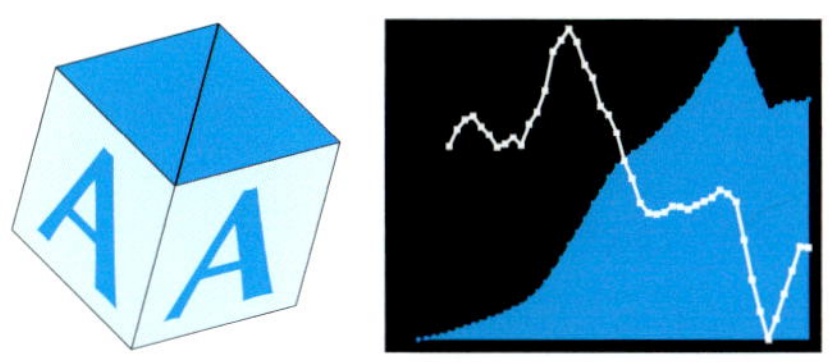

Assets Growth

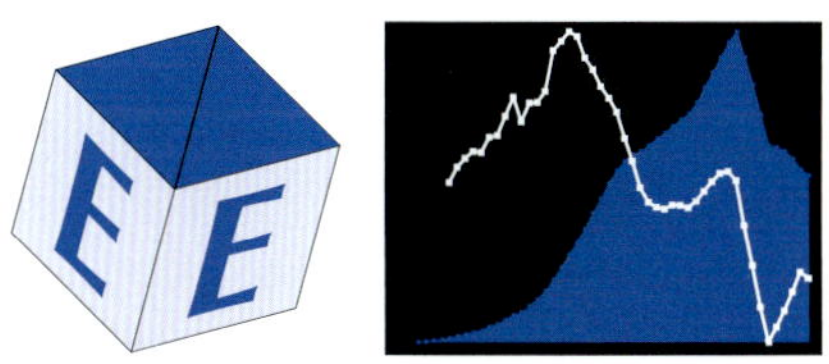

Equity Growth

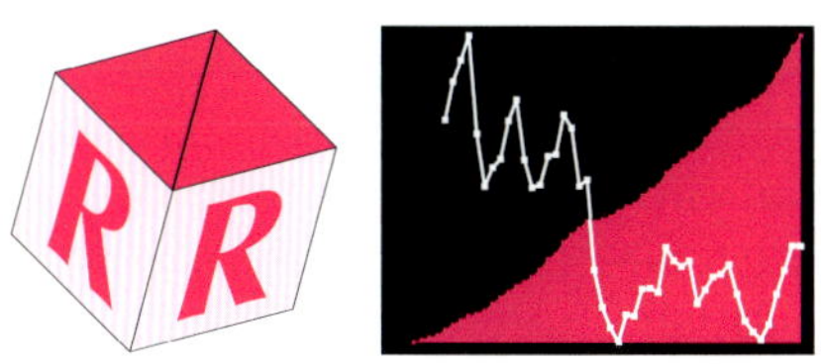

Revenue Growth

> Growth is always a component in the calculation of value (fair price), constituting a variable whose importance can range from negligible to enormous and whose impact can be negative as well as positive.
>
> Warren E. Buffett—*Letter to Berkshire Shareholders, 1992*

Evaluation became a lot easier once we discovered all equations of our *GAAP Structure* on the facing page and page 87 reduce to only four growth trends—income growth, assets growth, equity growth, revenue growth. These growth trends equal *Ratio Trends* on page 21 multiplied by corresponding *Change Trends* on page 35.

The Growth Hierarchy Riddle on page 104 reveals insights gained by condensing all the *SEC* data since 1993 from our *Quarterly Data Summary* into one *front cover* chart that compares the four growth trends.

You need growth trends (white) to see the rate of change in fundamentals. Fundamentals show you changes only in amounts—the rate of change is [(*new value* – *old value*) / *old value*] × 100. Each chart displays a growth trend—calculated from the fundamental datastream on its left. The *facing page* simplifies business thinking, showing you the datastreams used to calculate growth trends and the factors that are multiplied to cause each growth trend.

Although growth has no single correct value, the growth hierarchy describes the ideal company growing income as fast as possible, while growing equity, revenue, and assets equal to it. In real life, growth is optimized within this reasoned hierarchy.

The Best Numbers Riddle on page 100 shows why you want share price growth—influenced by popularity—to beat *S&P* price growth, and equity growth to beat *S&P* price growth. Ideally, you want the average growth of each fundamental to beat the *S&P* average of 11%.

Look at the four growth charts on the left. The naive investor sees colored income, assets, equity, and revenue going up. The savvy investor also sees revenue growth turning down first, simultaneously followed by growth of income, assets, and equity. People stare at colored datastreams—blind to aligned white growth turning points.

A pilot without instruments flies blind in the weather. An investor without growth trends makes blind decisions.

Income Growth

MICROSOFT

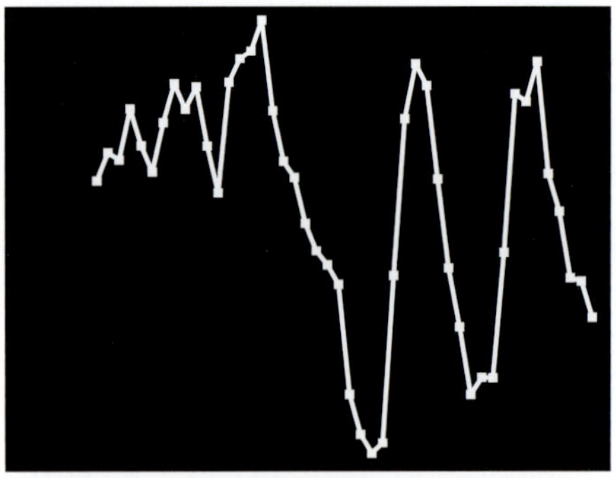

Income Growth

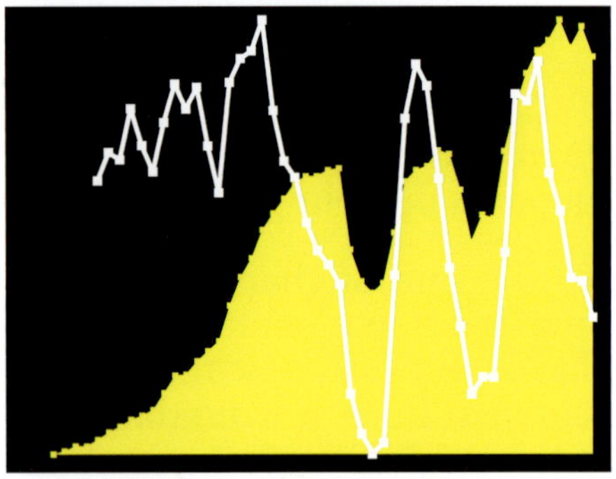

Income Growth—Income

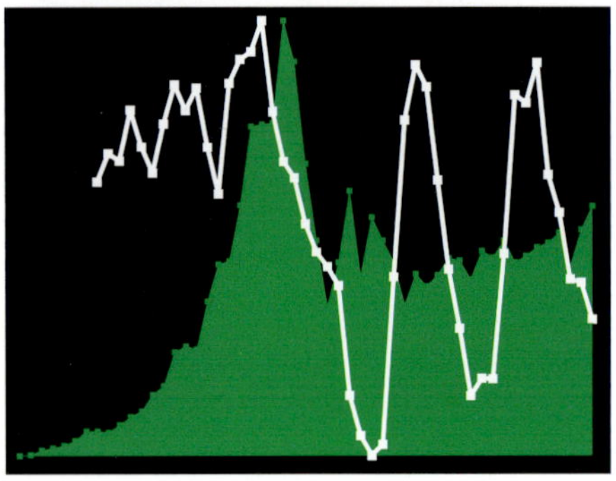

Income Growth—Share Price

You're better off ignoring 5-year compound (income) growth and profit margins exceeding the *Compustat* mean and focusing exclusively on stocks that show persistent (income) growth without regard to magnitude.

James P. O'Shaughnessy—*What Works on Wall Street*

Income growth shows the rate of change, stated as a percent. You can not see this rate in the fundamental—income.

Income (earnings) growth is change in income divided by income [(*new income* – *old income*) / *old income*] × 100. *The Per Share Growth Riddle* on page 107 shows we follow scholars using income per diluted share growth—not income per basic share growth.

Look for "persistent" income growth as in the middle chart. Notice O'Shaughnessy is very careful to say "persistent". He also says "without regard to magnitude", and avoids the word "consistent". Look at income (yellow). It is persistently increasing, so you see that income growth (white) is persistent. Keep in mind two facts about income: Not all income is reinvested to earn more income; High income growth—even if it is decreasing—may still provide more income added to equity than the company is able to reinvest.

You want to see the income growth trend. In the bottom chart, shortly after income growth turns steeply down, investors take the share price down. However, there is not always a correlation in direction or magnitude. Nevertheless, a downturn in revenue growth followed by a downturn in income growth should get you to pay close attention to your share price trend. Following are two reasons why investors may change share price.

First, income growth is the popular growth component for calculating the *Fair Price Estimate—Intrinsic Value* on page 85, though we argue in *The Growth Hierarchy Riddle* on page 104 for a reasoned number. If fair price goes down, investors may lower share price.

Second, income growth affects the amount of income available for reinvestment in assets and equity to fund revenue to earn more income. If revenue growth is going down—and the growth of income, assets, and equity turn down—investors may soon lower share price.

Despite volatility and other reservations about income growth, you see the additions of income to equity that become available for reinvestment when you look at *Equity Growth* on page 16. Martin S. Fridson says in *Financial Statement Analysis*, "As long as the amount of equity capital invested per share continues to rise, more income can be earned on that equity, and ... (income) per share can increase."

Income Growth Events

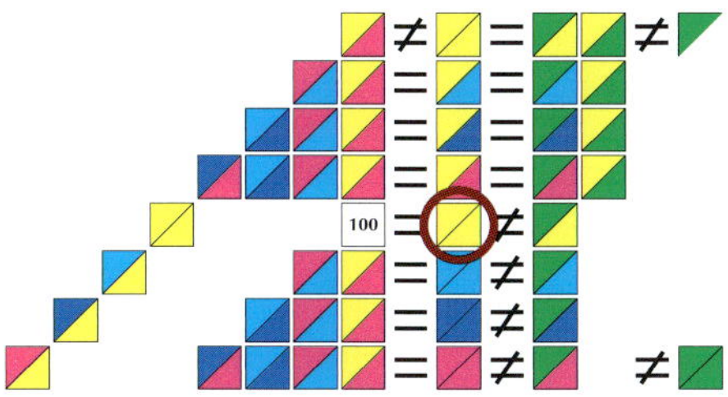

GAAP Structure

MICROSOFT

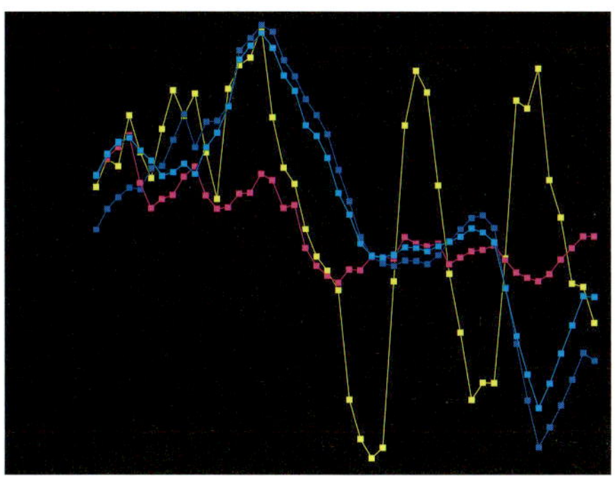

Income Growth
Equity Growth
Revenue Growth
Assets Growth

Income growth (circled) reduces your evaluation from 2 to 1 because it's the ***product*** of two factors to its left: *Income Change to Income* on page 36, and the factor 100. Leave the details of *GAAP Structure* on the left until page 87.

The Best Numbers Riddle on page 100 says ideally income growth equals equity growth, beating *S&P* price growth (averaging 11%)—as on the page facing *Share and Fair Price Trends* on page 77.

As you see in the growth hierarchy chart on the left—no sane investor would use volatile income growth in the estimate of fair price growth without considering the growth of revenue, assets, and equity.

During the *dot-com boom* the company increased income—probably through product pricing, not revenue growth. You see this in the chart on the left. During the boom, management kept revenue growth well below equity growth, so in the bust there was less decrease in revenue growth. Look at the chart below to see that income growth plummets. This causes the *Fair Price Estimate* on page 84 to plummet followed by share price. *The Growth Hierarchy Riddle* on page 104 proposes growth factors more realistic and consistent than income.

You see in the chart above from *The Growth Hierarchy Riddle* on page 104, that income growth (yellow) fluctuates around the more nearly equal growth paths of equity, revenue, and assets. You should form your own estimate of growth that is much more conservative than income growth. Consider its volatility and the fact that revenue (the source of equity) is growing much slower than income just after December 2004. Even if some formula calls for "income growth", don't blindly plug in income growth—think!

The December 2004 dividend made equity growth decrease, so equity growth is temporarily not the good estimate of fair price growth proposed in *The Best Numbers Riddle* on page 100.

MICROSOFT

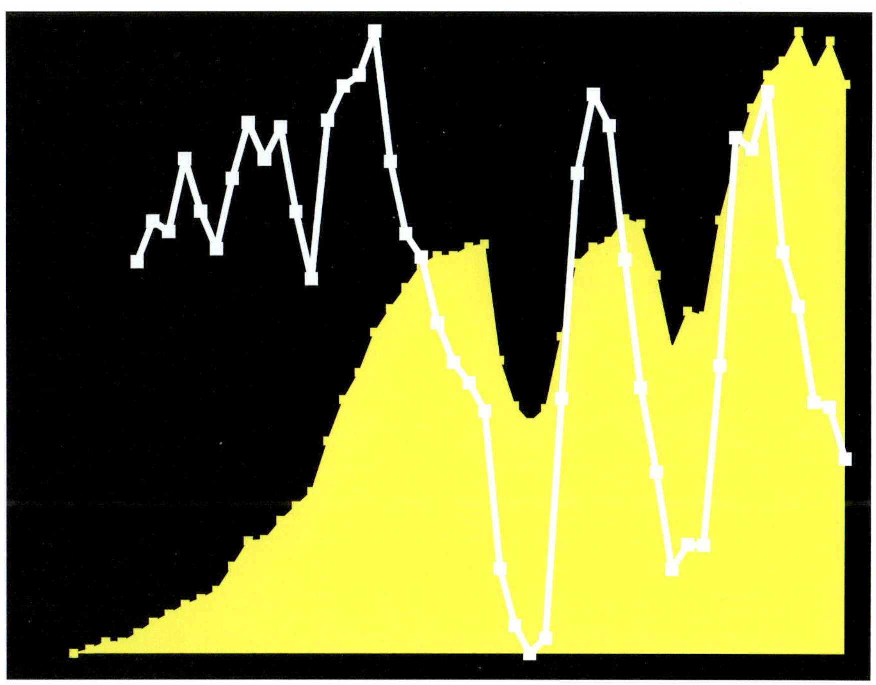

Income Growth—Income

Assets Growth

MICROSOFT

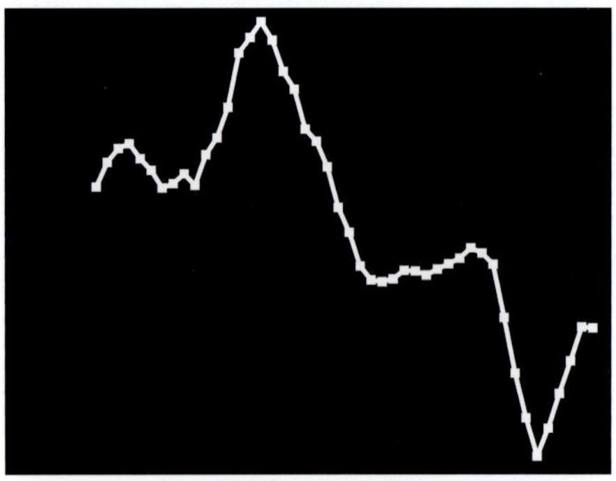

Assets Growth

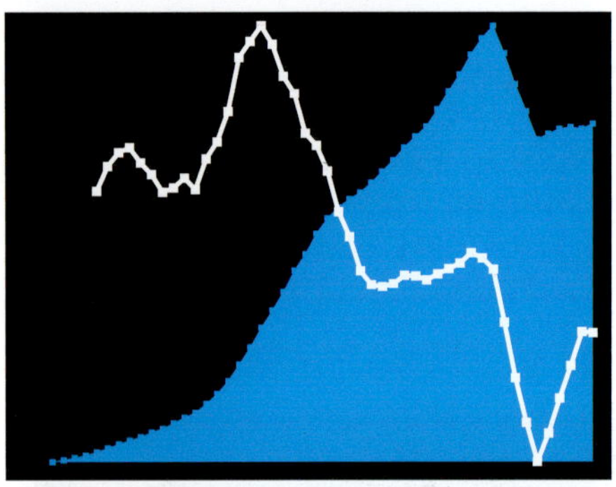

Assets Growth—Assets

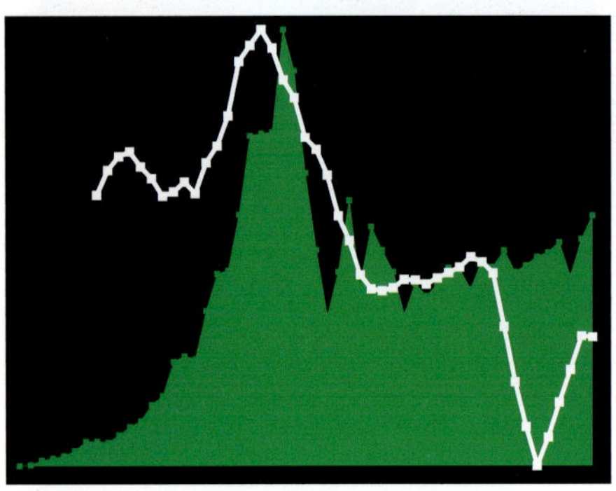

Assets Growth—Share Price

> We want to know what limits the rate at which the company...can increase (revenue)....Assuming, in effect, that all parts of a business expand in strict proportion like a balloon, what limits the rate of this expansion?....As equity grows, liabilities can increase proportionately without altering the capital structure; together, the growth of liabilities and the growth of equity determine the rate at which assets expand. This, in turn, limits the growth...in (revenue). So after all the dust settles, what limits the growth...in (revenue) is the rate at which....equity expands. A company's sustainable growth...therefore is nothing more than its growth...in equity.
>
> Robert C. Higgins—*Analysis for Financial Management*

Assets growth shows the rate of change, stated as a percent. You can not see this rate in the fundamental—assets.

Assets, also known as assets capital, growth is change in assets divided by assets [(*new assets* – *old assets*) / *old assets*] × 100.

Investors should be intrigued that early in the *Assets Growth—Share Price* chart assets growth is high and share price is climbing toward it. This is a clue for a good time to buy. Growth is high and the company is relatively unknown—as we infer from the share price and the early stage in company evolution.

Investors should also be intrigued by the vertical alignment of peaks followed by sharp downturns in all four *Growth Trends* on page 11. These are share price trend "clues" that help you follow one of Pat Dorsey's *Five Rules for Successful Stock Investing*—"Know when to sell: have fundamentals deteriorated" (in growth or size or both)? The December 2004 dividend payout is not a sign of deterioration.

Our charts allow us to delve further into the matter, with the help of Professor Higgins, in *Return on Assets—Income to Assets* on page 30, and *Return on Equity—Income to Equity* on page 32. Here though, look at the *front cover* and notice the strong similarity between the shapes of assets growth and return on assets. The reason is that they are related—as you will understand when you study *GAAP Structure* on the right and on page 87.

Revenue growth's peak and continuing downturn should alert you that less income will eventually flow into assets and equity—not yet affecting share price. Several quarters later, income peaked and turned down—in hindsight forecasting the plummet of share price. Still, you may wait. However, if share price is climbing steeply and you see aligned peaks followed by downturns in revenue, income, assets, and equity, informed investors may drop share price quickly.

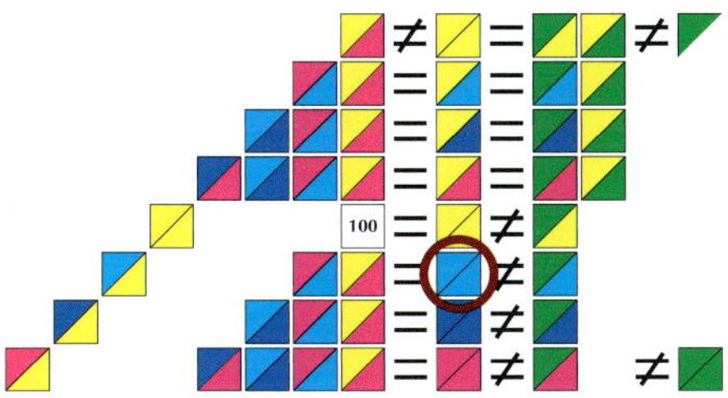

GAAP Structure

MICROSOFT

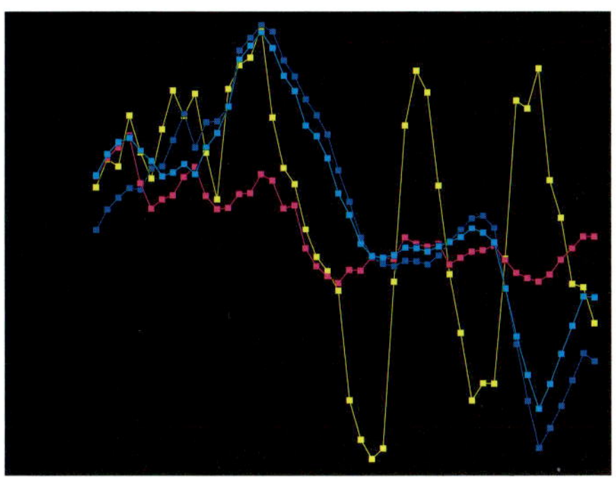

Income Growth
Equity Growth
Revenue Growth
Assets Growth

You see in the chart above, from *The Growth Hierarchy Riddle* on page 104, that the December 2004 dividend payout causes the expected sharp drop in assets growth (cyan). The drop continues for several quarters because assets are averaged, as in *The Assets and Equity Riddle* on page 103.

Investors have reason to believe that assets growth prior to the 2004 dividend may forecast growth several quarters after the dividend, as you can see in *GAAP Original Data* on page 91. Immediately after the dividend, quarterly assets increase, but average assets are decreasing as expected. Calculate quarterly assets growth—not average assets growth—to see assets growth close to the pre-dividend rate.

Assets Growth Events

Assets growth (circled) reduces your evaluation from 3 to 1 because it's the ***product*** of three factors to its left: *Assets Change to Income* on page 38, *Efficiency—Revenue to Assets* on page 24, and *Net Profit Margin—Income to Revenue* on page 22. Leave the details of *GAAP Structure* on the left until page 87.

The Best Numbers Riddle on page 100 says ideally assets growth equals equity growth, beating *S&P* price growth (averaging 11%)—as on the page facing *Share and Fair Price Trends* on page 77.

We know from *Assets* on page 4 that assets equal liabilities plus equity. Thus, if liabilities were zero, assets would equal equity and their growth would be equal. So, whatever we would say in *Equity Growth Events* on page 17 would repeat what we say here.

We begin discussing assets growth with a quote on equity growth because equity is usually the biggest portion of assets. Thus, equity growth usually accounts for most of assets growth, especially if liabilities and equity are expanding in strict proportion. You see this in the four growth chart on the left when the dividend causes assets growth to be slightly smaller than equity growth.

MICROSOFT

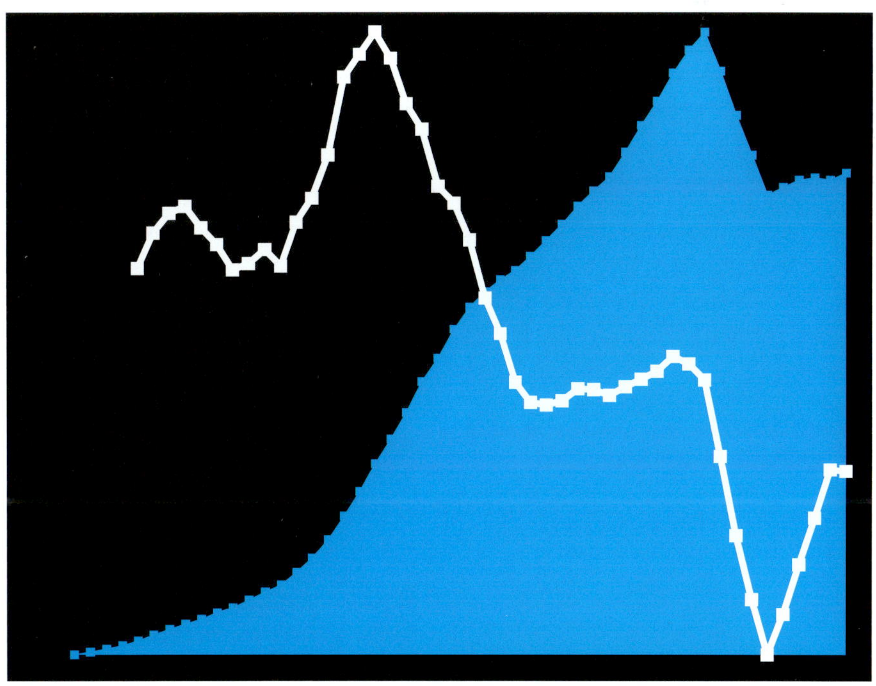

Assets Growth—Assets

Equity Growth

MICROSOFT

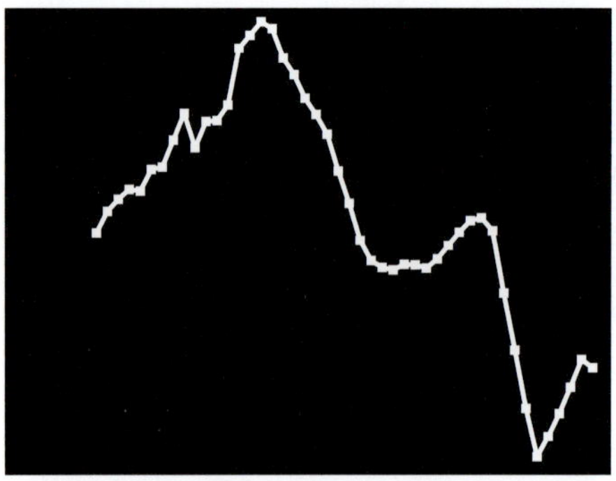

Equity Growth

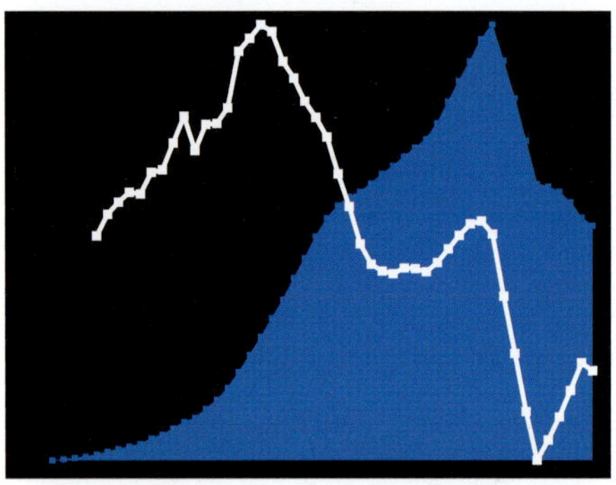

Equity Growth—Equity

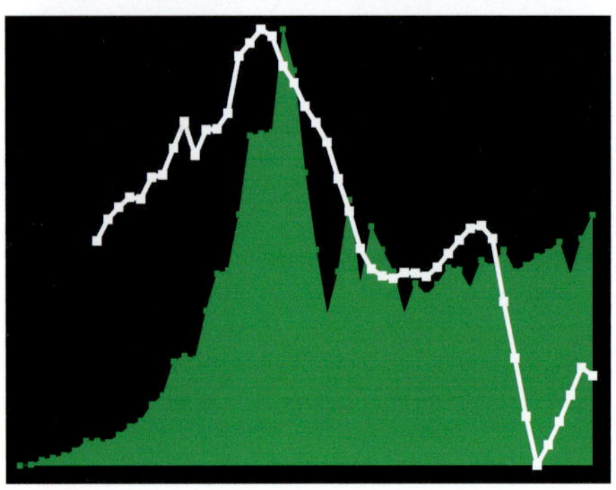

Equity Growth—Share Price

> We report our progress in terms of book value (equity growth per share) because in our case (though not, by any means, in all cases) it is a conservative but reasonably adequate proxy for growth in intrinsic business value (fair price growth per share)—the measurement that really counts. Book value's virtue as a score-keeping measure is that it is easy to calculate and doesn't involve the subjective (but important) judgments employed in calculation of intrinsic business value. It is important to understand, however, that the two terms—book value and intrinsic business value—have very different meanings.
>
> Warren E. Buffett—*Letter to Berkshire Shareholders, 1983*

Equity growth shows the rate of change, stated as a percent. You can not see this rate in the fundamental—equity.

Buffett features equity growth in his table beginning his *Letter to Berkshire Shareholders, 2005*. Who ever begins a letter with a table of numbers—unless those numbers are persuasively important? Investors want to understand equity growth because it's an easy proxy for fair price growth, as in the *Fair Price Estimate* on page 84. Equity growth limits sustainable revenue growth, as in *Equity Growth to Revenue Growth* on page 52—ultimately limiting income growth.

Equity growth, also known as book growth or book value growth or *progress in terms of book value*, is change in equity divided by equity [(*new equity* − *old equity*) / *old equity*] × 100.

Equity growth has even more names. For example, compare *EQUITY GROWTH* on our page facing *Share and Fair Price Trends* on page 77 to Buffett's *Annual Percentage Change in Per-Share Book Value of Berkshire* on page 1 of his *Letter to Berkshire Shareholders, 2005*.

Look for causes of equity growth going up and down—like volatile additions of income to equity, and dividend payouts such as December 2004 that decrease average equity growth for a few quarters, as in *The Assets and Equity Riddle* on page 103.

In the bottom chart, informed investors look for reasons that might drive down share price, like decreasing additions of income to *new equity* causing equity growth to decrease. However, when equity growth levels, investors level the share price—because management leaves enough equity after the December 2004 dividend payout to fund revenue growth and thus income growth.

Equity growth may be an easy-to-calculate proxy for fair price estimate growth (*intrinsic business value growth*)—and thus your share price growth—if you reason wisely from the facts.

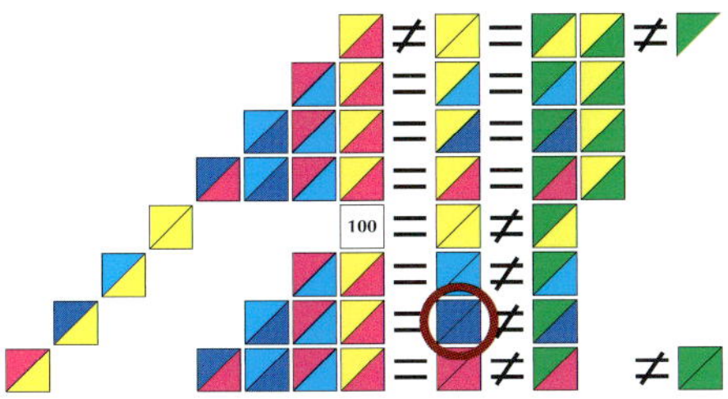

GAAP Structure

MICROSOFT

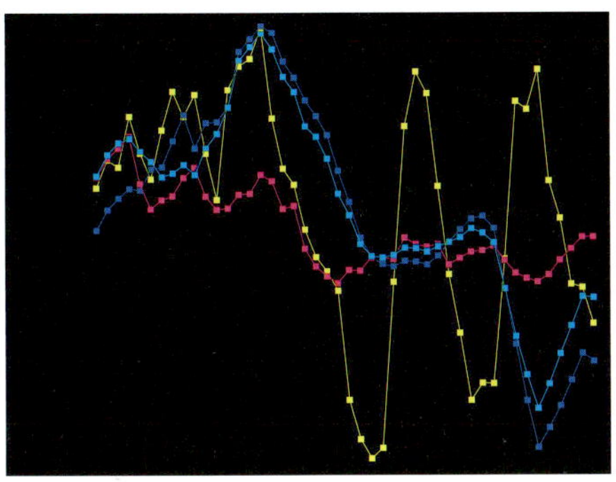

Income Growth
Equity Growth
Revenue Growth
Assets Growth

You see in the chart above, from *The Growth Hierarchy Riddle* on page 104, that equity growth (blue) is behaving about the same as assets growth (cyan). You would be more confident in estimating the growth of fair price and share price (excluding popularity) if you knew that growth of equity, assets, and revenue were likely to be nearly the same when they settle a few quarters after the December 2004 dividend.

Equity growth and assets growth can be calculated from quarterly data, as described in *Assets Growth Events* on page 15. You'll draw the same conclusion for both—they are likely to again be closer to the pre-dividend growth.

Equity Growth Events

Equity growth (circled) reduces your evaluation from 4 to 1 because it's the ***product*** of four factors to its left: *Equity Change to Income* on page 40, *Leverage—Assets to Equity* on page 26, *Efficiency—Revenue to Assets* on page 24, and *Net Profit Margin—Income to Revenue* on page 22. Leave the details of *GAAP Structure* on the left until page 87.

The Best Numbers Riddle on page 100 says we prefer average equity growth to beat *S&P* price growth (averaging 11%)—as equity growth does on the page facing *Share and Fair Price Trends* on page 77.

Equity growth is easy to calculate, and ideally is a proxy for a fair price estimate growth. You see the two are similar on the page facing *Share and Fair Price Trends* on page 77. Equity growth is more likely to be a proxy when the company reinvests much of equity in producing more revenue. This is known as *The Virtuous Cycle*.

Look for events that may cause equity growth to drop. For example, equity growth went into a long decline at the end of the *dot-com boom*, presumably because revenue decreased, earning less income to fuel assets and equity growth. Ultimately, equity limits growth.

MICROSOFT

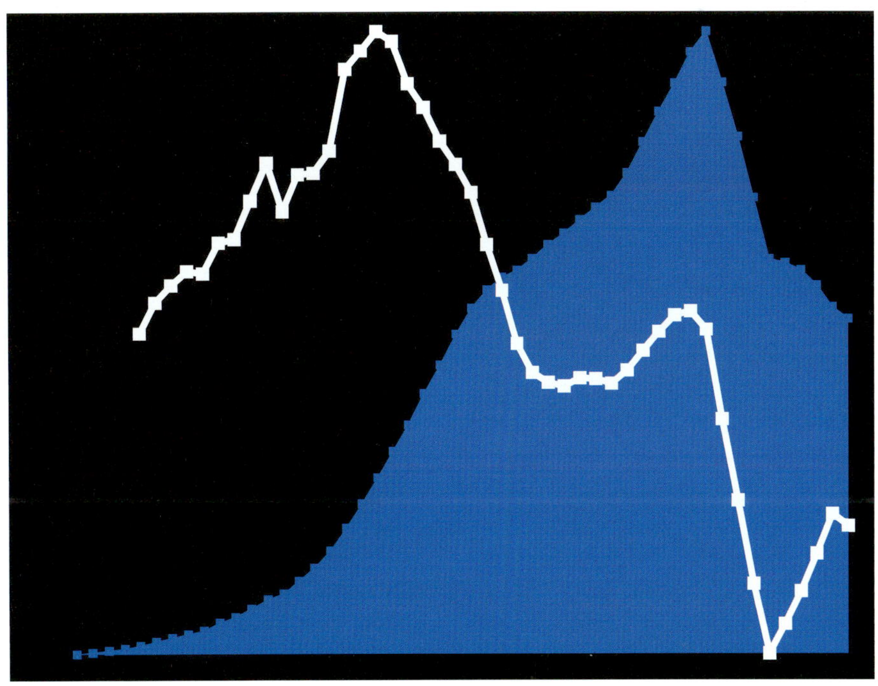

Equity Growth—Equity

Revenue Growth

MICROSOFT

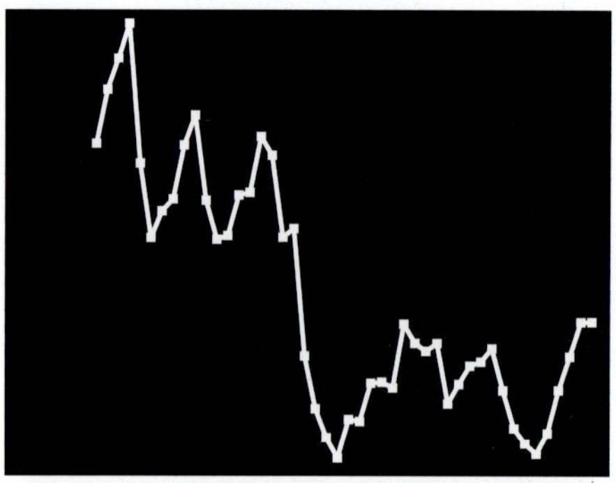

Revenue Growth

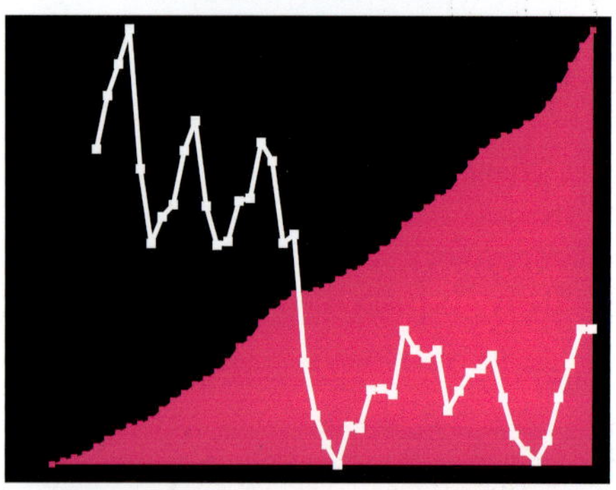

Revenue Growth—Revenue

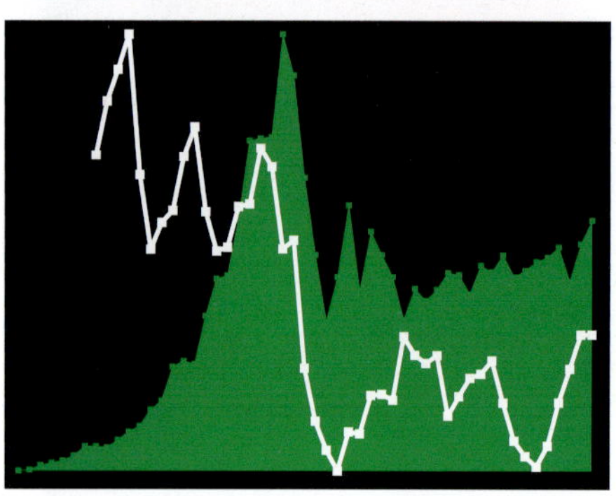

Revenue Growth—Share Price

> Growth in (revenue) drives everything else on the income statement and balance sheet. Good top-line growth means that investments in new products are paying off. Companies that meet this standard either are participating in a fast-growing business or are taking market share away from weaker competitors.
>
> Michael Murphy—*Every Investor's Guide to High-Tech Stocks*

Revenue growth shows the rate of change, stated as a percent. You can not see this rate in the fundamental—revenue.

Revenue (sales) growth is change in revenue divided by revenue [(*new revenue* − *old revenue*) / *old revenue*] × 100. As you'll see in *The Definitions Riddle* on page 111, Professor Higgins comments on revenue versus sales—"I've never found a meaningful distinction between these terms."

You want to see the revenue growth trend. Why? The middle chart is an example. Revenue (magenta) is increasing. However, revenue growth (white) is decreasing. It takes the same amount of time for you to see the magenta and white as it does to see only the magenta. Which investor do you believe is likely to make a more profitable decision—the investor who sees only the trend in size of revenue, or the investor who sees the trends in size and growth?

When you look at the trends in both size and growth, you see that growth has turned down. This should alert you to watch the growth of income, assets, and equity. If these also turn down, you should consider how far down you believe they will go before investors begin to lower the share price.

You can already infer from *The Best Numbers Riddle* on page 100 that revenue growth decreasing toward the *S&P* current price growth will alert investors. And, revenue growth decreasing toward the *S&P* 11% average price growth will cause informed investors to consider whether the *S&P*, bonds, or cash will be better investments.

A company report may tell you that management changed revenue growth to support their strategy of sustainable revenue growth, as in *Equity Growth to Revenue Growth* on page 52, or that the amount of business changed, or both.

There may be many reasons for changes in revenue growth. We'll see some of these reasons as we follow revenue through the business process—as its name changes to income, assets, and equity. The deeper we look into a company's finances, the more clearly we see that income, assets, and equity growth are fueled by revenue growth.

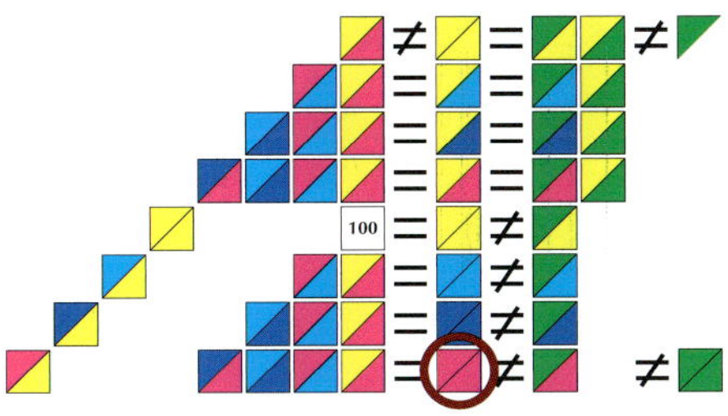

GAAP Structure

MICROSOFT

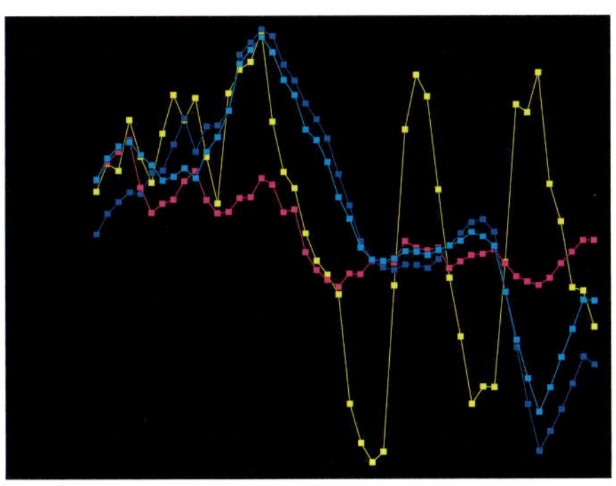

Income Growth
Equity Growth
Revenue Growth
Assets Growth

You see in the chart above from *The Growth Hierarchy Riddle* on page 104, that growth of revenue, assets, and equity are nearly equal approaching the December 2004 dividend payout. The dividend was paid from equity, leaving enough equity to fund revenue growth. So, the decline in revenue growth must be caused by lower demand, not lower equity. Thus, revenue growth looks like a good short-run estimate of fair price growth.

Revenue Growth Events

Revenue growth (circled) reduces your evaluation from 5 to 1 because it's the ***product*** of five factors to its left: *Revenue Change to Income* on page 42, *Equity to Revenue—Equity to Revenue* on page 28, *Leverage—Assets to Equity* on page 26, *Efficiency—Revenue to Assets* on page 24, *Net Profit Margin—Income to Revenue* on page 22. Leave the details of *GAAP Structure* on the left until page 87.

The Best Numbers Riddle on page 100 says ideally revenue growth equals equity growth, beating *S&P* price growth (averaging 11%)—as on the page facing *Share and Fair Price Trends* on page 77.

Revenue growth plays a unique role in estimating fair price growth when equity growth and assets growth are perturbed by an event like the December 2004 dividend payout. If the growths of revenue, assets, and equity have been nearly equal, as you see on the left, then revenue growth may be the best short-run estimate, when the other two run off the rails as following the dividend payout.

Look for events that may cause revenue to drop. Management may have recognized an unsustainable boom and decided to limit revenue. Or, revenue may simply have slowed.

MICROSOFT

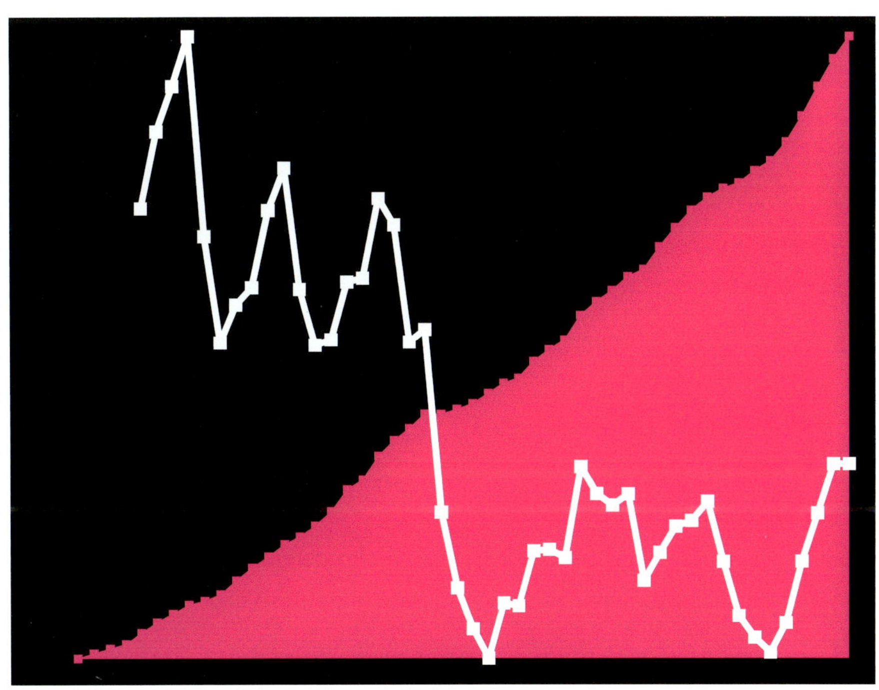

Revenue Growth—Revenue

GAAP Structure—Ratio Trends Datastreams

3 Ratio Trends

DATASTREAMS

MICROSOFT

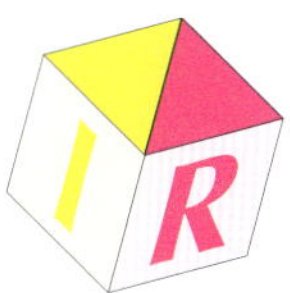

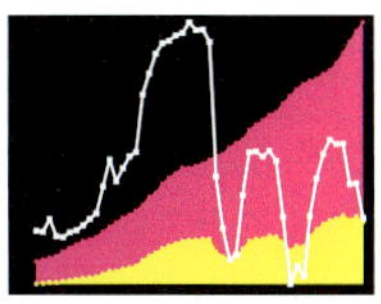

Net Profit Margin

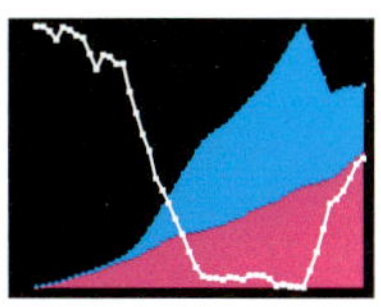

Efficiency

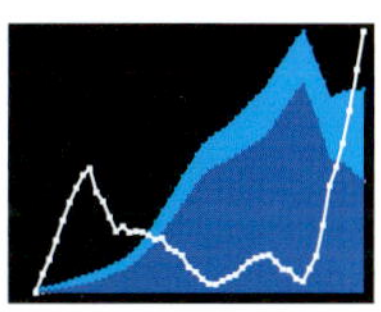

Leverage

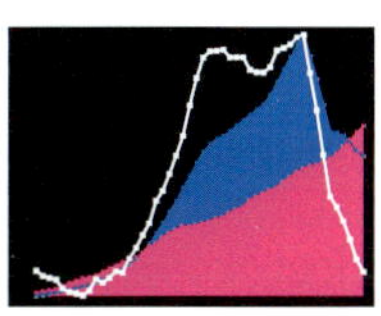

Equity to Revenue

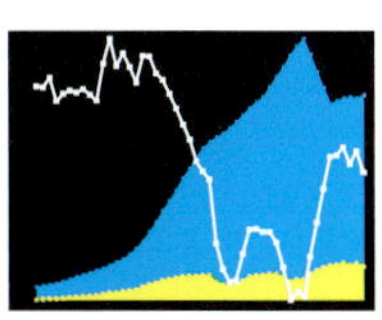

Return on Assets

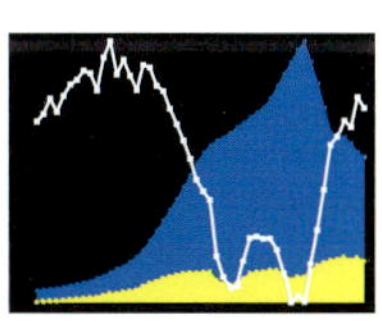

Return on Equity

The most useful way to evaluate ratios involves trend analysis: Calculate ratios for a company over several years, and note how they change over time. Trend analysis avoids the need for cross-company and cross-industry comparisons, enabling the analyst to draw firmer conclusions about the firm's financial health and its variation over time.

Robert C. Higgins—*Analysis for Financial Management*

Causes of *Growth Trends* on page 11 became obvious in our *GAAP Structure* on the facing page and page 87 when we discovered they result from ratio trends—net profit margin, efficiency, leverage, equity to revenue, return on assets, return on equity—multiplied by corresponding *Change Trends* on page 35.

The *front cover* displays key measures—including these ratio and growth trends—so you make quicker informed investment decisions.

The four fundamentals—revenue, income, assets, and equity—pair as six ratios defined in *The Ratios Riddle* on page 105. Each chart on the left displays a ratio trend (white)—the ratio of two colored fundamentals calculated from their datastreams. The *facing page* relates ratio trends as factors of resulting ratio trends to their right—and, ratio and change trends as factors of growth trends to their right.

Although a ratio has no single correct value, each has approximate limits described in *The Best Numbers Riddle* on page 100.

Ratio trends reveal competitive strategies, for example: high net profit margin—low efficiency; or low net profit margin—high efficiency.

Ratios enable you to compare companies of different sizes, because ratios express proportions of money, not amounts of money. Imagine identical ratios on the left, for a small company and a large company. The proportions (white) will be identical, and colored fundamentals will look identical—though amounts of money are small and large.

Our trend charts set a global standard by annualizing every datapoint every quarter, using all appropriate *SEC* data since 1993.

Higgins says: "It is useful to think of ratios as clues in a detective story. One or even several ratios might be misleading, but when combined with other knowledge of a company's management and economic circumstances, ratio analysis can tell a revealing story."

Net Profit Margin—Income to Revenue

MICROSOFT

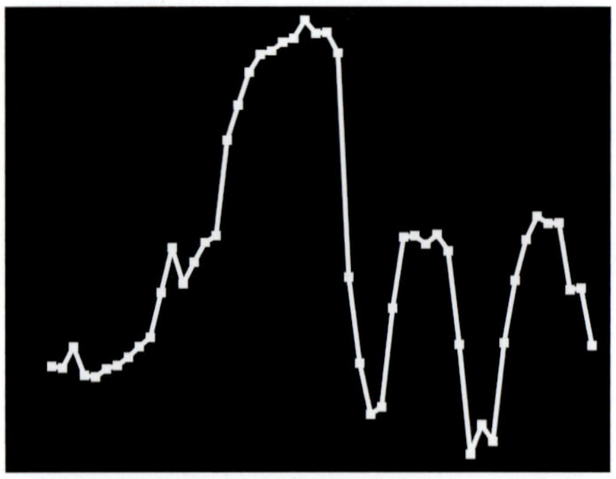

Net Profit Margin

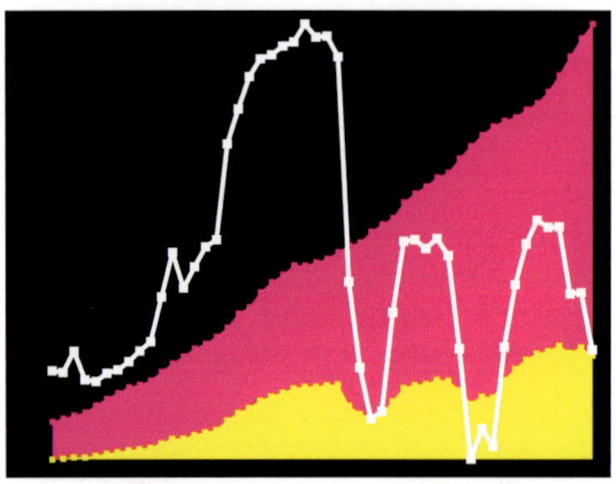

NPM—Income and Revenue

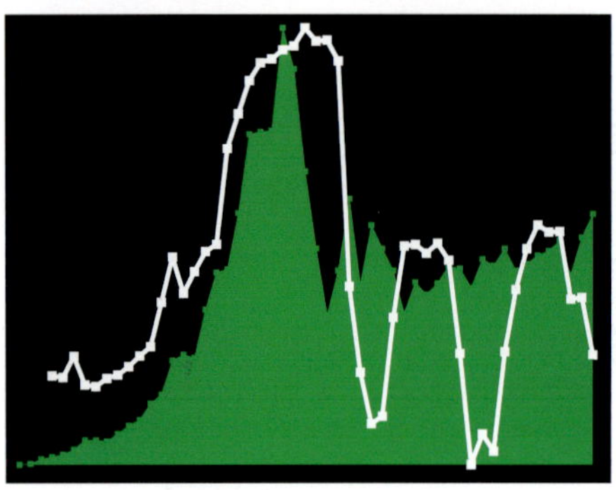

NPM—Share Price

> The profit margin measures the fraction of each dollar of (revenue) that trickles down through the income statement to profits. This ratio is particularly important to operating managers because it reflects the company's pricing strategy and its ability to control operating costs.
>
> Robert C. Higgins—*Analysis for Financial Management*

Net profit margin shows you the portion of revenue that is income (profit). The remaining portion of revenue is costs.

Net profit margin (NPM), also known as margin or return on revenue, is income divided by revenue (*income / revenue*) × 100. Net profit margin is a percent.

Look at the history of this excellent company. Net profit margin goes up for a while, then there's the *dot-com boom* and *bust*, then it may be approaching an approximate limit, "because too-fat margins will invite competition", Martin S. Fridson—*Financial Statement Analysis*.

Look for this limit. Why? You want to know if net profit margin has leveled—steadily contributing income—but not a factor causing the increase or decrease of other measures. Or, is net profit margin changing—thus contributing to change in assets growth, which limits equity growth, revenue growth, income growth, and fair price growth?

You want increases in net profit margin to be caused by increasing income, not by decreasing revenue. Look at the middle chart and you'll see revenue (magenta) increasing, while income (yellow) is also generally increasing. Once net profit margin is relatively steady near its limit, any decrease in revenue will drag income down with it.

Look at the bottom chart to see that skyrocketing net profit margin is followed by skyrocketing share price—until informed investors, watching the *Share and Fair Price Trends* on page 77, plummet the price a few quarters before net profit margin goes into free fall. However, in the life of a company that is evolving toward excellence, net profit margin will rise until costs and competition cause it to level at far less than its mathematical maximum of 100% of revenue.

Professor Higgins insightfully relates profit margin and efficiency:

> Net profit margins differ greatly among industries depending on the nature of the products sold and the company's competitive strategy.... Companies with high profit margins tend to have low asset turns (efficiency), and vice versa. This is no accident. Companies that add significant value to a product ... *can* demand high profit margins. However, because adding value to a product usually requires lots of assets, these same firms tend to have lower asset turns.

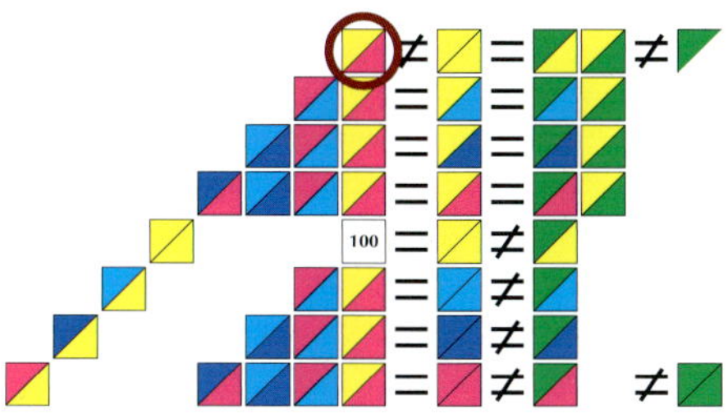

GAAP Structure

$$\frac{\delta\,equity}{income} \times \frac{assets}{equity} \times \frac{revenue}{assets} \times \frac{income}{revenue} = \frac{\delta\,equity}{equity}$$

Net profit margin is a factor on 6 of 8 rows of equations. Net profit margin and *Efficiency—Revenue to Assets* on page 24 are the two most frequent factors affecting company results. This should motivate you to understand.

Net profit margin answers questions.

Are fundamentals of net profit margin (return on revenue) related to fundamentals of return on assets and return on equity? Yes, row 4 completes the rows 1, 2, 3, 4 sequence by revealing the fundamentals of net profit margin.

Does net profit margin help make a place in the matrix for *Equity to Revenue—Equity to Revenue* (blue over magenta) on page 28? Yes, *The Ratios Riddle* on page 105 proves the requirement for equity to revenue in the matrix. Only when you place equity to revenue in column 5, rows 4 and 8, can you cross-cancel related colors—to complete the matrix.

Is equity to revenue a factor of revenue growth on row 8? Yes. As an investor, you want to know the factors influencing revenue growth, because revenue growth drives all other growth in the company. Equity to revenue is one factor. Or, revenue growth can be simplified to net profit margin times *Revenue Change to Income* on page 42.

Net Profit Margin Events

Net profit margin (circled) and efficiency are the most frequent factors of equations in the matrix on the left—visually relating measures. Leave details of *GAAP Structure* on the left until page 87.

The Best Numbers Riddle on page 100 shows why you want the equity growth equation from row 7 of *GAAP Structure* to average greater than the *S&P* 11% average. Specifically, in the equation on the left, you want net profit margin to multiply the factors to its left, so equity growth beats *S&P* price growth.

Look at the equation on the left. You want it to average greater than 11% (Microsoft 1993–2005, 26%; Buffett 1965–2005, 22%). This happens only when the left four numbers multiply to greater than 11%. For example, say equity change to income is 0.5, leverage is 1, efficiency is 2, and net profit margin is 20%, then equity growth is 20%—which obviously beats 11% and is close to Buffett's 22%.

Look for events that may affect the company, like correlating the early 2000 *Federal Communications Commission* announcement—it would not approve a monopoly over broadband-to-the-home channels—with the following plummet of net profit margin.

MICROSOFT

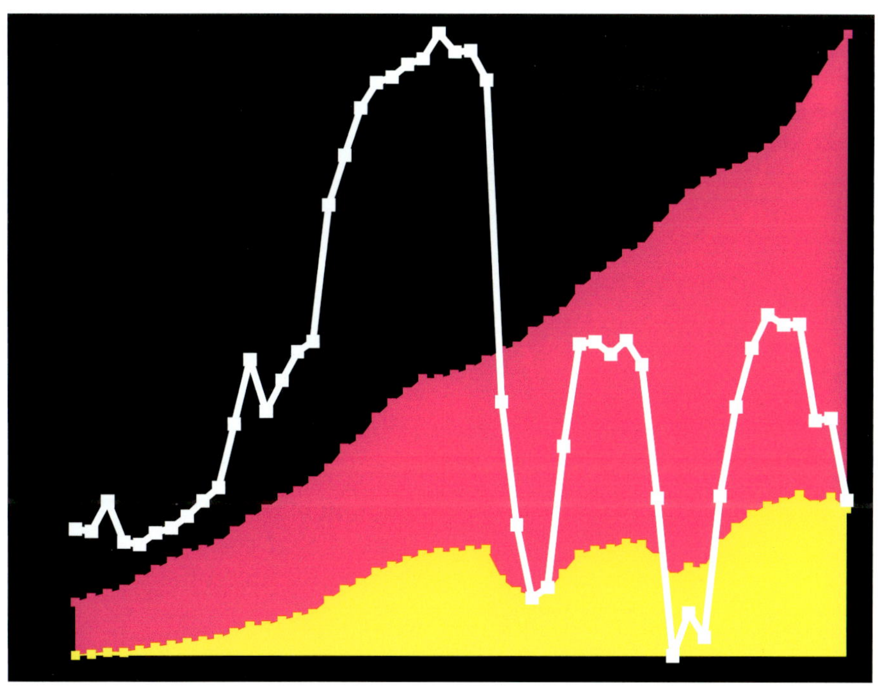

Net Profit Margin—Income and Revenue

Efficiency—Revenue to Assets

MICROSOFT

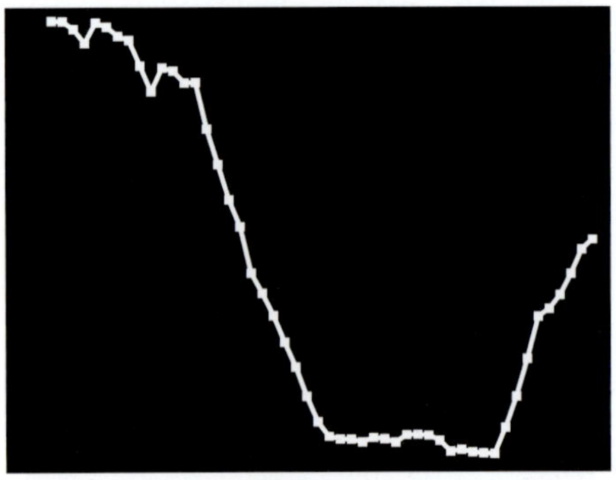

Efficiency

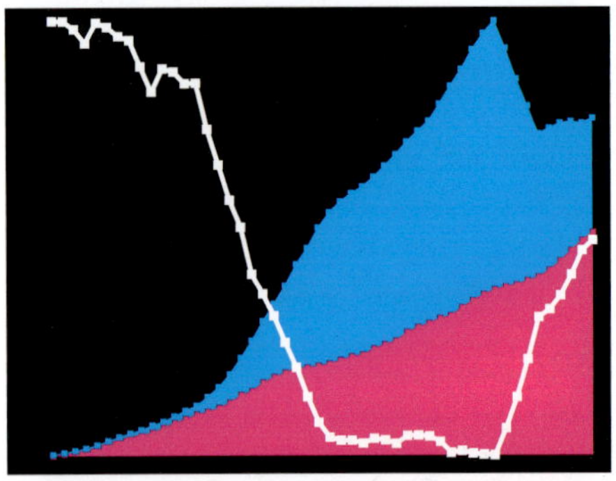

Efficiency—Revenue and Assets

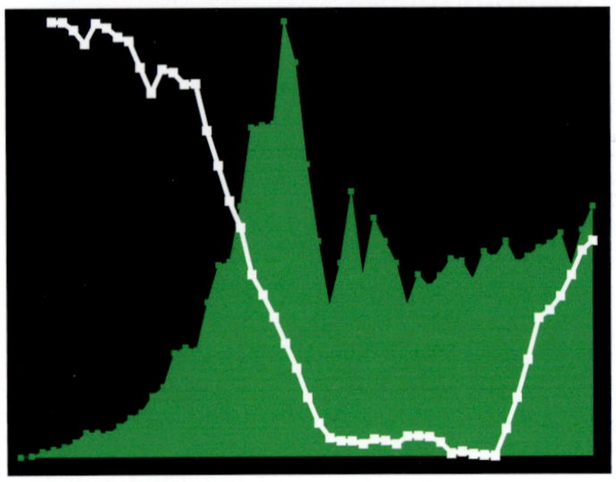

Efficiency—Share Price

> The asset turnover ratio (efficiency) measures the (revenue) generated per dollar of assets.... Companies with high profit margins tend to have low asset turns, and vice versa. This is no accident. Companies that add significant value to a product ...*can* demand high profit margins. However, because adding value to a product usually requires lots of assets, these same firms tend to have lower asset turns.... It should be apparent, therefore, that a high profit margin is not necessarily better or worse than a low one, for it all depends on the combined effect of the profit margin and the asset turnover.
>
> Robert C. Higgins—*Analysis for Financial Management*

Efficiency shows you how many dollars of revenue per year are produced for every dollar of assets.

Efficiency, also known as operational efficiency or total asset turnover or assets turnover or asset turns or turns, is revenue divided by assets (*revenue / assets*). Efficiency is a times-number.

Look at how decreasing efficiency displays an unusual signal of an excellent company. You see revenue (magenta) and assets (cyan) are increasing, so the company is earning revenue and reinvesting its income to increase revenue. What you see is the company's success. It's accumulating cash beyond what it needs to produce its products. If you retrieved data beyond these fundamental numbers, you'd expect to find cash efficiency to be lower than fixed assets (production) efficiency, because excellent companies earn more on products.

Aggressive management may boost asset turnover, but eventually the assets will reach the limits of their productive capacity, Martin S. Fridson—*Financial Statement Analysis*. Assets are increasing until the company pays its December 2004 dividend—sharply decreasing assets and increasing efficiency.

Of course, returning money to shareholders doesn't suddenly make the company more efficient at producing products. It just decreases cash assets earning lower returns than the returns on products, thus increasing efficiency until cash again increases assets. Excellent companies have different strategies—some keep the money, others pay.

Resist looking for the correct efficiency trend, and look instead for the efficiency trend that makes sense at each stage of the company's story. Legal risks led to increasing cash assets which decreased efficiency. Reduced risks led to a dividend payout, increasing efficiency.

Michael Pollan says in *The Omnivore's Dilemma*, "As the case of mushrooms suggests the omnivore's dilemma often comes down to a question of identification."

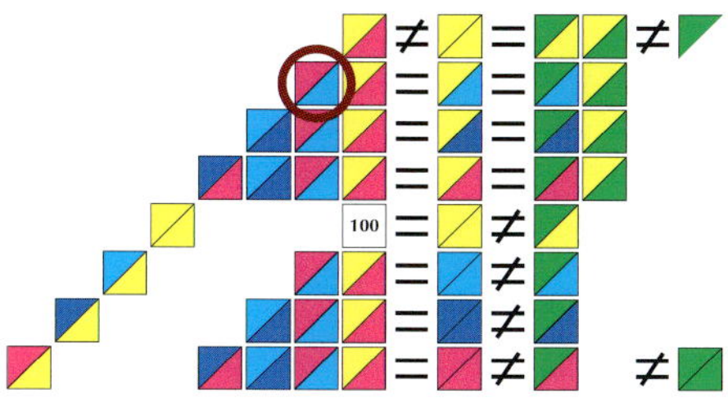

GAAP Structure

$$\frac{\delta equity}{income} \times \frac{assets}{equity} \times \frac{revenue}{assets} \times \frac{income}{revenue} = \frac{\delta equity}{equity}$$

What you really want is to see how factors combine to form results, and those results to form higher level results, until you reveal a condensed picture of a company. The factors show you what's causing the result, and the result enables you to move closer to knowing something important in that first 2 seconds.

GAAP Structure, row 2, shows you net profit margin and efficiency sharing revenue (magenta). Cross-cancel revenue to reveal their result—return on assets. The factors of *Return on Assets—Income to Assets* on page 30 are factors of other results that advance through the *GAAP Structure* matrix toward revealing a condensed picture of a company.

The condensed picture on the *front cover* shows a column beginning with net profit margin and efficiency that share magenta (revenue). Delete the revenue in each and realize that you've created their result—the fifth chart—return on assets.

Now you have the option to evaluate on a result level (return on assets), or on its factors level (net profit margin and efficiency)—result then detail. Divide fundamentals to get each ratio. Multiply the ratios to get their result.

Efficiency Events

Efficiency (circled) is the only factor management can use to cause return on assets to be different from net profit margin. You see this relationship on row 2 of *GAAP Structure* on the left, where efficiency times net profit margin equals return on assets.

The Best Numbers Riddle on page 100 says you want the equation from row 7 of *GAAP Structure* to average equity growth greater than the *S&P* 11% (Microsoft 1993–2005, 26%; Buffett 1965–2005, 22%).

Look at the page facing *Share and Fair Price Trends* on page 77 and you'll see that the *S&P* varies around its 11% average. Over the long run, this company does not always beat that average or even some current number. However, over that same long run, the product of the four factors of equity growth strongly beats the *S&P* average of 11%—as does share price growth. Shorter periods may be different.

Look at the chart below for events that send more income to equity for reinvestment, yet may never be headline news. For example, we know intuitively that the dividend of December 2004 did not suddenly improve the efficiency of production. But, improved efficiency indirectly increases income, if it's not countered by other factors.

MICROSOFT

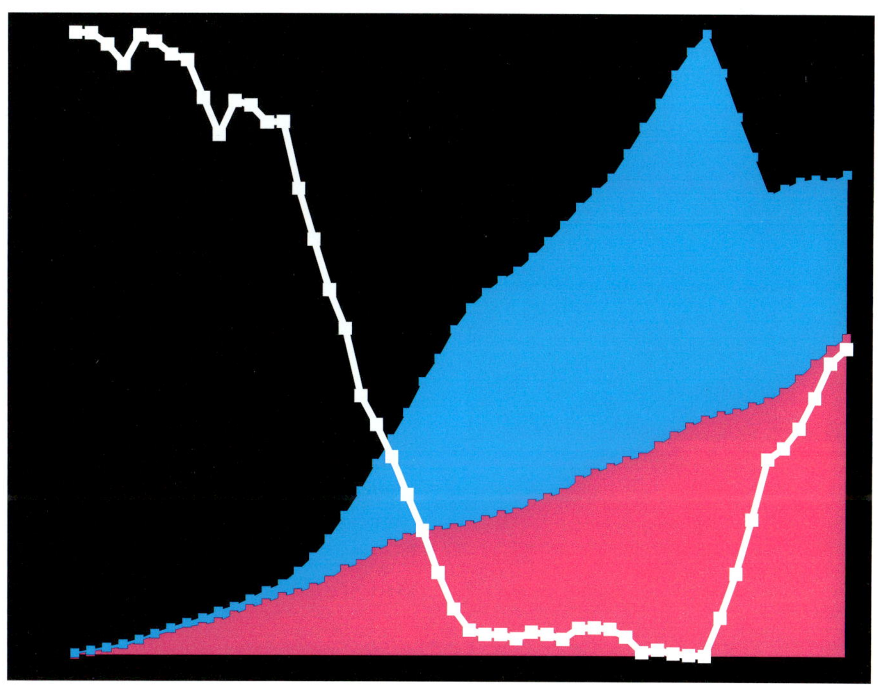

Efficiency—Revenue and Assets

Leverage—Assets to Equity

MICROSOFT

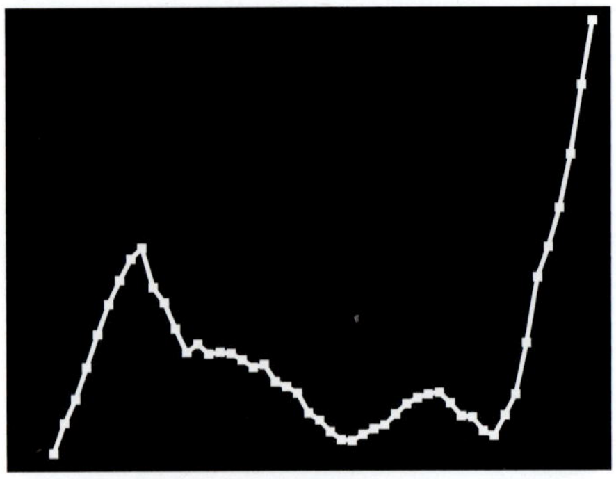

Leverage

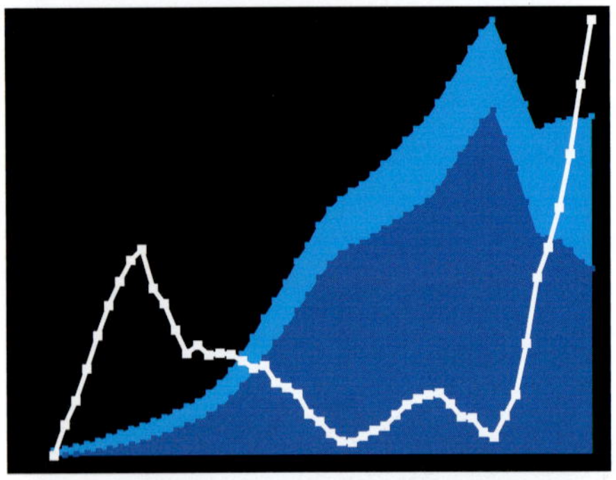

Leverage—Assets and Equity

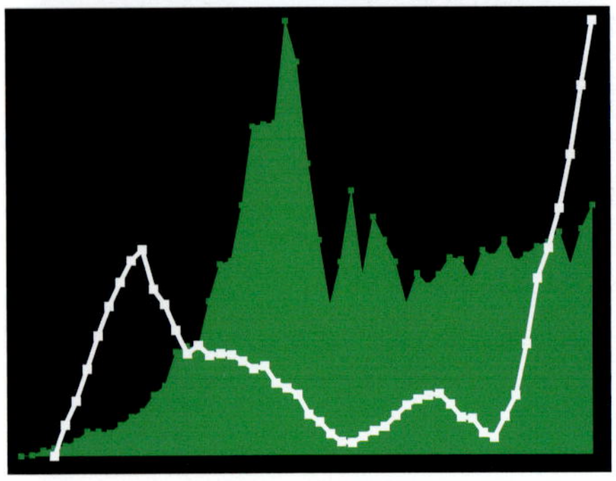

Leverage—Share Price

> We use debt (liabilities) sparingly and, when we do borrow, we attempt to structure our loans on a long-term fixed-rate basis. We will reject interesting opportunities rather than over-leverage our balance sheet. This conservatism has penalized our results but is the only behavior that leaves us comfortable, considering our fiduciary obligations to policyholders, lenders, and the many equity holders who have committed unusually large portions of their net worth to our care.
>
> Warren E. Buffett—*Berkshire Owner's Manual, Principle 7*

Leverage shows you "debt financing in hopes of increasing the rate of return on equity", Martin Fridson—*Financial Statement Analysis*. Only leverage causes return on equity larger than return on assets.

Leverage, also known as the equity multiplier or (1 + *debt / equity*), is assets divided by equity (*assets / equity*)—discussed in *The Leverage Riddle* on page 106.† Leverage is a times-number.

Look at how decreasing leverage displays an unusual signal of an excellent company. For a company with Microsoft's cash, decreasing leverage shows that the company has enough money to fund opportunities, so it chooses to decrease the ratio of assets (cyan) to equity (blue). You see that the difference (liabilities) is actually increasing. Leverage went down because this company decreased liabilities as a portion of equity—even though it increased the amount of liabilities.

Look how leverage went back up when the December 2004 dividend payout reduced cash—discussed in *Leverage Events* on page 27.

Consider these scholarly insights. Leverage "reaches a limit, since lenders will not continue advancing funds beyond a certain point as financial risk increases", Martin S. Fridson—*Financial Statement Analysis*. The "challenge of financial leverage is to strike a prudent balance between the benefits and costs of debt financing", Robert C. Higgins—*Analysis for Financial Management*. The "added risk to the shareholders from issuing more debt will raise required yields on the equity by just enough to offset the seeming gain from use of low-cost debt", Merton H. Miller, Nobel Prize winner—*M & M 30 Years Later*.

Look at share price to see if it appears affected by leverage. In this case, a quick look at the numbers in the chart on the next page reveals that there is very little difference between the lowest and highest leverage numbers—the steep slopes are due to scaling. So you should expect price to be unaffected by the changes in leverage.

† In Britain and other places, leverage is called *gearing*.

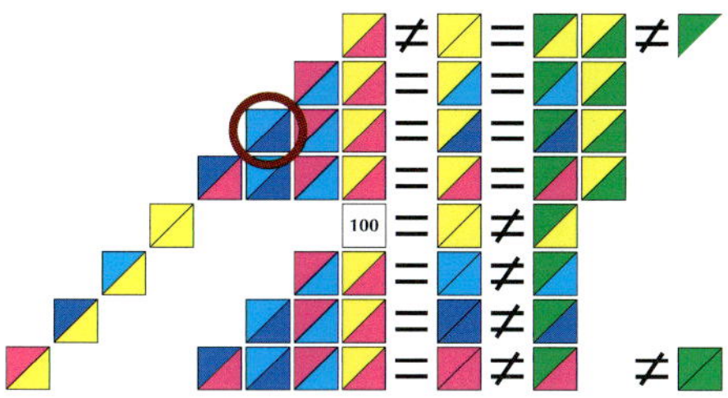

GAAP Structure

$$\frac{\delta\,equity}{income} \times \frac{assets}{equity} \times \frac{revenue}{assets} \times \frac{income}{revenue} = \frac{\delta\,equity}{equity}$$

Above is the equation for row 7 of the *GAAP Structure* matrix. You want both sides equal so you're using data from the appropriate time-period prescribed by the matrix. Then, you can confidently explore the factors to see what's causing the equity growth.

Looking left from the equal sign, net profit margin, efficiency, and leverage always use data from the time-period ending four quarters prior to the date equity growth is calculated. Our inference is, the company reinvests the money from these factors in the next four-quarter period to create equity growth. (Old factors fund new growth.)

Look at *GAAP Structure Verified by SEC Data* on page 93 to see that appropriate data should and does make sense in the financial puzzle. Look at *GAAP Original Data* on page 91 to see that net profit margin, efficiency, and leverage are four quarters older than *new equity* in return on equity.

Of course, our trend charts also show you the current numbers for net profit margin, efficiency, and leverage. However, to see the equity growth they will produce, you must wait four quarters. Then, *Equity Change to Income* described on page 40, as you see in the equation above, will bridge the gap.

Leverage Events

Leverage (circled) is the only factor management can use to cause return on equity to be greater than return on assets. Row 3 of *GAAP Structure* shows net profit margin and efficiency share revenue (magenta), while efficiency and leverage share assets (cyan). Cross-cancel revenue and assets to reveal the result—return on equity. On the *front cover* you see return on equity is the result of return on assets (net profit margin times efficiency) times leverage. Results are useful when you understand their factors.

The Best Numbers Riddle on page 100 shows you want the equation from row 7 of *GAAP Structure* to average greater than the *S&P* 11%.

July 20, 2004, Microsoft announced a plan "to return almost $75 billion of capital to our shareholders over the next four years . . . through a combination of dividends and buybacks (of shares)."

Look for events like the December 2004 dividend and buybacks of shares that cause leverage to rise. (Equity is smaller than assets, so subtracting the dividend from both increases assets to equity.) Equity to revenue in the next section shows enough equity retained to fund revenue growth—so investors leave share price unchanged.

MICROSOFT

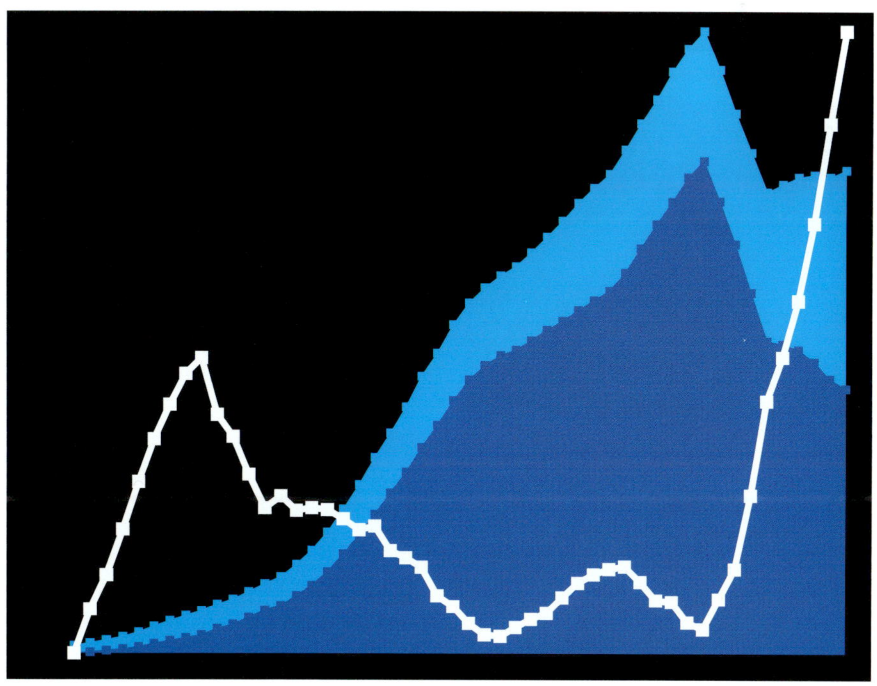

Leverage—Assets and Equity

Equity to Revenue—Equity to Revenue

MICROSOFT

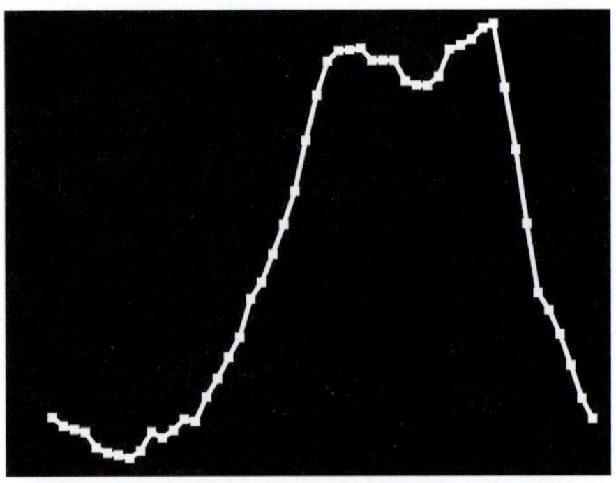

Equity to Revenue

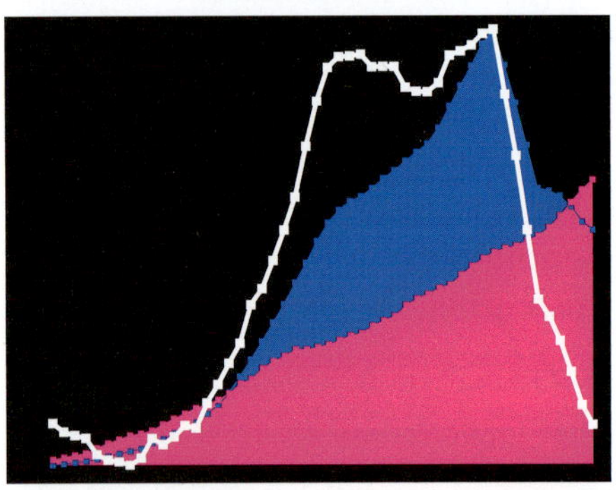

Equity to Revenue—Equity and Revenue

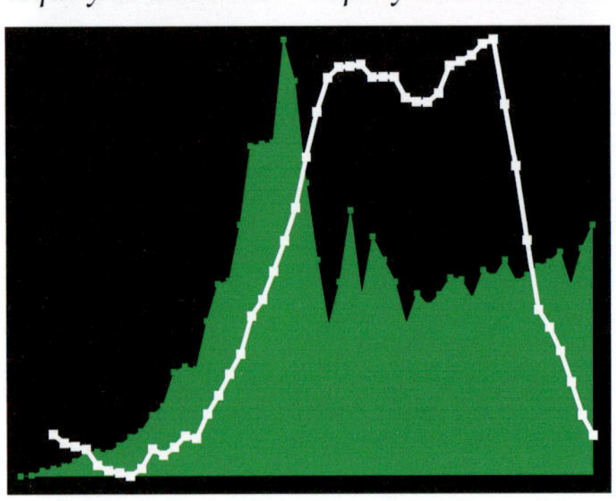

Equity to Revenue—Share Price

> If we reach the point that we can't create extra value by retaining earnings, we will pay them out and let shareholders deploy the funds.
>
> Warren E. Buffett—*Berkshire Owner's Manual, Principle 9*

Equity to revenue shows you equity in proportion to revenue. When there's more equity than company strategy prescribes—for revenue growth, opportunities, and safety—a company may buy back shares, reduce borrowing, or pay out dividends.

Equity to revenue, also known as the equity turnover reciprocal or the capital turnover reciprocal, is equity divided by revenue (*equity / revenue*). Equity to revenue is a times-number.

The beginning of the steep climb in equity to revenue (white) shows that the company is retaining income in equity (blue) much faster than it's increasing revenue (magenta).

In the middle chart, you see that neither retaining more income in equity—nor paying out equity in a dividend—is affecting revenue. This signals there is more than enough equity to fund revenue, and that the extra equity is not creating extra revenue, income, or value.

As equity becomes increasingly larger than revenue, you want an explanation. What's the company's strategy for creating extra value with large amounts of equity, beyond what it needs to fund production that generates revenue?

A company may believe it's in your best interest as a shareholder that it delay explanations or returns of significant resources until issues such as antitrust are resolved. However, you can easily read the news, know that legal rulings are one of many tools companies use to shape their competitive landscapes, and imagine that rational management requires appropriate reserves.

There are many paths to excellence. Microsoft paid a large dividend; whereas Buffett offered to return excess equity—shareholders asked him to keep it. Dividend or no dividend, the most remarkable chart feature is that equity increases faster than revenue to the *point* when management—for many reasons—returns money to shareholders.

Look at the *Equity to Revenue—Share Price* chart and you'll guess that after the dividend-payout-drop the company will strive for at least the minimum equity required to support revenue growth and for running equity parallel to revenue. Look at the charts on the *front cover* and you'll see after the *dot-com boom* that the company is consistently improving—reflected by informed investors in share price.

Equity to Revenue Events

Equity to revenue (circled) is the only factor management can use to cause net profit margin to be different from return on equity. You see this on row 4 of *GAAP Structure*, where equity to revenue times the factors of return on equity equals net profit margin.

What equity to revenue is best? You've read the *S&P* 11% argument earlier in this chapter. The July 20, 2004 *Teleconference Regarding New Microsoft Dividend and Stock Buyback Plans* clearly raises a related issue. The company decides how much cash to keep, based on its "capital management plan". As an investor watching equity to revenue rising, you can guess that new products, acquisitions, debt-paydowns, dividends, and stock buybacks are being considered.

Look for events like the point in the trend chart after which management retains enough income to cause equity greater than revenue. Management obviously wants the cash. The good news is that the company can generate cash beyond its needs. However, the chart reveals that within the focus of the business the company can fund opportunities beyond its ability or willingness to expand. This chart reveals the dynamic tension between retaining cash, paying a dividend like in December 2004, and risking investment in new arenas.

MICROSOFT

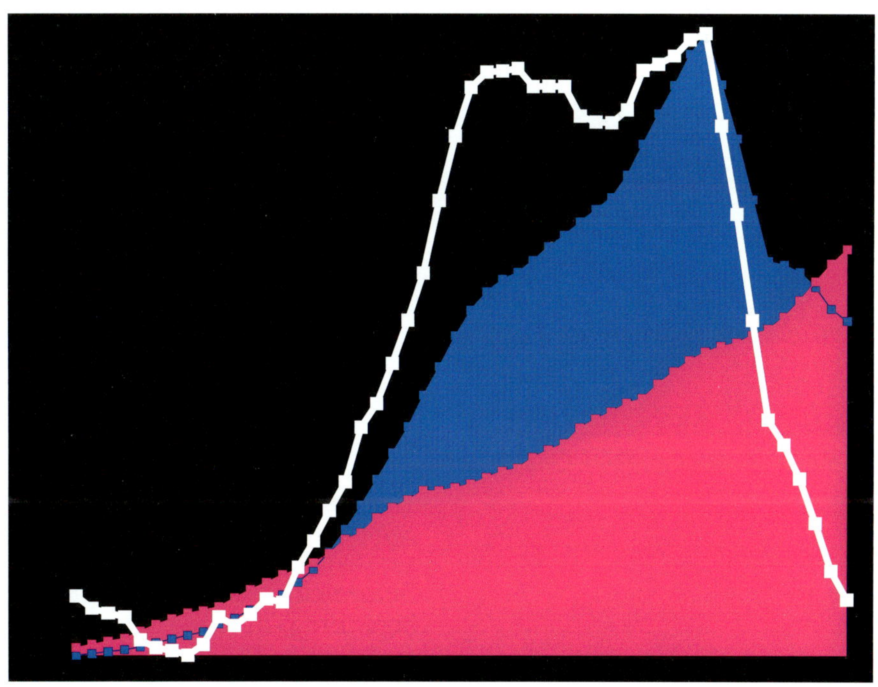

Equity to Revenue—Equity and Revenue

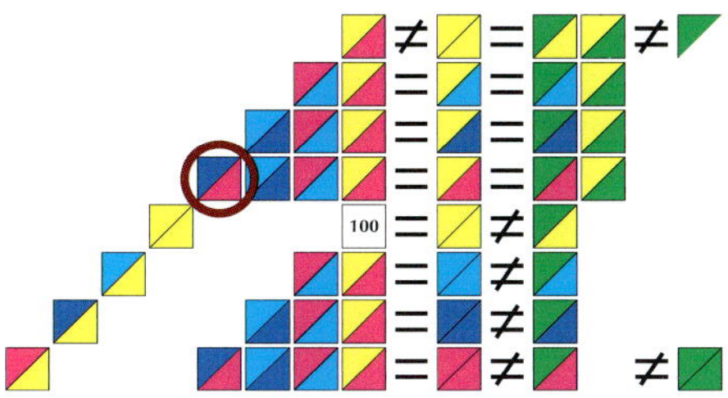

GAAP Structure

$$\frac{\delta equity}{income} \times \frac{assets}{equity} \times \frac{revenue}{assets} \times \frac{income}{revenue} = \frac{\delta equity}{equity}$$

In the margins of three prior subsections, we include the equation above from row 7 of *GAAP Structure* to show if the company's equity growth is beating the *S&P* price growth (averaging 11%).

It would be reasonable of you to expect that we should wrap up this subsection with the fourth factor that may cause the company to beat the *S&P*.

However, row 7 of *GAAP Structure* reveals that the factor is *Equity Change to Income* on page 40, instead of equity to revenue. *GAAP Structure Verified by SEC Data* on page 93 should convince you that equity change to income on row 7 is the appropriate factor.

Let's take one more look at our subject of equity to revenue. Who ever heard of equity to revenue? We hadn't until we explored a mathematical question: How many ratios are formed by the four fundamentals and satisfy *GAAP Structure*?

Six unique ratios is the answer—and equity to revenue is one of the six. We found that middle school students can follow the proof. In *The Ratios Riddle* on page 105, we use the binomial formula contributed to by Euclid and Pascal as part of the proof that equity to revenue indeed plays one of the unique roles in *GAAP Structure*.

Return on Assets—Income to Assets

MICROSOFT

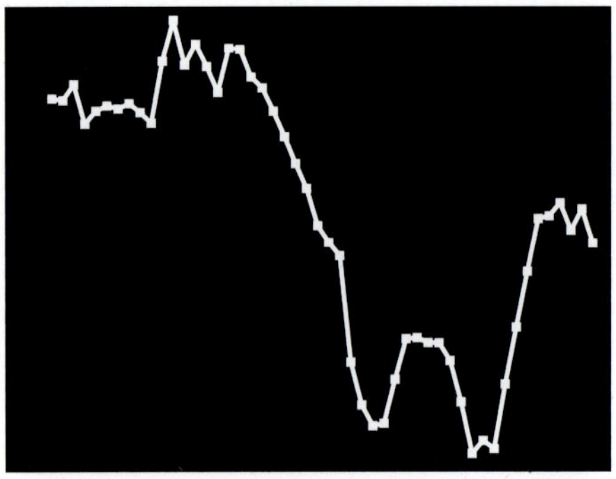

Return on Assets

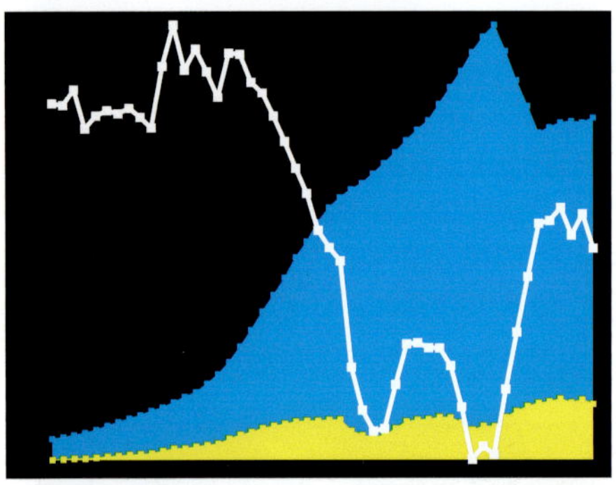

Return on Assets—Income and Assets

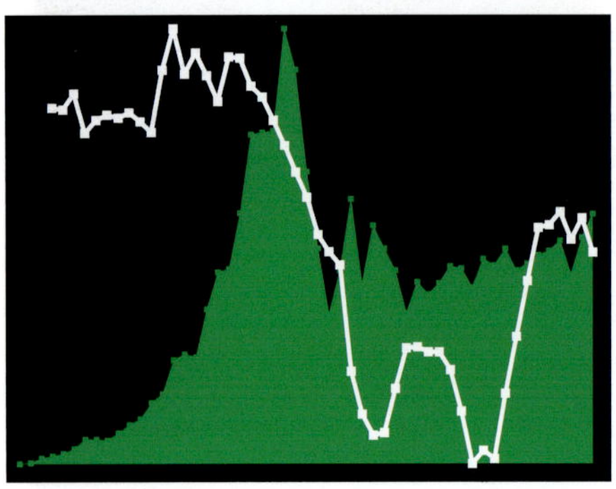

Return on Assets—Share Price

ROA is a basic measure of the efficiency with which a company allocates and manages its resources. It differs from ROE in that ROE measures profit as a percentage of the money provided by owners and creditors as opposed to only the money provided by owners.

Robert C. Higgins—*Analysis for Financial Management*

Return on assets is the result of two of four factors that help you determine if a company's business progress beats the *S&P*.

Return on assets (ROA) is income divided by assets (*income / assets*) × 100. ROA is the product of efficiency and net profit margin. Return on assets is a percent.

As an investor, you want to see measures like ROA that quickly show you high-level results of a company. Then you want the factors of each result—like efficiency and net profit margin—so you see if either are of concern or are excellent. Finally, you want the factors of these results to contribute to beating *S&P* average price growth of 11%, as in *The Best Numbers Riddle* on page 100.

As a shareholder, you might well ask why you should want both results—ROA and ROE. The answer is you want to compare them to see the role of liabilities in beating *S&P* price growth. ROA shows the return on owners' (shareholders') money, while ROE shows the return on owners' money plus creditors' money. For example, if ROA is 10% and ROE is 12%, then ROE is earned on 1 dollar of owners' money and 20 cents of creditors' money.

Leverage is the only bridge between ROA and ROE, as you see in ROA times leverage equals ROE. We explore *Leverage—Assets to Equity* on page 26, and the relationship between leverage and its components (including liabilities to equity) in *The Leverage Riddle* on page 106.

Investment opportunity exists when ROA is high, price is low, and the company is relatively unknown, as you see in the bottom chart when ROA is high while price is rising. Price plummets in early 2000 when the *FCC* decides against a low-cost broadband monopoly. In the middle chart, as you'll see on the next page, the company levels ROA closer to average numbers after its decline from very high numbers. The December 2004 spike in ROA results primarily from the dividend, not from slightly increasing income or improving efficiency.

Before calculating ROA and ROE, you must pick assets and equity as beginning, average, or ending a 4 quarter income period. *The Assets and Equity Riddle* on page 103 reveals the folly of ending, and compares the benefits of beginning and average as reasonable choices.

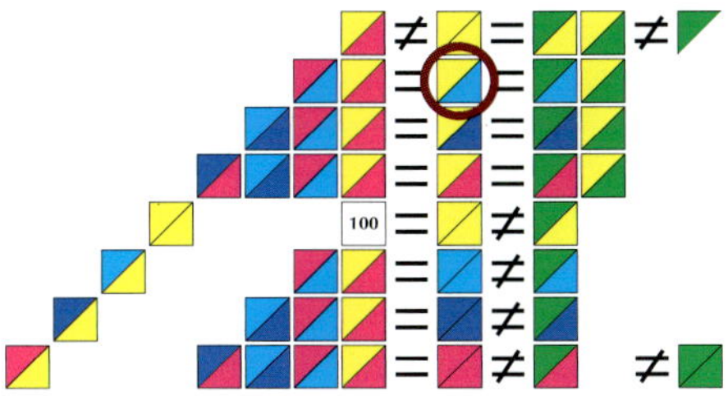

GAAP Structure

$$\frac{\delta\,\text{equity}}{\text{income}} \times \frac{\text{assets}}{\text{equity}} \times \frac{\text{revenue}}{\text{assets}} \times \frac{\text{income}}{\text{revenue}} = \frac{\delta\,\text{equity}}{\text{equity}}$$

Return on assets (ROA) reveals what you should expect from stockbrokers and financial websites. ***Their organizations and data resources, using our tools, can jump-start financial literacy.***

ROA results from net profit margin times efficiency—so you expect to see sides of the equation equal, as in *GAAP Structure Verified by SEC Data* on page 93.

ROA and its factors use revenue, income, and assets—so you wish to see charts of all our *GAAP Original Data* on page 91—data is free electronically since 1993 from our United States *Securities and Exchange Commission (SEC)*, as in *The Get Data Riddle* on page 113.

ROA and its factors are trend-slices—so you wish to see all measures in the context of their trend charts, as in our *GAAP Structure Graphics Verified* on page 95.

ROA and its factors use revenue, income, and assets—so you wish to see the most current data, as in our rolling quarterly updates of *The Annual Report Every Quarter Riddle* on page 101.

ROA and its factors use the same revenue, income, and assets used in growth measures—so you wish to see per-share ratio and growth measures as in *The Per Share Growth Riddle* on page 107; handling negative and zero numbers, as in *The Computable Riddle* on page 110.

Return on Assets Events

Return on assets (circled) is the product of the two factors on its left (efficiency and net profit margin). You see this relationship of factors and their result on row 2 of *GAAP Structure* on the left. Indeed, the factors of ROA are factors in six of seven results.

The Best Numbers Riddle on page 100 shows why you want the equity growth equation from row 7 of *GAAP Structure* to average greater than the *S&P* 11% average. In the equation on the left, you want change in equity to income and leverage to multiply the factors of return on assets, so equity growth beats *S&P* price growth.

Several ROA events should interest you as an investor. An excellent opportunity for investors occurred in the early four years of our data (and earlier), when ROA was high, and you might assume price was low because the company was relatively unknown. The chart would have scaled differently—you'd have had to read the numbers. The long decline in ROA was caused by the company's success. Increasing amounts of income were retained in assets—primarily as cash. Then, the December 2004 dividend was paid out of assets—but extends over several quarters due to averaging. This decrease in assets caused ROA to surge—resetting to above the industry average.

MICROSOFT

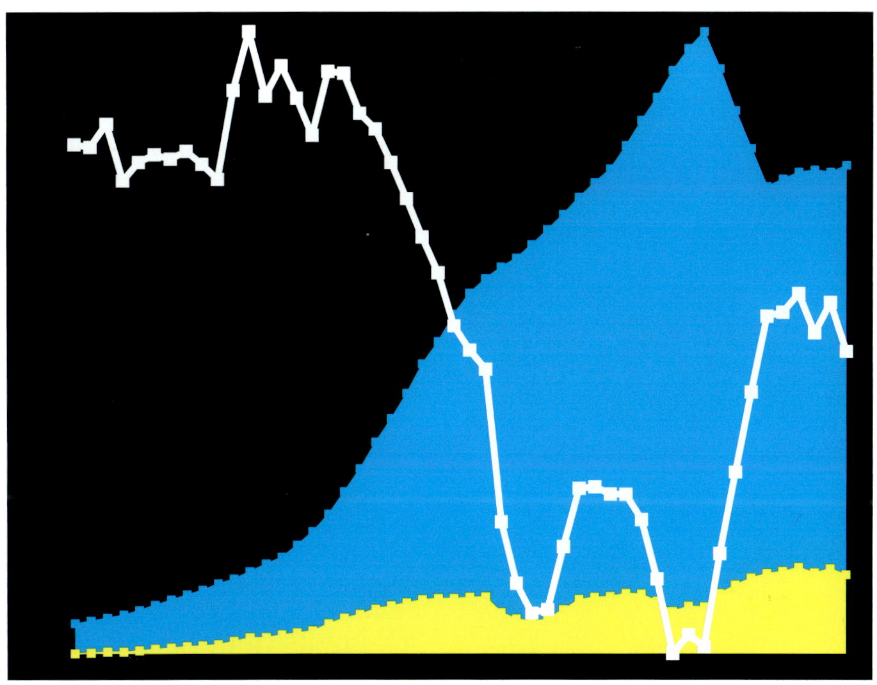

Return on Assets—Income and Assets

Return on Equity—Income to Equity

MICROSOFT

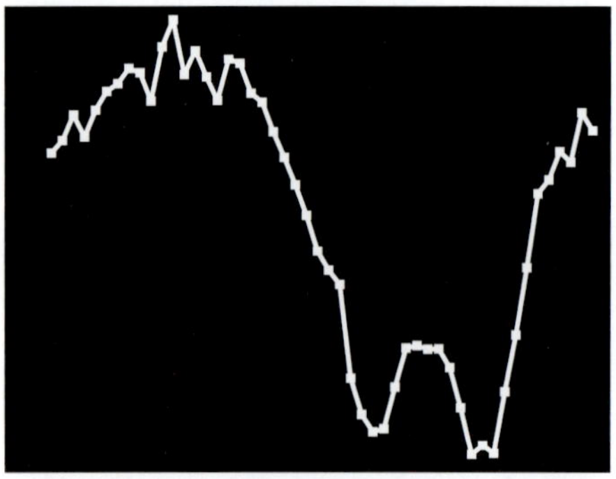

Return on Equity

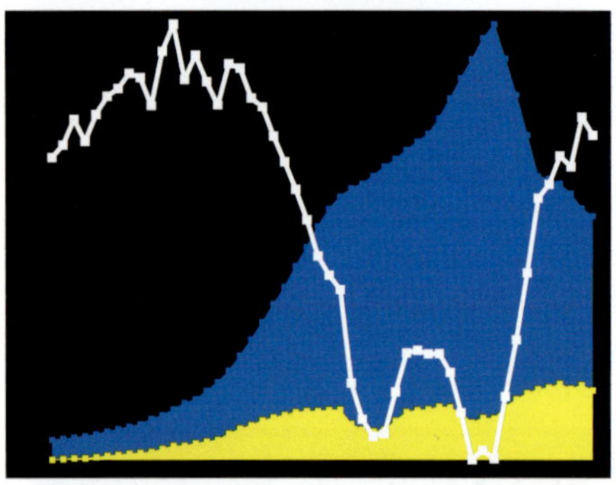

Return on Equity—Income and Equity

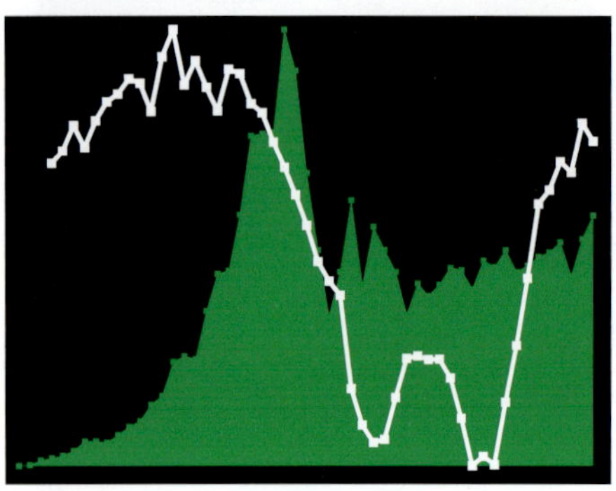

Return on Equity—Share Price

So even when ROE measures management's financial performance, it may not be synonymous with a high return on investment to shareholders. Thus, it is not enough for investors to find companies capable of generating high ROEs; these companies must be unknown to others, because once they are known, the possibility of high returns to investors will melt away in higher stock prices.

Robert C. Higgins—*Analysis for Financial Management*

Return on equity is the result of three of four factors that help you determine if a company's business progress beats the *S&P*.

Return on equity (ROE) is income divided by equity (*income / equity*) × 100. ROE is the product of leverage, efficiency, and net profit margin, or leverage times return on assets. Return on equity is a percent.

You want a company that is "capable of generating high ROEs", is "unknown", and whose "possibility of high returns to investors" will last a while. The high ROEs (white) meet the first criterion.

The bottom chart shows the early period of high ROEs with low yet increasing share price—so you infer the company must be relatively "unknown". In this period, informed investors made money—as you'll see in the table facing *Share and Fair Price Trends* on page 77.

Why does "the possibility of high returns to investors ... melt away in high stock prices"? First, in the bottom chart, as share price rises, optimistic shareholders become wary—especially when ROE peaks. Second, you see in the middle chart that this company's success is driving ROE down by retaining income in equity. When equity (blue) exceeds what's needed to fund revenue—whatever that number may be—investors are then inclined to decrease the share price.

High ROE may signal investors that the company has the benefits of high economic goodwill through its brand and reputation. Reputation is a free asset. Equipment and other assets are bought-assets that tend to cost more with inflation. An outstanding company may make its products with fewer bought-assets—so it has lower costs. However, reputation may enable it to sell products for the same or higher price as its less efficient competitor, earning more profit. Whenever you shop, you see reputation—economic goodwill.

Robert G. Hagstrom, Jr.—*The Warren Buffett Way* emphasizes that "Economic goodwill not only produces above-average returns on capital but its value tends to increase with inflation. This appreciation is fundamental in understanding Buffett's equity-investment strategy."

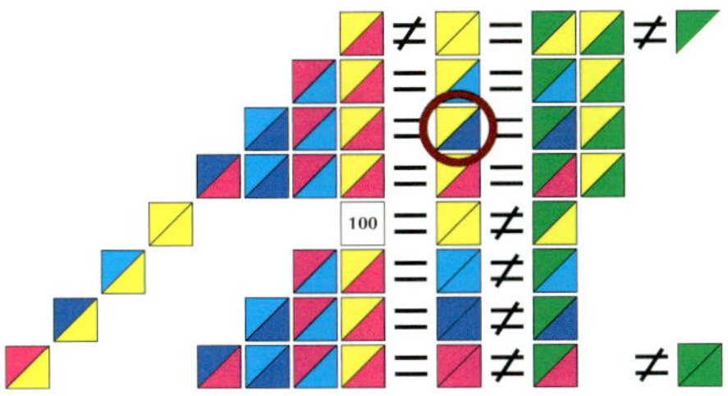

GAAP Structure

$$\frac{\delta equity}{income} \times \frac{assets}{equity} \times \frac{revenue}{assets} \times \frac{income}{revenue} = \frac{\delta equity}{equity}$$

For a company borrowing money on which it then measures its return, Robert C. Higgins offers a persuasive argument you can read for yourself in *Analysis for Financial Management*. He describes a measure in addition to ROE and ROA—that has its own limitations.

"To circumvent the distorting effects of leverage on ROE and ROA, I recommend calculating return on invested capital (ROIC), also known as return on net assets (RONA).... The numerator of this ratio is the earnings (income) after tax the company would report if it were all equity financed, and the denominator is the sum of all sources of cash to the company on which a return must be earned.... In essence, ROIC is the rate of return earned on the total capital invested in the business without regard for whether it is called debt (liabilities) or equity.... ROIC thus reflects the company's fundamental earning power before it is confounded by differences in financing strategies."

The numerators of ROE and ROIC are income (yellow). As you see in *The Definitions Riddle* on page 111, only the denominator (blue) changes from "equity" to invested capital (equity plus interest bearing debt). Here you see the flexibility of *GAAP Structure*.

Return on Equity Events

Return on equity (circled) is the product of the three factors on its left (leverage, efficiency, and net profit margin). You see this relationship on row 3 of *GAAP Structure*, where leverage times the factors of return on assets equals the resultant return on equity.

The Best Numbers Riddle on page 100 shows why you want the equity growth equation from row 7 of *GAAP Structure* to average greater than the *S&P* 11% average. In the equation on the left, you want *Equity Change to Income* on page 40 to multiply the factors of return on equity so equity growth beats *S&P* price growth.

"One or even several ratios might be misleading...." cautions Professor Higgins. For example, the December 2004 dividend has caused new equity to be smaller than old equity, causing *Equity Change to Income* on page 40 to be a negative number that multiplies ROE—a negative can't beat the *S&P* positive 11%.

Investors see in the chart below that company success first causes decreasing ROE due to increasing cash, then success causes increasing ROE due to decreasing cash from returning resources to shareholders. Thus, ROE trends may imply opportunities for the future.

MICROSOFT

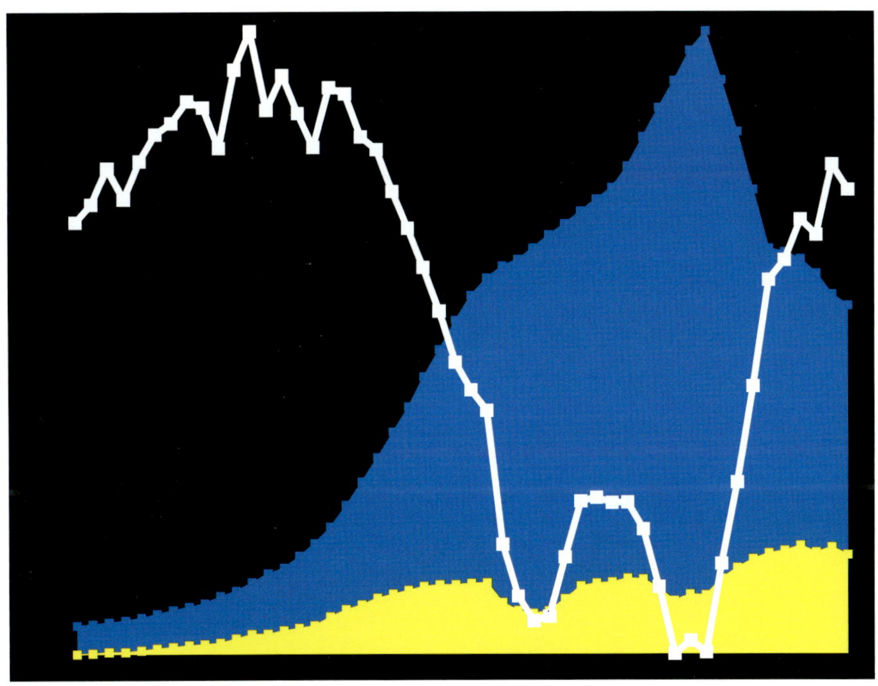

Return on Equity—Income and Equity

GAAP Structure—Change Trends Datastreams

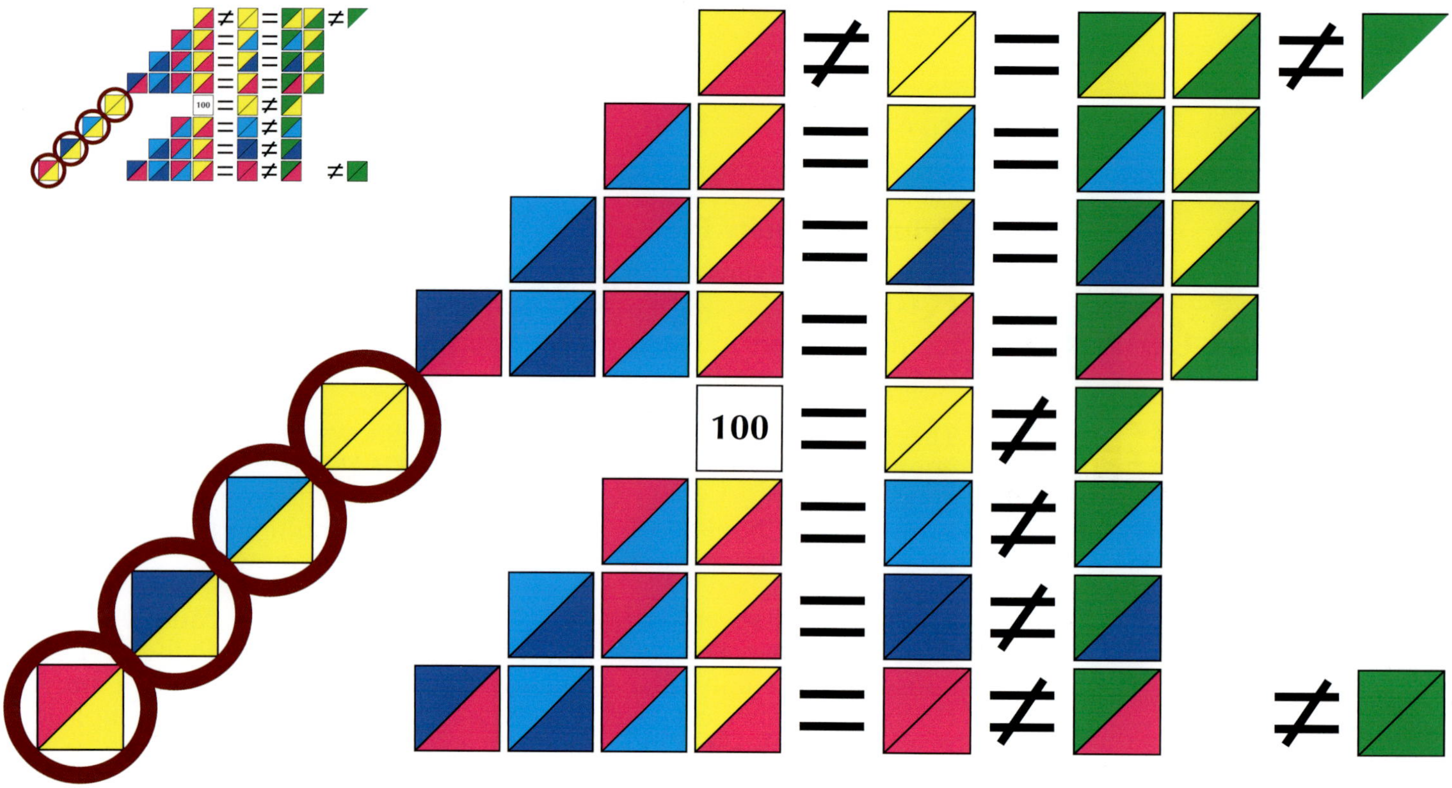

4 Change Trends

DATASTREAMS MICROSOFT

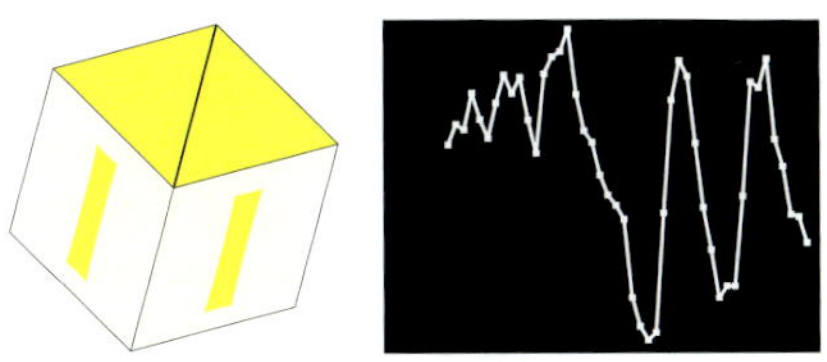

Inc Change/Income

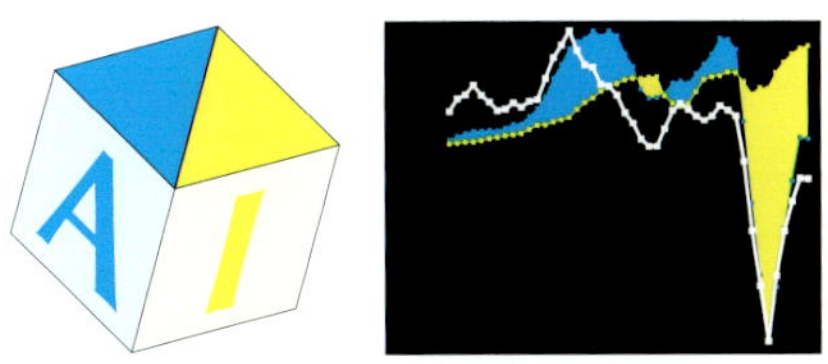

Ass Change/Income

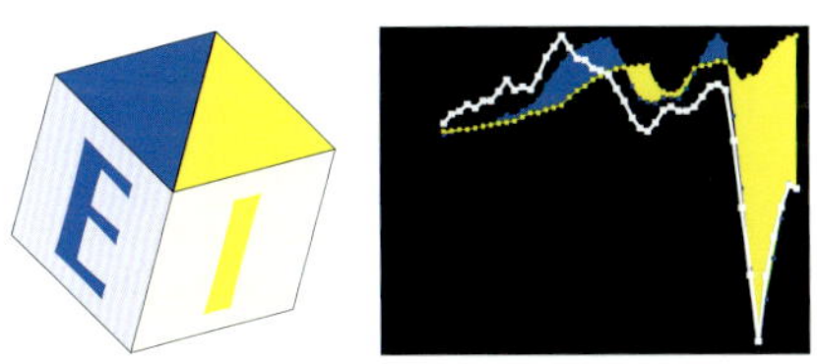

Eqt Change/Income

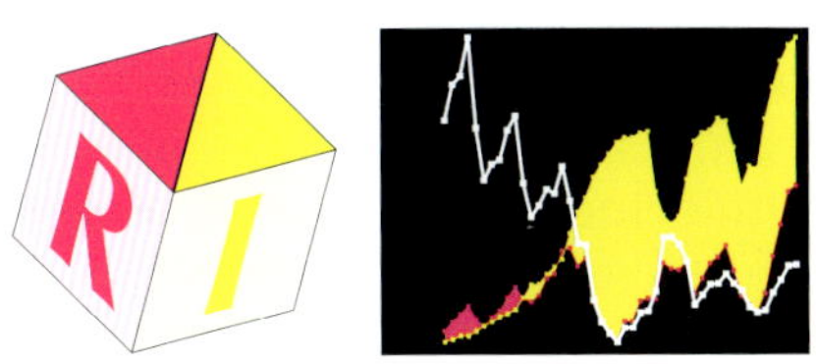

Rev Change/Income

The central stupendous truth about developed economies today is that they can have—in anything but the shortest run—the kind and scale of resources they decide to have. . . . It is no longer resources that limit decisions. It is decisions that make resources. This is the fundamental revolutionary change—perhaps the most revolutionary man has ever known.

U Thant—*Secretary-General of the United Nations, 1961–1971*

Causes of *Growth Trends* on page 11 became complete in our *GAAP Structure* on the facing page and page 87, when we discovered they equal *Ratio Trends* on page 21 times corresponding change trends—(except 100 times income change to income), assets change to income, equity change to income, revenue change to income.

Change trends show you decisions that make the resources. How much does a company decide to change a fundamental relative to old income to provide reinvestment that increases income?

You may be alerted to possible misappraisal when one *datastream* color is larger. The height of that color shows how much larger. The white line shows change to income as a ratio. For example, in *Eqt Change/Income*, the change in the equity datastream (blue) may be larger than income. How much? The height of the blue. A rising ratio (white) shows equity change to income is increasing.

Without change trends, evaluation is limited to a list. With change trends, you begin evaluation with the power of results related to causes. As Warren Buffett said in the *Financial Review*, December 9, 1985, "I can filter out 99 percent of the ideas in five minutes." Then, if a company passes your results-screening, you may want to see the factors. Your results-screens are the four growth trends. The factors are ratio trends and change trends—especially equity change.

Equity Change to Income shows "decisions that make resources" available to fund revenue growth and thus income growth. When net profit margin, efficiency, and leverage *Ratio Trends* on page 21 reach their limits, as Martin Fridson says in *Financial Statement Analysis*, "This leaves only (equity per share), which can rise unceasingly through additions to retained income (in equity change to income), as a source of sustainable growth in (income per share)"—provided the company finds profitable ways to use equity.

Income Change to Income

MICROSOFT

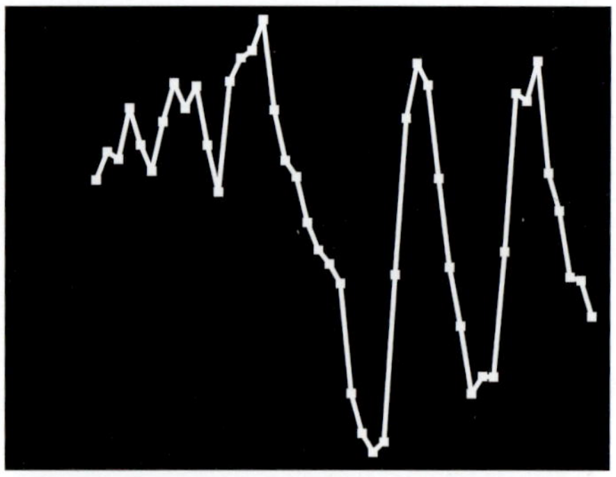

Income Change / Income

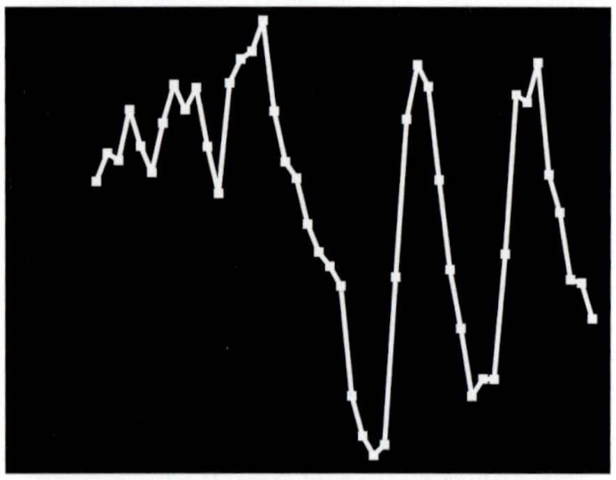

Inc Chg / Inc—without Inc Chg and Inc

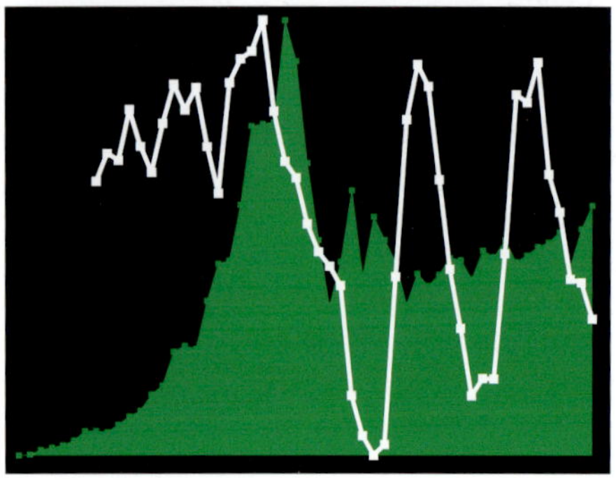

Inc Chg / Inc—Share Price

> To achieve sustainable growth in (income) per share, then, a company must retain a portion of its (income). The higher the portion retained, the more (equity) is accumulated per share and the higher can be the (income per share) growth.
>
> Martin S. Fridson—*Financial Statement Analysis*

Income change to income multiplies the factor 100 to reveal itself as its own result. You see this on the right in row 5 of *GAAP Structure*. Our middle chart is without components of income change and income, because they're hard to distinguish with one color (yellow).

Income change to income is income change divided by income [(*new income* – *old income*) / *old income*]. Income change to income is a times-number—so many times income.

Income is the common denominator that impacts the four growth results—income growth (yellow), assets growth (cyan), equity growth (blue), and revenue growth (magenta). Obviously, income change to income impacts the common denominator—income. What's not obvious is that income change to income is one—but not the only—influence on the numerators. You can picture the sweeping affect of income change to income only when you focus on the factors of the four growth results—not the results.

If this seems too complex, think simply. Each of the four change to income rows of *GAAP Structure* equals a growth measure. You know from *The Best Numbers Riddle* on page 100 that you want growth to beat the *S&P* 11% average price growth. An increasing change to income ratio helps. When the other factors in a growth equation have reached their limits described in *Ratio Trends* on page 21, the change to income ratios become the only sources for increasing the four growth measures. Finally, a positive income change to income makes a positive contribution to the four growth measures—ideally income change to income is increasing.

This can happen only when management retains income in equity and uses equity to make more income. Here you see why Martin Fridson says, "To achieve sustainable growth in (income) per share, then, a company must retain a portion of its (income)."

We intended that the middle chart overlay income change to income (white) on the interplay of income change and income—but couldn't code it right. Instead, look at *Income* on page 2. Income (yellow) is persistently increasing. This shows you that management is making decisions that retain a portion of income to flow all the way to equity—then to reinvest that income to achieve more income.

Income Change Events

Income change to income (circled) and 100 are the only two factors of income growth. You see this on row 5 of *GAAP Structure*, where income change to income times 100 equals income growth.

The Best Numbers Riddle on page 100 says you want the equation from row 5 of *GAAP Structure* on the left to average greater than the *S&P* 11% average price growth.

The big event for income change to income (white) is the persistent increase in income (yellow)—resulting from management deciding on profitable markets, deciding to have flexible product pricing and low costs, deciding to send income to equity, deciding to reinvest that income to fund more revenue and return some to shareholders.

As an investor, you prefer income change to income to be increasing or remain level.

Income change to income enables investors to imagine the changes in each of the four fundamentals proportional to the common denominator of income—ideally, a portion the company can reinvest to grow more income, fair price, and share price.

MICROSOFT

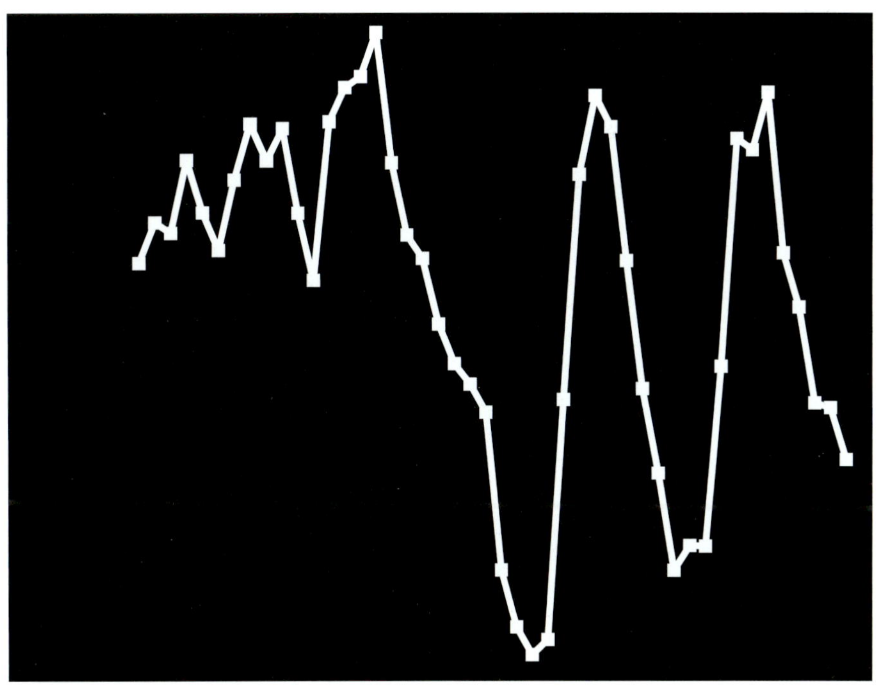

Income Change to Income—without Income Change and Income

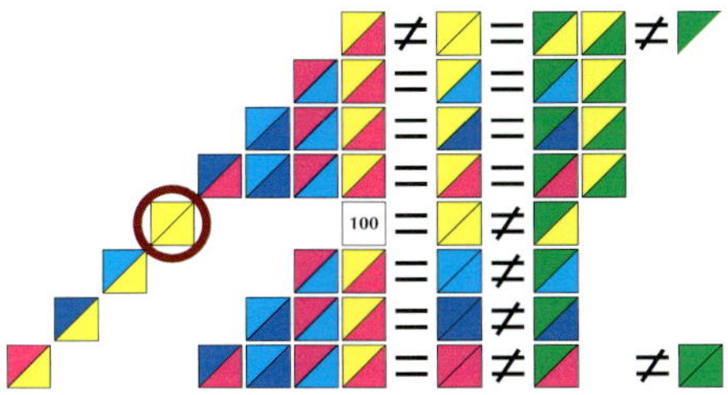

GAAP Structure

In the *GAAP Structure* above, you see that various forms of income play a dominant role in completing the matrix. All forms of income are calculated from the *inside front cover Data Summary*.

There is a persuasive alternative to income—owner earnings—explained by Warren Buffett at the end of his *Letter to Berkshire Shareholders, 1986*. http://www.berkshirehathaway.com/

Here's the approximate equation: (*owner earnings = income + depreciation – net change in property, plant, equipment – net change in working capital*).

GAAP Structure is flexible. Once you have calculated the owner earnings datastream, you can substitute owner earnings for income. However, we use income so you have fewer data-items to understand and retrieve.

Notice that income is a component in the owner earnings equation. Buffett emphasizes that owner earnings may be significantly more or less than income.

Buffett says: *Our owner-earnings equation does not yield the deceptively precise figures provided by GAAP.... We consider the owner earnings figure, not the GAAP figure, to be the relevant item for valuation purposes—both for investors in buying stocks and for managers in buying entire businesses. We agree with Keynes's observation: "I would rather be vaguely right than precisely wrong."*

Assets Change to Income

MICROSOFT

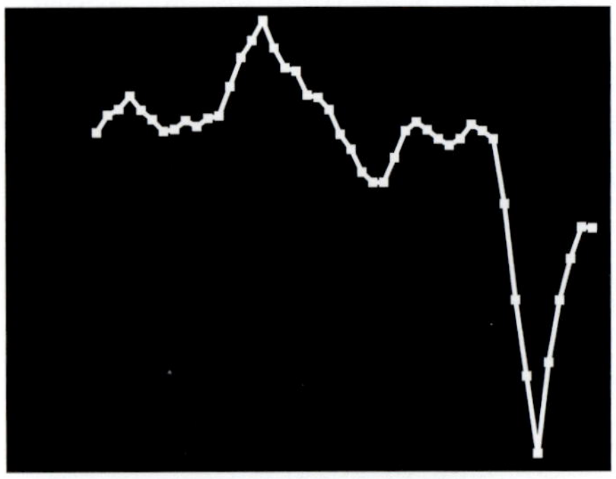

Assets Change / Income

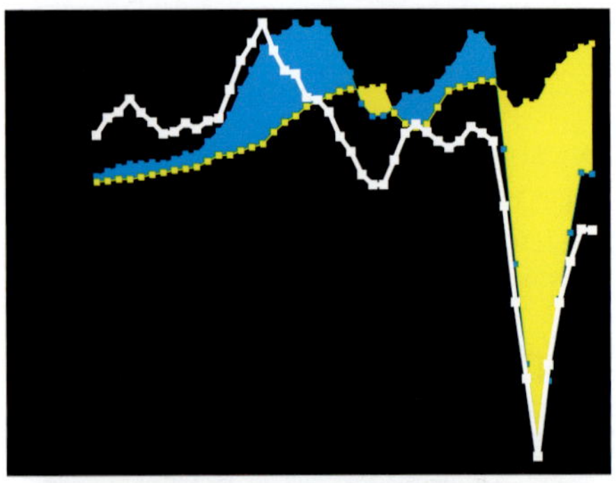

Ass Chg / Inc—Ass Chg and Income

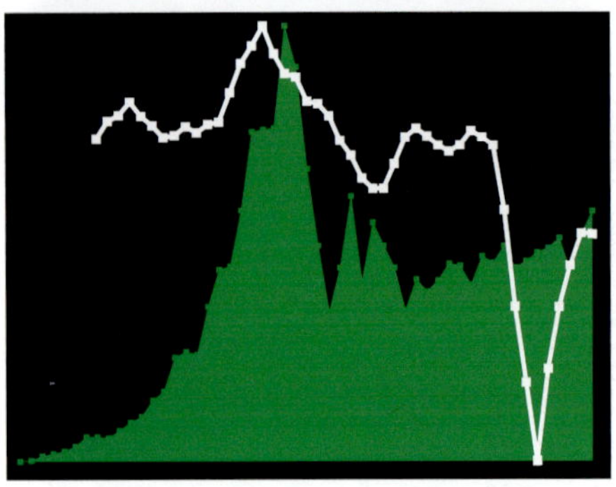

Ass Chg / Inc—Share Price

> As equity grows, liabilities can increase proportionately without altering the capital structure; together, the growth of liabilities and the growth of equity determine the rate at which assets expand. This, in turn, limits the growth in (revenue).
>
> Robert C. Higgins—*Analysis for Financial Management*

Assets change to income multiplies the two factors of *Return on Assets—Income to Assets* on page 30, freeing you from four apparently unrelated measures to reveal three factors and one result. You see this on the right in row 6 of *GAAP Structure*.

Assets change to income is assets change divided by income [(*new assets* – *old assets*) / *old income*]. Assets change to income is a times-number—so many times income.

In *GAAP Structure Verified by SEC Data* on page 93, assets change to income multiplies the factors of return on assets (ROA)—efficiency and net profit margin—to equal their result, assets growth.

As you should infer from *Assets* on page 4, assets change and equity change have a common element—equity. If there are liabilities, they are subtracted from assets. If new and old liabilities are zero, assets change to income and equity change to income will be equal.

Differences between assets growth and *Return on Assets—Income to Assets* on page 30 are caused by assets change to income, as you see in row 6 of *GAAP Structure* on the right and on page 87.

Martin Fridson, in his quote beginning *Equity Change Events* on page 41, is careful not to say that additions of income to assets will definitely cause sustainable income growth. In fact, as we see in the *Assets Change to Income* charts on the left, the company paid out a significant amount of additions of income to assets in the form of its December 2004 dividend—income obviously not reinvested.

On the other hand, look at the rebound after the dividend. The company is continuing to add income to assets. However, even when income—in the form of cash equivalents—is retained in assets, the company may not be able to reinvest all of it in the business. Thus, cash equivalents are a minor source of sustainable growth in income when compared with the income from the sale of company products.

Professor Higgins says that assets (equity plus liabilities) growth limits its revenue growth, which it does. However, as you should infer from *Leverage—Assets to Equity* on page 26, liabilities reach a limit beyond which only equity growth ultimately limits revenue growth.

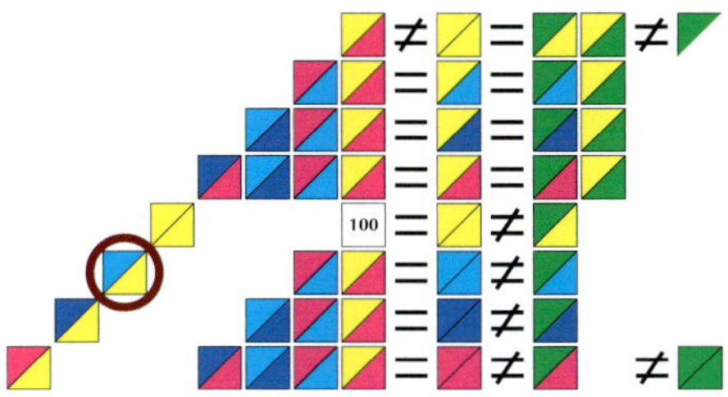

GAAP Structure

In the *GAAP Structure* matrix above, assets change to income is a factor in the assets growth equation on row 6. A brief discussion below of liabilities, and of asset that are undesirable versus desirable, will add to your practical understanding of assets.

We begin with liabilities—which excellent companies "use sparingly" as Buffett says in his *Berkshire Owner's Manual, Principle 7*. Liabilities are the only difference between assets change and equity change—discussed in *Assets* on page 4, *Equity* on page 6, and *The Assets and Equity Riddle* on page 103.

Next, we describe undesirable versus desirable assets—"operations maintenance assets" versus "cash equivalent assets". Excellent companies create persistent income, don't spend it all on maintaining operations, and allocate a significant portion to cash reserves, business growth, shares buyback, debt paydown, or dividends.

Companies always prefer cash equivalents—desirable assets—to undesirable assets (for example, waves of aging airliners rendered uncompetitive by the next generation of more fuel-efficient models).

Now, expand Professor Higgins' quote in *Assets* on page 4: "Indeed, the ideal company would be one that produced income without any assets"—except assets for cash reserves, business growth, or return to shareholders.

Assets Change Events

Assets change to income (circled) is the only factor management can use to cause assets growth to be different from return on assets. You see this on row 6 of *GAAP Structure*, where assets change to income times the factors of return on assets equals assets growth.

The Best Numbers Riddle on page 100 says you want the equation from row 6 of *GAAP Structure*—which includes assets change to income—to average greater than the *S&P* 11% average price growth.

The December 2004 dividend temporarily caused new assets to be smaller than old assets, causing assets change to income to be a negative number that multiplies ROA—a negative can't beat the *S&P* positive 11%. Investors want sustainable assets growth not limiting revenue growth as in *Equity Growth to Revenue Growth* on page 52.

Some income is spent before arriving in the equity portion of assets, and some after arriving. The liabilities portion of assets may also change. Only assets change to income measures net additions to assets as a portion of income—picturing company and creditor money available for cash, business growth, or return to shareholders.

MICROSOFT

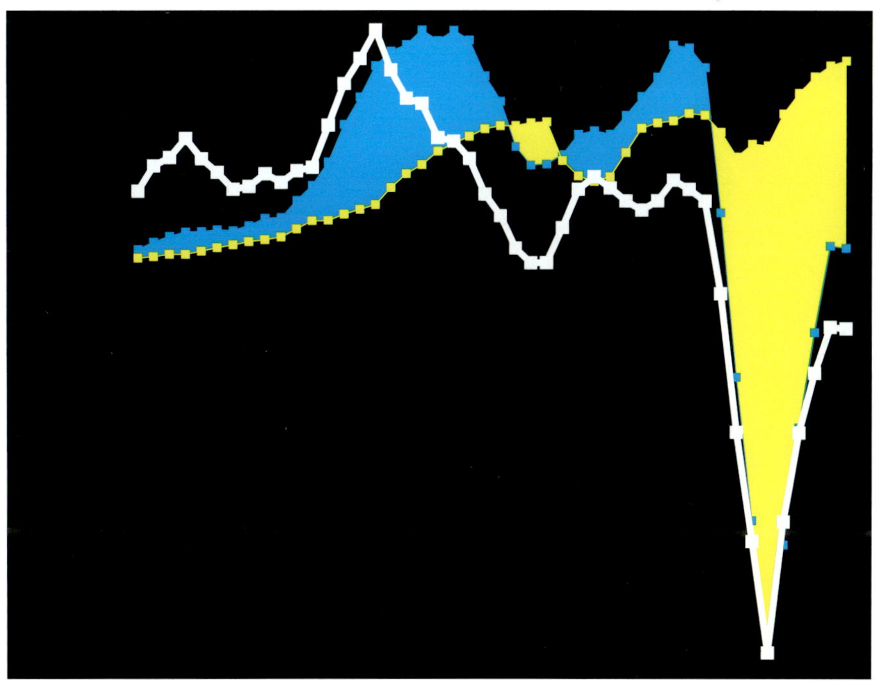

Assets Change to Income—Assets Change and Income

Equity Change to Income

MICROSOFT

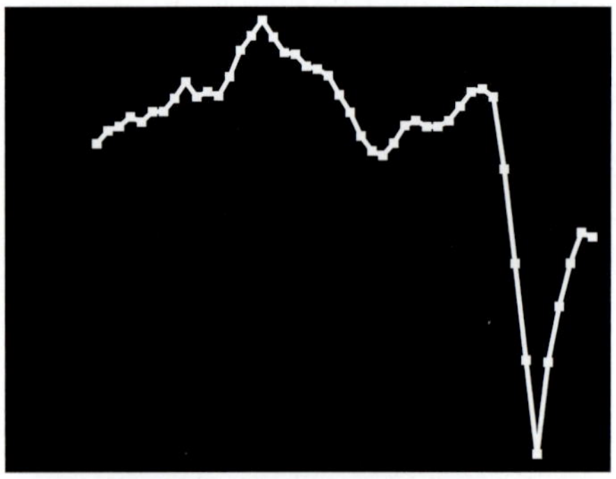

Equity Change / Income

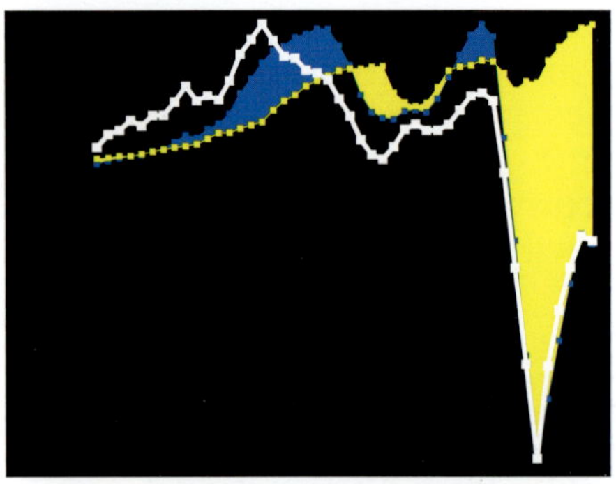

Eqt Chg / Inc—Eqt Chg and Income

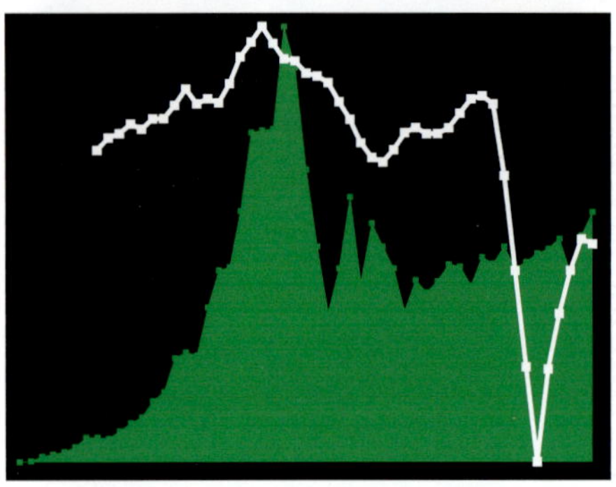

Eqt Chg / Inc—Share Price

> This leaves only (equity per share), which can rise unceasingly through additions to retained income (in equity change to income), as a source of sustainable growth in (income per share).
>
> Martin S. Fridson—*Financial Statement Analysis*

Equity change to income multiplies the three factors of *Return on Equity—Income to Equity* on page 32, freeing you from five apparently unrelated measures to reveal four factors and one result. You see this on the right in row 7 of *GAAP Structure*.

Equity change to income is equity change divided by income [(*new equity* – *old equity*) / *old income*]. Equity change to income is a times-number—so many times income.

In *GAAP Structure Verified by SEC Data* on page 93, equity change to income multiplies the factors of return on equity (ROE)—leverage, efficiency, net profit margin—to equal their result, equity growth.

Equity change to income can cause equity growth to vary, even when leverage, efficiency, and net profit margin have settled near their limits. You might make different investment decisions if the factors of ROE appear to be near their limits than if they are still improving.

Informed investors look not only for excellent companies, but also for great investment opportunities. Equity change to income in the early period of the bottom chart reveals a possible great opportunity. The actual numbers show that equity change to income is high and rising, possibly before the company's excellence becomes well known causing the price to rise. Some investors obviously made money.

Fridson is careful not to say that additions of income to equity will definitely cause sustainable income growth. For example, as we see in the *Equity Change to Income* charts on the left, the company paid out a significant amount of additions of income to equity in the form of its December 2004 dividend—decreasing net additions to equity.

On the other hand, look at the rebound after the dividend. The company is continuing to add income into equity. However, even when income—in the form of cash equivalents—is retained in equity, the company may not be able to reinvest all of it in the business. Thus, cash equivalents are a minor source of sustainable growth in income when compared with the income from the sale of company products.

Martin Fridson synthesizes all these views in one point—Additions of income into equity are the only unceasing source of sustainable growth in income per share.

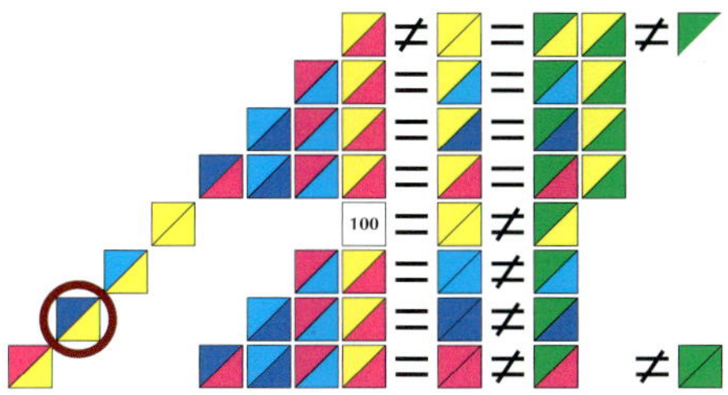

GAAP Structure

In the *GAAP Structure* matrix above, equity change to income influences the equity growth equation on row 7, thus playing a role in revealing the matrix.

Why not calculate equity growth as change in equity divided by equity, and skip its factors? Here are two reasons.

Equity growth is a result of the factors to its left. Forward-looking investors want to know how much of equity growth is caused by leverage, efficiency, and net profit margin—which are limited, and how much by equity change to income—which can rise unceasingly.

Informed investors cross check their computations to establish confidence in the internal consistency of their numbers for investment decisions.

You can quickly convince yourself that *SEC* data makes sense by using *GAAP Structure* to cross-check computations.

Pull out your calculator and turn to the page facing *GAAP Structure Verified by SEC Data* on page 93. Go to row 7. From the left side of the equity growth equation, multiply equity change to income times the three factors of return on equity. Confidence requires that they equal the right side—equity growth.

Now that you understand what's happening, estimate equity change to income in your head. Just ask yourself this: "What number (equity change to income) multiplies return on equity to equal equity growth?"

Equity Change Events

Equity change to income (circled) is the only factor management can use to cause equity growth to be different from return on equity. You see this on row 7 of *GAAP Structure*, where equity change to income times the factors of return on equity equals equity growth.

The Best Numbers Riddle on page 100 says you want the equation from row 7 of *GAAP Structure*—which includes equity change to income—to average greater than the *S&P* 11% average price growth.

The December 2004 dividend temporarily caused new equity to be smaller than old equity, causing equity change to income to be a negative number that multiplies ROE—a negative can't beat the *S&P* positive 11%. In the long run, investors want sustainable equity growth that doesn't limit revenue growth as in *Equity Growth to Revenue Growth* on page 52, and excess that is returned to shareholders.

Some income is spent as it flows to equity, and some is spent from equity. Only equity change to income measures net additions to equity as a portion of income—ideally, the portion the company can reinvest to increase income, fair price, and share price.

MICROSOFT

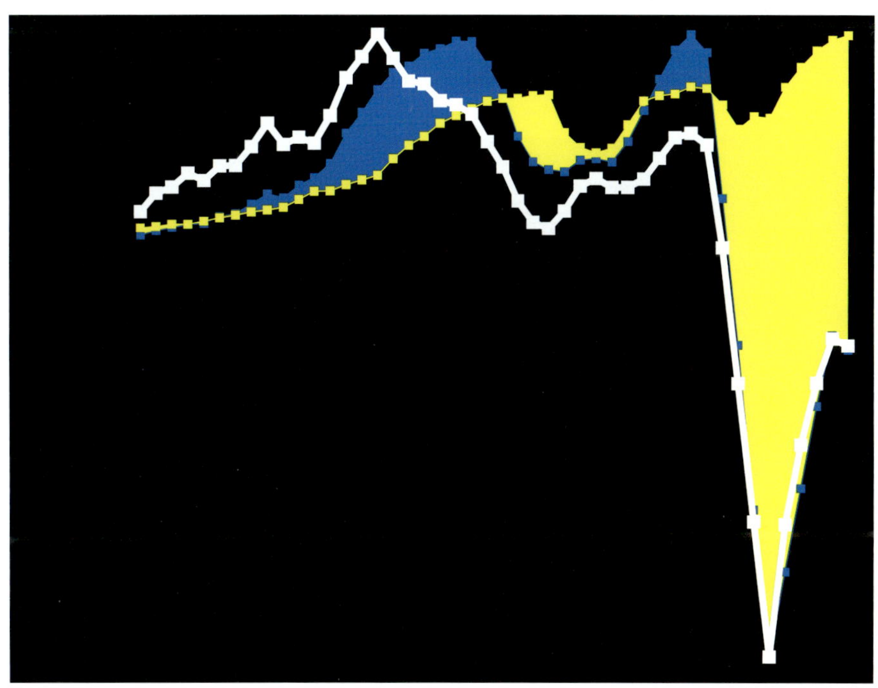

Equity Change to Income—Equity Change and Income

Revenue Change to Income

MICROSOFT

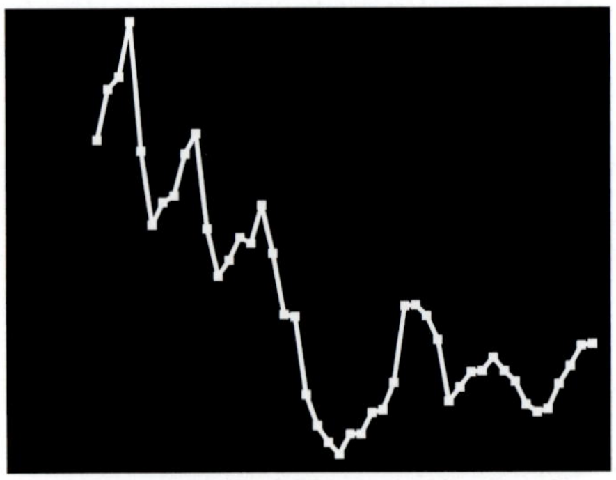

Revenue Change/Income

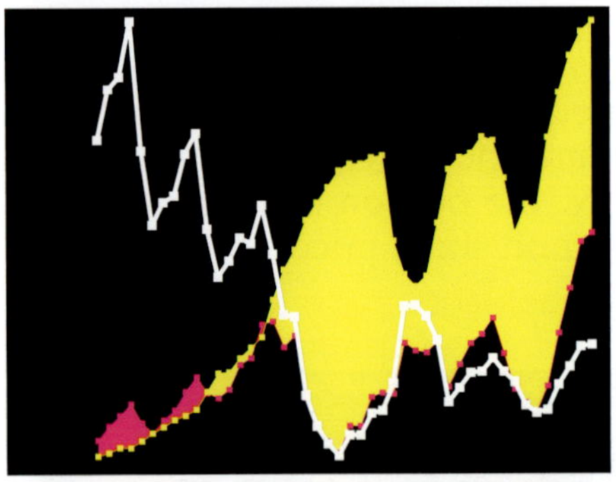

Rev Chg/Inc—Rev Chg and Income

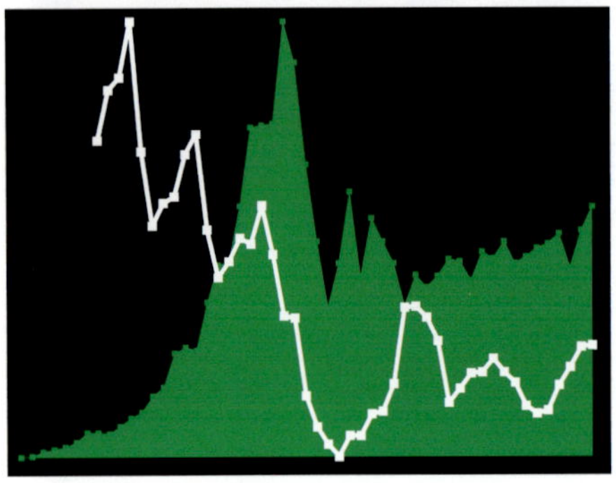

Rev Chg/Inc—Share Price

> By definition, a product that experiences higher-than-GNP (Gross National Product) growth captures a larger percentage of GNP each year. As the numbers get larger, it becomes increasingly difficult to switch consumers' spending patterns to accommodate continued high growth of a particular product.
>
> Martin S. Fridson—*Financial Statement Analysis*

Revenue change to income multiplies the four factors of *Net Profit Margin—Income to Revenue* on page 22, freeing you from six apparently unrelated measures to reveal five factors and one result. You see this on the right in row 8 of *GAAP Structure*.

Revenue change to income is revenue change divided by income [(*new revenue* – *old revenue*) / *old income*]. Revenue change to income is a times-number—so many times income.

In *GAAP Structure Verified by SEC Data* on page 93, revenue change to income multiplies the factors of return on revenue (also known as net profit margin)—equity to revenue, leverage, efficiency, and oddly net profit margin itself—to equal their result, revenue growth.

Revenue change to income can cause revenue growth to vary, even when equity to revenue, leverage, efficiency, and net profit margin have settled near their limits. You might make different investment decisions if the factors of net profit margin appear to be near their limits than decisions you'd make if they are still improving.

Informed investors look not only for excellent companies, but also for great investment opportunities—like early in the bottom chart. The actual numbers show that revenue change to income is high and rising, possibly before the company's excellence becomes well known causing the price to rise. Some investors obviously made money.

Fridson is careful not to say that additions to revenue will cause sustainable income growth. Even if additions to revenue result in additions to income, management still decides how much of that income they will add to equity and then decides how much of that portion of income to reinvest to grow more income.

As revenue change to income (white) is decreasing, revenue (magenta) and income (yellow) continue increasing—but slower than their fastest rates. The revenue change to income trend illustrates Fridson's classic point—"it becomes increasingly difficult to switch consumers' spending patterns to accommodate continued high growth of a particular product."

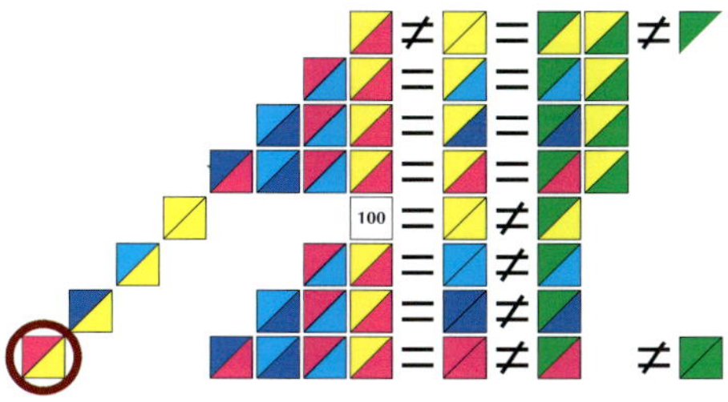

GAAP Structure

In the *GAAP Structure* matrix above, revenue change to income and all other measures are influenced by inflation. If the focus of our book was amounts of money—rather than picturing company finances—we would have adjusted money for inflation.

If inflation was zero, then our trend charts would not be affected. But, inflation is usually not zero. You can mentally adjust our trend charts by knowing the percentage of inflation at a particular datapoint and subtracting (or adding which is rare) that percentage.

The importance of considering inflation is emphasized by Edward R. Tufte in his standard-setting book, *The Visual Display of Quantitative Information, Second Edition*.

"The only way to think clearly about money over time is to make comparisons using inflation-adjusted units of money. Several distinguished graphic designers did express the price in real dollars—and they also avoided other sources of design variation. The stars were *Business Week*, the *Sunday Times* (London), and *The Economist*. In the graphic we saw first, the two sources of design variation covered up an intriguing, non-obvious aspect of the data: in the four years prior to the 1979–1980 increases, the real price of oil had *declined*. Busy with decoration, the graphic had missed the news."

Revenue Change Events

Revenue change to income (circled) is the only factor management can use to cause revenue growth to be different from return on revenue (net profit margin). You see this on row 8 of *GAAP Structure*, where revenue change to income times the factors of return on revenue equals revenue growth.

The Best Numbers Riddle on page 100 says you want the equation from row 8 of *GAAP Structure*—which includes revenue change to income—to average greater than the *S&P* 11% average price growth.

The December 2004 dividend was followed by a short period of slightly reduced revenue—probably due to reduced product demand, not reduced equity to fund revenue. You would expect this to be true. If management had needed more equity reserves to fund post-dividend revenue, they would have made a smaller dividend payout.

Revenue change to income enables investors to imagine all revenue changes as a portion of income—ideally, the portion the company can reinvest to grow more income, fair price, and share price. However, some revenue gets spent as it flows to equity or is in equity.

MICROSOFT

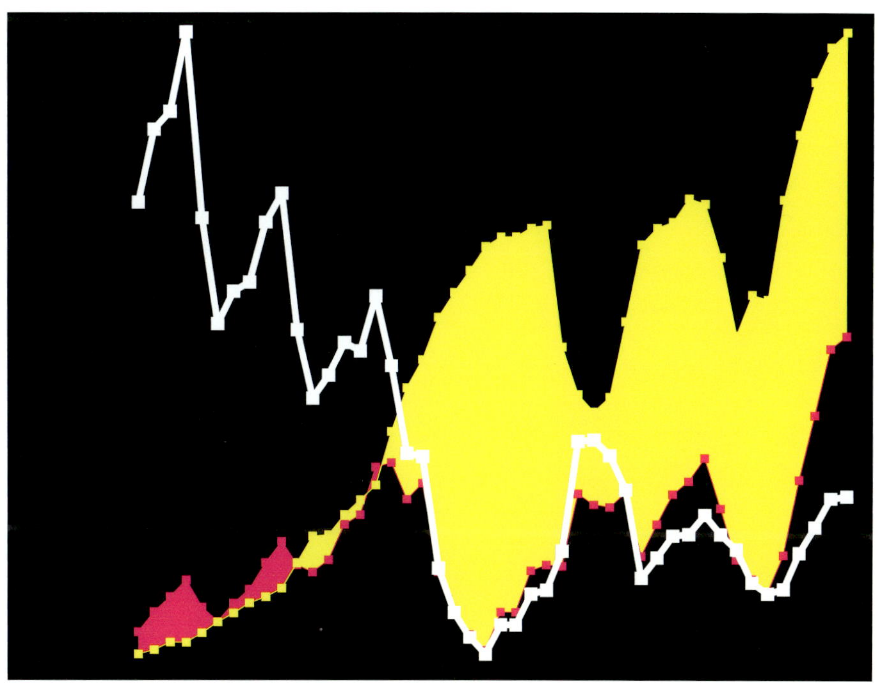

Revenue Change to Income—Revenue Change and Income

GAAP Structure—Sustainable Trends Datastreams

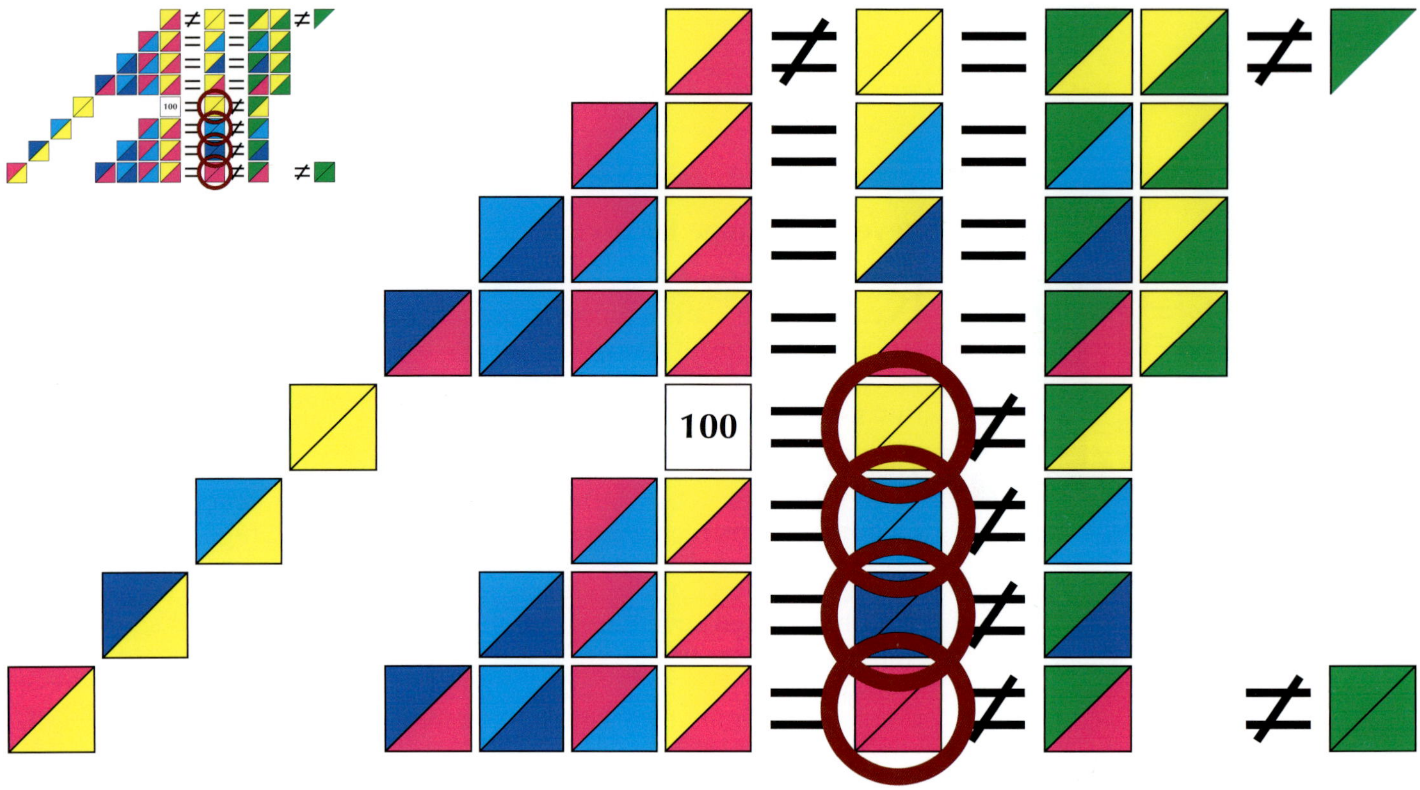

5 Sustainable Trends

DATASTREAMS

MICROSOFT

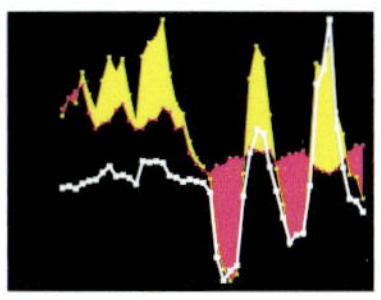

Inc Gro / Rev Gro

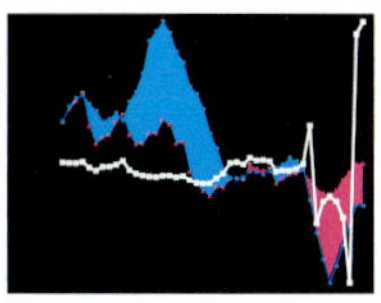

Rev Gro / Ass Gro

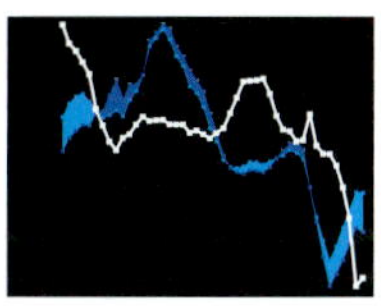

Ass Gro / Eqt Gro

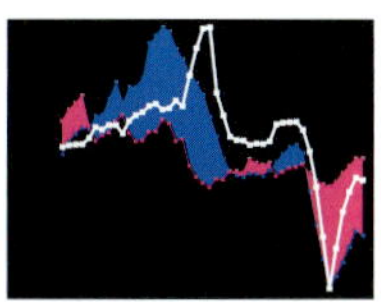

Eqt Gro / Rev Gro

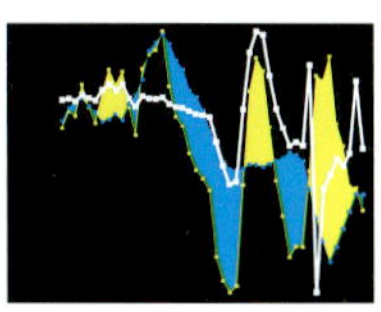

Inc Gro / Ass Gro

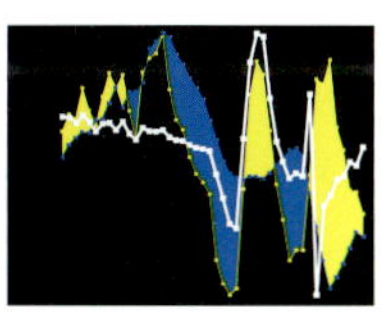

Inc Gro / Eqt Gro

Robert Solow showed mathematically—the basis for his 1987 Nobel Prize—that in the long run growth in gross national product per worker is not due so much to capital investment, the traditional pillar of classic economic analysis. Instead, such growth is in very large part the result of technological progress. In a nutshell, advanced economies grow largely on the strength of what one can call New Knowledge—in most cases the high-tech fruits of research and development.

Robert Buderi—*Engines of Tomorrow*

There is a balance maintained in the affairs of a healthy company. It is reflected in the six sustainable growth ratios which parallel the six *Ratio Trends* on page 21. We wanted to see when growth is sustainable, so we used *The Growth Hierarchy Riddle* on page 104 to build six pairs—income growth and revenue growth, revenue growth and assets growth, assets growth and equity growth, equity growth and revenue growth, income growth and assets growth, income growth and equity growth.

We assume sustainable growth of a fundamental must eventually be reflected in the growth of its mates. For a fairly appraised company—adjusted by "business thinking"—share and fair price growth may approximate the shape of the four-growth chart.

For example, informed investors assume that growth of the *Fair Price Estimate* on page 84 may approximate the growth of equity and revenue of an excellent monopoly—except when an event like the December 2004 dividend pulls equity growth down, or a great investment opportunity arises because the company is misappraised.

You may be alerted to possible misappraisal when one *datastream* color is growing faster. The height of that color shows how much faster. The white line shows a growth pair as a ratio. For example, in the *Eqt Gro/Rev Gro* ratio, the equity growth datastream (blue) may grow faster than revenue. How much? The height of the blue. A rising ratio (white) shows sustainable revenue growth is increasing.

As more customers want the company's current products, equity growth faster than revenue growth may increase fair price and share price. However, the December 2004 dividend was paid because revenue growth requires more than sustainability. Even companies that can fund revenue growth ultimately depend on new knowledge.

Income Growth to Revenue Growth

MICROSOFT

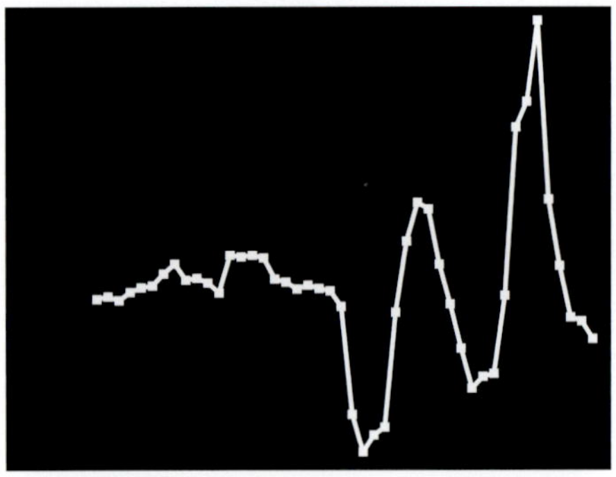

Income Growth / Revenue Growth

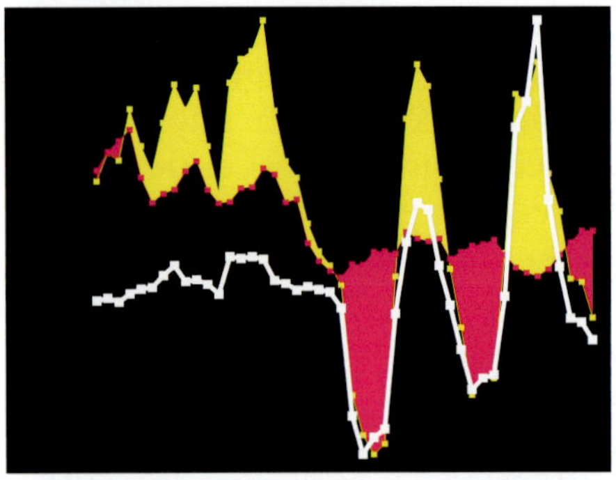

IG / RG—Inc Gro and Rev Gro

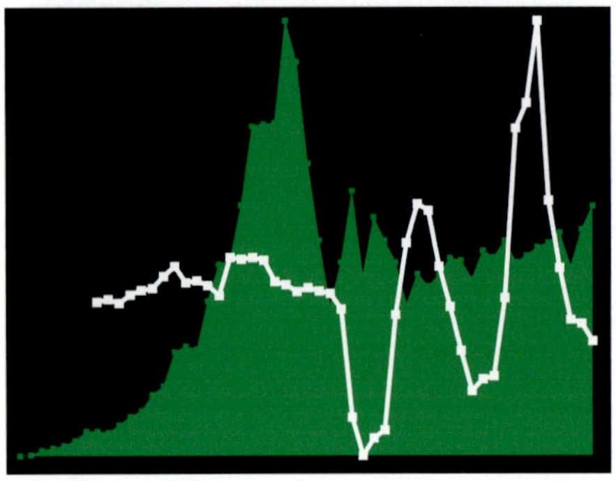

IG / RG—Share Price

An important implication of the sustainable growth equation is that (sustainable growth) *is the only growth in (revenue) that is consistent with stable values of the four ratios.* This means that when a company grows at a rate in excess of its sustainable growth, it had better improve operations (represented by an increase in the profit margin or the operating efficiency) or prepare to alter its financial policies (represented by increasing its equity to revenue or its financial leverage).

Robert C. Higgins—*Analysis for Financial Management*

Income growth to revenue growth shows you income growth in proportion to revenue growth. Management can grow income faster than revenue until *Net Profit Margin—Income to Revenue* on page 22 reaches its market limit.

Then, as you see in the *GAAP Structure Molecule* on the right and on page 89, only factors other than net profit margin increase returns on assets, equity, and revenue; and growth of assets, equity, and revenue.

Income growth to revenue growth (IG/RG) is income growth divided by revenue growth (*income growth / revenue growth*). Income growth to revenue growth is a times-number—income growth is so many times revenue growth.

Learn to read the income growth and revenue growth pair in the *front cover* four-growth chart from *The Growth Hierarchy Riddle* on page 104. Only the growth hierarchy uses all the data—except price—in the *Quarterly Data Summary*. For a fairly appraised company, the general shape of the growth hierarchy may forecast its share price trend. With "business thinking", use the growth hierarchy to adjust reasoned estimates of your short-term future share price growth.

In the middle chart on the left, the color shows the datastream that's growing faster. The height of the color shows how much faster. As an investor, the ideal chart color would be yellow—because income is growing faster than revenue causing net profit margin to increase.

However, yellow is unsustainable because income growth can increase only until the proportion of income to revenue reaches its market limit. This market limit for net profit margin depends on costs, pricing, and competition—and is some percentage far below the defined maximum of 100%, at which costs would have to be zero.

Great investment opportunities may exist when the chart is yellow. Investors like more income flowing to equity which management may be able to reinvest to make more income. But, more income doesn't guarantee increasing equity or reinvestment to make more income.

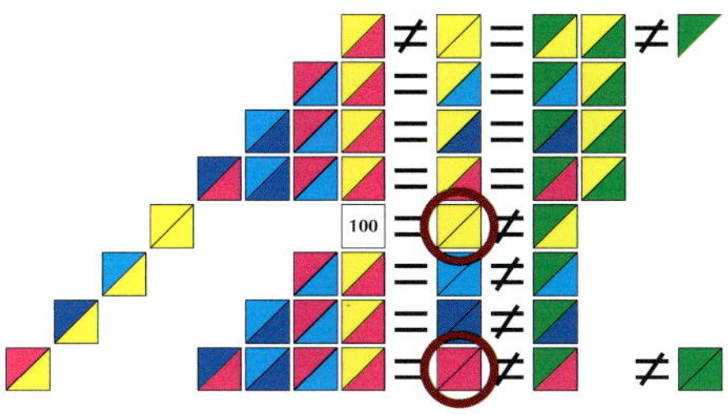

GAAP Structure

MICROSOFT

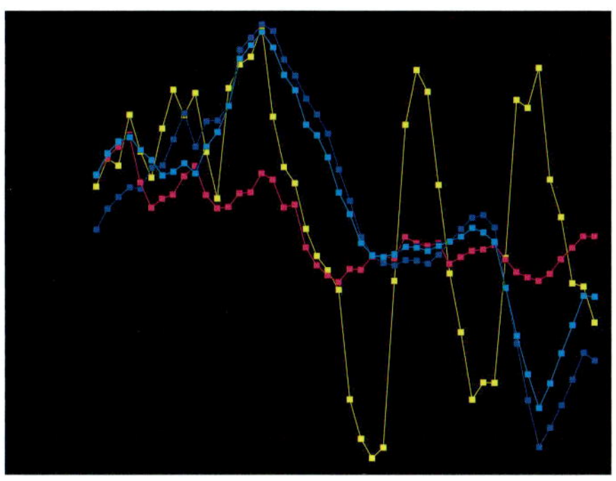

Income Growth
Equity Growth
Revenue Growth
Assets Growth

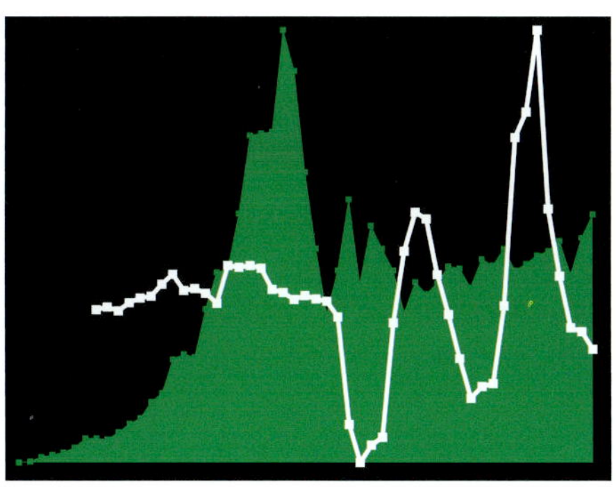

IG/RG—Share Price

Is profit margin sustainable? Or, was Albert Einstein right in *Ideas and Opinions*: "It may intimidate the human race to bring order into its international affairs, which, without the pressure of fear, it undoubtedly would not do."

Income Growth to Revenue Growth Events

Income growth (circled) and revenue growth (circled) result from factors to the left of each as you see in *GAAP Structure* on the left. Thus, fundamentals form related factors resulting in growth. All are condensed on the left and on the *front cover* in the chart from *The Growth Hierarchy Riddle* on page 104—simplifying your evaluation.

Look at the *IG/RG—Share Price* chart. There is one big event for the relationship between income growth and revenue growth. Management has, on the average, grown income slightly faster than revenue. This means that on the average, management has been increasing net profit margin for many quarters. You see the correlation in share price rising at about the same rate.

You know that increasing income on revenue (net profit margin) is not enough to influence investors to continually raise the share price. The income on that revenue must make the trip all the way to equity. Even that is not enough to influence shareholders to raise their price. Shareholders want some benefit that increases the *Fair Price Estimate* of their shares, as on page 84—new knowledge with higher profit.

MICROSOFT

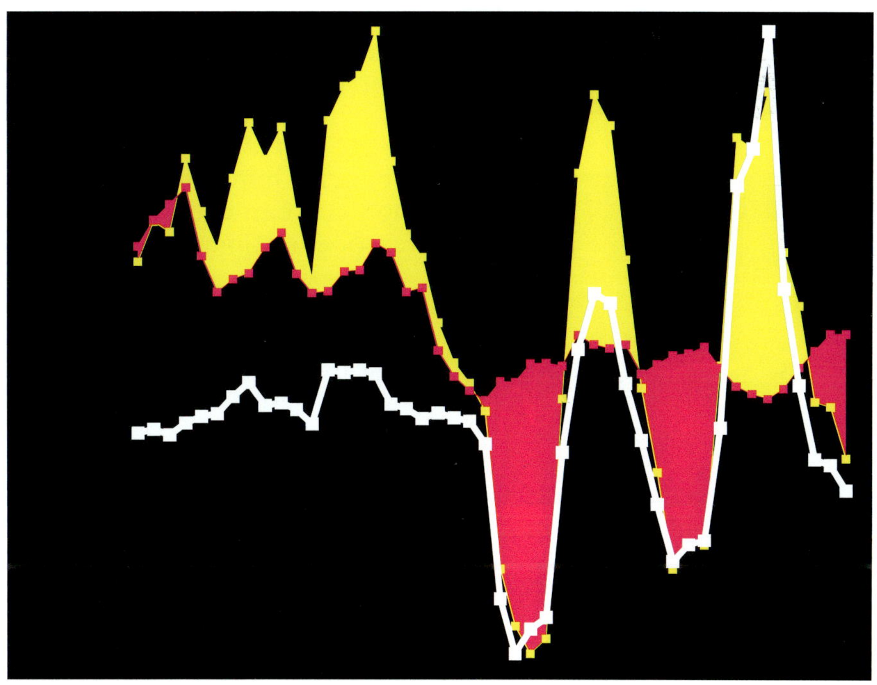

Income Growth to Revenue Growth—Inc Gro and Rev Gro

Revenue Growth to Assets Growth

MICROSOFT

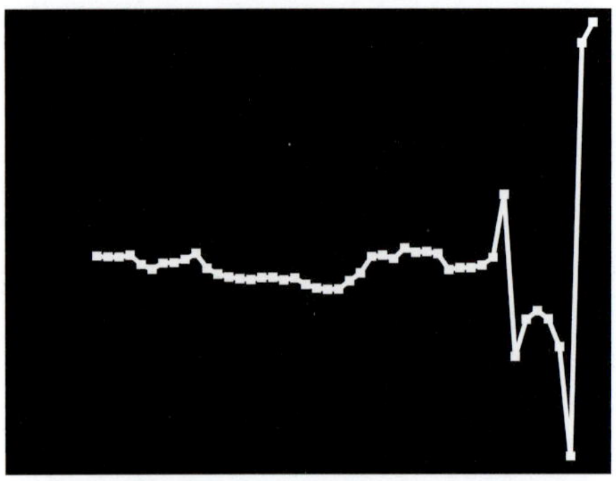

Revenue Growth / Assets Growth

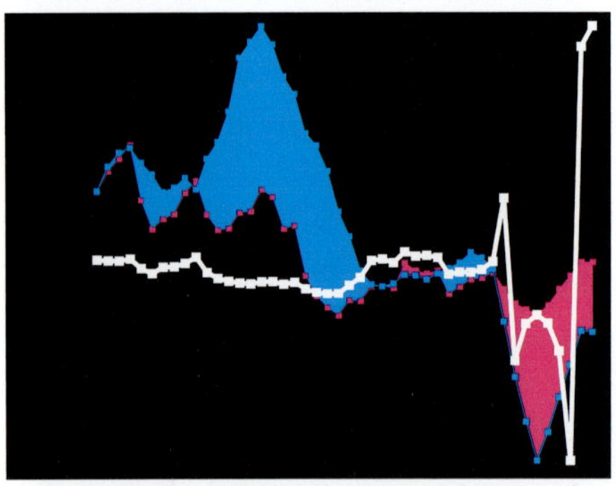

RG / AG—Rev Gro and Ass Gro

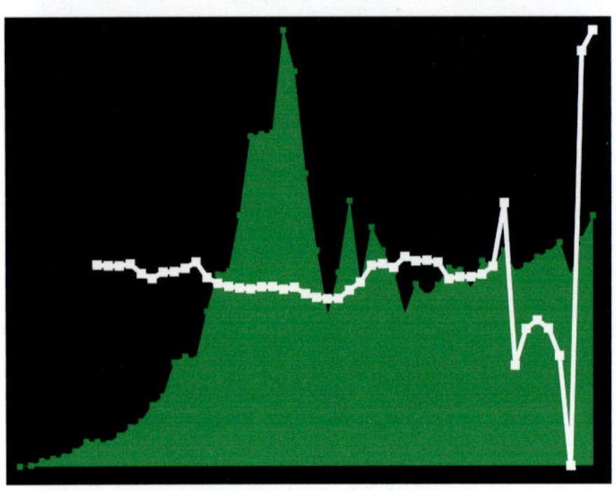

RG / AG—Share Price

> Because increasing operating efficiency is not always possible and altering financial policies is not always wise, we see that it is entirely possible for a company to grow too fast for its own good. This is particularly true for smaller companies, which may do inadequate financial planning. Such companies see (revenue) growth as something to be maximized and think too little of the financial consequences.
>
> Robert C. Higgins—*Analysis for Financial Management*

Revenue growth to assets growth shows you revenue growth in proportion to assets growth. Management can grow revenue faster than assets until *Efficiency—Revenue to Assets* on page 24 reaches its limit of productivity.

Then, as you see in the *GAAP Structure Molecule* on the right and on page 89, only factors other than efficiency increase returns on assets, equity, and revenue; and growth of assets, equity, and revenue.

Revenue growth to assets growth (RG/AG) is revenue growth divided by assets growth (*revenue growth / assets growth*). Revenue growth to assets growth is a times-number—revenue growth is so many times assets growth.

Sustainable trends are growths of numerators and denominators of *Ratio Trends* on page 21. You'll see these growth pairs shed intuitive light on sustainability. Growth pairs also condense into the *front cover* four-growth chart from *The Growth Hierarchy Riddle* on page 104. For a fairly appraised company, the general shape of the growth hierarchy may forecast its share price trend. With "business thinking", you can use the revenue growth and assets growth pair to adjust reasoned estimates of your short-term future share price growth.

In the middle chart on the left, the color shows the datastream that's growing faster. The height of the color shows how much faster. As an investor, the ideal chart color would be magenta—because revenue is growing faster than assets causing efficiency to increase.

However, when efficiency, leverage, and net profit margin reach their limits, *Equity Change to Income* on page 40 limits sustainable revenue growth by additions of income to equity.

As an investor, there may be a great investment opportunity during times when the chart is magenta. Investors like more efficiency, especially if there is a history of a large portion of revenue that is income flowing to equity, which management may be able to reinvest to make more income. But, more efficiency doesn't guarantee increasing equity and its reinvestment to make more income.

Revenue Growth to Assets Growth Events

Revenue growth (circled) and assets growth (circled) result from factors to the left of each as you see in *GAAP Structure* on the left. Thus, fundamentals form related factors resulting in growth. All are condensed on the left and on the *front cover* in the chart from *The Growth Hierarchy Riddle* on page 104—simplifying your evaluation.

Look at the *RG/AG—Share Price* chart. There is one big event for the relationship between revenue growth and assets growth. Management has, on the average, grown revenue slightly slower than assets. This means that on the average, management has been decreasing efficiency for many quarters.

Naive investors may expect efficiency and net profit margin to rise unceasingly. However, as Professor Higgins explains: lower *Efficiency—Revenue to Assets* on page 24 is compensated for by higher *Net Profit Margin—Income to Revenue* on page 22. For this company, a big event is that share price is rising in the last half of the chart even though the product of efficiency and net profit margin, *Return on Assets—Income to Assets* on page 30, isn't. Share price may be rising because informed investors realize that cash accumulating in assets only artificially reduced acceptable returns.

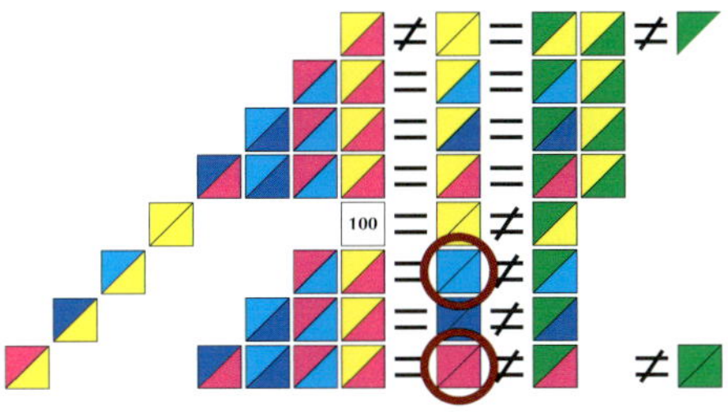

GAAP Structure

MICROSOFT

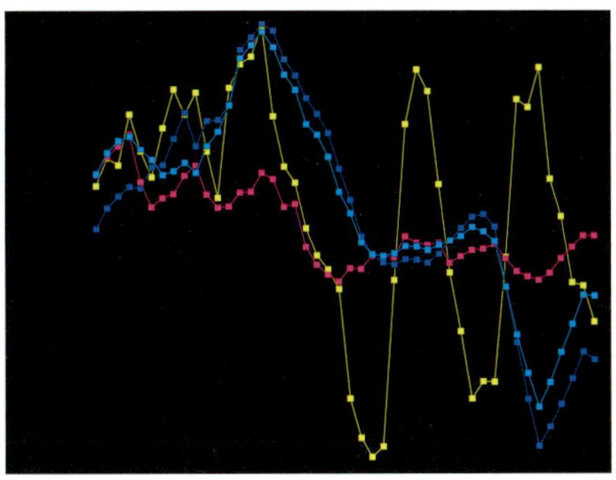

- *Income Growth*
- *Equity Growth*
- *Revenue Growth*
- *Assets Growth*

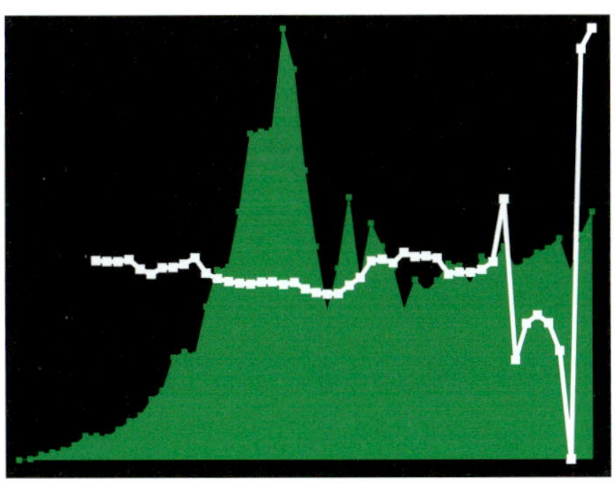

RG/AG—Share Price

Is efficiency sustainable? Or, was Albert Einstein right in *Ideas and Opinions*: "It may intimidate the human race to bring order into its international affairs, which, without the pressure of fear, it undoubtedly would not do."

MICROSOFT

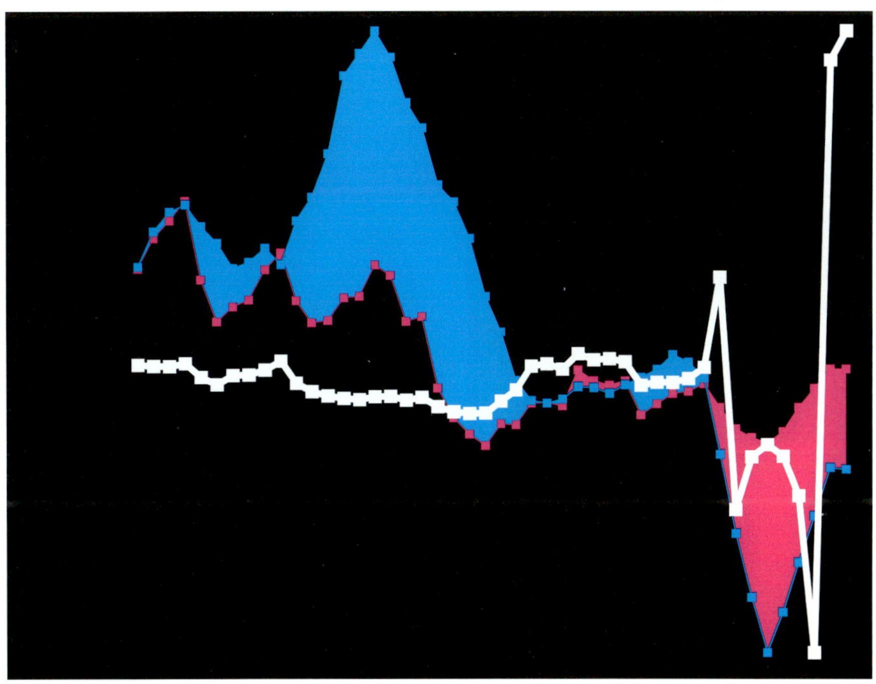

Revenue Growth to Assets Growth—Rev Gro and Ass Gro

Assets Growth to Equity Growth

MICROSOFT

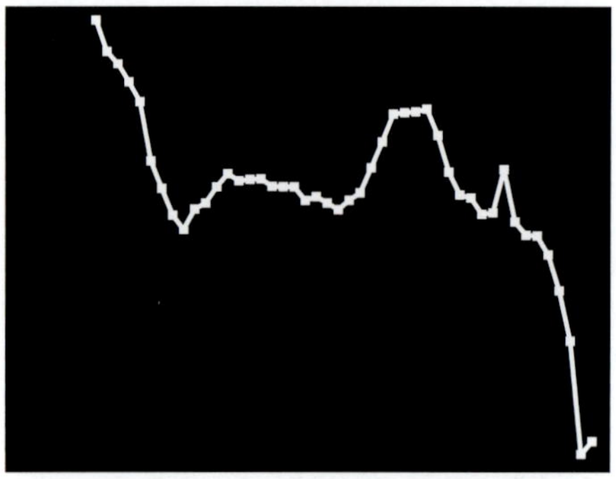

Assets Growth / Equity Growth

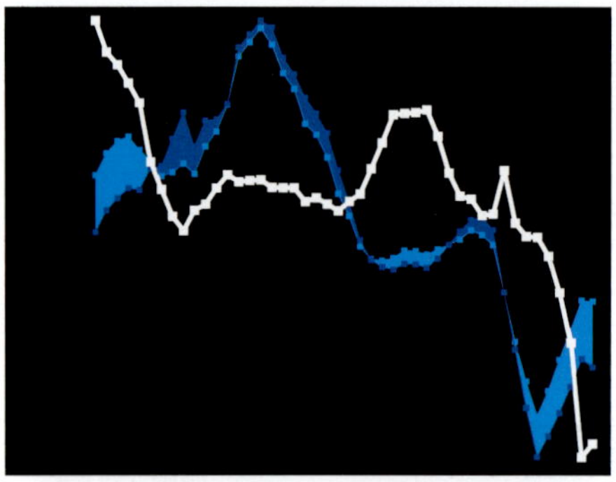

AG / EG—Ass Gro and Eqt Gro

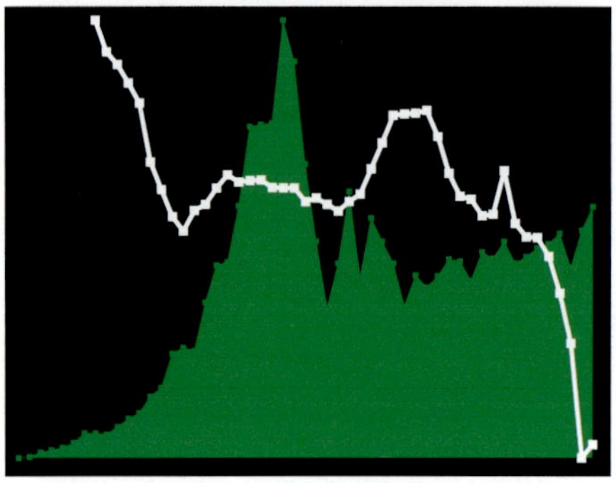

AG / EG—Share Price

> They do not realize that rapid growth has them on a treadmill; the faster they grow, the more cash they need, even when they are profitable. They can meet this need for a time by increasing leverage, but eventually they will reach their debt capacity, lenders will refuse additional credit requests, and the companies will find themselves without the cash to pay their bills. All of this can be prevented if managers understand that growth above the company's sustainable rate creates financial problems that must be anticipated and solved.
>
> Robert C. Higgins—*Analysis for Financial Management*

Assets growth to equity growth shows you assets growth in proportion to equity growth. Management can grow assets faster than equity until *Leverage—Assets to Equity* on page 26 reaches its limit due to debt paydown, company financial policy, or lender's policy.

Then, as you see in the *GAAP Structure Molecule* on the right and on page 89, only factors other than leverage increase returns on equity and revenue; and growth of equity and revenue.

Assets growth to equity growth (AG/EG) is assets growth divided by equity growth (*assets growth / equity growth*). Assets growth to equity growth is a times-number—assets growth is so many times equity growth.

You may be trying to get a grip on how an investor might make more money using the six sustainable trends. Sustainable trends deepen your understanding of *Ratio Trends* on page 21, which multiply their respective *Change Trends* on page 35 to equal *Growth Trends* on page 11. All are condensed into one four-growth chart explained in *The Growth Hierarchy Riddle* on page 104. Understanding the causes of growth helps you choose the most believable growth to compute your *Fair Price Estimate* on page 84. You want to know the fair price.

In the middle chart on the left, the color shows the datastream that's growing faster. The height of the color shows how much faster. The naive investor might think the ideal chart color is cyan—because then assets are growing faster than equity causing leverage to increase. This increases returns on equity and revenue, and the growth of equity and revenue. However, Warren Buffett says in his *Berkshire Owner's Manual—Principle 7*, "We will reject interesting opportunities rather than over-leverage our balance sheet."

Cyan is unsustainable because the company may be paying down debt, its capital policy may set a limit, or lenders may not continue advancing funds as financial risk increases. Similar to increasing net profit margin and efficiency, increasing leverage doesn't guarantee that increasing assets will be reinvested to make more income.

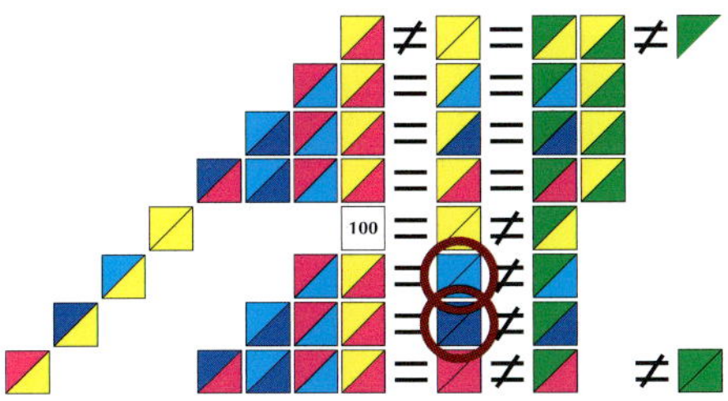

GAAP Structure

MICROSOFT

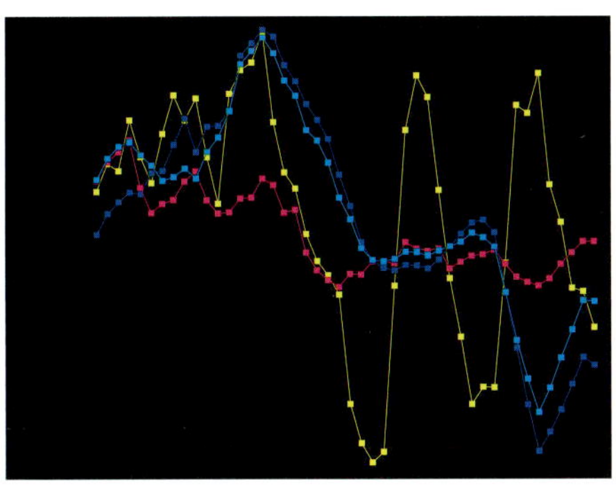

Income Growth
Equity Growth
Revenue Growth
Assets Growth

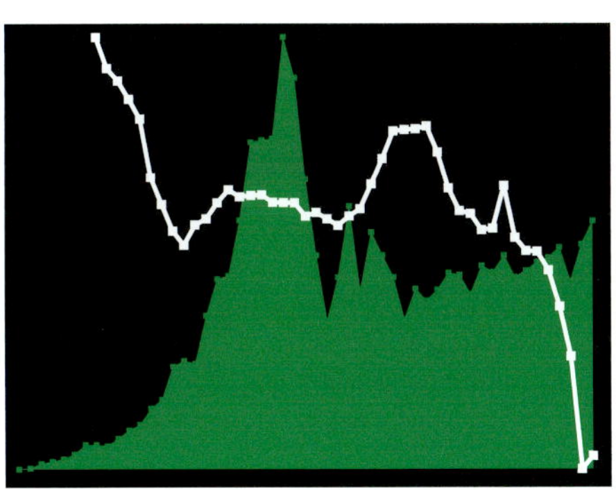

AG/EG—Share Price

Is leverage sustainable? Or, was Albert Einstein right in *Ideas and Opinions*: *It may intimidate the human race to bring order into its international affairs, which, without the pressure of fear, it undoubtedly would not do.*

Assets Growth to Equity Growth Events

Assets growth (circled) and equity growth (circled) result from factors to the left of each as you see in *GAAP Structure* on the left. Thus, fundamentals form related factors resulting in growth. All are condensed on the left and on the *front cover* in the chart from *The Growth Hierarchy Riddle* on page 104—simplifying your evaluation.

Look at the *AG/EG—Share Price* chart. The December 2004 dividend was a bigger event for equity growth than assets growth, because equity is always smaller than assets. You might reasonably expect this to cause equity growth to be smaller than assets growth. Confirm dataplots using *GAAP Original Data* facing page 91.

Naive investors may expect leverage, efficiency, and net profit margin to rise unceasingly. However, as Professor Higgins explains: *Leverage—Assets to Equity* on page 26 has limits, whereas lower *Efficiency—Revenue to Assets* on page 24 is compensated for by higher *Net Profit Margin—Income to Revenue* on page 22. A big event is share price rising in the last half of the chart even though the product of leverage, efficiency, and net profit margin, *Return on Equity—Income to Equity* on page 32, isn't. Share price may be rising because cash only artificially reduced acceptable returns.

MICROSOFT

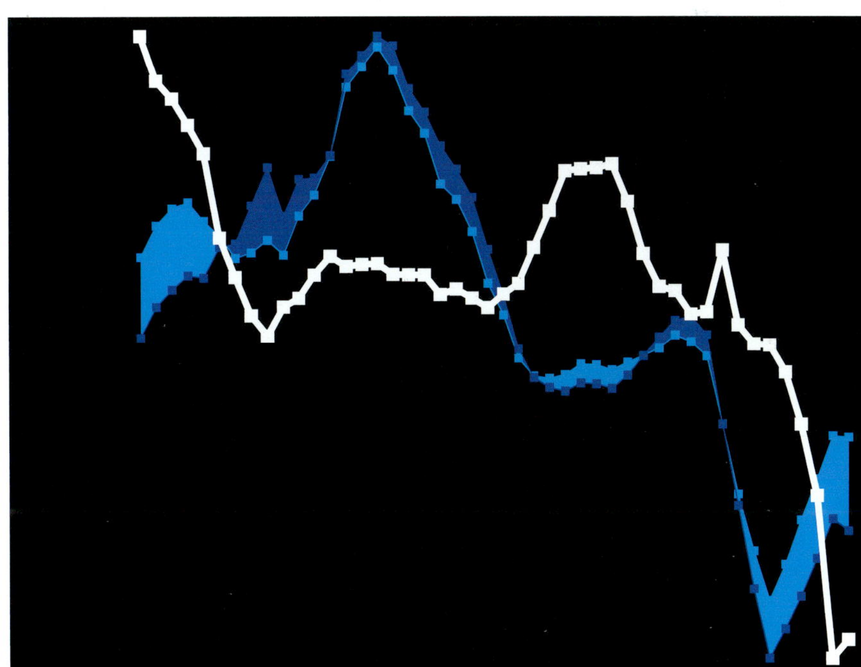

Assets Growth to Equity Growth—Ass Gro and Eqt Gro

Equity Growth to Revenue Growth

MICROSOFT

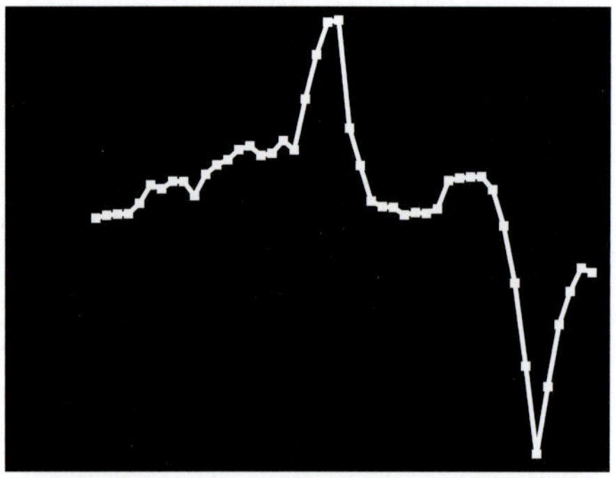

Equity Growth / Revenue Growth

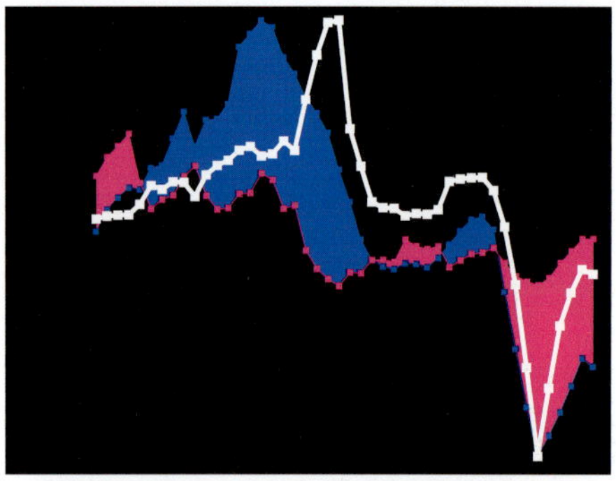

EG / RG—Eqt Gro and Rev Gro

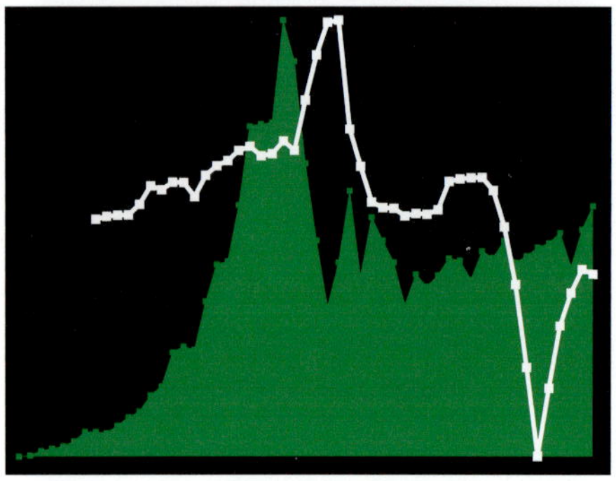

EG / RG—Share Price

> So after all the dust settles, what limits the growth in (revenue) is the rate at which owner's equity expands. A company's sustainable growth therefore is nothing more than its growth in equity.
>
> Robert C. Higgins—*Analysis for Financial Management*

Equity growth to revenue growth shows you equity growth in proportion to revenue growth. Management can grow equity faster than revenue until *Equity to Revenue—Equity to Revenue* on page 28 reaches its limit, beyond which investors want their money returned so they can reinvest it more profitably.

Then, as you see in the *GAAP Structure Molecule* on the right and on page 89, only factors other than equity to revenue increase net profit margin; and growth of revenue.

Equity growth to revenue growth (EG/RG), also known as sustainable revenue growth, is equity growth divided by revenue growth (*equity growth / revenue growth*). Equity growth to revenue growth is a times-number—equity growth is so many times revenue growth.

In the middle chart on the left, the color shows the datastream that's growing faster. The height of the color shows how much faster. As an investor, the ideal chart color would be blue—because equity growing slightly faster than revenue provides funds for increasing revenue.

As an investor, you see that management sometimes increases equity growth (blue) faster than revenue growth (magenta). However, even if there is money to fund more revenue, there may not be enough demand for the company's products. Also, the company may want equity growth to exceed revenue growth to build equity reserves.

Famous and obscure companies have ***grown broke***, as Professor Higgins describes in his chapter on *Managing Growth* in *Analysis for Financial Management*. In the course of healthy business, companies increase—and decrease—their cash and other reserves to continue equity growth that funds revenue growth.

Increasing equity growth enables management to increase income growth and thus the *Fair Price Estimate* described on page 84—which means the fair price is increasing. Only equity per share growth can rise unceasingly through additions to *Equity Change to Income* on page 40 as a source of sustainable growth of income per-share.

From the investor's perspective, increasing the wealth and progress of a company requires growing equity that funds revenue growth to produce more income to fund more equity. This is the ***Virtuous Cycle***.

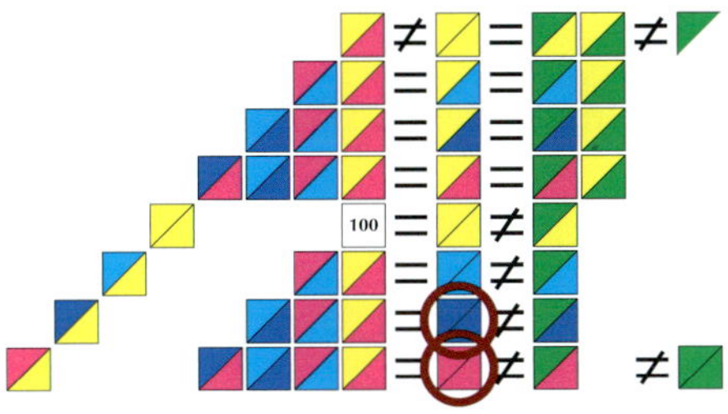

GAAP Structure

MICROSOFT

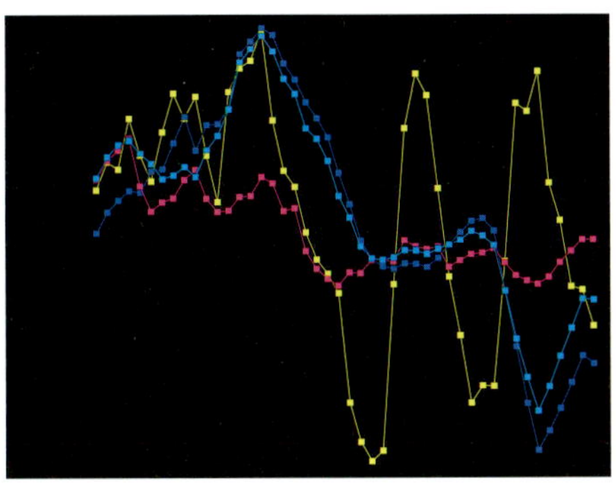

Income Growth
Equity Growth
Revenue Growth
Assets Growth

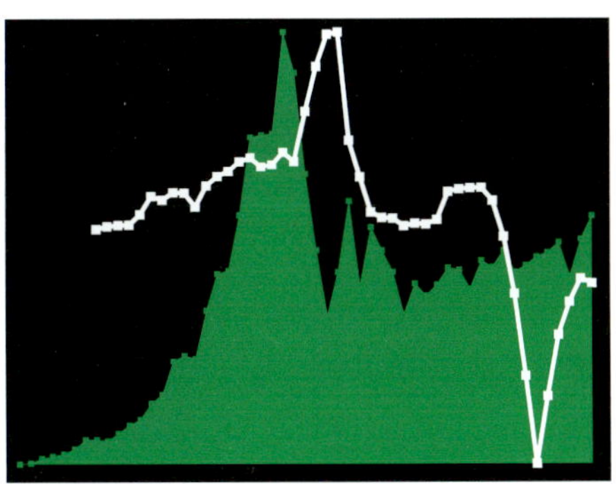

EG/RG—Share Price

Is revenue growth sustainable? Or, was Albert Einstein right in *Ideas and Opinions*: "It may intimidate the human race to bring order into its international affairs, which, without the pressure of fear, it undoubtedly would not do."

Equity Growth to Revenue Growth Events

Equity growth (circled) and revenue growth (circled) result from factors to the left of each as you see in *GAAP Structure* on the left. Thus, fundamentals form related factors resulting in growth. All are condensed on the left and on the *front cover* in the chart from *The Growth Hierarchy Riddle* on page 104—simplifying your evaluation.

Look at the *EG/RG—Share Price* chart. You'll realize the December 2004 dividend is not a big event for revenue growth—when equity growth dropped, price kept on climbing, except for the automated drop as in *The Split-Adjusted Close Price Riddle* on page 108.

The big event is not equity growth (blue) above revenue growth, though equity grew from income that came from revenue. Neither is the big event the *dot-com boom* and *bust* that produced more equity.

There are two big events. The dividend signaled the company didn't need large reserves for anti-trust penalties. Paradoxically, the biggest event for company survival and prosperity, through many opportunities and challenges, may be that management kept revenue growth below equity growth—yet grew average equity at a phenomenal rate.

MICROSOFT

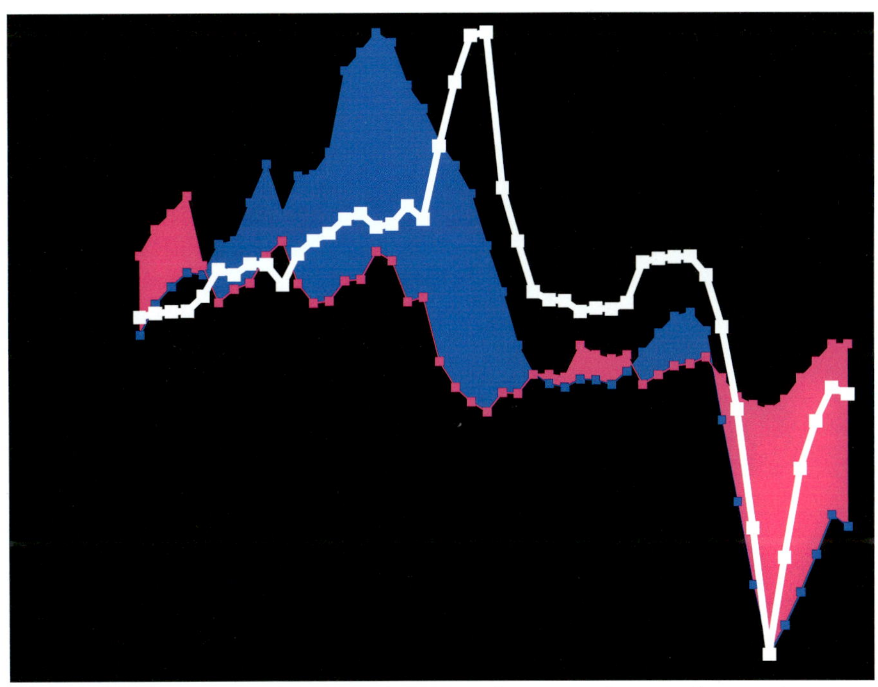

Equity Growth to Revenue Growth—Eqt Gro and Rev Gro

Income Growth to Assets Growth

MICROSOFT

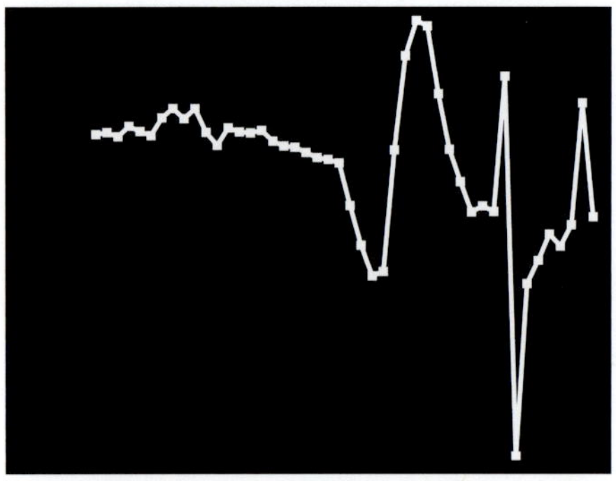

Income Growth / Assets Growth

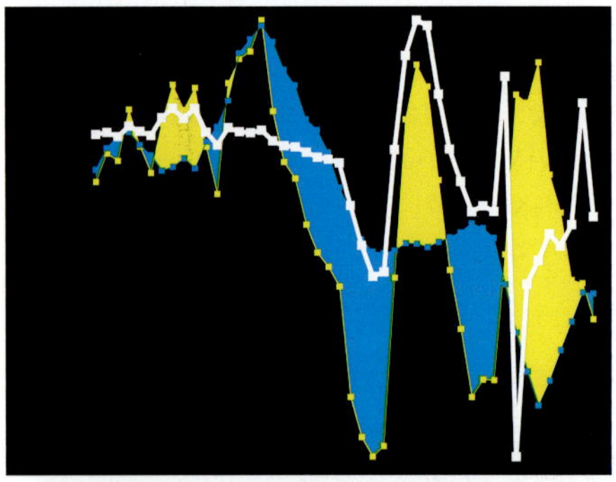

IG / AG—Inc Gro and Ass Gro

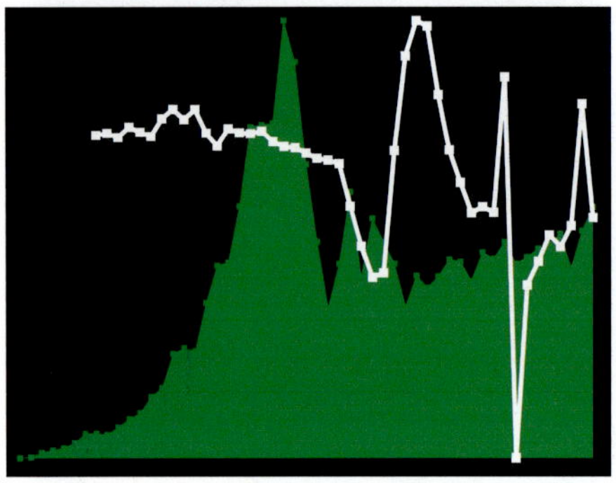

IG / AG—Share Price

> When a company experiences unbalanced growth of either the surplus or the deficit variety, it can move toward the balanced growth line in any of three ways: It can change its growth, alter its return on assets, or modify its financial policies.
>
> Robert C. Higgins—*Analysis for Financial Management*

Income growth to assets growth shows you income growth in proportion to assets growth.

Management can grow income faster than assets only to the point at which *Return on Assets—Income to Assets* on page 30 reaches the limits of its factors: *Efficiency—Revenue to Assets* on page 24, and *Net Profit Margin—Income to Revenue* on page 22.

Then, as you see in the *GAAP Structure Molecule* on the right and on page 89, only factors other than return on assets increase growth of assets, equity, and revenue.

Income growth to assets growth (IG/AG) is income growth divided by assets growth (*income growth / assets growth*). Income growth to assets growth is a times-number—so many times assets growth.

In the middle chart on the left, the color shows the datastream that's growing faster. The height of the color shows how much faster. As an investor, the ideal chart color would be yellow—because income is growing faster than assets causing return on assets to increase. However, yellow is unsustainable because return on assets can increase only to the limits of its factors.

A healthy return on assets, even if limited or decreasing, can provide a source of large income that may flow to equity for reinvestment in production. We recall Martin Fridson in *Financial Statement Analysis*, "This leaves only (equity per share), which can rise unceasingly through additions to retained income (in equity change to income), as a source of sustainable growth in (income per share)."

Some investors are obsessed with ever-higher returns. You're better off, as O'Shaughnessy says, focusing on persistent *Income Growth* on page 12, flowing into equity in *Equity Change to Income* on page 40, for reinvestment in production and new knowledge.

The many charts in this book are insight generators that help you understand the *front cover* charts, and look beyond the specifics of this company to the specifics of your company. When income grows slower than assets or equity, investors should look for increasing cash that isn't being reinvested in more profitable production assets.

Income Growth to Assets Growth Events

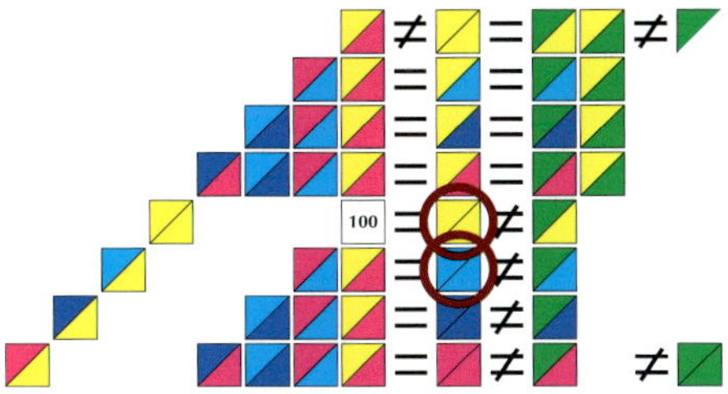

GAAP Structure

MICROSOFT

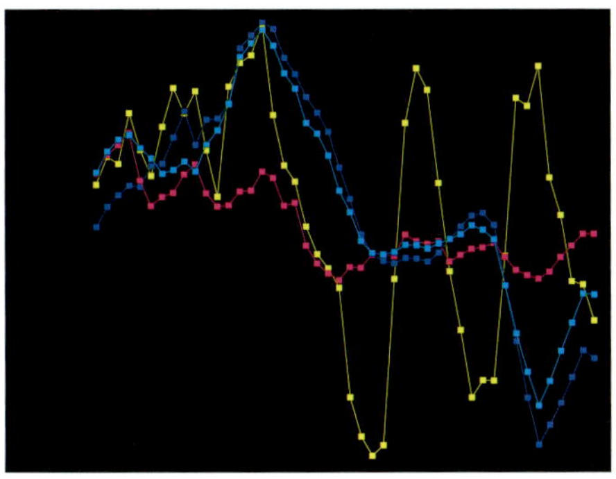

Income Growth
Equity Growth
Revenue Growth
Assets Growth

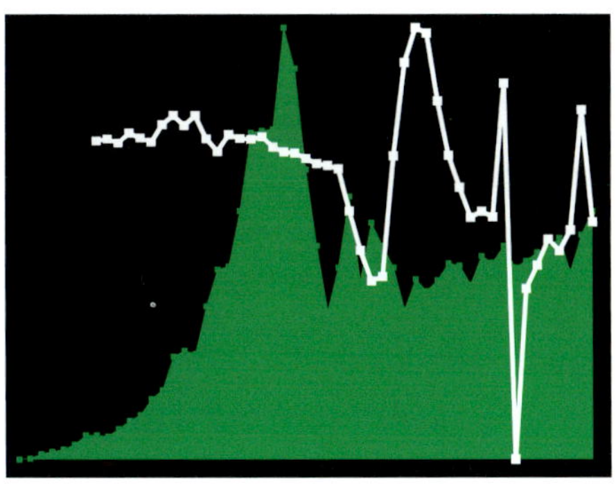

IG/AG—Share Price

Is return on assets sustainable? Or, was Albert Einstein right in *Ideas and Opinions*: "It may intimidate the human race to bring order into its international affairs, which, without the pressure of fear, it undoubtedly would not do."

Income growth (circled) and assets growth (circled) result from factors to the left of each as you see in *GAAP Structure* on the left. Thus, fundamentals form related factors resulting in growth. All are condensed on the left and on the *front cover* in the chart from *The Growth Hierarchy Riddle* on page 104—simplifying your evaluation.

Look at the *IG/AG—Share Price* chart. There is one big event for the relationship between income growth and assets growth. Management has, on the average, grown income slightly slower than assets. However, investors are steadily increasing share price. Even though income growth and assets growth have been generally decreasing, *Income* on page 2 continues to increase. There are plenty of assets invested in production to keep income increasing—so investors are willing to increase price.

Income Growth to Assets Growth—Inc Gro and Ass Gro below reveals three distinct shifts in company strategy—marked by shifts from mostly yellow to cyan to mostly yellow. If yellow continues, it may indicate that management is able to convert more cash assets to production assets. Customers are ready for the next product cycle, and the company's new applications are earning good reviews.

MICROSOFT

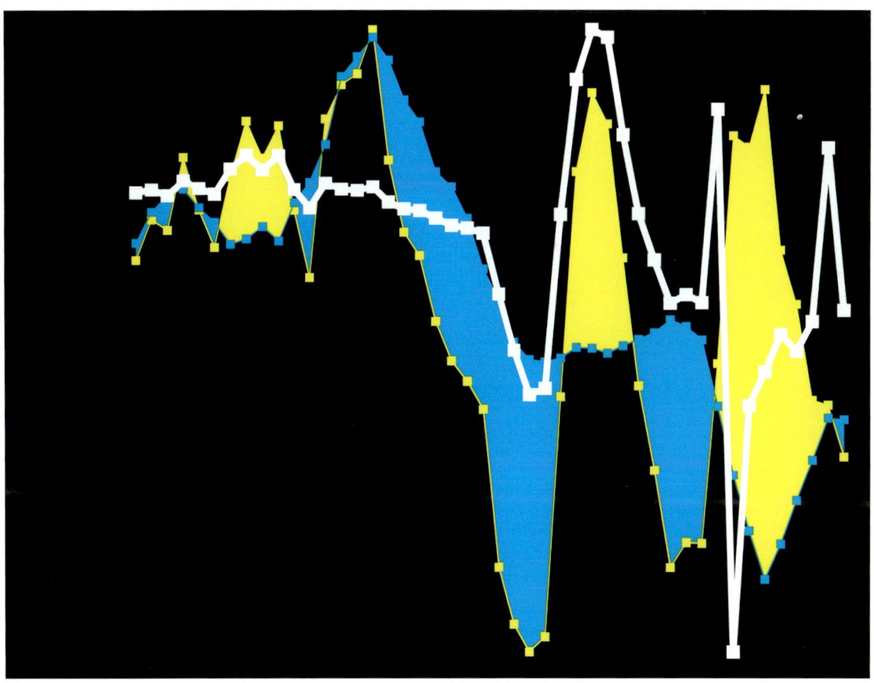

Income Growth to Assets Growth—Inc Gro and Ass Gro

Income Growth to Equity Growth

MICROSOFT

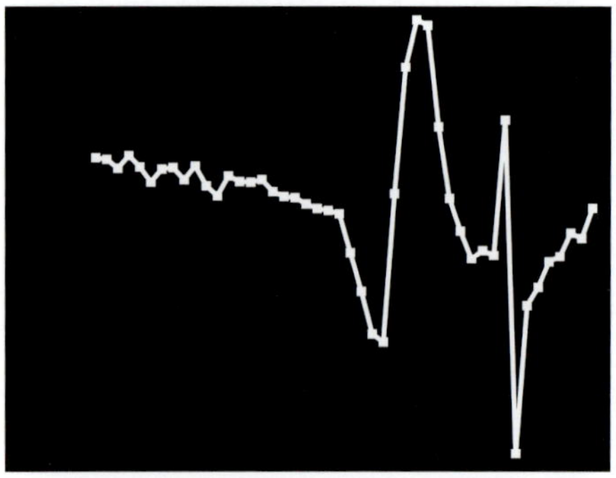

Income Growth / Equity Growth

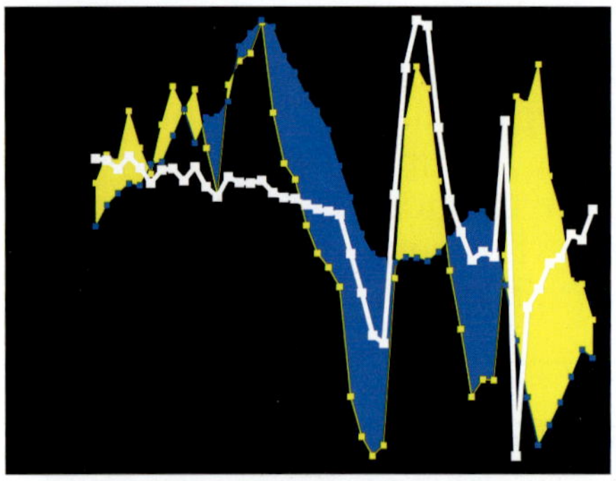

IG / EG—Inc Gro and Eqt Gro

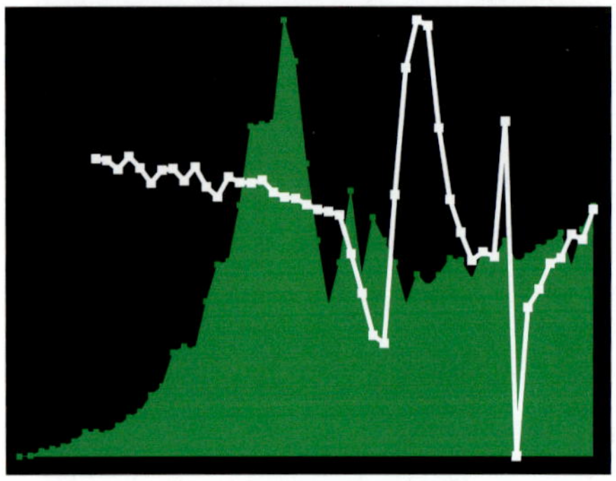

IG / EG—Share Price

> This leaves only (equity per share), which can rise unceasingly through additions to retained income (in equity change to income), as a source of sustainable growth of (income per share).
>
> Martin S. Fridson—*Financial Statement Analysis*

Income growth to equity growth shows you income growth in proportion to equity growth.

Management can grow income faster than equity only to the point at which *Return on Equity—Income to Equity* on page 32 reaches the limits of its factors: *Leverage—Assets to Equity* on page 26, *Efficiency—Revenue to Assets* on page 24, and *Net Profit Margin—Income to Revenue* on page 22.

Then, as you see in the *GAAP Structure Molecule* on the right and on page 89, only factors other than return on equity increase growth of equity and revenue.

Income growth to equity growth (IG/EG) is income growth divided by equity growth (*income growth / equity growth*). Income growth to equity growth is a times-number—so many times equity growth.

In the middle chart on the left, the color shows the datastream that's growing faster. The height of the color shows how much faster. As an investor, the ideal chart color would be yellow—because income is growing faster than equity causing return on equity to increase. However, yellow is unsustainable because return on equity can increase only to the limits of its factors.

A healthy return on equity, even if limited or decreasing, can provide a source of large income that may flow to equity for reinvestment in production. We again recall Martin Fridson in *Financial Statement Analysis*, "This leaves only (equity per share), which can rise unceasingly through additions to retained income (in equity change to income), as a source of sustainable growth in (income per share)."

Some investors are obsessed with ever-higher returns. You're better off, as O'Shaughnessy says, focusing on persistent *Income Growth* on page 12, flowing into equity in *Equity Change to Income* on page 40, for reinvestment in production and new knowledge.

The many charts in this book are insight generators that help you understand the *front cover* charts, and look beyond the specifics of this company to the specifics of your company. When income grows slower than assets or equity, investors should look for increasing cash that isn't being reinvested in more profitable production equity.

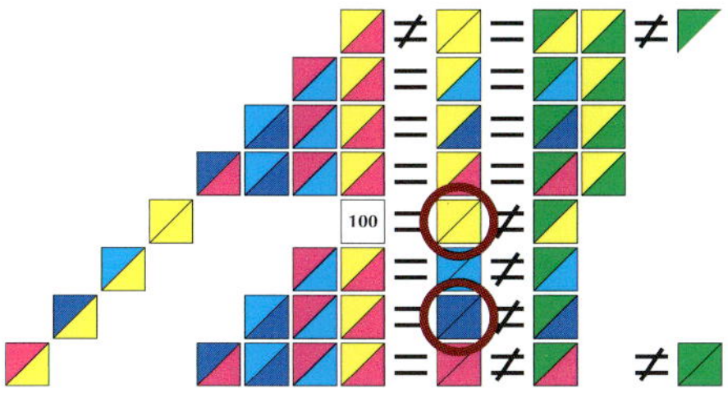

GAAP Structure

MICROSOFT

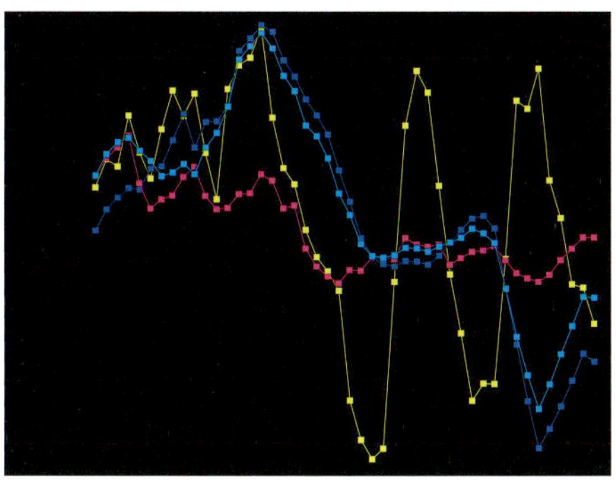

Income Growth
Equity Growth
Revenue Growth
Assets Growth

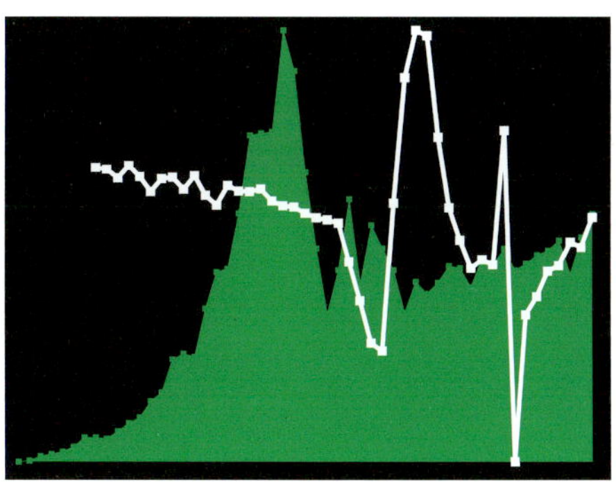

IG/EG—Share Price

Is return on equity sustainable? Or, was Albert Einstein right in *Ideas and Opinions*: "It may intimidate the human race to bring order into its international affairs, which, without the pressure of fear, it undoubtedly would not do."

Income Growth to Equity Growth Events

Income growth (circled) and equity growth (circled) result from factors to the left of each as you see in *GAAP Structure* on the left. Thus, fundamentals form related factors resulting in growth. All are condensed on the left and on the *front cover* in the chart from *The Growth Hierarchy Riddle* on page 104—simplifying your evaluation.

Look at the *IG/EG—Share Price* chart. There is one big event for the relationship between income growth and equity growth. Management has, on the average, grown income slightly slower than equity. However, investors are steadily increasing share price. Even though income growth and equity growth have been generally decreasing, *Income* on page 2 continues to increase. There is plenty of equity invested in production to keep income increasing—so investors are willing to increase price.

Income Growth to Equity Growth—Inc Gro and Eqt Gro below reveals three distinct shifts in company strategy—marked by shifts from mostly yellow to blue to mostly yellow. If yellow continues, it may indicate that management is able to convert more cash equity to production equity. Customers are ready for the next product cycle, and the company's new applications are earning good reviews.

MICROSOFT

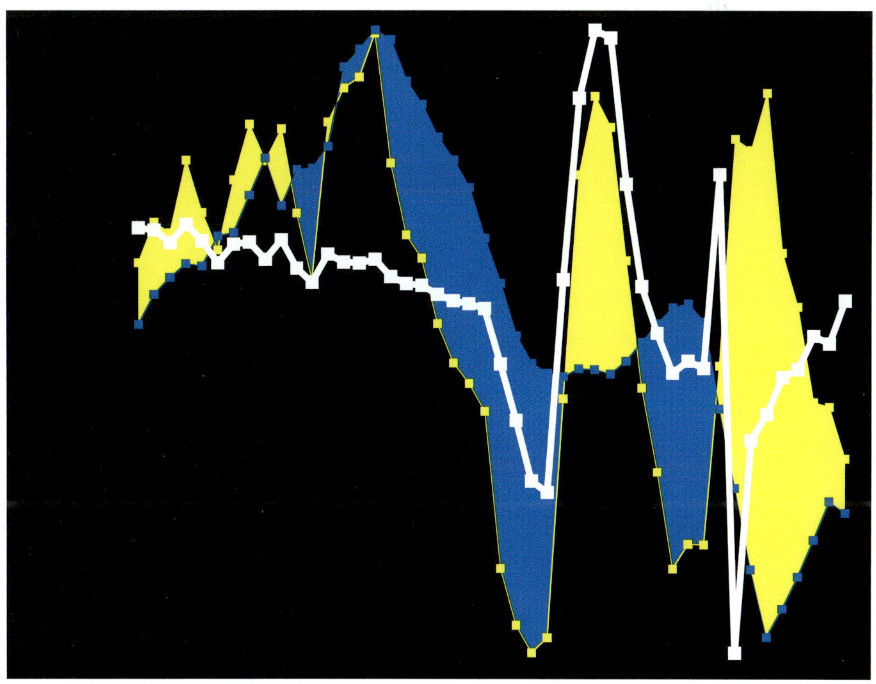

Income Growth to Equity Growth—Inc Gro and Eqt Gro

MICROSOFT

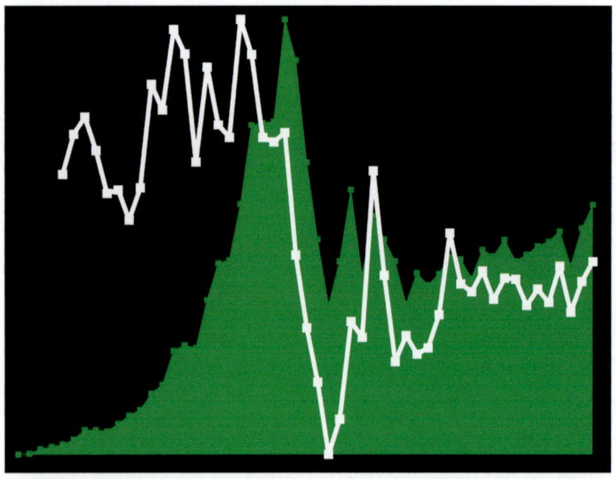

Share Price Growth (white)—Share Price

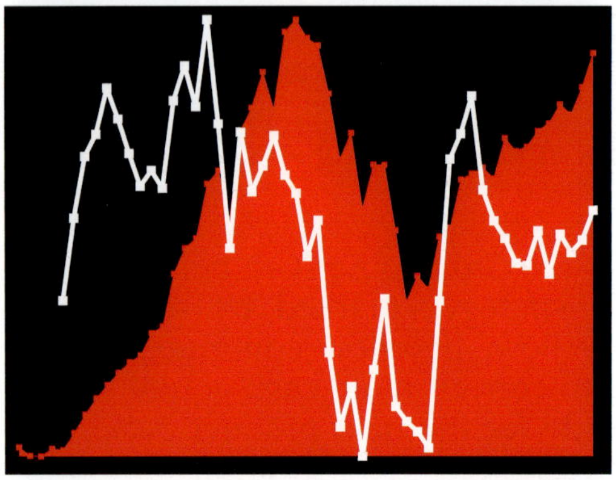

S & P Price Growth (white)—S & P Price

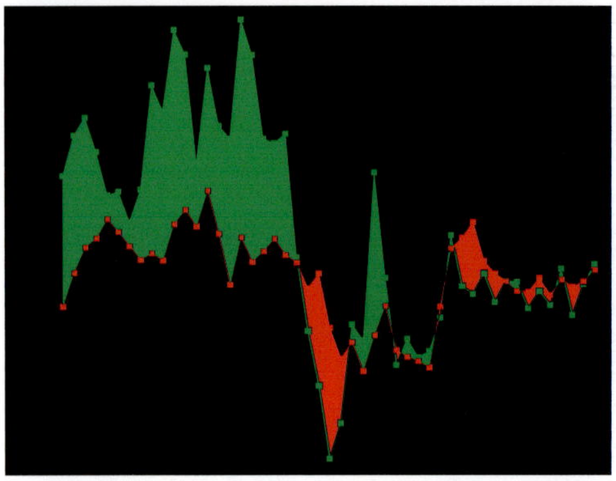

Share Price Growth—S & P Price Growth

QUARTER ENDED	SHARE	PRICE GROWTH S&P	SHARE *minus* S&P
OVERALL GROWTH	1270	204	1066
AVERAGE GROWTH	29	11	18
2006-12-31	15.83	13.62	2.21
2006-09-30	7.79	8.71	(0.92)
2006-06-30	(4.93)	6.62	(11.55)
2006-03-31	13.98	9.68	4.30
2005-12-31	(0.92)	3.00	(3.92)
2005-09-30	4.68	10.25	(5.57)
2005-06-30	(2.17)	4.43	(6.60)
2005-03-31	8.70	4.83	3.87
2004-12-31	9.14	8.99	0.15
2004-09-30	0.33	11.91	(11.58)
2004-06-30	12.02	17.07	(5.05)
2004-03-31	3.58	32.78	(29.20)
2003-12-31	6.81	26.38	(19.57)
2003-09-30	27.47	22.16	5.31
2003-06-30	(5.97)	(1.55)	(4.42)
2003-03-31	(19.47)	(26.08)	6.61
2002-12-31	(21.99)	(23.37)	1.38
2002-09-30	(14.49)	(21.68)	7.19
2002-06-30	(25.06)	(19.16)	(5.91)
2002-03-31	10.29	(1.12)	11.41
2001-12-31	52.75	(13.04)	65.79
2001-09-30	(15.17)	(27.54)	12.37
2001-06-30	(8.74)	(15.83)	7.08
2001-03-31	(48.54)	(22.57)	(25.97)
2000-12-31	(62.84)	(10.14)	(52.71)
2000-09-30	(33.40)	11.99	(45.39)
2000-06-30	(11.30)	5.97	(17.27)
2000-03-31	18.55	16.50	2.06
1999-12-31	68.37	19.53	48.84
1999-09-30	64.56	26.13	38.44
1999-06-30	66.41	21.07	45.34
1999-03-31	100.31	16.76	83.55
1998-12-31	114.62	26.67	87.96
1998-09-30	66.39	7.36	59.03
1998-06-30	71.55	28.10	43.46
1998-03-31	95.15	45.52	49.63
1997-12-31	56.39	31.01	25.38
1997-09-30	100.56	37.82	62.74
1997-06-30	110.49	31.99	78.51
1997-03-31	77.74	17.29	60.45
1996-12-31	88.19	20.26	67.92
1996-09-30	45.90	17.61	28.29
1996-06-30	32.79	23.11	9.68
1996-03-31	45.05	28.92	16.14
1995-12-31	43.64	34.11	9.53
1995-09-30	61.06	26.30	34.75
1995-06-30	74.91	22.62	52.29
1995-03-31	67.69	12.32	55.36
1994-12-31	51.38	(1.54)	52.92
1994-09-30	....	....	....
1994-06-30	....	....	....
1994-03-31	....	....	....
1993-12-31	....	....	....

6 Popularity Trends

DATASTREAMS

MICROSOFT

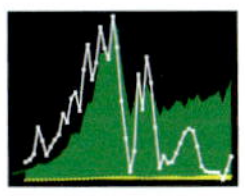
P / Income

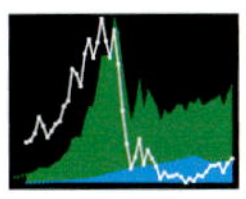
P / Assets

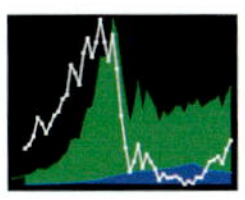
P / Equity

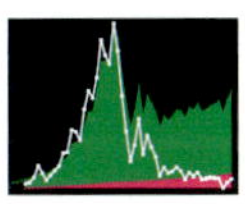
P / Revenue

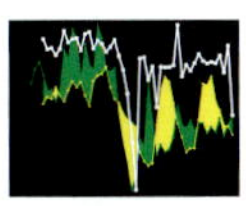
PG / IG

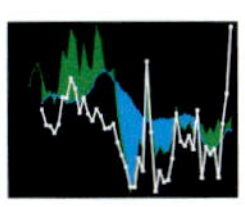
PG / AG

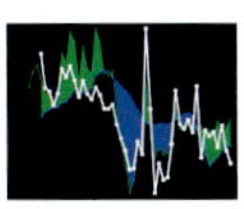
PG / EG

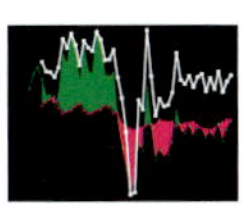
PG / RG

> We value businesses, and not just stocks, and we invest in them long-term. We do not buy stocks based primarily on accounting-based relationships such as price earnings (price to income) or price to book value (price to equity) or price to cash flow (although we carefully consider these metrics and many others besides), and we do not sell when the securities we own reach some pre-determined target based on the relation of price to such metrics as may have prevailed in the past (though we also take that into consideration).
>
> Bill Miller—*Letter to Legg Mason Value Trust Shareholders, 2005*

Popularity trends show the multiple price is of each fundamental, and the multiple price growth is of each fundamental's growth.

Popularity trends may alert you to exaggerations in measures of company evolution. These mark unusual circumstances that may cause the stock to be misappraised in your *Fair Price Estimate* on page 84.

The green price-spike in the top four charts is one of several examples you'll see influencing the popularity of a company with investors. This price-spike marks the ending of the *dot-com boom* in early 2000. The unsustainable exaggeration in fundamental measures and then in share price may reveal great investment opportunities that depart from the steady progress you see in the overall price trend.

Numerators are quarter-end split-adjusted close price (P) or price growth (PG). Denominators are fundamentals or growth (IG, AG, EG, RG). Fundamentals and growth are per average diluted share.

The Split-Adjusted Close Price Riddle on page 108 explains why only quarter-end price makes sense when comparing to other quarter-end measures—and why we measure per diluted shares.

The *facing page* shows you trends in price and price growth for share price and *S&P* price. These give you a market context to understand the price or price growth numerator of popularity measures.

You look for great investment opportunities when stock is misappraised. You see opportunities to buy or sell when price is increasing or decreasing at a rate different from a fundamental or its growth.

Price to Income

MICROSOFT

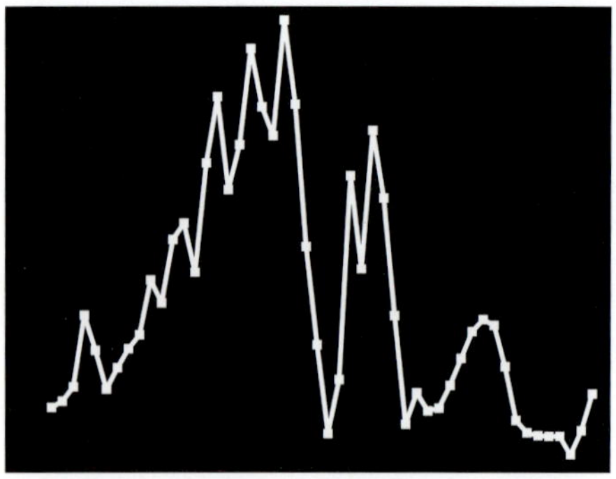

Price / Income

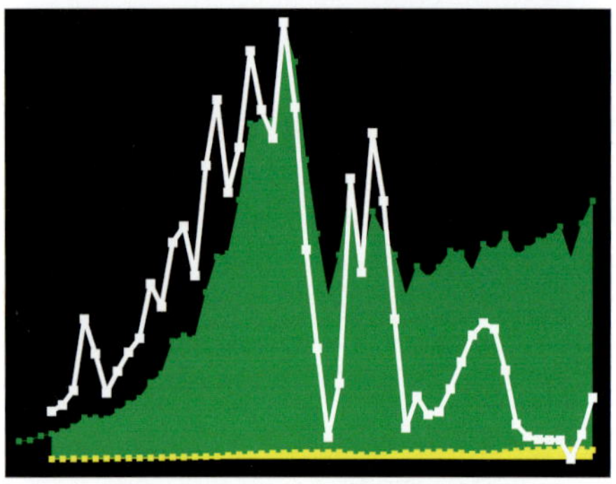

Prc / Inc—Price and Income

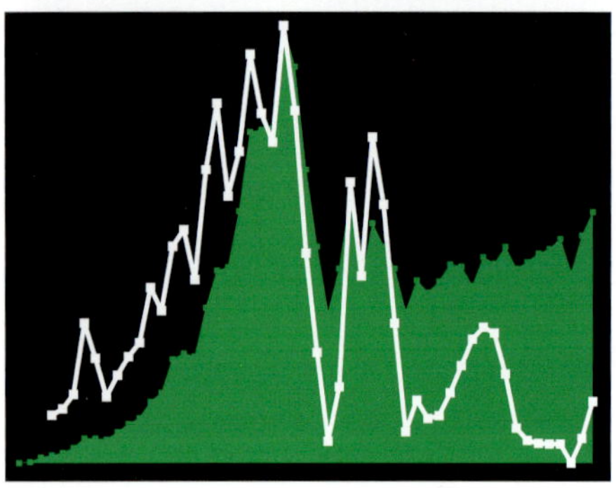

Prc / Inc—Share Price

Warren is buying Old Economy businesses and stocks at seven times earnings (income), so he is not about to start buying New Economy stocks at 25 times earnings just because Bill Gates is on his board.

Robert P. Miles, *Warren Buffett Wealth—Seattle Times, April 29, 2005*

Price to income shows you the multiple share price is of income per average diluted share.

Price to income (Prc/Inc), also known as P/I or price to earnings (P/E) or the price earnings multiple or the earnings multiple, is share price divided by income (*price / income*). Price to income is a times number—so many times income.

In *Valuing Wall Street*, Smithers and Wright say a price to income of 13 is the geometric average since 1871.

Some charts require more than one vertical scale. In the middle chart, one scale compares values for *Prc/Inc* as the white dataplot. A second scale compares *Price* (green) and *Income* (yellow). Different scales may use different values and units of measure.

Informed investors use the *Fair Price Estimate* on page 84 to calculate fair price. P/I is not a price, it's the ratio of price to income. Investors may use P/I when considering the time and price to buy or sell. If you want to calculate current P/I, use current price, not quarter end price, divided by your current estimate of annualized income.

The popularity of changes in income can cause investors to set a share price that is above or below fair price resulting in the stock being misappraised and opening opportunities for great investment.

Why do we devote your time or ours to giving the long-standing name P/E the new name P/I? The deeper question is—Why does Wall Street use P/E rather than P/I, when the fundamental is named ***income***—not ***earnings***—in the official government source for public company data—the *SEC EDGAR Archives*? Alternate names are also used for the other fundamentals—revenue, assets, and equity. The standardized name helps you find the data you want, quickly.

We believe that financial literacy requires the end of such financial Latin. The medical world is putting an end to medical Latin. The financial world will put an end to financial Latin—when it's serious about supporting the public to make informed investment decisions.

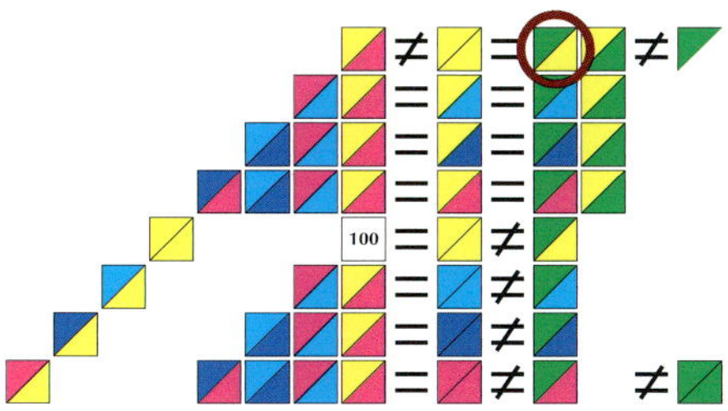

GAAP Structure

MICROSOFT

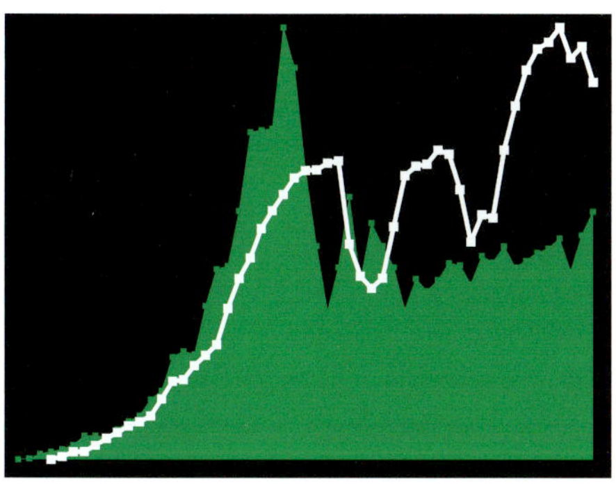

Income—Share Price

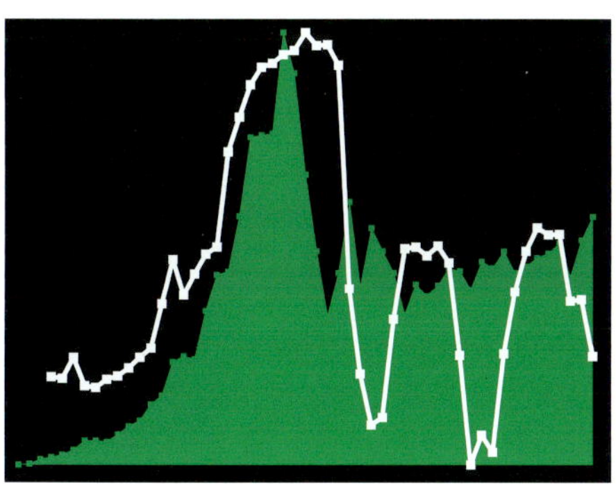

Net Profit Margin—Share Price

Price to Income Events

Price to income is circled on row 1 of *GAAP Structure*. To its right, the income to price (income yield) column relates the market to results, as you'll see in the *GAAP Structure Molecule* on page 89.

Price to Income below signals an unusual circumstance during the *dot-com boom* peaking in early 2000—price to income is increasing.

Income—Share Price on the left reveals the cause. Before the peak, investors increase price (green) faster than the company increases income (white). Compare green and white profiles—don't consider price and income numbers because they're in different contexts. Why would investors move green above white?

Net Profit Margin—Share Price on the left reveals one influence on investors. During the boom, the company increases net profit margin by increasing income faster than revenue. It reinvested much of that income in production assets that earned more income than cash assets—probably making income more popular with investors. For many quarters, investors enjoyed this great investment opportunity.

MICROSOFT

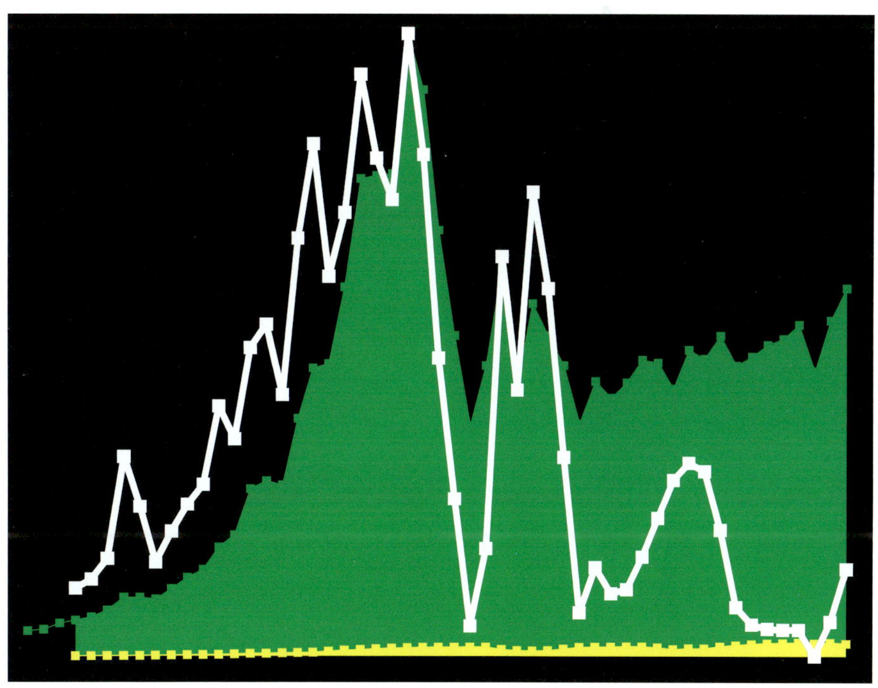

Price to Income—Price and Income

Price to Assets

MICROSOFT

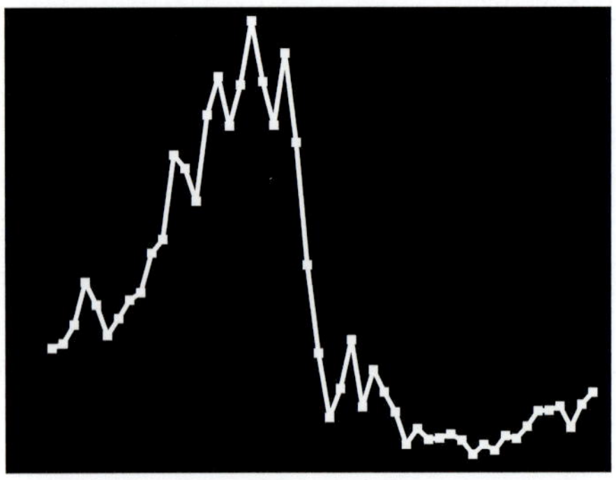

Price / Assets

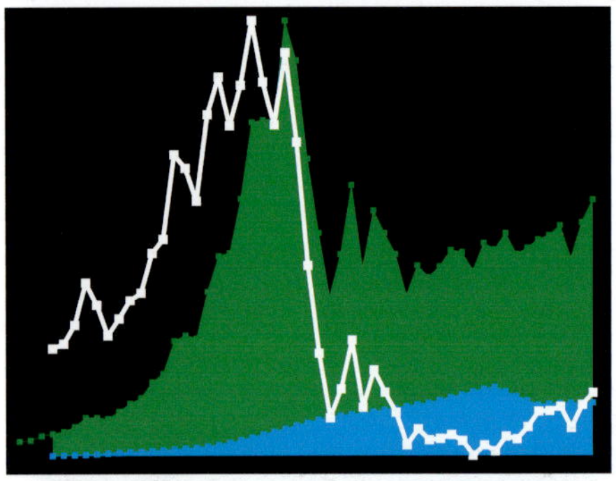

Prc / Ass—Price and Assets

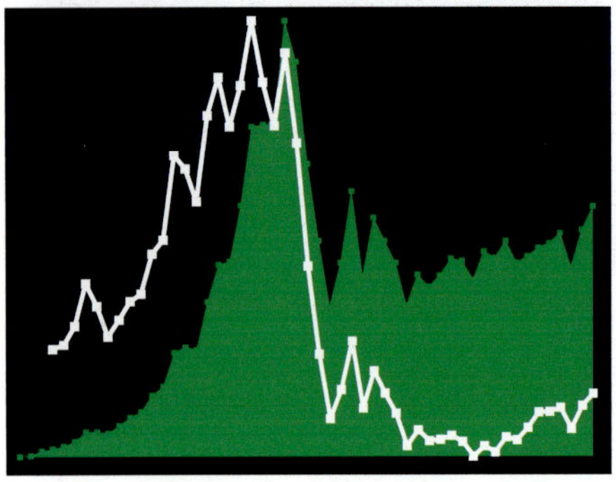

Prc / Ass—Share Price

> Graham laid out four components of stock evaluation: expected income, expected dividends, a method for valuing expected income, and asset value. All are still widely used. He repeatedly cautions the practitioner to tie the four firmly to the record of the past.
>
> David Dreman—*Contrarian Investment Strategies: The Next Generation*

Price to assets shows you the multiple share price is of assets per average diluted share.

Price to assets (Prc/Ass), also known as price to assets capital or the price assets multiple or the assets multiple, is share price divided by assets (*price / assets*). Price to assets is a times number—so many times assets.

Now that you have access to fundamentals and price data and their derived trends, you can quickly dismiss at least a few assumptions not supported by fact or reason, and get closer to the causes.

In the case of this company, when price to assets on the left increases to its peak, you know the cause must be increasing price, not decreasing assets. Why? Look at the *Assets—Share Price* chart on the page to the right. The assets white line is increasing steadily, except for the December 2004 averaged dividend.

Some charts require more than one vertical scale. In the middle chart, one scale compares values for *Prc/Ass* as the white dataplot. A second scale compares *Price* (green) and *Assets* (cyan). Different scales may use different values and units of measure.

In the *Assets—Share Price* chart on the right, you see that the company pays a large dividend in December 2004, causing assets (white) to change from increasing to decreasing.

So, the increase you see in *Price—Assets* charts on the left is caused by increasing price. Since the price increases faster than assets, the price may be driven by a cause in addition to increasing assets.

The company did not suddenly become worth more, then peak, then suddenly become worth less. Ignoring both fact and reason are characteristic of market mania. Here there may be a great investment opportunity to buy at an unreasonably low price and sell at an unreasonably high price.

Price to Assets Events

Price to assets is circled on row 2 of *GAAP Structure*. Multiply by income to price to complete the return on assets equation.

Price to Assets below signals an unusual circumstance during the increase of assets—price to assets begins decreasing.

Assets—Share Price on the left reveals the cause. After a certain point on the assets line (white), investors increase price (green) slower than the company increases assets. Compare green and white profiles—don't consider price and assets numbers because they're in different contexts. Why would investors move green below white?

Return on Assets—Share Price on the left reveals one influence on investors. During the time before the December 2004 dividend, the company experiences a long decrease in return on assets. However, assets probably become less popular with investors when the company begins retaining more of income in cash assets to fund possible anti-trust awards, and less in production assets to earn more income. Developing markets and new knowledge are also becoming issues.

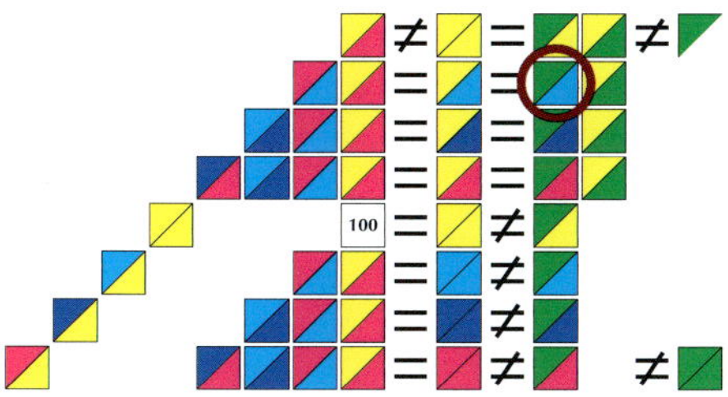

GAAP Structure

MICROSOFT

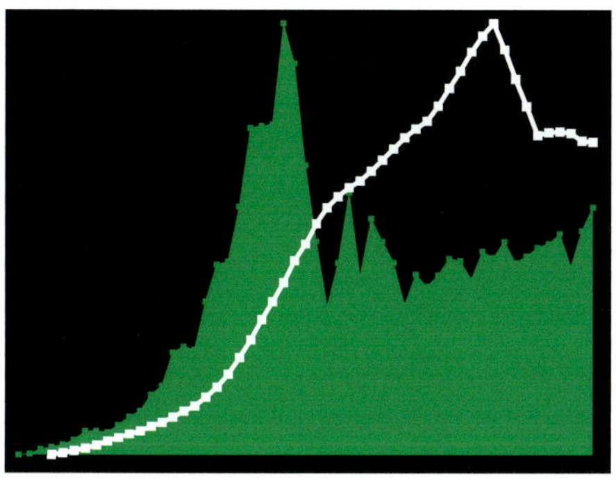

Assets—Share Price

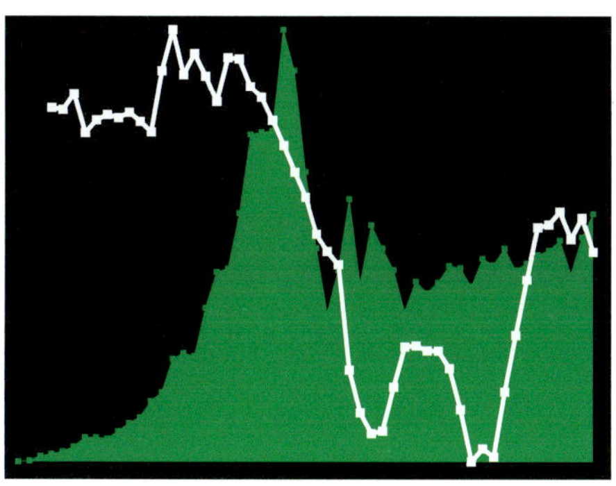

Return on Assets—Share Price

MICROSOFT

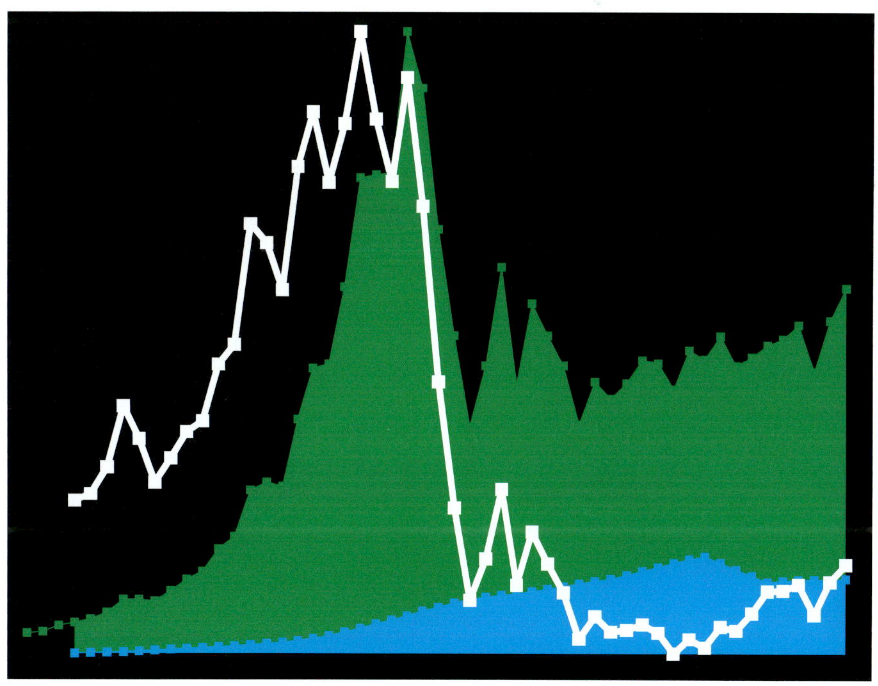

Price to Assets—Price and Assets

Price to Equity

MICROSOFT

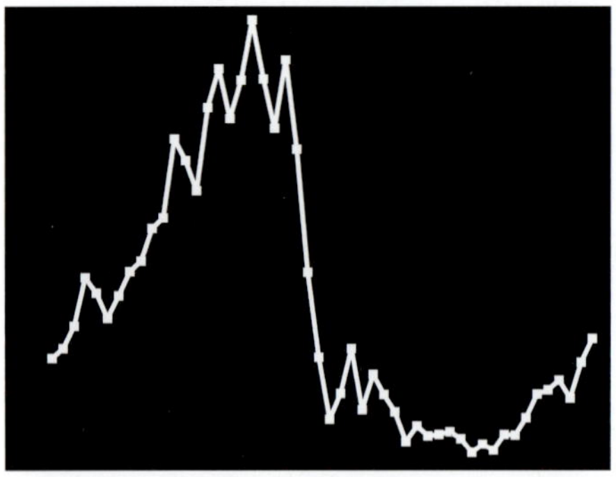

Price / Equity

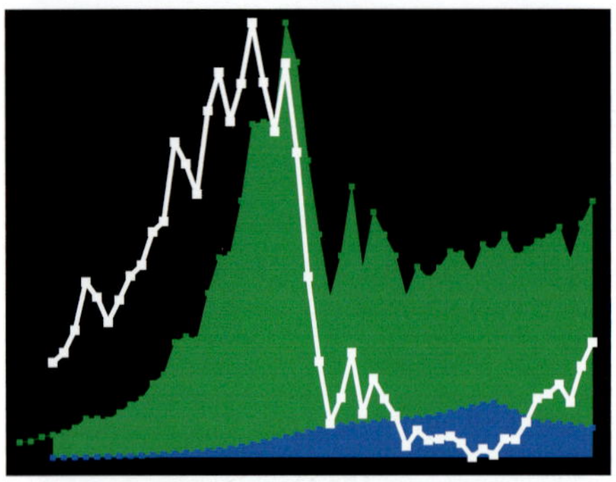

Prc / Eqt—Price and Equity

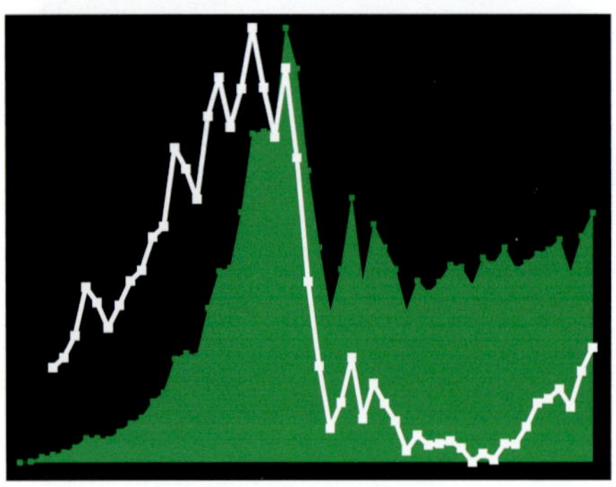

Prc / Eqt—Share Price

> "Value" investors observed the same Coca-Cola that Buffett purchased and because its price to income, price to equity, and price to cash flow were all so high, considered Coca-Cola overvalued.
>
> Robert G. Hagstrom, Jr.—*The Warren Buffett Way*

Price to equity shows you the multiple share price is of equity per average diluted share.

Price to equity (Prc/Eqt), also known as price to book value or price to net assets or price to equity capital or the price equity multiple or the equity multiple, is share price divided by equity (*price / equity*). Price to equity is a times number—so many times equity.

Some charts require more than one vertical scale. In the middle chart, one scale compares values for *Prc/Eqt* as the white dataplot. A second scale compares *Price* (green) and *Equity* (blue). Different scales may use different values and units of measure.

Now, read again Robert Hagstrom's phrase above—"were all so high". High relative to what? The market average! But, Hagstrom implies that Buffett invested on the basis of a *Fair Price Estimate* of the present value of future cash flow like on page 84, rather than on the basis of price to equity per average diluted share.

Price to equity, by definition, can't estimate future cash flow. All it can show you is what the market is paying for equity. It can't show you an estimate of income that may flow from that equity.

How can you as an investor benefit from all this? Assume that Buffett correctly estimated that the company was undervalued, whereas other investors improperly inferred from price to equity that the company was overvalued. You'd buy at a discount and ride the price up.

How could price to equity become unjustifiably high? Investors could misappraise the relation between income and equity by assuming they always move in lock-step. If that were true, income to equity (white) in the *Return on Equity—Share Price* chart to the right would always be a horizontal line—which return on equity clearly is not.

Naive investors may assume that increased equity can always be invested to increase income and influence an increase in price. A glance at the *Equity—Share Price* chart to the right invites you to consider why price may increase faster or slower than equity.

Price to Equity Events

Price to equity is circled on row 3 of *GAAP Structure*. Multiply by income to price to complete the return on equity equation.

Price to Equity below signals an unusual circumstance at the December 2004 dividend—price to equity begins increasing.

Equity—Share Price on the left reveals the cause. Investors increase price (green) while the company decreases average equity (white). Compare green and white profiles—don't consider price and equity numbers because they're in different contexts. Why would investors increase green while the company decreases white?

Return on Equity—Share Price (income to equity) on the left reveals one influence on investors. The December 2004 dividend payout causes a decrease in average equity—but a dividend doesn't improve productivity. The savvy investor realizes that a large dividend payout is expected to cause a surge in *Return on Equity—Income to Equity* on page 32 and *Return on Assets—Income to Assets* on page 30, probably making equity temporarily more popular with investors.

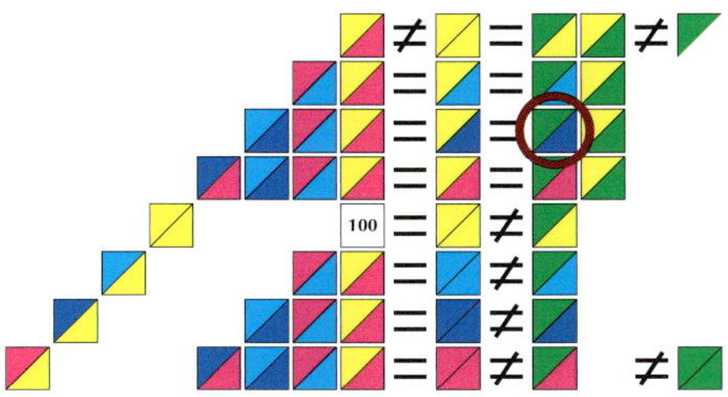

GAAP Structure

MICROSOFT

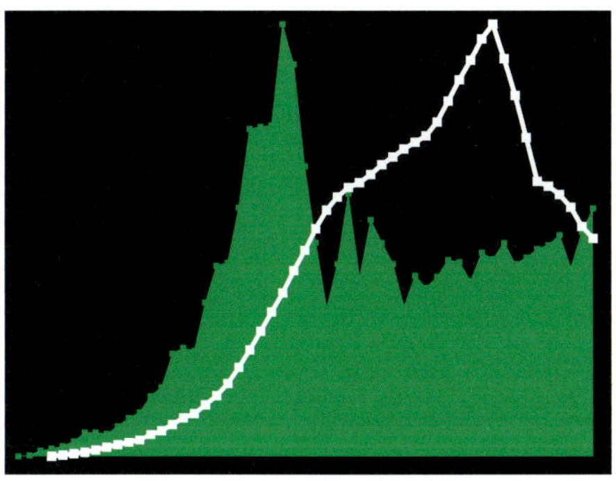

Equity—Share Price

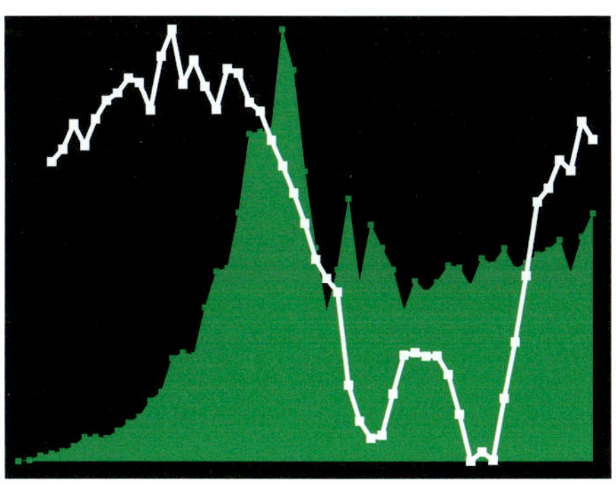

Return on Equity—Share Price

MICROSOFT

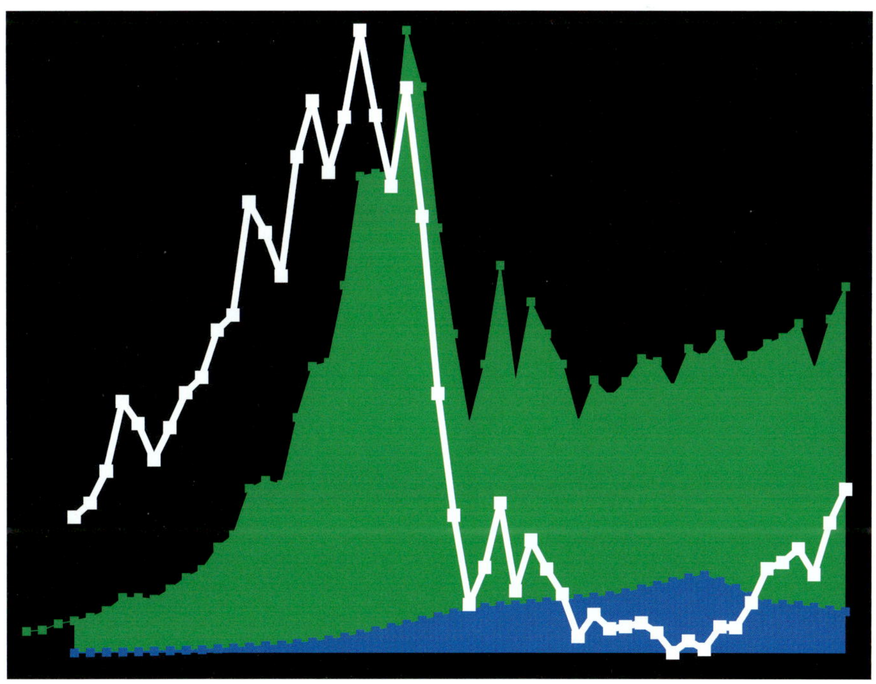

Price to Equity—Price and Equity

Price to Revenue

MICROSOFT

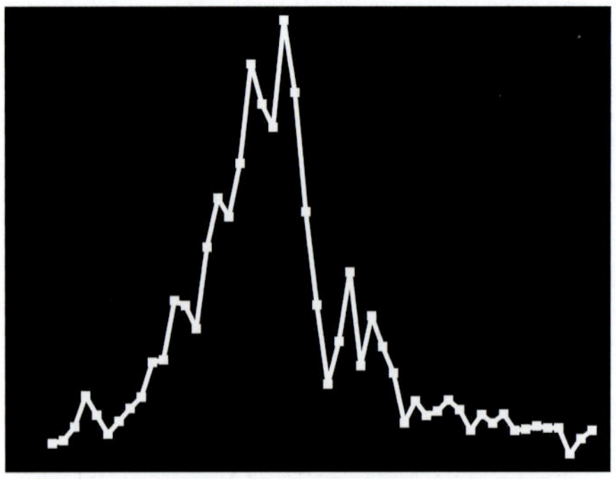

Price / Revenue

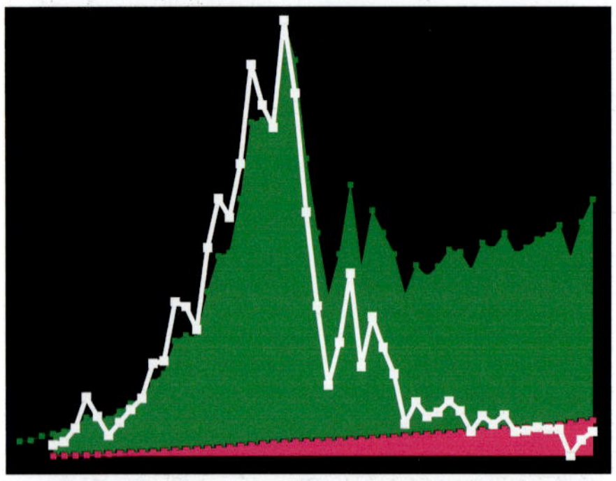

Prc / Rev—Price and Revenue

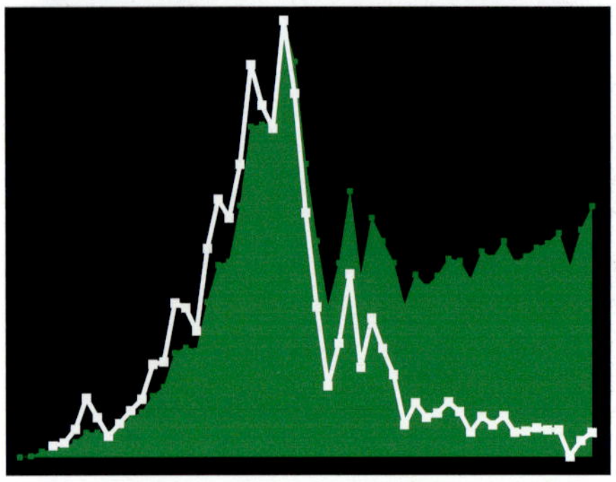

Prc / Rev—Share Price

> They are almost a perfect measure of popularity.
>
> Kenneth L. Fisher—*Super Stocks*

Price to revenue shows you the multiple share price is of revenue per average diluted share.

Price to revenue (Prc/Rev), also known as P/R or price to sales (P/S), is share price divided by revenue (*price / revenue*). Price to revenue is a times number—so many times revenue.

This ratio is not as popular as the better-known price to income, but has come to be regarded as a more useful ratio in recent years. One reason to use price to revenue is that, theoretically, revenue is harder to manipulate (unless of course management is just lying).

Some charts require more than one vertical scale. In the middle chart, one scale compares values for *Prc/Rev* as the white dataplot. A second scale compares *Price* (green) and *Revenue* (magenta). Different scales may use different values and units of measure.

The *Prc/Rev—Price and Revenue* chart on the left may tempt you to believe that price to revenue predicts price. A glance at the chart shows it sometimes does and it sometimes does not. But, the other measures in this book can help you benefit from the picture painted by the price to revenue ratio.

Increasing popularity does not show you that the company is worth more as a business. For example, increasing price does not necessarily mean increasing revenue. On the other hand, if other measures like net profit margin on the facing page are improving significantly, then increasing price to revenue does reveal that investors are recognizing and paying for an improvement in the business. An improvement that is recognized is a reason for you as an investor to notice.

Ken Fisher reminds us that

> People forget. In their careless abandon of fundamentals, they ignore any sense of long-term value.... Just as the market reaches high levels, people forget that stocks go down. Based on hopes and dreams, they pay prices that have little resemblance to what a private buyer would pay for the whole business.

After the *dot-com peak*, the shape of the price trend is not so close to the shape of the price to revenue trend.

Price to Revenue Events

Price to revenue is circled on row 4 of *GAAP Structure*. Multiply by income to price to complete the return on revenue equation.

Price to Revenue below signals an unusual circumstance during the increase of revenue—price to revenue increases and decreases.

Revenue—Share Price on the left reveals the cause. Before the peak, investors increase price (green) faster than the company increases revenue (white). After a point on the revenue line, investors increase price slower. Compare green and white profiles—don't consider price and revenue numbers because they're in different contexts. Why would investors move green above white, and then below?

Net Profit Margin on the left reveals two influences on investors. Before a point on the revenue line, the company increases net profit margin by increasing income faster than revenue—and reinvests much of that income in production to earn more income. After the point, revenue becomes less popular with investors because the company retains more of net profit margin's income in cash assets.

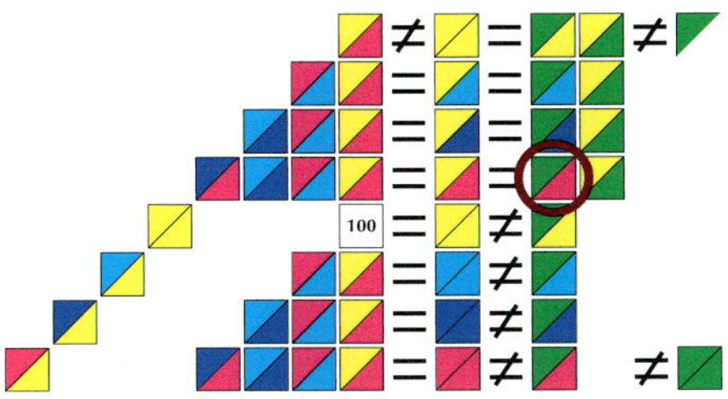

GAAP Structure

MICROSOFT

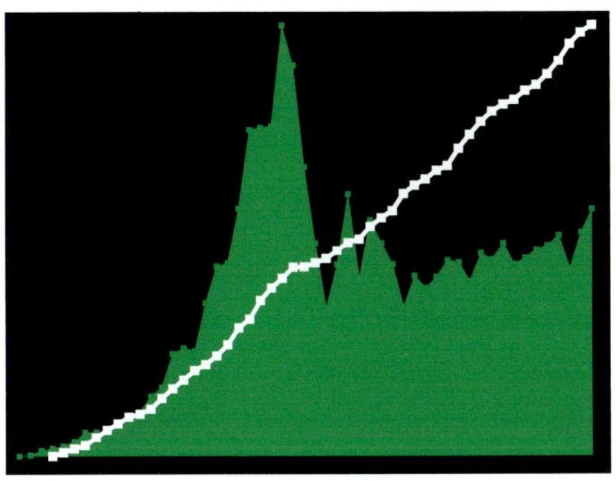

Revenue—Share Price

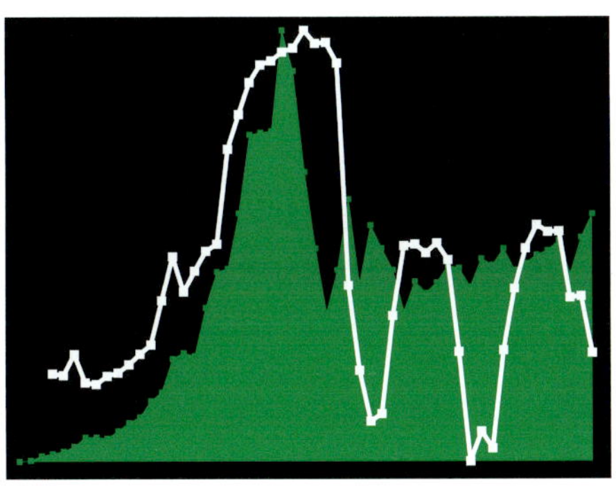

Net Profit Margin—Share Price

MICROSOFT

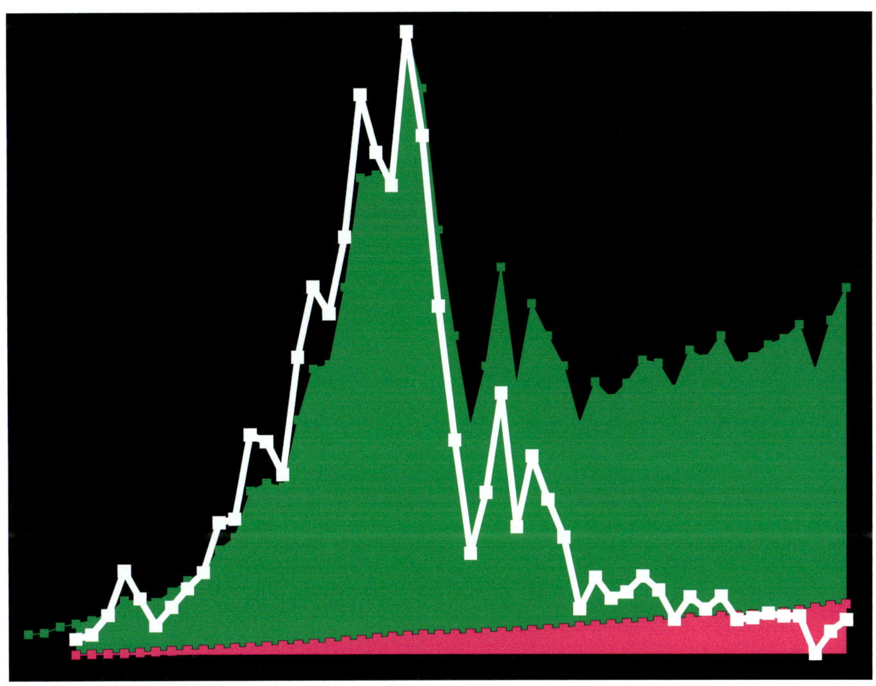

Price to Revenue—Price and Revenue

Price Growth to Income Growth

MICROSOFT

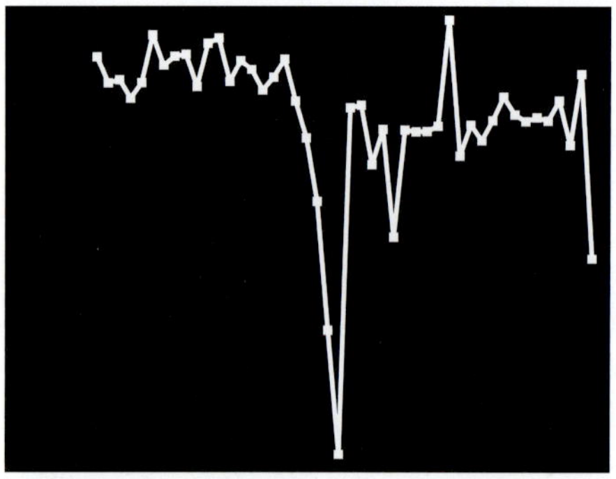

Price Growth / Income Growth

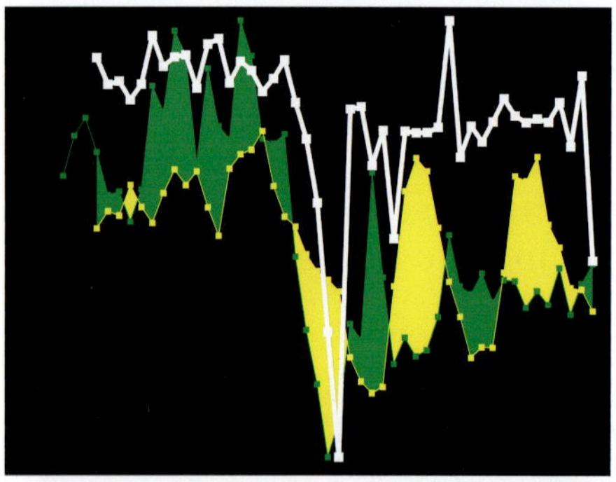

PG/IG—Prc Growth and Inc Growth

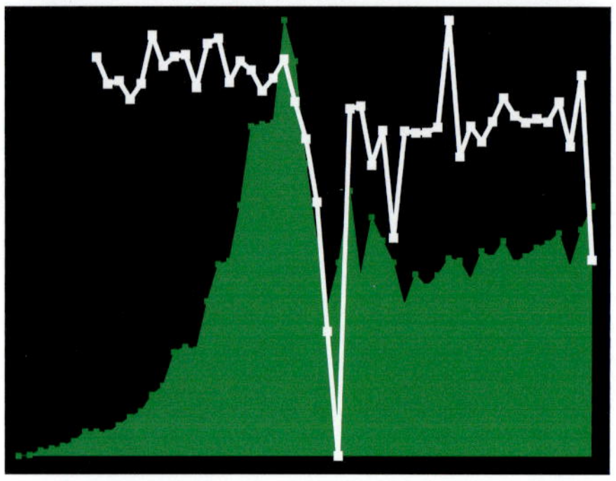

PG/IG—Share Price

With low P/Is, yields between 4.5% and 6.5%, and growth, even in a worst case, well above the *S&P 500*, the stocks proved to be a screaming buy, doubling in less than two years.

David Dreman—*Contrarian Investment Strategies: The Next Generation*

Price growth to income growth shows you the multiple share price growth is of income growth per average diluted share.

Price growth to income growth (PG/IG) is price growth divided by income growth (*price growth / income growth*). Price growth to income growth is a times number—so many times income growth.

In the middle chart on the left, the color shows the datastream that's growing faster. The height of the color shows how much faster. When the fill is green, price is growing faster than income—indicating income growth is popular with investors. Why?

Before and during the *dot-com boom*, the company is growing income rapidly and reinvesting it in production—on which this company earns more profit than on cash. When this company's fill is more often green, the corresponding balance sheets in quarterly and annual reports show cash is a smaller proportion of assets than it is later on.

When this company's fill changes to more often yellow, you'll find its cash is a larger proportion of assets. Investors lower price growth, possibly indicating that income growth is less popular. *The Monopoly Riddle* on page 99 offers insights into why this company shifts more of its income flow from production assets to cash assets.

In the bottom chart on the left, after the *dot-com boom*, price (green) is increasing at about the same rate as PG/IG (white)—possibly on optimism that the company is increasing the proportion of income reinvested in production versus flowing into cash.

The Company achieved a temporary consumer monopoly as a *cultural imperative* through its Windows operating system dominating 90 percent of the world's personal computers. The company protected its investors by conservatively retaining cash to pay penalties for its boldness, even at the temporary expense of its share price popularity. The company retained cash also because it found it increasingly difficult to expand markets and discover new knowledge.

Price Growth to Income Growth Events

Price growth to income growth is circled on row 5 of *GAAP Structure*—using income growth from the equation on its left.

Price Growth to Income Growth (white) below signals an unusual circumstance along the income growth line—income growth switches from more often popular (green fill) to less often popular (yellow fill).

Income Growth—Share Price on the left reveals the cause. The chart focuses on income growth (IG) from *PG/IG—Share Price* on the facing page. The company begins averaging lower income growth, influencing investors to react by lowering price growth. However, as income growth increases, investors continue increasing price (green).

The four-growth chart on the left reveals one influence on investors. During the period approaching the December 2004 dividend payout, the growth of revenue, assets, and equity proceed steadily along a common path. Revenue growth—which flows income into assets and equity—may influence less yellow with bursts of green. But, investors want increasing proportions of income flowing to production.

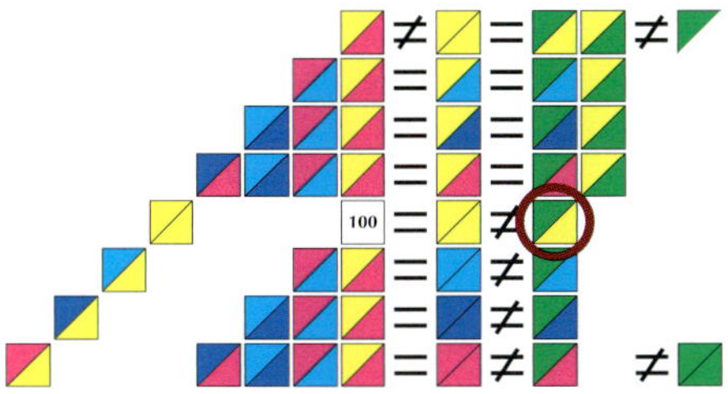

GAAP Structure

MICROSOFT

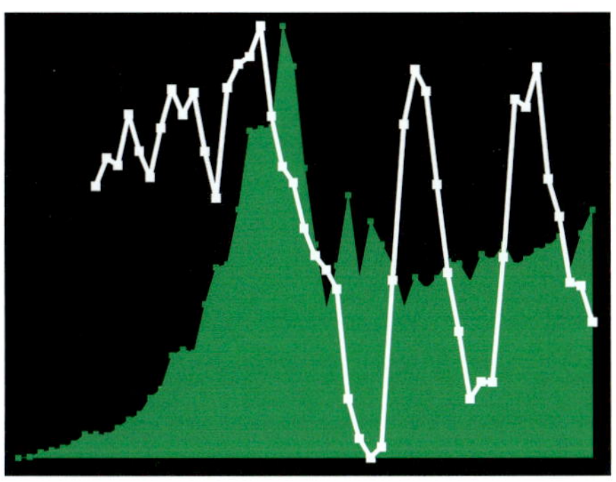

Income Growth—Share Price

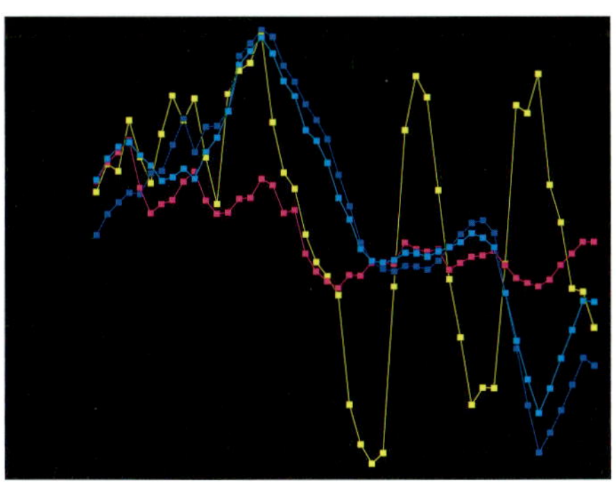

Income Growth
Equity Growth
Revenue Growth
Assets Growth

MICROSOFT

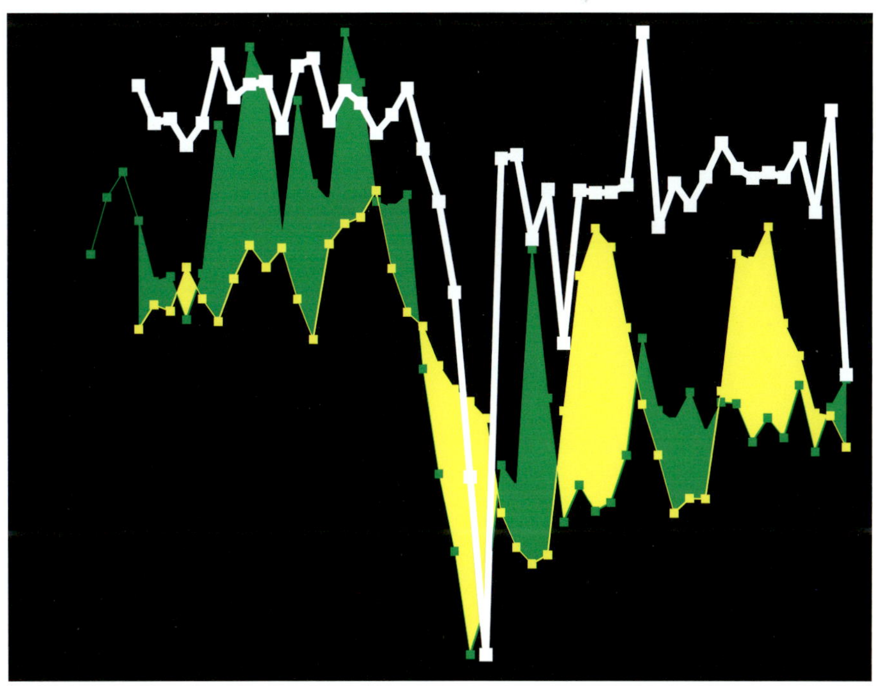

Price Growth to Income Growth—Prc Growth and Inc Growth

Price Growth to Assets Growth

MICROSOFT

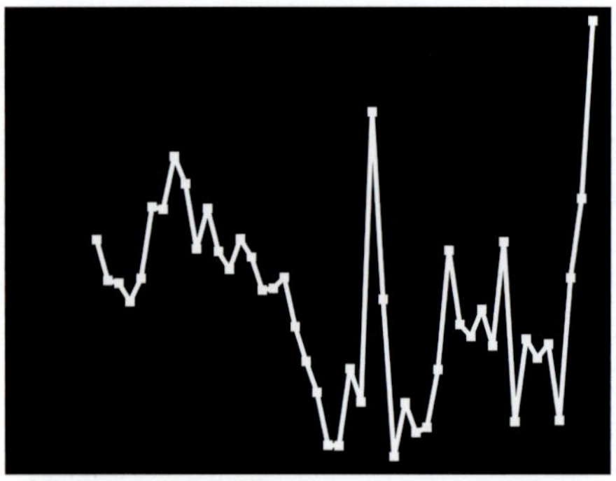

Price Growth / Assets Growth

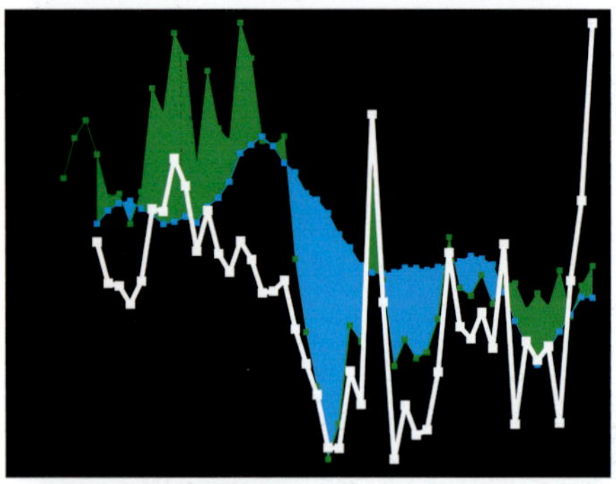

PG / AG—Prc Growth and Ass Growth

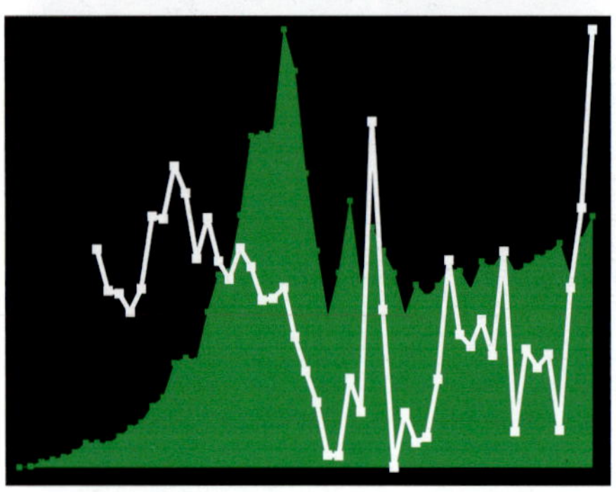

PG / AG—Share Price

> In both funds, however, I was struck by something else: The managements seemed excessively focused on assets growth, rather than performance. The two families that the funds are part of each oversees well over $800 billion. Fidelity alone manages more than 20 large-cap growth funds. What's the point of this slicing and dicing, except to accumulate assets? Why not focus one's best skills so as to maximize the returns?
>
> Louis Lowenstein, *Rifkind Professor Emeritus of Finance and Law at Columbia University—Barrons, A Recipe for Weak Results, July 10, 2006*

Price growth to assets growth shows you the multiple share price growth is of assets growth per average diluted share.

Price growth to assets growth (PG/AG) is price growth divided by assets growth (*price growth / assets growth*). Price growth to assets growth is a times number—so many times assets growth.

In the middle chart on the left, the color shows the datastream that's growing faster. The height of the color shows how much faster. When the fill is green, price is growing faster than assets—indicating assets growth is popular with investors. Why?

Before and during the *dot-com boom*, the company is growing assets rapidly by reinvesting income in production—on which this company earns more profit than on cash. When the fill is more often green, the corresponding balance sheets in quarterly and annual reports show cash is a smaller proportion of assets than it is later on.

When this company's fill changes to more often cyan, you'll find its cash is a larger proportion of assets. Investors lower price growth, possibly indicating that assets growth is less popular. *The Monopoly Riddle* on page 99 offers insights into why this company shifts the balance of its income flow from production assets to cash assets.

In the bottom chart on the left, after the *dot-com boom*, price (green) is increasing at about the same rate as PG/AG (white)—possibly on optimism that the company is increasing the proportion of income reinvested in production assets versus flowing into cash assets.

In the preceding *Price Growth to Income Growth* section of this chapter you see the obvious shift in the pattern of color from green to yellow. Now you see a similar pattern-shift for price growth to assets growth, from green to cyan. You will see that equity and revenue make similar pattern-shifts. Informed investors insist that income be reinvested in production to earn more income on increasing revenue.

Price Growth to Assets Growth Events

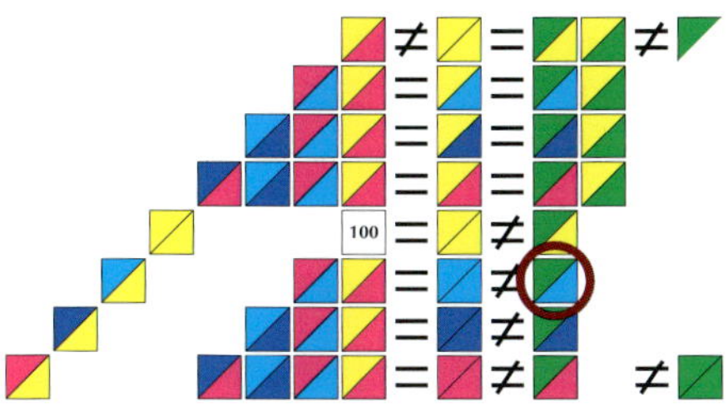

GAAP Structure

MICROSOFT

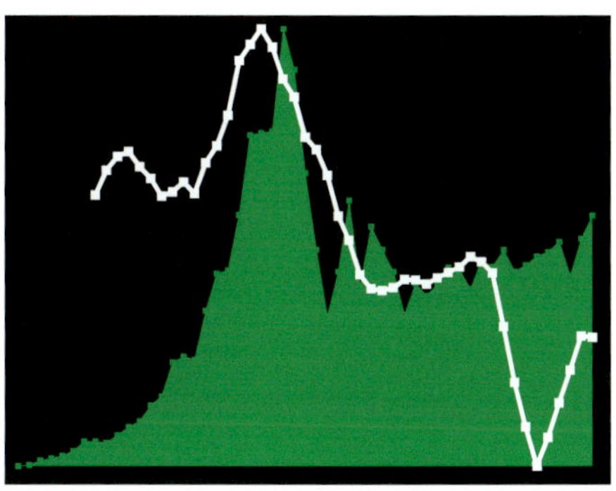

Assets Growth—Share Price

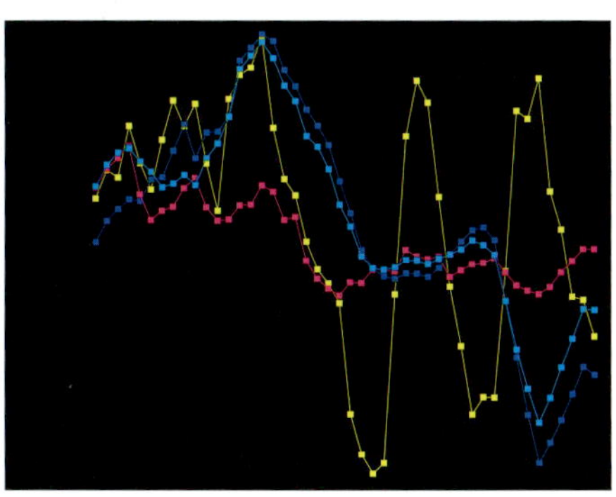

Income Growth
Equity Growth
Revenue Growth
Assets Growth

Price growth to assets growth is circled on row 6 of *GAAP Structure*—using assets growth from the equation on its left.

Price Growth to Assets Growth (white) below signals an unusual circumstance along the assets growth line—assets growth switches from more often popular (green fill) to less often popular (cyan fill).

Assets Growth—Share Price on the left reveals the cause. The chart focuses on assets growth (AG) from *PG/AG—Share Price* on the facing page. Assets growth turns down before the *dot-com peak* because income growth turns down—feeding less income into assets.

The four-growth chart on the left reveals one influence on investors. During the period approaching the December 2004 dividend payout, the growth of revenue, assets, and equity proceed steadily along a common path—around which income growth vascillates. Assets growth plummets—due to the relatively large dividend payout. Price (green) isn't affected much by the payout from assets, because the payout is from cash assets not assets earning production income.

MICROSOFT

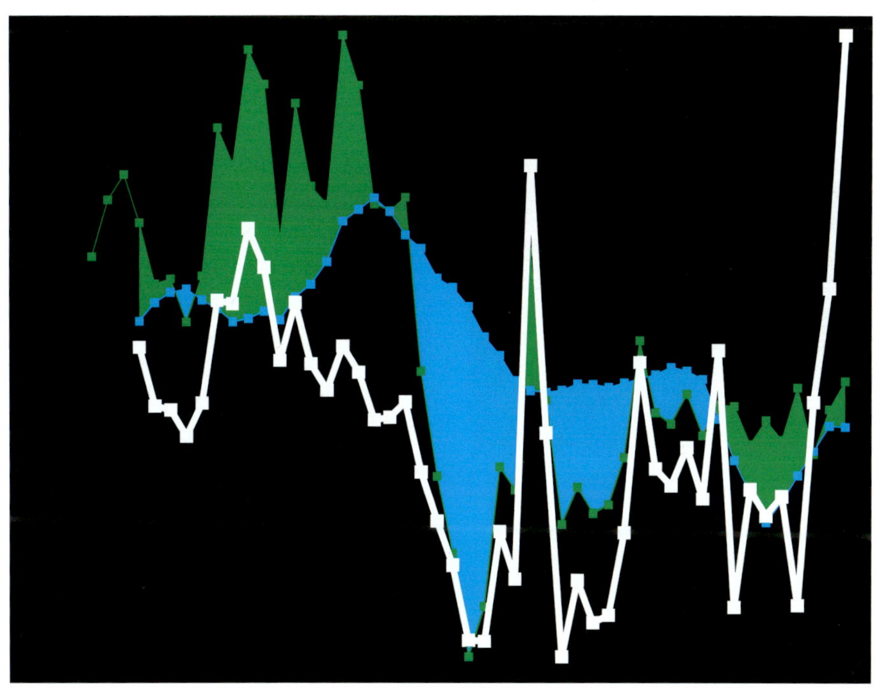

Price Growth to Assets Growth—Prc Growth and Ass Growth

Price Growth to Equity Growth

MICROSOFT

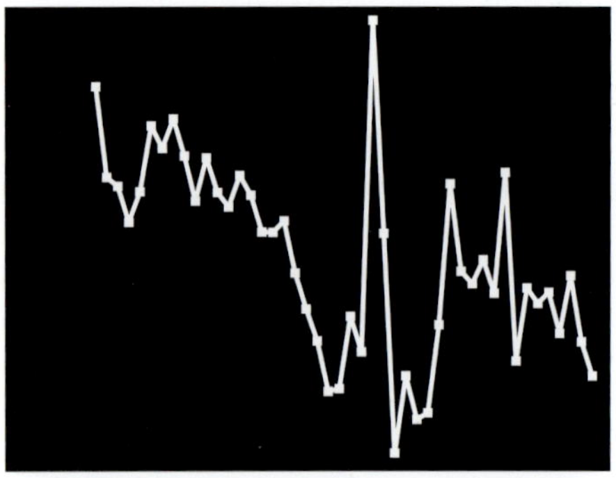

Price Growth / Equity Growth

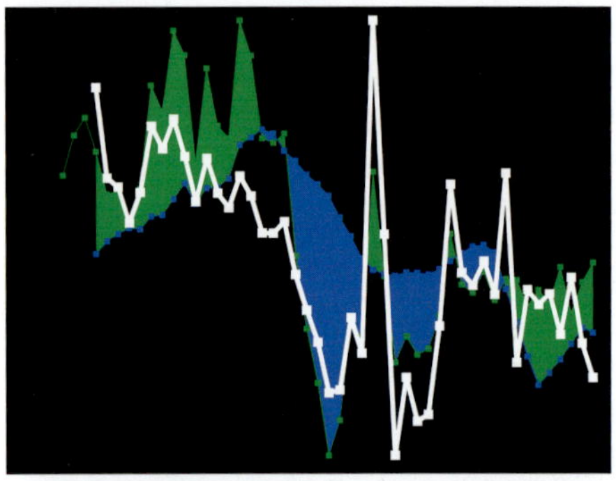

PG / EG—Prc Growth and Eqt Growth

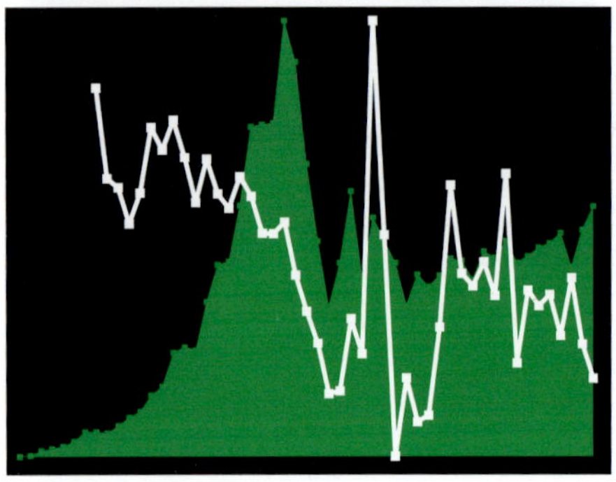

PG / EG—Share Price

To sum up, price to book value (price to equity per diluted share) was an excellent criterion for banks who stepped up and took their medicine early. At the bottom of the banking crisis they traded at the lowest financial ratios since the 1930s. In the case of Fleet, the stock rose from as low as $9 in October of 1990 to over $24 by April of 1991, a gain of 160%. By late December of 1997 it had appreciated 700% to $73.

David Dreman—*Contrarian Investment Strategies: The Next Generation*

Price growth to equity growth shows you the multiple share price growth is of equity growth per average diluted share.

Price growth to equity growth (PG/EG) is price growth divided by equity growth (*price growth / equity growth*). Price growth to equity growth is a times number—so many times equity growth.

In the middle chart on the left, the color shows the datastream that's growing faster. The height of the color shows how much faster. When the fill is green, price is growing faster than equity—indicating equity growth is popular with investors. Why?

Before and during the *dot-com boom*, the company is growing equity rapidly by reinvesting income in production—on which this company earns more profit than on cash. When the fill is more often green, the corresponding balance sheets in quarterly and annual reports show cash is a smaller proportion of equity than it is later on.

When this company's fill changes to more often blue, you'll find its cash is a larger proportion of equity. Investors lower price growth, possibly indicating that equity growth is less popular. *The Monopoly Riddle* on page 99 offers insights into why this company shifts the balance of its income flow from production equity to cash equity.

In the bottom chart on the left, after the *dot-com boom*, price (green) is increasing at about the same rate as PG/EG (white)—possibly on optimism that the company is increasing the proportion of income reinvested in production equity versus flowing into cash equity.

Remember that in the four price growth ratios, the price growth numerator is the same for any given datapoint. Only the denominators can cause the four dataplots (white) to be different. Simply speaking, when the company was growing equity—in the absence of an equal demand for increased production—investors lowered price growth, turning the chart from green to blue.

Price Growth to Equity Growth Events

Price growth to equity growth is circled on row 7 of *GAAP Structure*—using equity growth from the equation on its left.

Price Growth to Equity Growth (white) below signals an unusual circumstance along the equity growth line—equity growth switches from more often popular (green fill) to less often popular (blue fill).

Equity Growth—Share Price on the left reveals the cause. The chart focuses on equity growth (EG) from *PG/EG—Share Price* on the facing page. Equity growth turns down before the *dot-com peak* because income growth turns down—feeding less income into equity.

The four-growth chart on the left reveals one influence on investors. During the period approaching the December 2004 dividend payout, the growth of revenue, assets, and equity proceed steadily along a common path—around which income growth vascillates. Equity growth plummets—due to the relatively large dividend payout. Price (green) isn't affected much by the payout from equity, because the payout is from cash equity not equity earning production income.

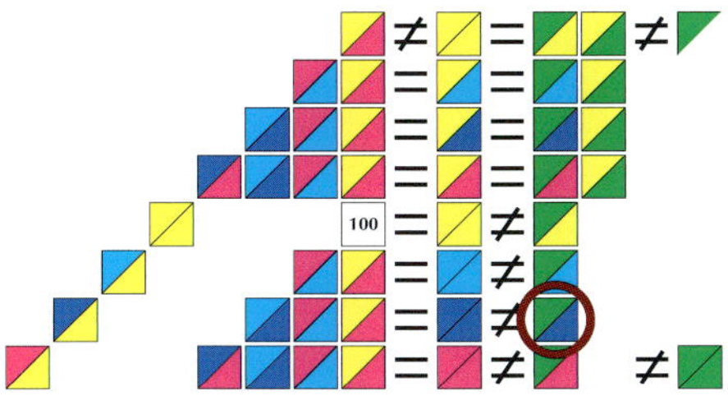

GAAP Structure

MICROSOFT

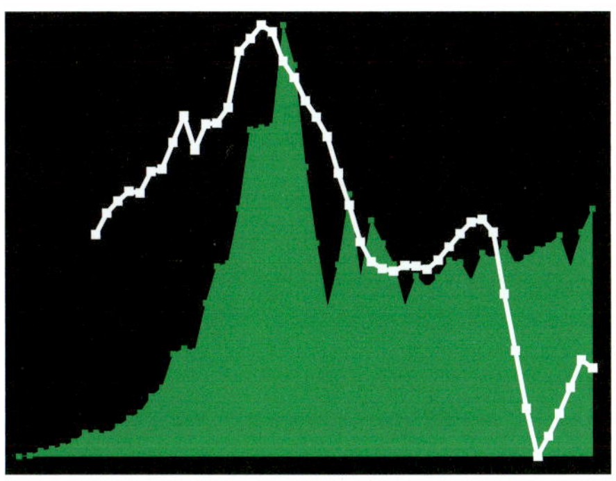

Equity Growth—Share Price

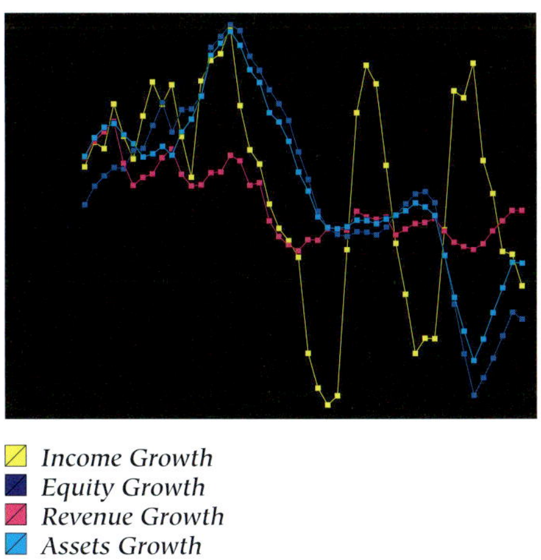

MICROSOFT

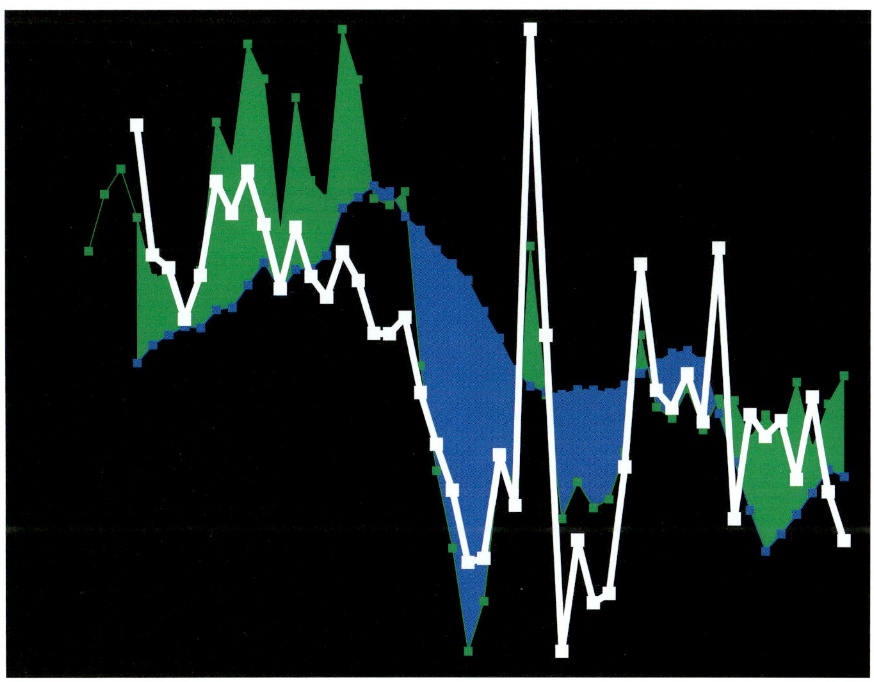

Price Growth to Equity Growth—Prc Growth and Eqt Growth

Price Growth to Revenue Growth

MICROSOFT

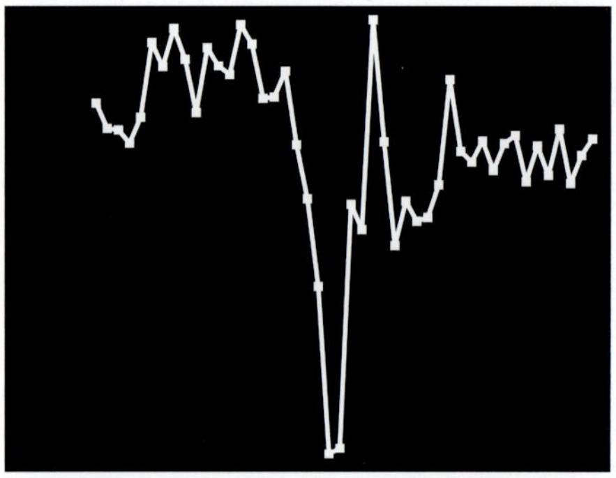

Price Growth / Revenue Growth

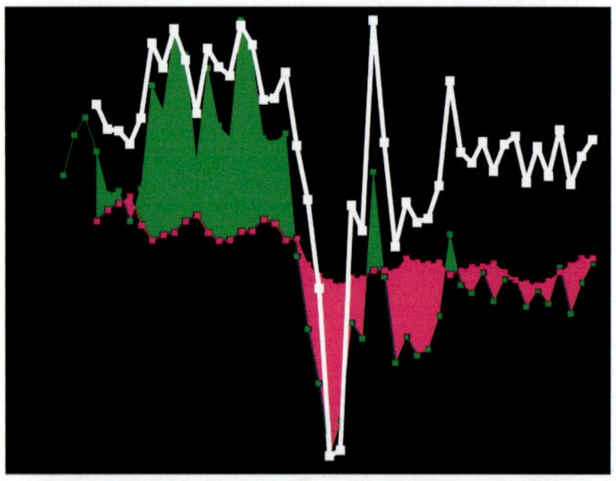

PG / RG—Prc Growth and Rev Growth

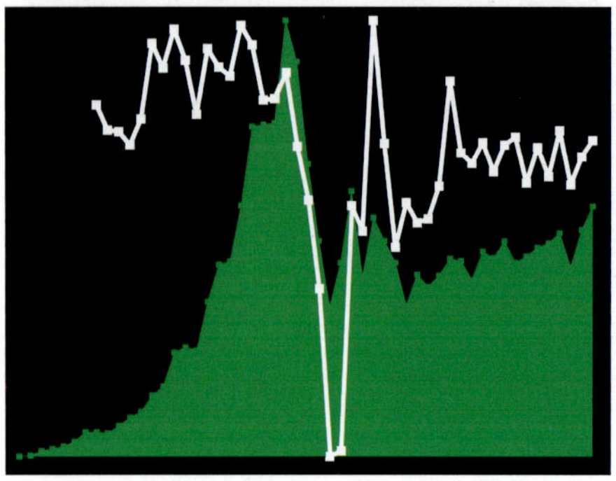

PG / RG—Share Price

> A study I did in collaboration with Eric Lufkin pinpoints exactly how powerful the psychological effects of overreaction are. It shows how overpriced the "best" (and underpriced the "worst") stocks become before they correct, as well as how small the underlying changes in a stock's fundamentals actually are that cause such major price moves.
>
> David Dreman—*Contrarian Investment Strategies: The Next Generation*

Price growth to revenue growth shows you the multiple share price growth is of revenue growth per average diluted share.

Price growth to revenue growth (PG/RG) is price growth divided by revenue growth (*price growth / revenue growth*). Price growth to revenue growth is a times number—so many times revenue growth.

In the middle chart on the left, the color shows the datastream that's growing faster. The height of the color shows how much faster. When the fill is green, price is growing faster than revenue—indicating revenue growth is popular with investors. Why?

Before and during the *dot-com boom*, the company is growing revenue rapidly and reinvesting it in production—on which this company earns more profit than on cash. When the fill is more often green, the corresponding balance sheets in quarterly and annual reports show cash is a smaller proportion of assets than it is later on.

When this company's fill changes to more often magenta, you'll find its cash is a larger proportion of assets. Investors lower price growth, possibly indicating that revenue growth is less popular. *The Monopoly Riddle* on page 99 offers insights into why this company shifts the balance of its revenue flow from production assets to cash assets.

In the bottom chart on the left, after the *dot-com boom*, price (green) is increasing at about the same rate as PG/RG (white)—possibly on optimism that the company is increasing the proportion of revenue reinvested in production versus flowing into cash.

The Company achieved a temporary consumer monopoly as a *cultural imperative* through its Windows operating system dominating 90 percent of the world's personal computers. The company protected its investors by conservatively retaining cash to pay penalties for its boldness, even at the temporary expense of its share price popularity. It retained cash also because large companies find it increasingly difficult to expand markets and discover new knowledge.

Price Growth to Revenue Growth Events

Price growth to revenue growth is circled on row 8 of *GAAP Structure*—using revenue growth from the equation on its left.

Price Growth to Revenue Growth (white) below signals an unusual circumstance along the revenue growth line—revenue growth switches from more often popular (green fill) to less (magenta fill).

Revenue Growth—Share Price on the left reveals the cause. The chart focuses on revenue growth (RG) from *PG/RG—Share Price* on the facing page. When revenue growth decreases, that influences investors to lower price growth. However, as revenue growth increases, investors tend to increase price (green).

The four-growth chart on the left reveals one influence on investors. During the period approaching the December 2004 dividend payout, the growth of revenue, assets, and equity proceed steadily along a common path. Revenue growth—which flows income into assets and equity—may influence less magenta with bursts of green. But, investors want increasing portions of revenue reinvested in production.

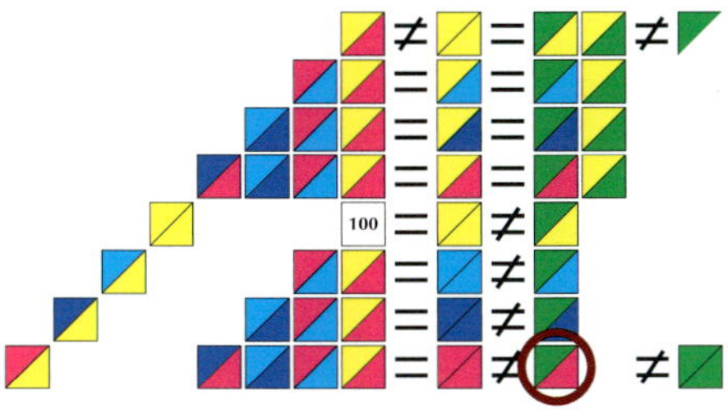

GAAP Structure

MICROSOFT

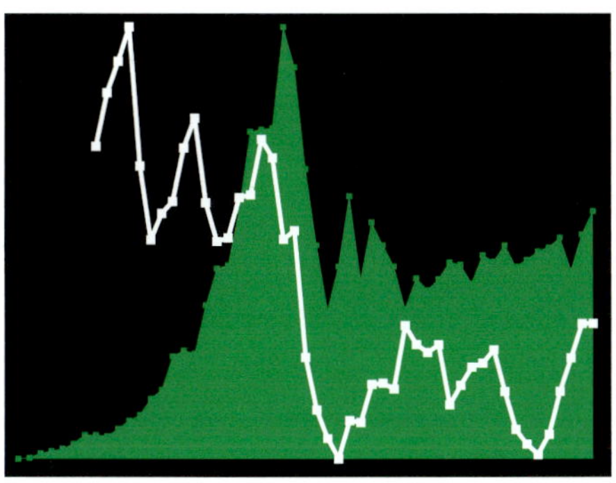

Revenue Growth—Share Price

MICROSOFT

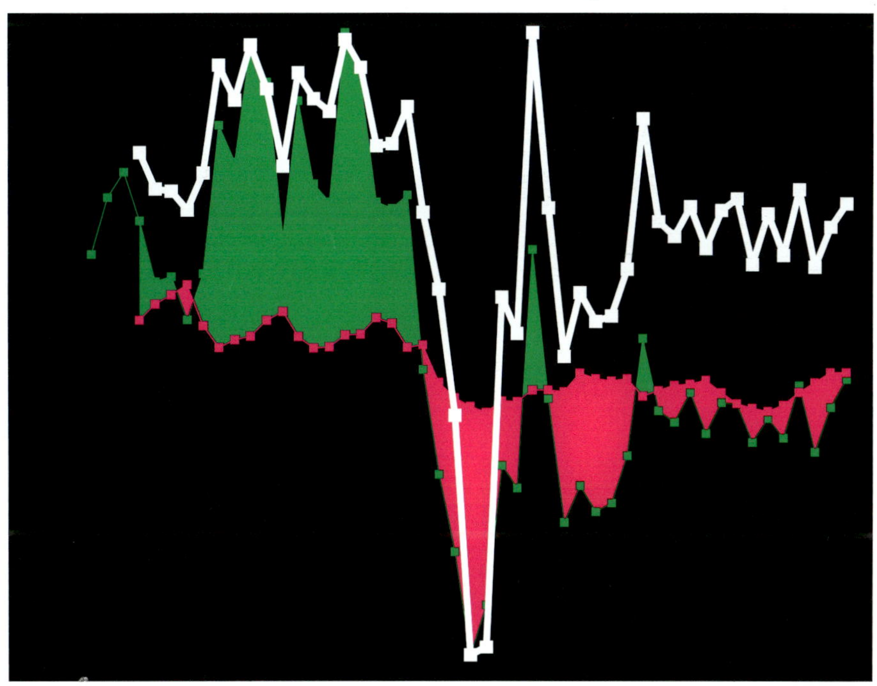

Price Growth to Revenue Growth—Prc Growth and Rev Growth

MICROSOFT

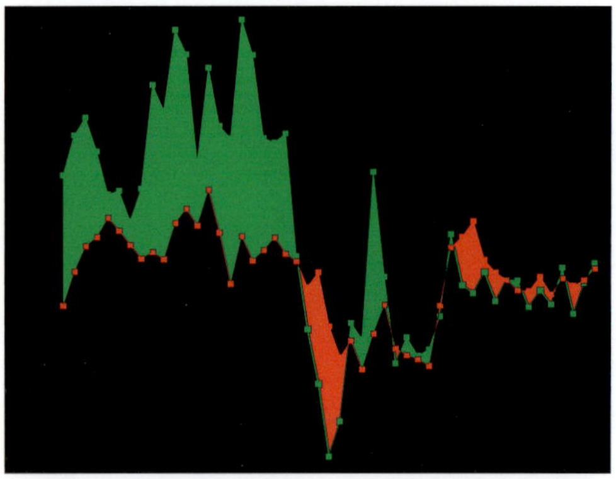

Share Price Growth—S&P Price Growth

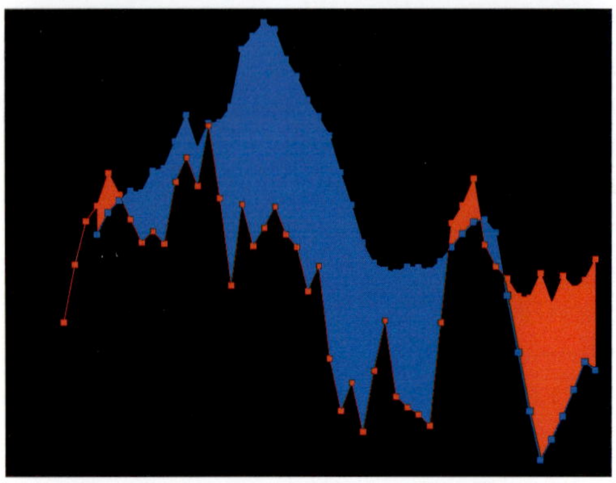

Equity Growth—S&P Price Growth

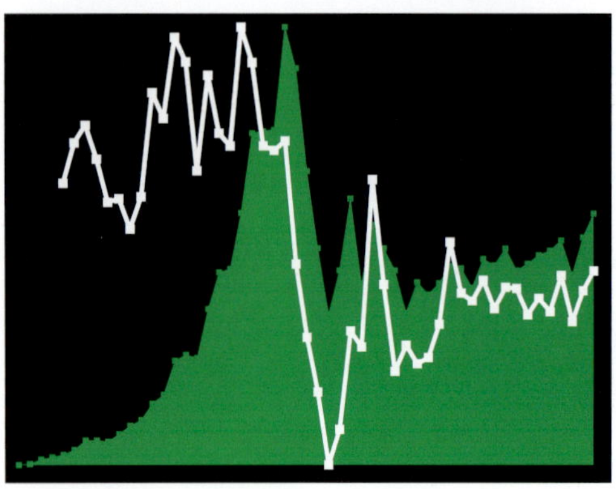

Share Price Growth (white)—Share Price

QUARTER ENDED	EQUITY GROWTH	PRICE GROWTH SHARE	S&P	SHARE *minus* S&P
OVERALL GROWTH	791	1270	204	1066
AVERAGE GROWTH	23	29	11	18
2006-12-31	(12.90)	15.83	13.62	2.21
2006-09-30	(10.94)	7.79	8.71	(0.92)
2006-06-30	(17.56)	(4.93)	6.62	(11.55)
2006-03-31	(23.86)	13.98	9.68	4.30
2005-12-31	(29.38)	(0.92)	3.00	(3.92)
2005-09-30	(34.27)	4.68	10.25	(5.57)
2005-06-30	(22.62)	(2.17)	4.43	(6.60)
2005-03-31	(8.69)	8.70	4.83	3.87
2004-12-31	4.96	9.14	8.99	0.15
2004-09-30	19.97	0.33	11.91	(11.58)
2004-06-30	23.07	12.02	17.07	(5.05)
2004-03-31	22.40	3.58	32.78	(29.20)
2003-12-31	19.63	6.81	26.38	(19.57)
2003-09-30	16.41	27.47	22.16	5.31
2003-06-30	13.13	(5.97)	(1.55)	(4.42)
2003-03-31	10.93	(19.47)	(26.08)	6.61
2002-12-31	11.70	(21.99)	(23.37)	1.38
2002-09-30	11.83	(14.49)	(21.68)	7.19
2002-06-30	10.48	(25.06)	(19.16)	(5.91)
2002-03-31	11.09	10.29	(1.12)	11.41
2001-12-31	12.74	52.75	(13.04)	65.79
2001-09-30	17.60	(15.17)	(27.54)	12.37
2001-06-30	26.55	(8.74)	(15.83)	7.08
2001-03-31	34.25	(48.54)	(22.57)	(25.97)
2000-12-31	43.04	(62.84)	(10.14)	(52.71)
2000-09-30	47.75	(33.40)	11.99	(45.39)
2000-06-30	51.66	(11.30)	5.97	(17.27)
2000-03-31	57.29	18.55	16.50	2.06
1999-12-31	61.27	68.37	19.53	48.84
1999-09-30	68.41	64.56	26.13	38.44
1999-06-30	70.05	66.41	21.07	45.34
1999-03-31	66.80	100.31	16.76	83.55
1998-12-31	63.68	114.62	26.67	87.96
1998-09-30	50.05	66.39	7.36	59.03
1998-06-30	46.32	71.55	28.10	43.46
1998-03-31	46.10	95.15	45.52	49.63
1997-12-31	39.83	56.39	31.01	25.38
1997-09-30	48.06	100.56	37.82	62.74
1997-06-30	41.65	110.49	31.99	78.51
1997-03-31	35.23	77.74	17.29	60.45
1996-12-31	34.63	88.19	20.26	67.92
1996-09-30	29.49	45.90	17.61	28.29
1996-06-30	29.87	32.79	23.11	9.68
1996-03-31	27.51	45.05	28.92	16.14
1995-12-31	24.62	43.64	34.11	9.53
1995-09-30	19.47	61.06	26.30	34.75
1995-06-30	....	74.91	22.62	52.29
1995-03-31	....	67.69	12.32	55.36
1994-12-31	....	51.38	(1.54)	52.92
1994-09-30	....	....	....	....
1994-06-30	....	....	....	....
1994-03-31	....	....	....	....
1993-12-31	....	....	....	....

7 Share and Fair Price Trends

MICROSOFT

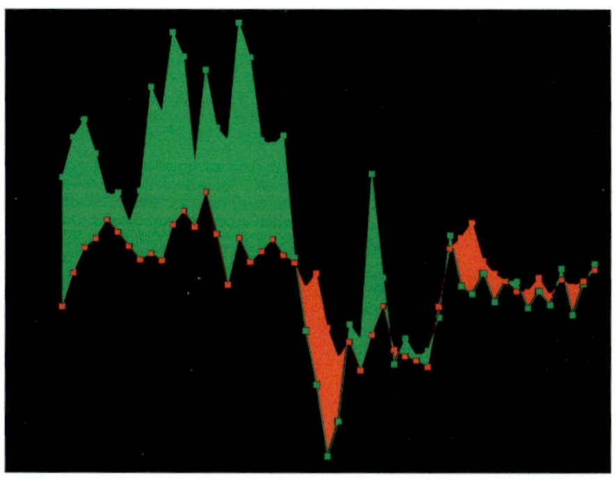

Share Price Growth—S&P Price Growth

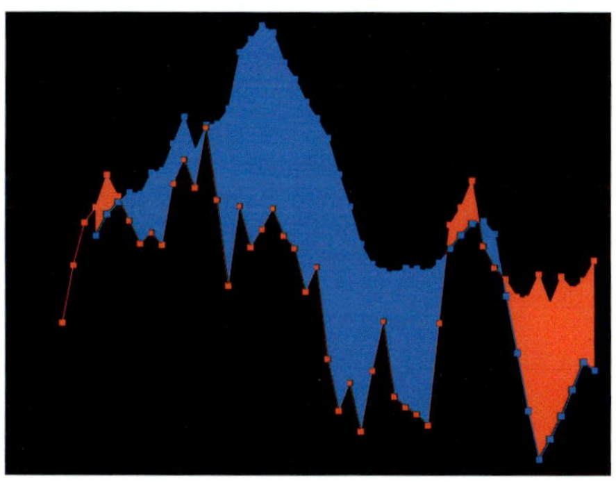

Equity Growth—S&P Price Growth

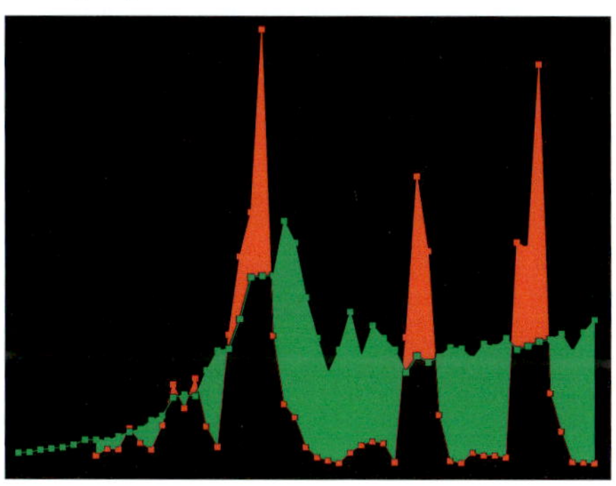

Share Price—Fair Price
Margin of Safety—Margin of Risk

> The most common error in investing is confusing business fundamentals with investment merit. A company that is doing terrifically well, that has great management and returns on capital, and great products and prospects, may be a terrible investment, if the expectations embedded in the current valuation are in excess of those fundamentals. A company with poor business fundamentals, a mediocre management, and indifferent prospects may be a great investment if the market is even more pessimistic about the business than is warranted.
>
> Bill Miller—*Letter to Legg Mason Value Trust Shareholders, 2005*

Share and fair price trends on the left deserve *front cover* charts because they answer three questions about "doing well":

- ❑ Is share price growth beating the market (*S&P*)—green fill?
- ❑ Is equity growth beating the market (*S&P*)—blue fill?
- ❑ Is share price below fair price—red fill? or above—green fill?

Share Price Growth shows you a company is "doing well" when share price growth is beating the *Standard & Poor's 500 Index* (*S&P*) price growth—green fill. The *facing page* shows average growth for 1993–2006 share price at 29% beating the *S&P* at 11%.

Equity Growth shows you a company is "doing well" when equity growth is beating the market (*S&P*)—blue fill. Why? You want to see equity average growth that makes share price average growth believable. *Equity Growth* on page 16 may be a proxy for growth of the *Fair Price Estimate* on page 84. The *facing page* shows average growth for 1993–2006 equity at 23% beating the *S&P* at 11%.

Share Price—Fair Price shows you a company is "doing well" if share price continues to rise—especially if there are opportunities to buy at a substantial discount and sell at a substantial premium (if your sell price is also well above your buy price). Red fill shows you are buying at a discount (margin of safety) when a share price (green marker) is below a fair price estimate (red marker). Green fill shows you are selling at a premium when share price is above fair price.

The *facing page* shows differences in overall growth compounded for 1993–2006 *S&P* at 204%, equity at 791%, and share price at 1270%.

Share Price Growth and S&P Price Growth

MICROSOFT

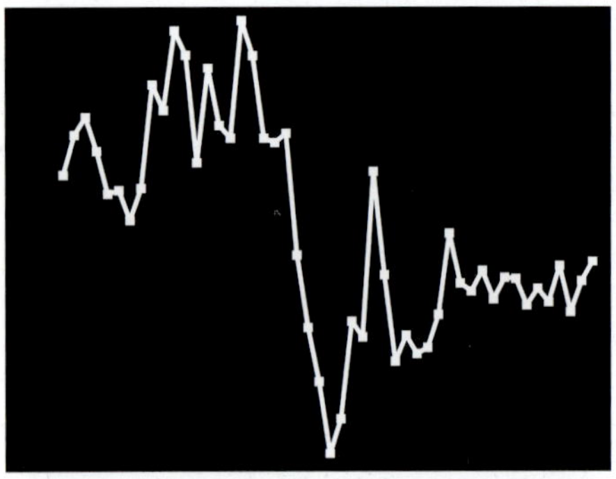

Share Price Growth

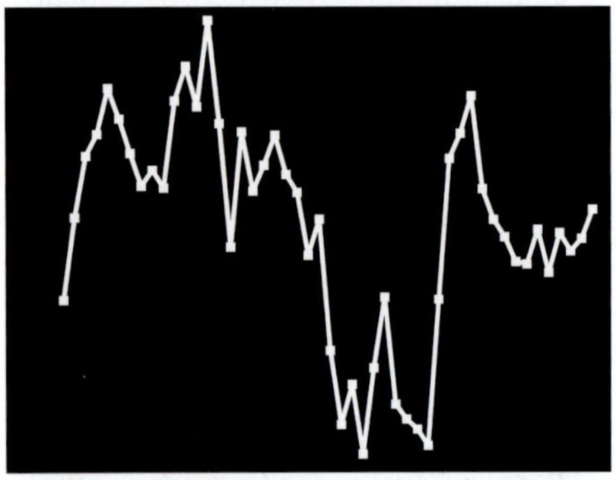

S&P Price Growth

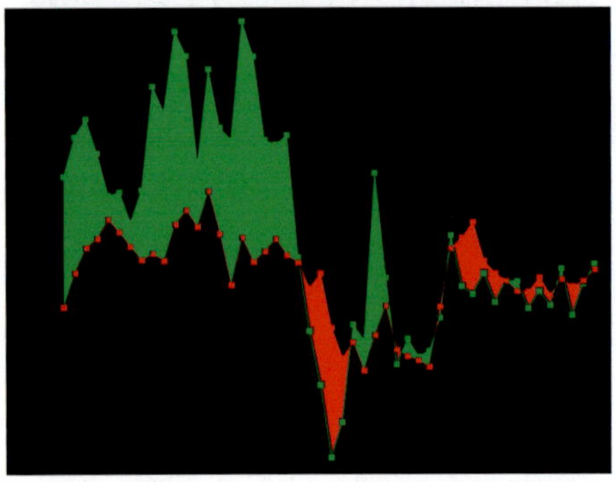

Share Price Growth—S&P Price Growth

> Our shareholders can buy the *S&P* through an index fund at very low cost. Unless we achieve gains in per-share intrinsic value (fair price growth, and eventually share price growth) in the future that outdo the *S&P*, Charlie and I will be adding nothing to what you can accomplish on your own.
>
> Warren E. Buffett—*Letter to Berkshire Shareholders, 2004*

Share price growth and *S&P* price growth show you if a company is beating the market—green fill—when and by how much.

Share Price Growth—S&P Price Growth deserves to be a *front cover* chart. Buffett implies that unless a company achieves share price growth outdoing *S&P* price growth, that company "will be adding nothing to what you can accomplish on your own" if you just buy an *S&P* index fund.

Share Price Growth—S&P Price Growth shows you when and by how much share price growth is beating the market. Share price growth is beating *S&P* price growth when green fill shows you that share price growth (green markers) are above *S&P* price growth (red markers).

The page facing *Share and Fair Price Trends* on page 77 shows average growth for 1993–2006 share price at 29% outdoing *S&P* price at 11%—as you see. The table gives you a feel for how quarterly growth rolls up to become average growth (29% versus 11%), and how these average growth numbers compound over time to become overall growth (1270% versus 204%). Realistic expectations are laid out by Bill Miller in his *Letter to Legg Mason Value Trust Shareholders*, 2005:

> If your expectation is that we will outperform the market (S&P) every year, you can expect to be disappointed.... Unfortunately, when we purchase companies we believe are mispriced, it is often difficult to determine when the market will agree with us and close the discount to intrinsic value (fair price estimate). Our goal is to construct portfolios that have the potential to outperform the market over an investment time horizon of 3–5 years without assuming undue risk.

Share price growth and *S&P* price growth are calculated by [(*new value* – *old value*) / *old value*] × 100, expressed as growth is this percent. The simple message of growth is this—When share price growth beats *S&P* price growth you have one important reason to believe that a company *is doing well*. Even better is an unknown company growing sharply toward beating *S&P* price growth.

Share Price Growth and S&P Price Growth Events

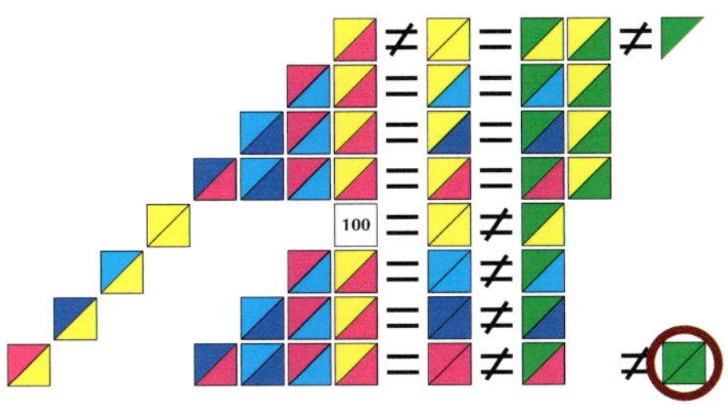

GAAP Structure

MICROSOFT

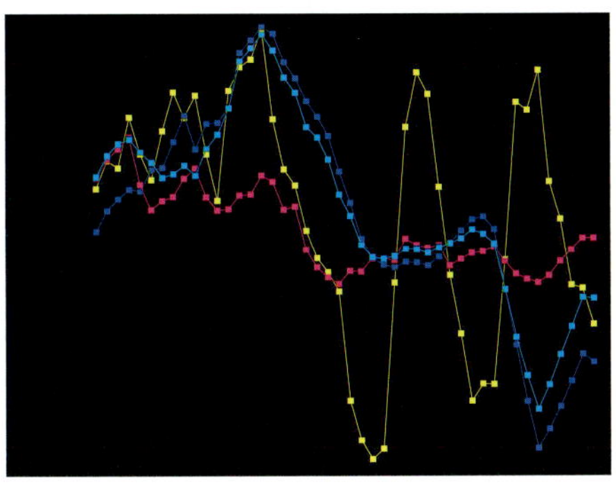

Income Growth
Equity Growth
Revenue Growth
Assets Growth

Share price growth (circled) is preceded by a not equal sign. This pictures that share price growth is not proportionally connected to other financial growth measures of a company. Share price growth is also not proportionally connected to the *S&P*—one approximation of the market—except that the company is a very small part of the market. Leave the details of *GAAP Structure* on the left until page 87.

Compare the dominant shape of the chart on the left from *The Growth Hierarchy Riddle* on page 104 to *Share Price Growth—S&P Price Growth* below. Refine your view by mentally removing volatile income growth, and the drops in growth of assets and equity due to the December 2004 dividend. Resulting similar shapes imply that the company reasonably used economic conditions to manage *Sustainable Trends* on page 45—the market signaled agreement in price.

The Best Numbers Riddle on page 100 says ideally share price growth beats *S&P* price growth (averaging 11%)—as on the page facing *Share and Fair Price Trends* on page 77. The chart below shows if the company is beating the market—when and by how much.

MICROSOFT

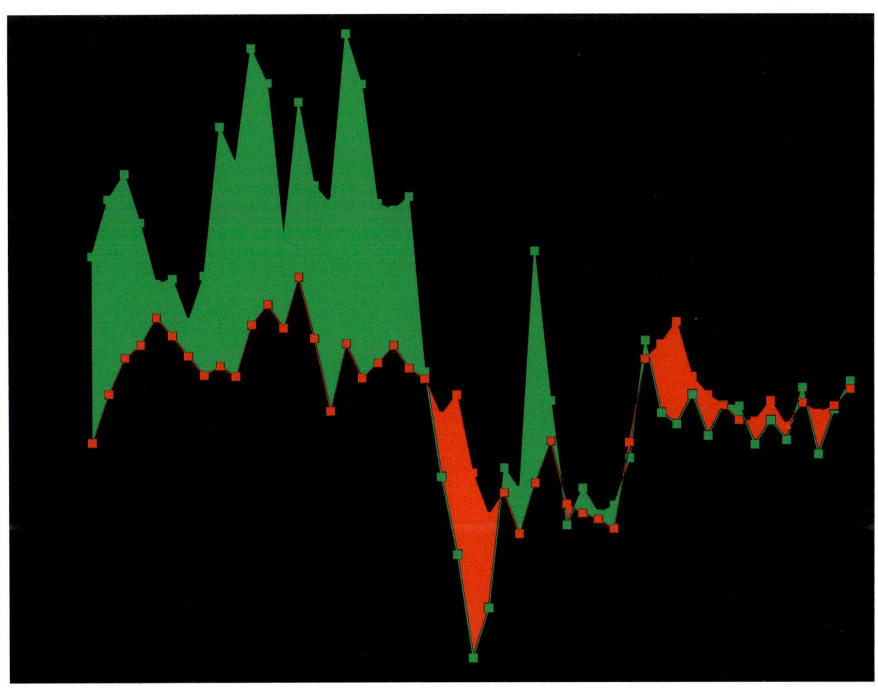

Share Price Growth—S&P Price Growth

Equity Growth and S&P Price Growth

MICROSOFT

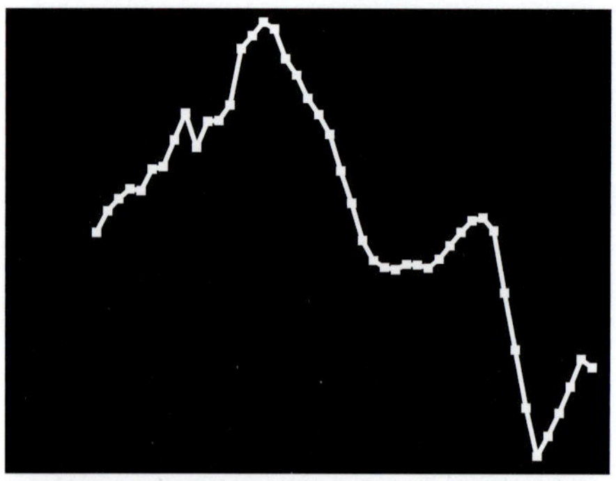

Equity Growth (Fair Price Growth Proxy)

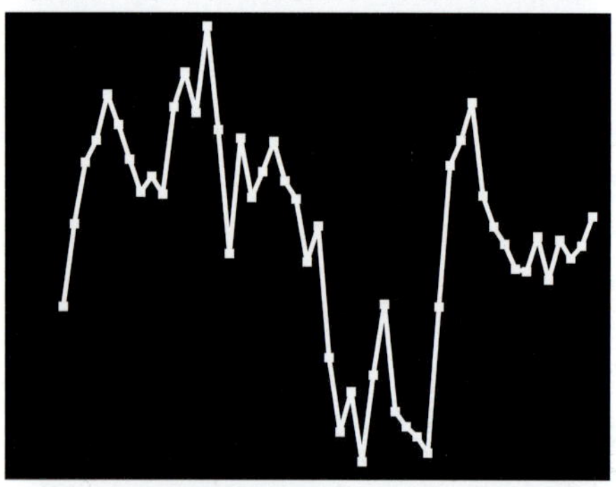

S&P Price Growth

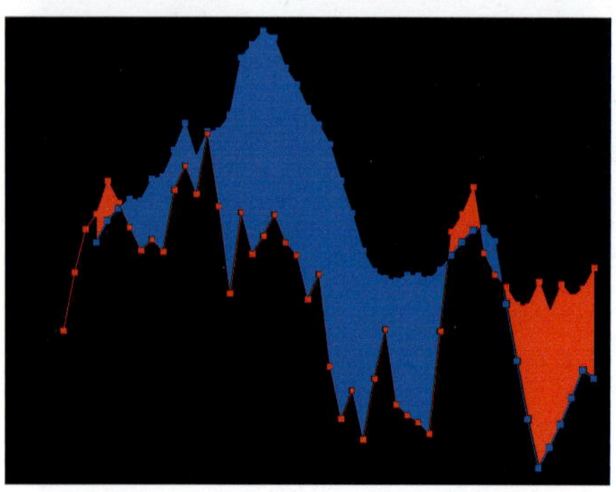

Equity Growth—S&P Price Growth

We report our progress in terms of book value (per-share equity growth) because in our case (though not, by any means, in all cases) it is a conservative but reasonably adequate proxy for growth in intrinsic business value (fair price growth)—the measurement that really counts. Book value's virtue as a score-keeping measure is that it is easy to calculate and doesn't involve the subjective (but important) judgments employed in calculation of intrinsic business value. It is important to understand, however, that the two terms—book value and intrinsic business value—have very different meanings.

Warren E. Buffett—*Letter to Berkshire Shareholders, 1983*

Equity growth and *S&P* price growth compare *Equity Growth* on page 16 to the market (*S&P* price growth). Equity growth may be an adequate proxy for growth of the *Fair Price Estimate* on page 84.

You want share price growth consistent with company growth, because you're going to measure your estimate of future share price growth using company growth and business thinking.

How close is share price growth to the equity growth proxy? The page facing *Share and Fair Price Trends* on page 77 shows average growth for 1993–2006 of share price at 29% and equity at 23%.

However, Buffett says "not, by any means, in all cases". The averaging of equity from the December 2004 dividend payout contributed to minus 34% equity growth on 2005-09-30. Considering the current sound financial success of Microsoft, no sane investor would use minus 34% equity growth as a proxy for near future share price growth. In the same breath, the longer historical 23% may be high.

Equity Growth—S&P Price Growth deserves to be a *front cover* chart because it represents your insistence that share price growth be upheld by equity growth—both being close and beating the market.

Calculate growth as [(*new value* – *old value*) / *old value*] × 100. When equity growth is approaching or beats the growth of *S&P* and share price, you have an investment merit explained as economic goodwill in *Return on Equity—Income to Equity* on page 32.

Robert G. Hagstrom—*The Warren Buffett Way*—implies that share price growth greater than equity growth signals shareholders believe "Economic goodwill not only produces above-average returns on capital but its value tends to increase with inflation. This appreciation is fundamental in understanding Buffett's equity-investment strategy."

Equity Growth and S&P Price Growth Events

Equity growth (circled) and *S&P* price growth compare company fundamental progress to the market. Leave the details of *GAAP Structure* on the left until page 87.

Equity growth may be a proxy for share price growth until the company accumulates more equity than it needs for revenue growth. Then, revenue growth is limited by demand for products, not by equity growth as in *Equity Growth to Revenue Growth* on page 52.

We believe that Microsoft's *SEC* numbers are true, and that our charts present those numbers—we make conceptual points with facts, not with hypothetical numbers. However, we do ask you for a thought exercise that makes the facts you see more useful. For example, in the chart on the left, look at the plummet in assets and equity growth due to the December 2004 dividend. These are not reasons to believe that decreased capital will decrease revenue growth. In fact, though the growth paths of assets and equity do drop sharply, the path of revenue growth (magenta) continues nearly level. Thus, in this case, revenue growth is a short-run proxy for fair price growth.

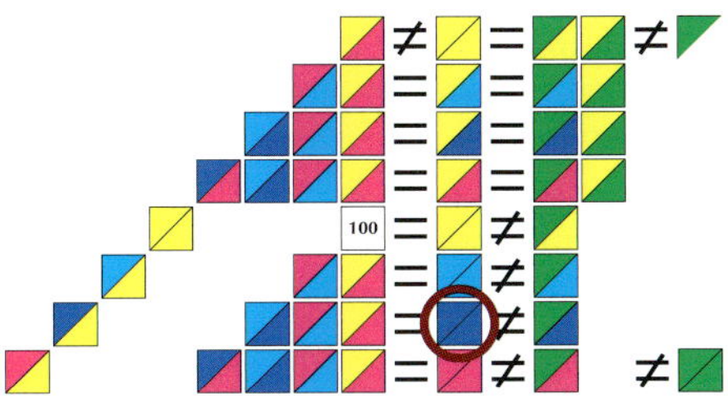

GAAP Structure

MICROSOFT

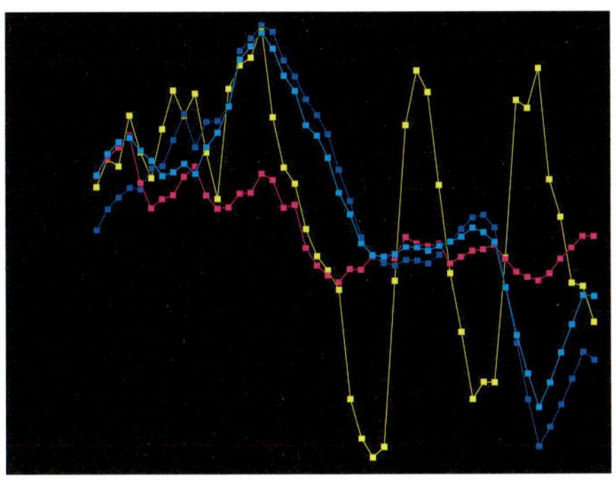

Income Growth
Equity Growth
Revenue Growth
Assets Growth

The chart above is from *The Growth Hierarchy Riddle* on page 104. From this chart, you want a number that estimates future share price growth. It is named *income growth* in the formula for *Fair Price Estimate* on page 84.

The four growth measures are candidates. Income growth (yellow) is less meaningful because it's volatile. However, our charts use income growth. Assets growth (cyan) and equity growth (blue) are not meaningful because they plummet after the December 2004 dividend. In this case, you can make a better choice. Revenue growth (magenta) runs close to pre-dividend assets and equity growth. Business thinking might say, "Post-dividend revenue growth is the best short-run proxy for the fair price estimate."

MICROSOFT

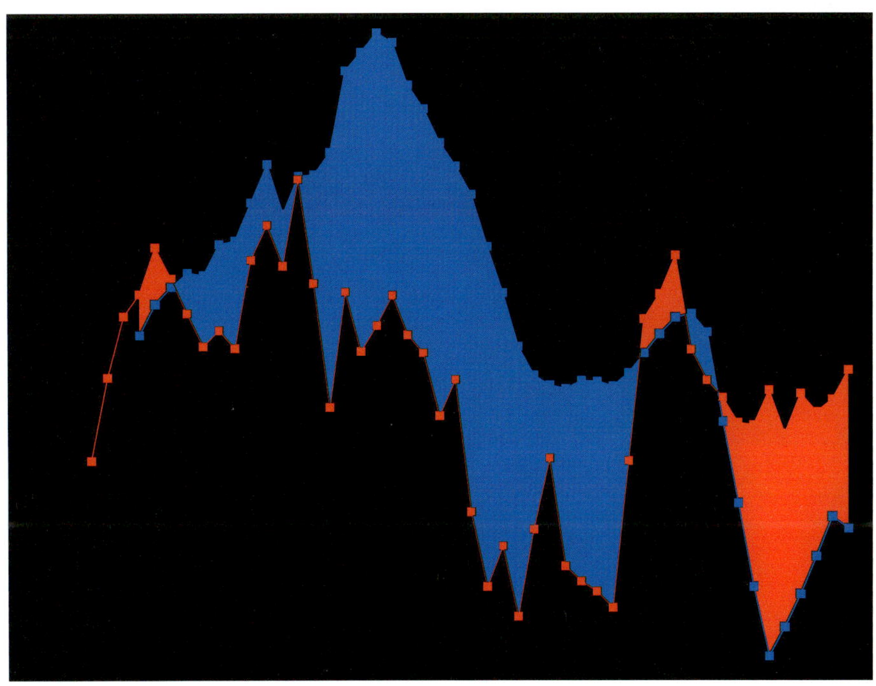

Equity Growth—S&P Price Growth

Share Price and Fair Price

MICROSOFT

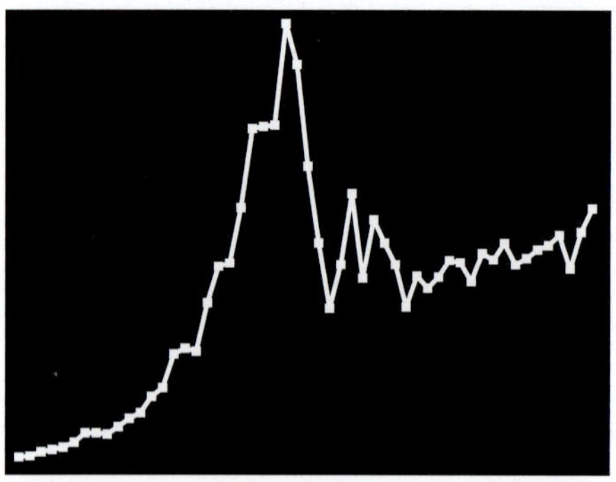

Share Price

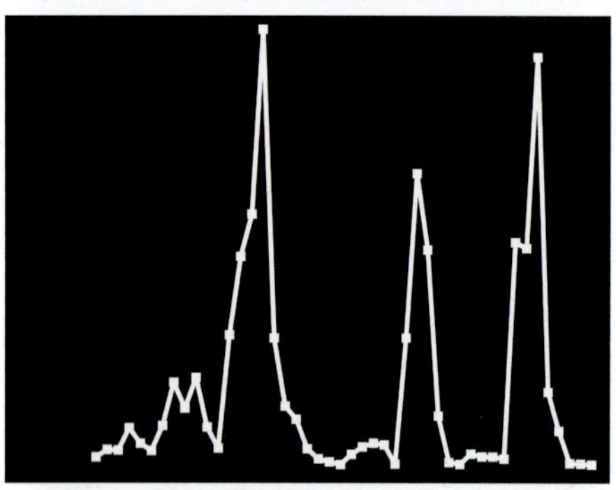

Fair Price

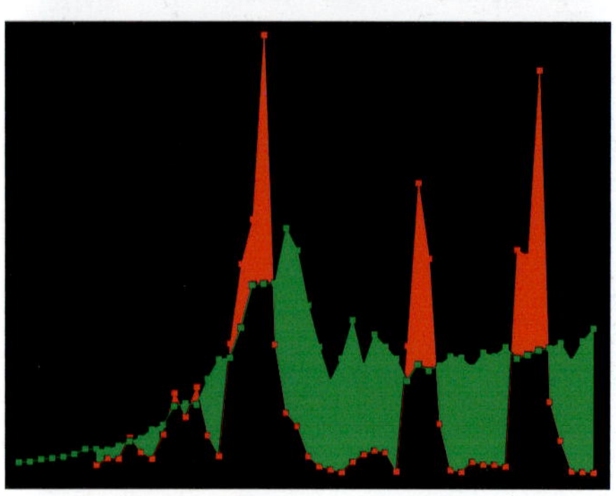

Share Price—Fair Price
Margin of Safety—Margin of Risk

To the extent possible, we would like each Berkshire shareholder to record a gain or loss in market value (share price) during his period of ownership that is proportional to the gain or loss in per-share intrinsic value (fair price) recorded by the company during that holding period.

For this to come about, the relationship between the intrinsic value (fair price) and the market price (share price) of a Berkshire share would need to remain constant, by our preference at 1-to-1 . . . .

Obviously, Charlie and I can't control Berkshire's price (share price) . . . .

Our it's-as-bad-to-be-overvalued-as-to-be-undervalued approach may disappoint some shareholders.

We believe, however, that it affords Berkshire the best prospect of attracting long-term investors who seek to profit (share price growth) from the progress (fair price growth) of the company rather than from the investment mistakes of their partners.

Warren E. Buffett—*Berkshire Owner's Manual, An Added Principle*

Share price and fair price define the reality of stock you buy or sell. Are you paying a share price that gives you a substantial margin of safety below your estimate of fair price? Investors like Buffett uncover and buy at discounts sometimes greater than 50%.

Share price is the money shareholders have paid for one share of the company's stock. Fair price is a calculated estimate of the price an informed investor would consider to be a fair price. As an investor, you may prefer to buy below fair price and to sell above fair price. Ideally—in a company and a society—share price would always equal fair price so investors would profit only from the evolution of the company, rather than from the mistakes of their societal partners.

Share price in the top left chart, also known as market price or stock price, is listed in the *inside front cover Quarterly Data Summary*, and defined in *The Split-Adjusted Close Price Riddle* on page 108.

Fair price in the middle chart, also known as intrinsic value per share or present value of future cash flow per share, is the *Fair Price Estimate* described on page 84. *Share Price—Fair Price* deserves to be a *front cover* chart because it shows whether you are buying at a discount relative to your fair price estimate, or selling at a premium.

Share price and fair price are plotted together in the bottom chart. For an investor buying stock, share price (green markers) below fair price (red markers) reveals a margin of safety (red fill). Buffett prefers his own company to show no red fill or green fill. He prefers to buy companies in the red fill and sell at a profit in the green fill.

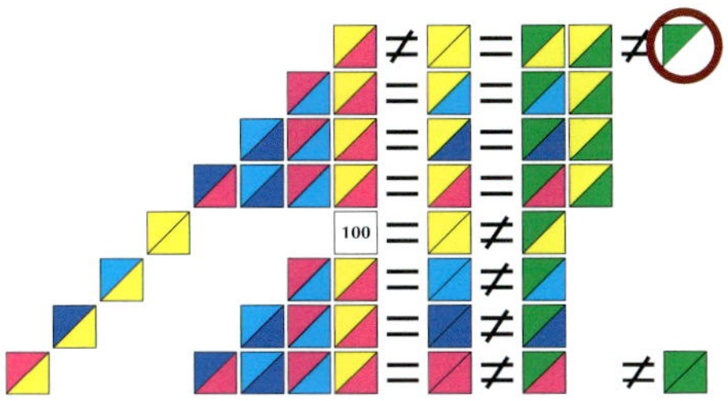

GAAP Structure

MICROSOFT

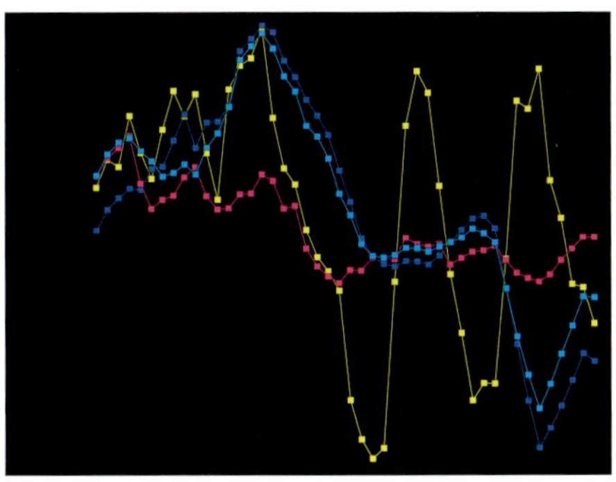

Income Growth
Equity Growth
Revenue Growth
Assets Growth

The December 2004 dividend made equity growth decrease, so it's not the good estimate of fair price growth proposed in *The Best Numbers Riddle* on page 100. Income growth is volatile.

However, in the chart above from *The Growth Hierarchy Riddle* on page 104, revenue, assets, and equity growth are nearly equal approaching December 2004. Management paid the dividend from equity, and left enough equity to fund revenue growth. So, the decline in revenue growth must be caused by lower demand, not lower equity. Thus, a thoughtful investor might say that revenue growth looks better than the growth of income, assets, or equity as a short-run estimate of fair price growth.

Share Price and Fair Price Events

Share price (circled) is preceded by a not equal sign. This visualization emphasizes that share price is not mathematically driven by other financial measures of a company. Share price is also not mathematically connected to the *S&P*—one approximation of the market—except that the company is a very small part of the market. Leave the details of *GAAP Structure* on the left until page 87.

Share Price—Fair Price chart spikes are caused by our use of the traditional *Fair Price Estimate—Intrinsic Value* formula on page 85, dominated by income and income growth—both are volatile. Fair price spikes align with income growth spikes in the hierarchy chart.

As a thought experiment, revenue growth could play a unique role in estimating fair price—and thus fair price growth—when equity growth and assets growth are perturbed by an event like the December 2004 dividend. If the recent pre-dividend growths of revenue, assets, and equity have been nearly equal—as you see on the left—then revenue growth may be your best short-run estimate.

MICROSOFT

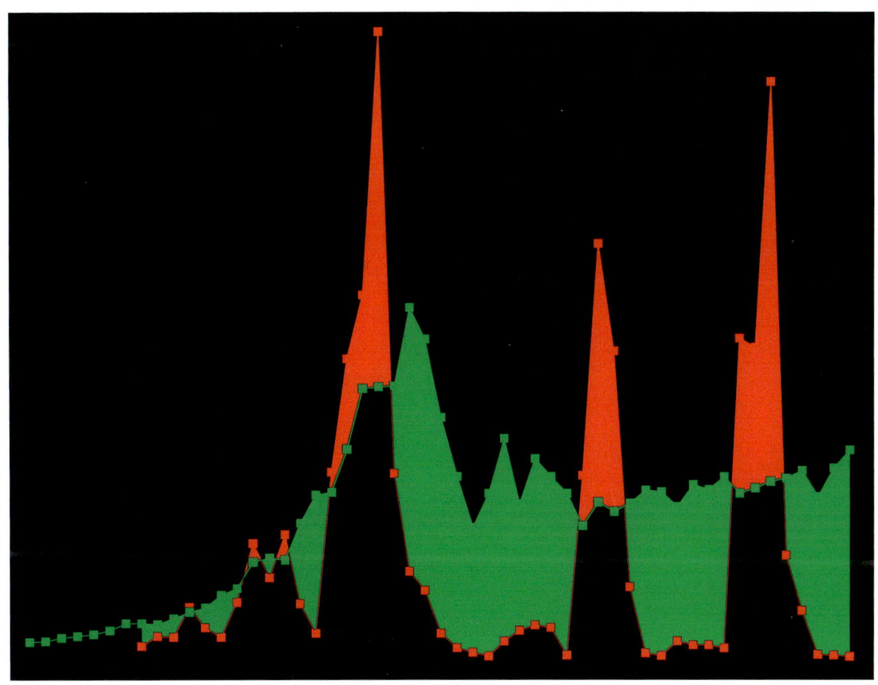

Share Price—Fair Price
Margin of Safety—Margin of Risk

Fair Price Estimate

MICROSOFT

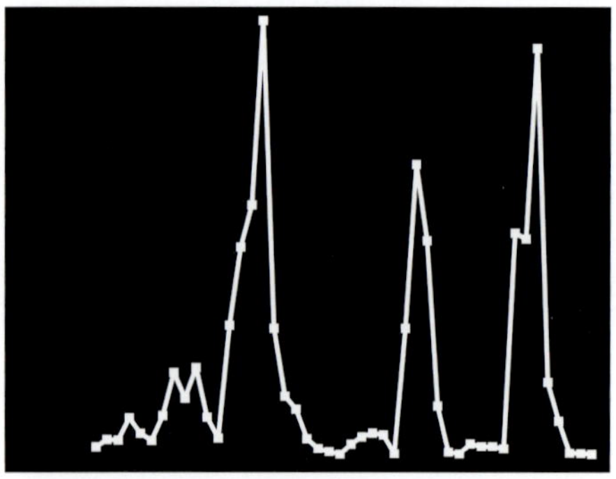

Fair Price

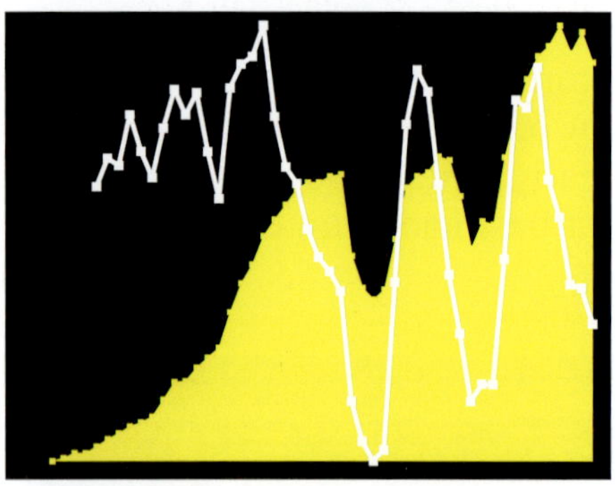

Income Growth—Income

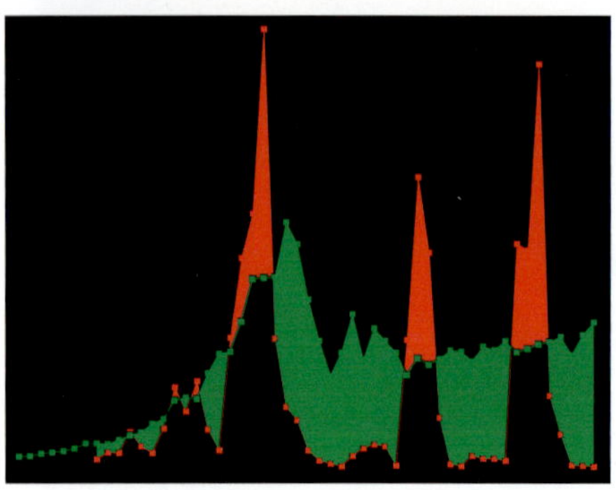

Share Price—Fair Price
Margin of Safety—Margin of Risk

> This is the purest form of fundamental securities analysis, since it links the value of the company directly to the economic returns it can generate from its businesses and assets.
>
> McKinsey & Company, Inc./Tom Copeland, Tim Koller, Jack Murrin; *Valuation: Measuring and Managing the Value of Companies*

Fair price estimate is your best calculation of a criterion against which you compare share price. It's subjective. However, the authors of *Valuation* present understandable, detailed, and persuasive arguments for simple and complex estimates of fair price.

Fair price estimate, like share price, is expressed in units of money. It is not growth like you have seen for share price growth, *S&P* price growth, and equity growth—which are expressed as percentages. You could use a growth formula to calculate fair price estimate growth, but we have used equity growth instead.

Fair price estimate is a subjective method for calculating a price against which you can compare share price to see if you can buy at a discount—less than your fair price estimate. Fair price estimate is also a price against which you can compare share price to see if you can sell at a premium—more than your fair price estimate. Share price streams from the trading floor in contrast to fair price estimate which may change only when new quarterly numbers are available.

We use the formula on the *right facing page* to calculate fair price estimate per share, also known as intrinsic value per share or present value of future cash flow per share. We use rolling sum four quarters income per sum four quarters average diluted shares—and growth of that same income. Thus, you expect the shape of fair price to be influenced by income. In fact, overlay a straight edge on the three charts to the left and observe that the three income growth peaks occur at the same time as the the three fair price estimate peaks. If you have a better number than income growth, use it!

In a clamoring world, we've focused requests for your attention mostly on topics in the evaluation system derived from *SEC* data. We can't justify saying that you must consider fair price. However, we can justify asking you this—If not fair price, then to what criterion will you compare share price to decide if you're about to buy at a discount or sell at a premium? If not all the charts and data in this book boiled down to only two pages—the *front cover* and *inside front cover*—then how will you make informed investment decisions?

MICROSOFT

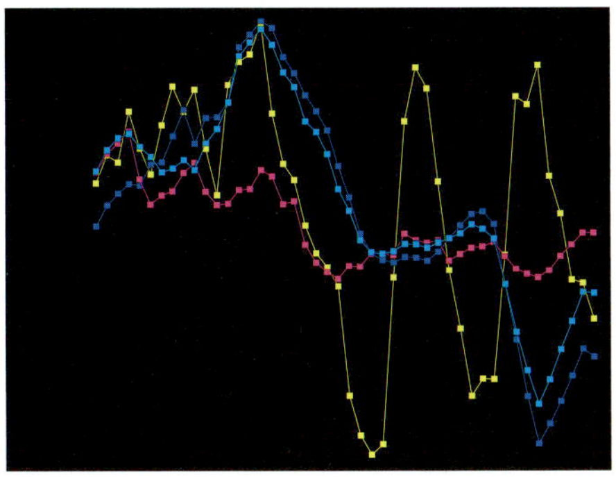

Income Growth
Equity Growth
Revenue Growth
Assets Growth

Fair Price Estimate—Intrinsic Value

Fair price estimate—intrinsic value per share is quickly calculated using free, Internet, *Intrinsic Value Online Calculators*. The intrinsic value formula below is a framework for assumptions you'll make that determine numbers for the few components you'll enter:

- Initial Income per Share—*GAAP Original Data* facing page 91;
- Discount Rate—Your estimate, possibly a long term *US* bond;
- Long Term Liabilities per Share—Microsoft's *Balance Sheet*;
- Growth—Consider the Growth Hierarchy chart to the left.

Warren Buffett says in his *Letter to Berkshire Shareholders*, 1992:

> Growth is always a component in the calculation of value (fair price), constituting a variable whose importance can range from negligible to enormous and whose impact can be negative as well as positive.

The chart to the left from *The Growth Hierarchy Riddle* on page 104 shows you volatile income growth compared to believable growth of revenue, assets, and equity prior to the December 2004 dividend. Enter a believable growth and a discount rate in a calculator to see a believable fair price estimate you'll compare to share price.

Intrinsic Value per Share—Fair Price Estimate is a simple equation:

$$Intrinsic\ Value\ per\ Average\ Diluted\ Share = Discounted\ Value + Continuing\ Value - Long\ Term\ Liabilities$$

$$Discounted\ Value = \sum_{year\ =\ 1 \cdots first\ stage\ years} \left[\frac{Initial\ Income \times (1 + Income\ Growth_{first\ stage})^{year}}{(1 + Discount\ Rate_{first\ stage})^{year}} \right]$$

$$plus\ Continuing\ Value = \frac{\dfrac{Initial\ Income \times (1 + Income\ Growth_{first\ stage})^{1 + first\ stage\ years}}{(Discount\ Rate_{second\ stage} - Income\ Growth_{second\ stage})}}{(1 + Discount\ Rate_{first\ stage})^{first\ stage\ years}}$$

$$minus\ Long\ Term\ Liabilities = Long\ Term\ Liabilities\ per\ Average\ Diluted\ Share$$

GAAP Structure—Datastreams Identified

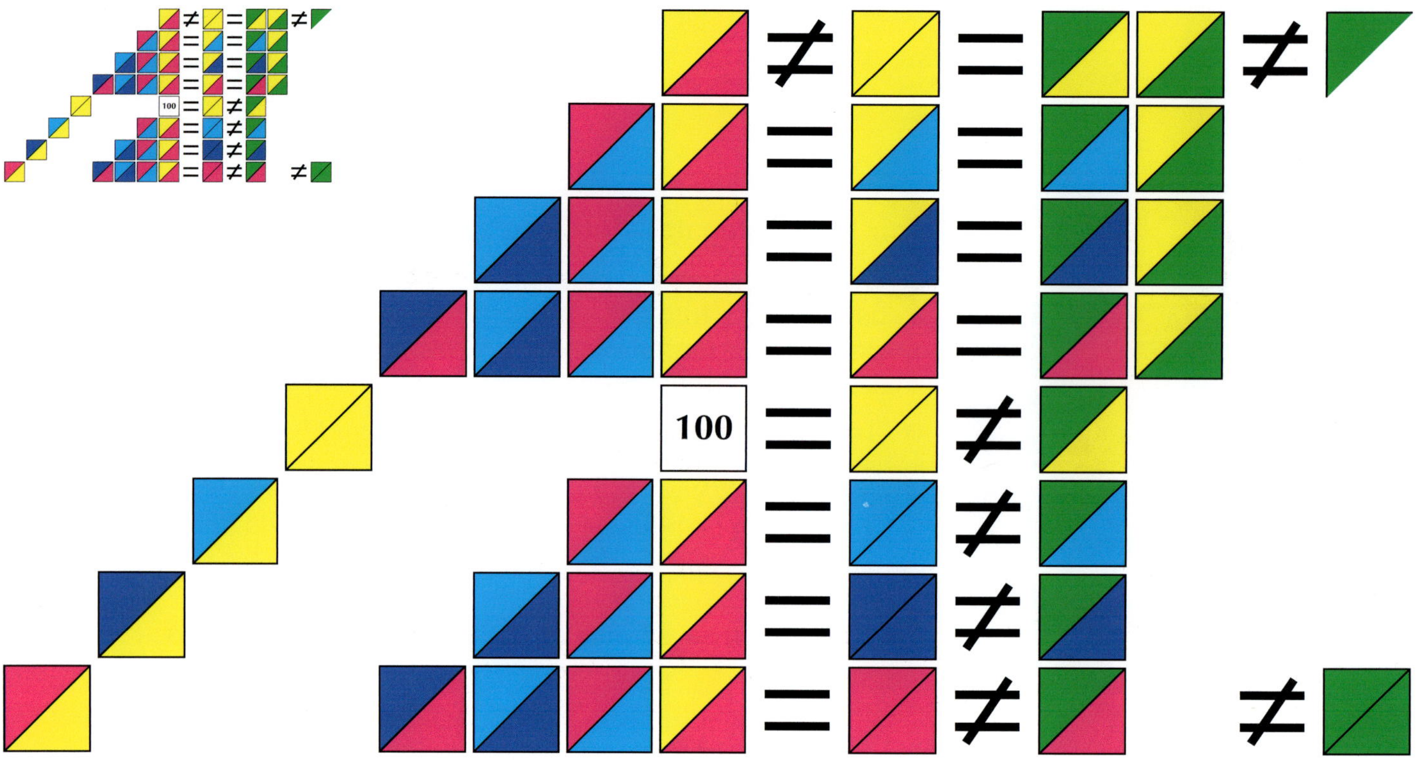

8 GAAP Structure

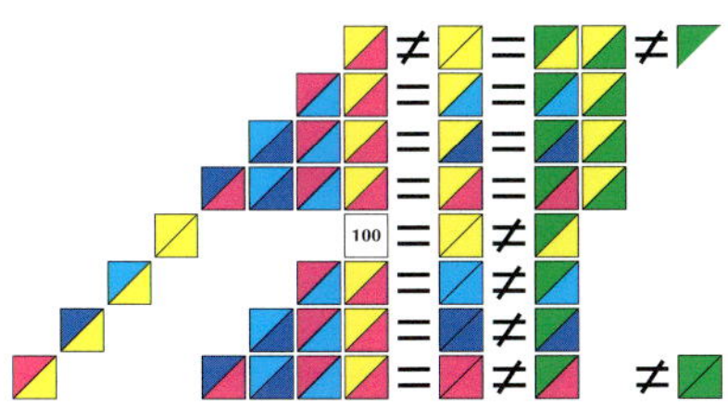

GAAP Structure

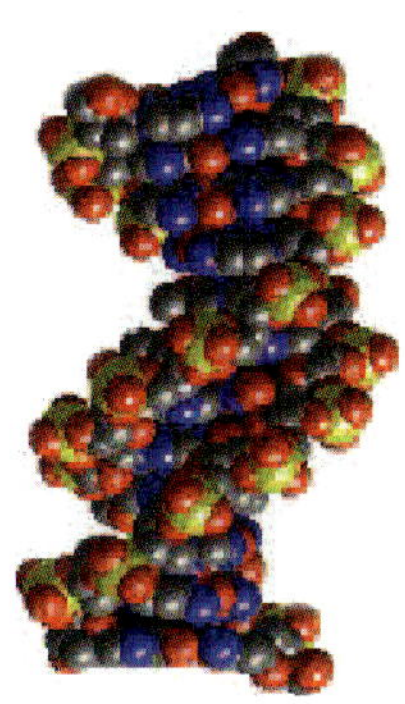

DNA Structure

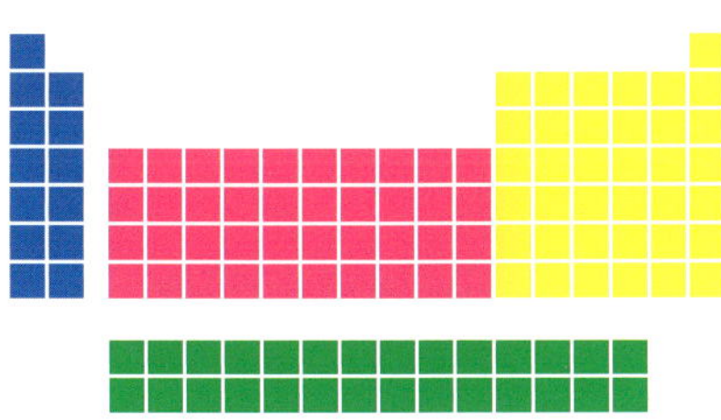

Atomic Structure

Without our ability to arrange things in ordered succession little progress could have been made.

Tobias Dantzig—*Number, The Language of Science*

GAAP† *Structure* reveals order in the financial puzzle you can't see in its fundamentals. It predicts factors on rows, and the bottom five factors on its diagonal—equity to revenue, and four change to income ratios. These previously unpublished relations expand results to reveal their causes—enabling astute investment decisions.

The truth of the numbers is essential to your confidence in the trend charts. We all know some companies lie—but they must lie consistently for sides of the equations to be equal in *GAAP Structure*.

GAAP Structure is built with income (yellow), assets (cyan), equity (blue), revenue (magenta), and for public companies price (green).

Some investors know that leverage times efficiency times net profit margin causes return on equity. Now, the *GAAP Structure* matrix expands your understanding of relations to see the causes of growth.

The *facing page* begins our proof—which derives *GAAP Structure* from *SEC* data, then proves *GAAP Structure* is verified by *SEC* data.

When you look closely at the structures on the left, you find only a few fundamental concepts. As Jacob Bronowski says, "simplicity triumphs, however complex the worlds within worlds may appear":

GAAP Structure—income, assets, equity, revenue;
DNA Structure—adenine, thymine, guanine, cytosine;
Atomic Structure—atoms ordered by atomic weights.

Globally, billions of people communicate with alphabetic systems of only a few letters. *The GAAP Alphabet Riddle* on page 98 describes how *GAAP Structure* brings financial communication to everyday life.

---

† United States *Generally Accepted Accounting Principles* (US GAAP)
Financial Accounting Standards Board (FASB) at **http://www.fasb.org/st/**

GAAP Structure—Dimensions Verified

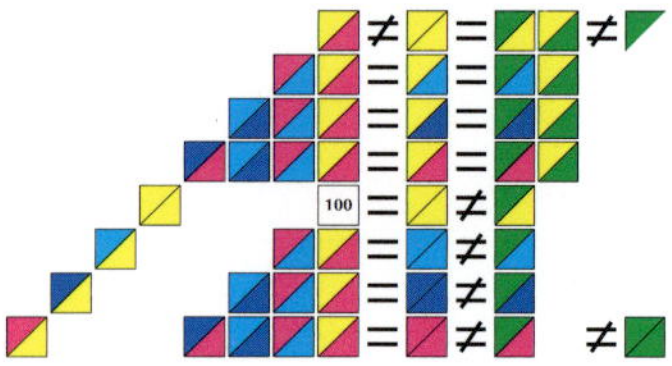

$$\frac{I_5}{R_5} \neq \frac{I_5}{I_5} = \frac{P_5}{I_5} \times \frac{I_5}{P_5} \neq P_5$$

$$\frac{R_5}{A_5} \times \frac{I_5}{R_5} = \frac{I_5}{A_5} = \frac{P_5}{A_5} \times \frac{I_5}{P_5}$$

$$\frac{A_5}{E_5} \times \frac{R_5}{A_5} \times \frac{I_5}{R_5} = \frac{I_5}{E_5} = \frac{P_5}{E_5} \times \frac{I_5}{P_5}$$

$$\frac{E_5}{R_5} \times \frac{A_5}{E_5} \times \frac{R_5}{A_5} \times \frac{I_5}{R_5} = \frac{I_5}{R_5} = \frac{P_5}{R_5} \times \frac{I_5}{P_5}$$

$$\frac{I_1 - I_5}{I_5} \times 100 = \frac{I_1 - I_5}{I_5} \neq \frac{\frac{P_1 - P_5}{P_5}}{\frac{I_1 - I_5}{I_5}}$$

$$\frac{A_1 - A_5}{I_5} \times \frac{R_5}{A_5} \times \frac{I_5}{R_5} = \frac{A_1 - A_5}{A_5} \neq \frac{\frac{P_1 - P_5}{P_5}}{\frac{A_1 - A_5}{A_5}}$$

$$\frac{E_1 - E_5}{I_5} \times \frac{A_5}{E_5} \times \frac{R_5}{A_5} \times \frac{I_5}{R_5} = \frac{E_1 - E_5}{E_5} \neq \frac{\frac{P_1 - P_5}{P_5}}{\frac{E_1 - E_5}{E_5}}$$

$$\frac{R_1 - R_5}{I_5} \times \frac{E_5}{R_5} \times \frac{A_5}{E_5} \times \frac{R_5}{A_5} \times \frac{I_5}{R_5} = \frac{R_1 - R_5}{R_5} \neq \frac{\frac{P_1 - P_5}{P_5}}{\frac{R_1 - R_5}{R_5}} \neq \frac{P_1 - P_5}{P_5}$$

GAAP Structure Molecule

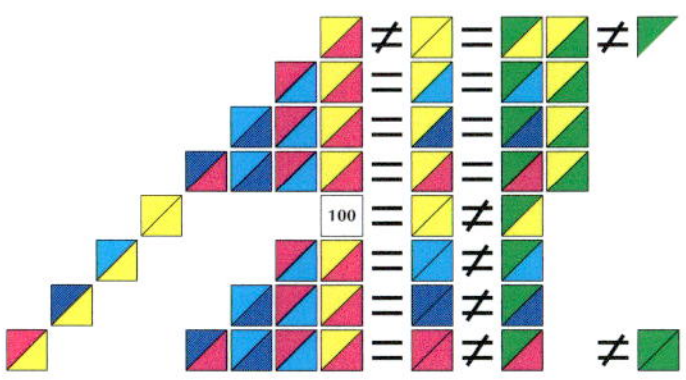

GAAP Structure

We derive *GAAP Structure* from *SEC* data by deriving four fundamentals that form four ratio trends (with their results), and four change trends—all reduce, in ordered succession, to equal the four growth results on rows 5, 6, 7, 8.

The Best Numbers Riddle on page 100 shows you want growth measures—and thus products of their factors—to beat the *S&P* price growth (averaging 11%).

Company—measures the company. Stepping down the diagonal are the first four *Ratio Trends* from page 21, then the four *Change Trends* from page 35.

Results—measures the company at a glance. A result equals the product of the factors on its row, as in *GAAP Structure Verified by SEC Data* on page 93.

Market—measures what the market is "paying up" for each fundamental and the growth of each fundamental. The market column of four is ***income yield***.

Price—measures price and growth.

In *GAAP Structure*, revenue and income sum 4 quarters per average 4 quarters diluted shares, as in *The Revenue and Income Riddle* on page 102. Assets and equity average 4 quarters per average 4 quarters diluted shares, as in *The Assets and Equity Riddle* on page 103. Price is within the quarter, nearest the end, as in *The Get Data Riddle* on page 113.

> I think both Crick and I realized we were famous because the double helix was the most important molecule of life, and therefore we got our names associated with it.
>
> James Watson—*Nobel Prize Winner, Discover Dialogue, July 2003*

GAAP † *Structure* is the most important molecule of business because it reveals the arrangement of fundamentals—income, assets, equity, and revenue—in ordered succession, deriving from *SEC* data a tool for systematic evaluation of company evolution.

Colored, per-share income, assets, equity, revenue, and price build 45 measures, minus duplicates, into the 26-measure *GAAP Structure*.

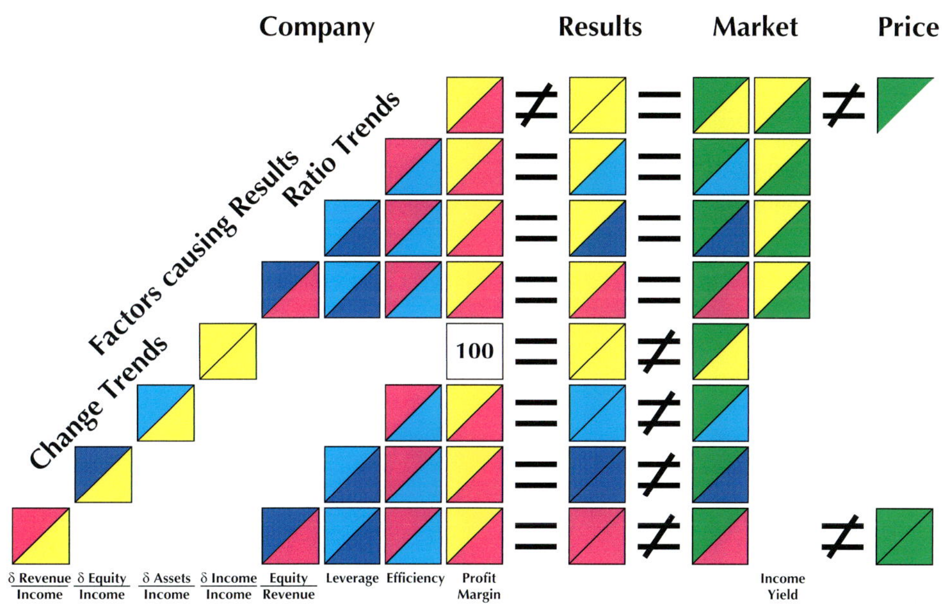

The *GAAP Structure* molecule on the *facing page* requires only two versions of the five measures—income, assets, equity, revenue, and price—I_1, A_1, E_1, R_1, P_1; and I_5, A_5, E_5, R_5, P_5. *GAAP Structure* shows which number to pick from *GAAP Original Data* facing page 91. For example, R_5 is the number at *row 5, column* R_{s4q} / S_{a4q}. *GAAP Structure* growth formulas require sub 5, implying that all rows must use sub 5. Charts, however, show you all the data!

† United States *Generally Accepted Accounting Principles (US GAAP)*
Financial Accounting Standards Board (FASB) at **http://www.fasb.org/st/**

GAAP Structure—Original Data

	QUARTER	REVENUE		INCOME		ASSETS		EQUITY		SHARES DILUTED		ADJUSTED PRICE	
ROW	ENDED	RqB	Rs4q/Sa4q	IqB	Is4q/Sa4q	AqB	Aa4q/Sa4q	EqB	Ea4q/Sa4q	SqB	Sa4q	SHARE	S & P
1	2006-12-31	12.542	4.505	2.626	1.165	66.371	6.557	36.634	3.787	9.942	10.224	29.86	1418.30
2	2006-09-30	10.811	4.361	3.478	1.244	65.354	6.469	36.101	3.906	10.010	10.398	27.26	1335.85
3	2006-06-30	11.804	4.182	2.828	1.190	69.597	6.497	40.104	4.124	10.531	10.589	23.14	1270.20
4	2006-03-31	10.900	3.991	2.977	1.261	66.854	6.468	42.038	4.275	10.415	10.683	26.91	1294.87
5	2005-12-31	11.837	3.825	3.653	1.208	67.257	6.378	44.208	4.348	10.638	10.812	25.78	1248.29
6	2005-09-30	9.741	3.704	3.141	1.181	71.462	6.278	48.327	4.385	10.772	10.891	25.29	1228.81
7	2005-06-30	10.161	3.641	3.700	1.121	70.815	6.778	48.115	5.002	10.906	10.928	24.34	1191.33
8	2005-03-31	9.620	3.562	2.563	1.029	66.275	7.274	47.373	5.615	10.931	10.925	23.61	1180.59
9	2004-12-31	10.818	3.528	3.463	0.917	64.941	7.825	47.232	6.156	10.956	10.907	26.02	1211.92
10	2004-09-30	9.189	3.471	2.528	0.742	94.268	8.317	75.946	6.672	10.920	10.892	24.16	1114.58
11	2004-06-30	9.292	3.384	2.690	0.750	92.389	8.094	74.825	6.465	10.894	10.883	24.88	1140.84
12	2004-03-31	9.175	3.273	1.315	0.680	89.767	7.802	70.580	6.149	10.856	10.880	21.72	1126.21
13	2003-12-31	10.153	3.149	1.549	0.816	85.937	7.449	69.343	5.865	10.899	10.883	23.84	1111.92
14	2003-09-30	8.215	3.004	2.614	0.909	84.281	7.146	66.680	5.561	10.885	10.869	24.08	995.97
15	2003-06-30	8.065	2.958	1.921	0.918	79.571	6.816	61.020	5.253	10.882	10.881	22.21	974.50
16	2003-03-31	7.835	2.869	2.794	0.877	74.482	6.508	58.282	5.024	10.864	10.937	20.97	848.18
17	2002-12-31	8.541	2.798	2.552	0.867	72.359	6.330	55.812	4.903	10.846	11.003	22.32	879.82
18	2002-09-30	7.746	2.709	2.726	0.838	70.235	6.135	53.516	4.777	10.933	11.070	18.89	815.28
19	2002-06-30	7.253	2.551	1.525	0.704	67.646	5.908	52.180	4.643	11.106	11.120	23.62	989.82
20	2002-03-31	7.245	2.488	2.738	0.572	68.379	5.704	54.300	4.529	11.129	11.131	26.04	1147.39
21	2001-12-31	7.741	2.412	2.283	0.546	65.387	5.507	51.548	4.390	11.112	11.130	28.61	1148.08
22	2001-09-30	6.126	2.304	1.283	0.577	61.367	5.331	48.505	4.272	11.134	11.137	22.09	1040.94
23	2001-06-30	6.577	2.272	0.065	0.660	58.830	5.215	47.289	4.203	11.148	11.132	31.52	1224.38
24	2001-03-31	6.403	2.207	2.451	0.872	59.605	5.063	48.090	4.077	11.126	11.113	23.61	1160.33
25	2000-12-31	6.550	2.141	2.624	0.867	57.691	4.872	46.422	3.894	11.140	11.103	18.73	1320.28
26	2000-09-30	5.766	2.105	2.206	0.851	56.089	4.595	45.343	3.632	11.114	11.087	26.04	1436.51
27	2000-06-30	5.804	2.073	2.409	0.851	51.694	4.230	41.368	3.321	11.072	11.072	34.54	1454.60
28	2000-03-31	5.656	2.075	2.385	0.834	50.895	3.938	39.792	3.037	11.086	11.045	45.88	1498.58
29	1999-12-31	6.112	1.982	2.436	0.793	45.093	3.551	34.589	2.722	11.076	11.030	50.41	1469.25
30	1999-09-30	5.384	1.905	2.191	0.755	39.672	3.221	31.340	2.458	11.054	10.991	39.10	1282.71
31	1999-06-30	5.764	1.804	2.202	0.711	38.321	2.913	28.438	2.190	10.964	10.944	38.94	1372.71
32	1999-03-31	4.595	1.652	1.917	0.638	33.561	2.562	25.722	1.931	11.024	10.884	38.70	1286.37
33	1998-12-31	5.195	1.587	1.983	0.588	30.049	2.255	22.578	1.688	10.920	10.813	29.94	1229.23
34	1998-09-30	4.193	1.446	1.683	0.513	25.569	1.961	19.124	1.460	10.868	10.750	23.76	1017.01
35	1998-06-30	3.995	1.354	1.357	0.420	22.357	1.732	16.627	1.288	10.724	10.699	23.40	1133.84
36	1998-03-31	3.774	1.284	1.337	0.394	19.545	1.554	14.676	1.157	10.740	10.640	19.32	1101.75
37	1997-12-31	3.585	1.236	1.133	0.367	16.840	1.396	12.344	1.031	10.668	10.599	13.95	970.43
38	1997-09-30	3.130	1.157	0.663	0.332	15.366	1.308	11.464	0.973	10.664	10.540	14.28	947.28
39	1997-06-30	3.175	1.086	1.057	0.330	14.387	1.207	10.777	0.880	10.488	10.462	13.64	885.14
40	1997-03-31	3.208	1.004	1.042	0.284	12.613	1.111	9.134	0.792	10.576	10.401	9.90	757.12
41	1996-12-31	2.680	0.915	0.741	0.240	12.786	1.047	9.642	0.737	10.432	10.313	8.92	740.74
42	1996-09-30	2.295	0.873	0.614	0.225	10.740	0.963	7.277	0.657	10.352	10.257	7.12	687.33
43	1996-06-30	2.255	0.848	0.559	0.215	10.093	0.903	6.908	0.621	10.244	10.229	6.48	670.63
44	1996-03-31	2.205	0.790	0.562	0.197	9.590	0.837	6.595	0.586	10.224	10.176	5.57	645.50
45	1995-12-31	2.195	0.733	0.575	0.182	9.106	0.767	6.180	0.548	10.208	10.124	4.74	615.93
46	1995-09-30	2.016	0.666	0.499	0.162	8.160	0.693	5.739	0.507	10.240	10.072	4.88	584.41
47	1995-06-30	1.621	0.594	0.368	0.145	7.210	0.635	5.333	0.478	10.032	10.000	4.88	544.75
48	1995-03-31	1.587	0.565	0.396	0.146	6.592	0.593	4.930	0.459	10.016	9.932	3.84	500.71
49	1994-12-31	1.482	0.534	0.373	0.133	5.961	0.555	4.443	0.440	10.000	9.860	3.30	459.27
50	1994-09-30	1.247	0.502	0.316	0.125	5.637	0.521	4.430	0.425	9.952	9.792	3.03	462.71
51	1994-06-30	1.293	....	0.362	....	5.363	....	4.450	....	9.760	....	2.79	444.27
52	1994-03-31	1.244	....	0.256	....	4.926	....	4.012	....	9.728	....	2.29	445.77
53	1993-12-31	1.129	....	0.289	....	4.486	....	3.746	....	9.728	....	2.18	466.45

GAAP Original Data

MICROSOFT

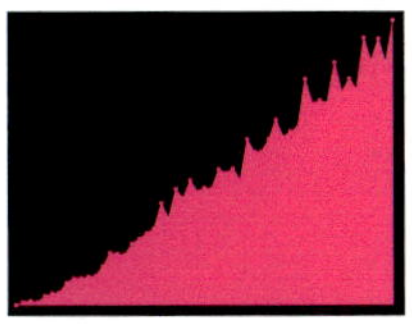

Revenue Quarterly

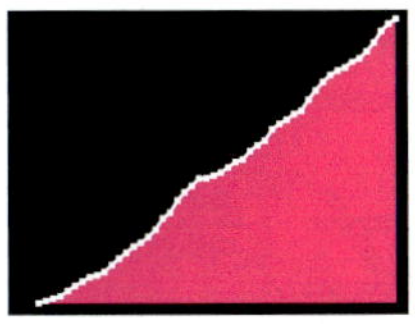

$R_{s\,4q} \,/\, S_{a\,4q}$

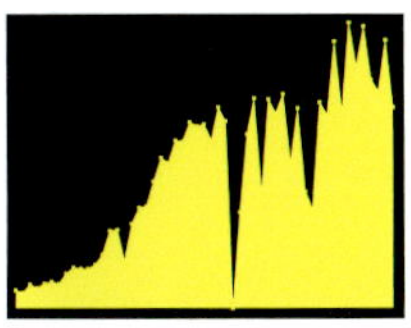

Income Quarterly

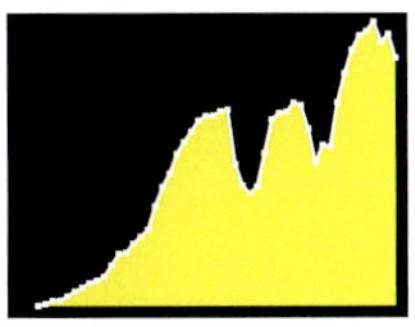

$I_{s\,4q} \,/\, S_{a\,4q}$

Assets Quarterly

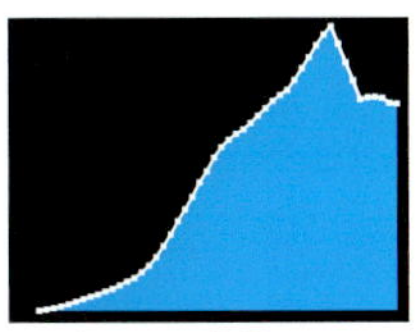

$A_{a\,4q} \,/\, S_{a\,4q}$

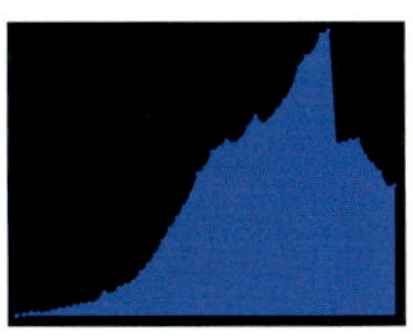

Equity Quarterly

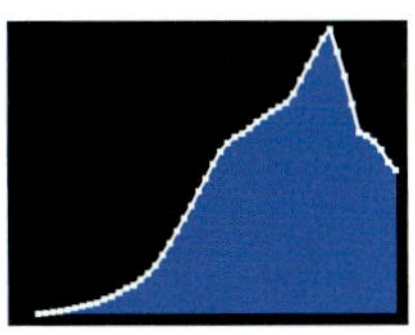

$E_{a\,4q} \,/\, S_{a\,4q}$

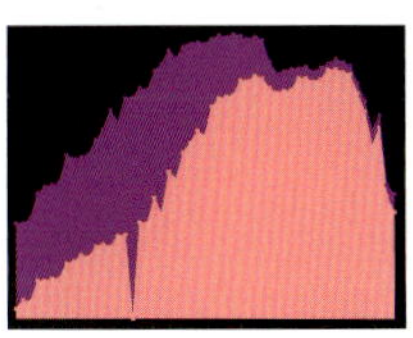

Shares Quarterly

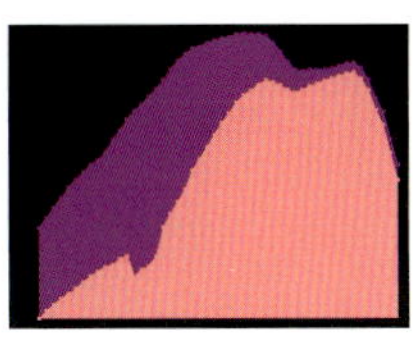

$S_{a\,4q}$

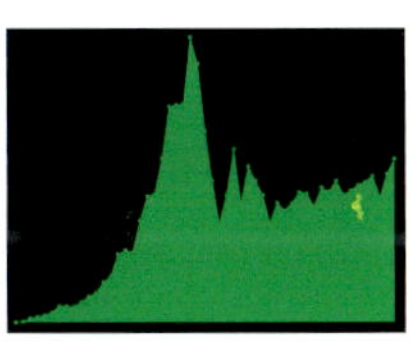

Price Quarterly

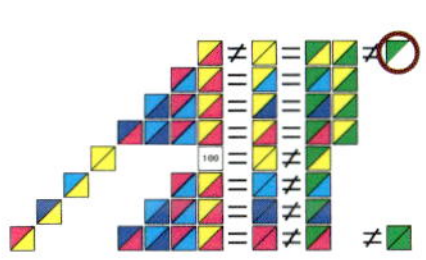

GAAP Structure

Accounting numbers, of course, are the language of business and as such are of enormous help to anyone evaluating the worth of a business and tracking its progress. Charlie and I would be lost without these numbers: they invariably are the starting point for us in evaluating our own businesses and those of others. Managers and owners need to remember, however, that accounting is but an aid to business thinking, never a substitute for it.

Warren E. Buffett—*Letter to Berkshire Shareholders, 1986*

GAAP † *Original Data*—date, revenue, income, assets, equity, shares, and adjusted close price (except *S&P*)—are required by the *GAAP Structure Molecule* on page 89 to make charts in this book.

Can any of you show us the *facing page*—quarterly updating 8 items (6 plus 2 prices) causing related tables and charts to update automatically for all quarters electronically available from the *SEC*?

The Get Data Riddle on page 113 shows you how to replicate 8 top row items on the *facing page*. Enter quarter ended (not filing) date; quarterly (q) *SEC* data in billions (B) for $R_q B$, $I_q B$, $A_q B$, $E_q B$, $S_q B$; and quarterly adjusted prices for share price and *S&P* price.

Next, compute *row 1 REVENUE* $R_{s\,4q} / S_{a\,4q}$ or *INCOME* $I_{s\,4q} / S_{a\,4q}$: sum the top four rows of $R_q B$ or $I_q B$, then divide by *SHARES* $S_{a\,4q}$ (top four rows of $S_q B$ averaged). Compute *row 1 ASSETS* $A_{a\,4q} / S_{a\,4q}$ or *EQUITY* $E_{a\,4q} / S_{a\,4q}$: average the top four rows of $A_q B$ or $E_q B$, then divide by *SHARES* $S_{a\,4q}$. On the next page, income over revenue uses *row 5*—not *row 1*—computed data: 100 times I_5 divided by R_5.

On the *facing page*, revenue is greater than income because the company has costs. Assets are greater than equity because the company has liabilities. Costs and liabilities are inferred—revenue minus income and assets minus equity. Diluted shares (purple) are greater than basic shares (pink, from the *inside front cover*), because diluted shares add dilutive instruments (such as warrants) to basic shares.

Tools used to make this book can instantly update and chart company data. Someday, in an Internet tool, you'll enter a company symbol like *MSFT*, select a *GAAP* measure, view its chart.

† United States *Generally Accepted Accounting Principles* (US GAAP)
Financial Accounting Standards Board (FASB) at **http://www.fasb.org/st/**

GAAP Structure—Verified by SEC Data

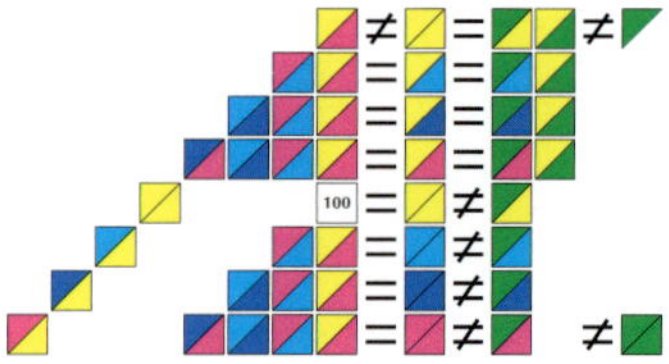

δ revenue	δ equity	δ assets	δ income											
							income / revenue 31.57%	≠	income / income 100.00%	=	price / income 21.347	income / price 4.685%	≠	price $25.78
						revenue / assets 0.5998	income / revenue 31.57%	=	income / assets 18.94%	=	price / assets 4.042	income / price 4.685%		
					assets / equity 1.4669	revenue / assets 0.5998	income / revenue 31.57%	=	income / equity 27.78%	=	price / equity 5.930	income / price 4.685%		
				equity / revenue 1.1365	assets / equity 1.4669	revenue / assets 0.5998	income / revenue 31.57%	=	income / revenue 31.57%	=	price / revenue 6.739	income / price 4.685%		
			δ income / income –0.0355				100.00%	=	δ income / income –3.55%	≠	prc gro / inc gro –4.454			
		δ assets / income 0.1488				revenue / assets 0.5998	income / revenue 31.57%	=	δ assets / assets 2.82%	≠	prc gro / ass gro 5.618			
	δ equity / income –0.4643				assets / equity 1.4669	revenue / assets 0.5998	income / revenue 31.57%	=	δ equity / equity –12.90%	≠	prc gro / eqt gro –1.227			
δ revenue / income 0.5624				equity / revenue 1.1365	assets / equity 1.4669	revenue / assets 0.5998	income / revenue 31.57%	=	δ revenue / revenue 17.76%	≠	prc gro / rev gro 0.891		≠	prc gro 15.83%

GAAP Structure Verified by SEC Data

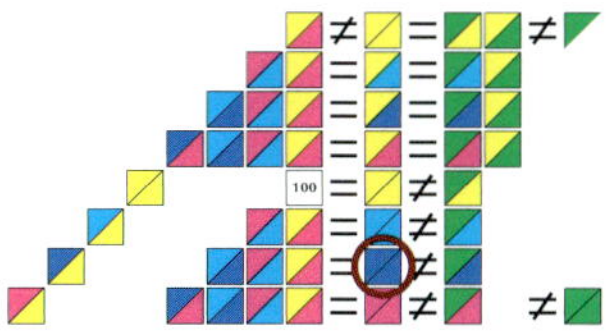

GAAP Structure

MICROSOFT

IG Slice

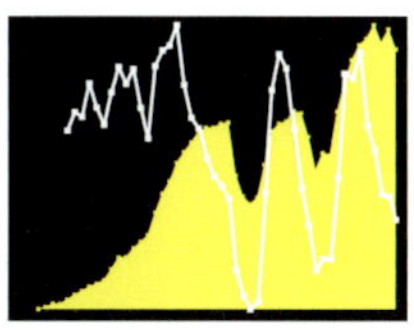

Income Growth

AG Slice

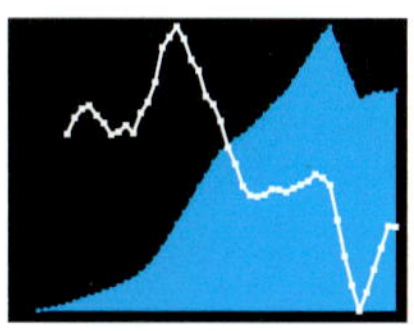

Assets Growth

EG Slice

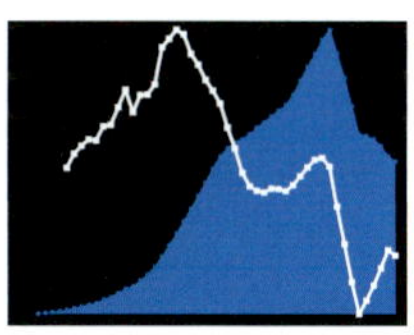

Equity Growth

RG Slice

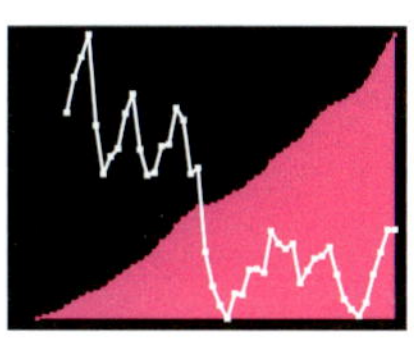

Revenue Growth

> I never looked at the original data;
> I only read those reports, like a dope....
> Since then I never pay any attention to anything by "experts";
> I calculate it all myself.
>
> Richard P. Feynman—*Physicist, Nobel Prize Winner, Bongo Drummer, Safe Cracker, Visionary—Surely You're Joking, Mr. Feynman!*

GAAP † *Structure* verified by *SEC* data is the moment of truth. It proves you should have confidence that *GAAP Original Data* facing page 91 implies the computations. Each growth on the *facing page* is seen on the left as the current *Slice* from its full chart.

The evidence proof of computations requires only one equation from the *facing page, row 7*—because this equation includes all four fundamentals, reds cross-cancel, and *SEC* data verifies *GAAP Structure*.

$$\frac{\text{equity change}}{\text{income}} \times \frac{\text{assets}}{\text{equity}} \times \frac{\text{revenue}}{\text{assets}} \times \frac{\text{income}}{\text{revenue}} = \frac{\text{equity change}}{\text{equity}}$$

In the equation above, leverage, efficiency, and net profit margin use *Original Data* from *row 5*—not *row 1*—because growth formulas in the *GAAP Structure Molecule* facing page 89 imply that all rows must use sub 5. Sub 5 ripples through the structure, revealing old ratios as factors of new growth. Charts, however, use all data including *row 1*.

The equity growth equation confirms the self-consistent *GAAP* matrix. The probability of accidental equality for all equations on the *facing page* for many quarters for thousands of companies is inconceivable.

If a company fails the test, confirm you've chosen numbers directed by the *GAAP Structure Molecule* facing page 89 from *GAAP Original Data* facing page 91. If you're correct, then the company made an error, is incompetent, or lied. Napoleon reminds us, "Never ascribe to malice that which is adequately explained by incompetence."

Peter Schwartz might say our *GAAP Structure* is an "inevitable surprise"—United States *Securities and Exchange Commission (SEC)* reports are governed by self-consistent US *Generally Accepted Accounting Principles (GAAP)*—a tribute to the millions of company people reporting, to *FASB*, to the *EDGAR Archives*, and to the *SEC*.

† United States *Generally Accepted Accounting Principles (US GAAP)*
Financial Accounting Standards Board (FASB) at **http://www.fasb.org/st/**

GAAP Structure—Graphics Verified

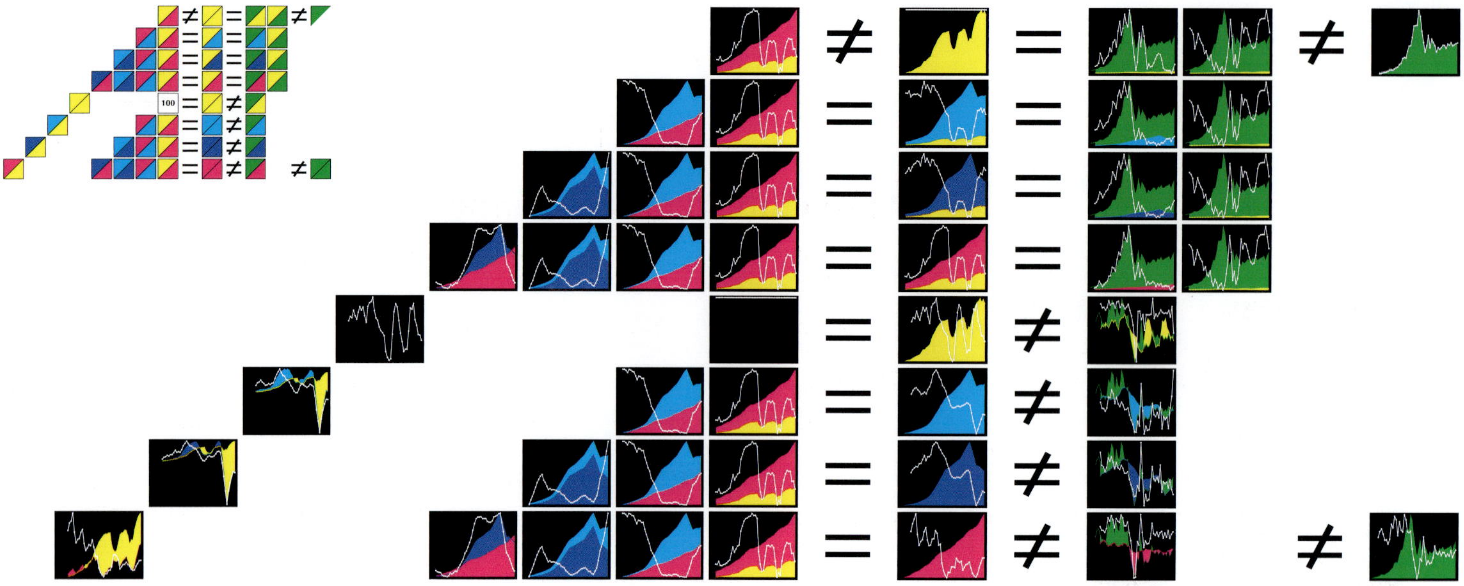

GAAP Structure Graphics Verified

MICROSOFT

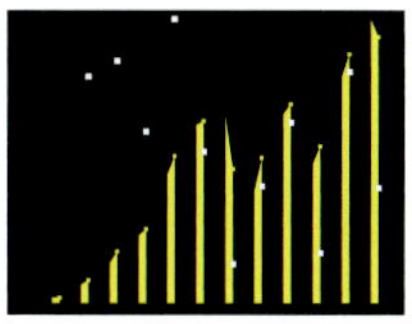

IG Annual Slices

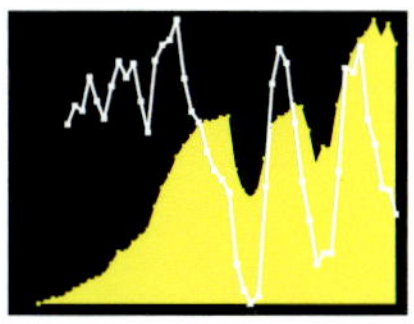

Income Growth

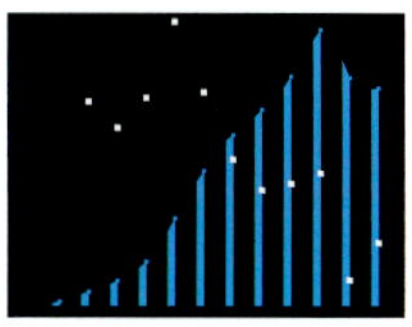

AG Annual Slices

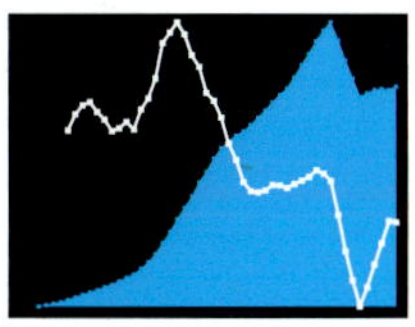

Assets Growth

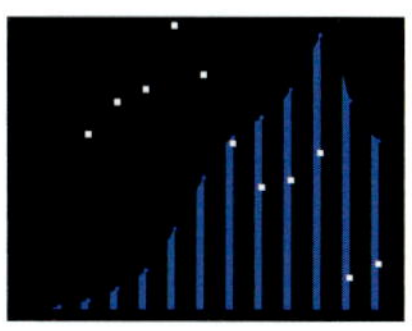

EG Annual Slices

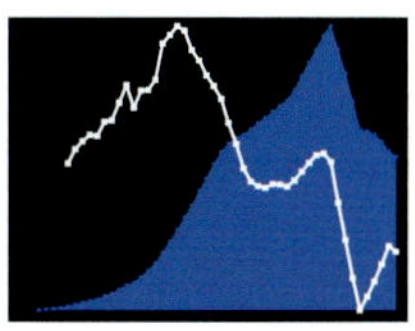

Equity Growth

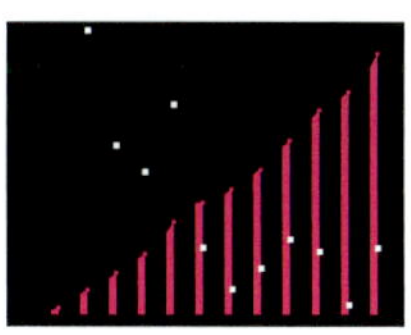

RG Annual Slices

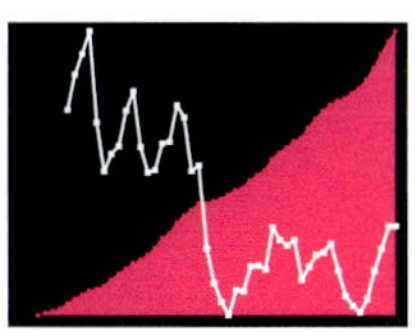

Revenue Growth

I want to reach that state of condensation of sensations which constitutes a picture.

Henri Matisse—*Notes of a Painter*

Finally, in one picture on the *facing page*, we reach that condensation of sensations which unites the data through its structure.

In one composite picture—instead of traditional annual slices—we deploy our rolling quarterly trend charts from *The Annual Report Every Quarter Riddle* on page 101 to "Above all else show the data." †

From this graphics verified picture you explore a story of company evolution, confident you've made sense by deriving from *GAAP Original Data* facing page 91 both the *GAAP Structure Molecule* facing page 89 and *GAAP Structure Verified by SEC Data* facing page 93.

Your hawk's-eye-view of the *facing page* shows its four sections related by equal or not-equal signs. Colored components on each row are calculated from *GAAP Original Data* facing page 91—then used to calculate white trend factors, which multiply to equal white results.

We could reduce *GAAP Structure* to only the *Results* column. Instead, we show that the *Company* diagonal heads eight columns—each displaying one measure. The *Results* column shows each result that equals the product of factors on its row. The *Market* section is two columns: the left column is price and price growth ratios, and the right column is income to price (income yield) revealing relations between sections. The *Price* column shows price and price growth.

Each pair of trend charts on the left uses all the data from one datastream in *GAAP Original Data* facing page 91. The left column displays annualized slices computed annually. In contrast, the right column displays annualized slices computed quarterly—the most frequent available from the data, and the most timely for evaluation.

GAAP Structure reveals how the factors on each row unite in mathematical relations, enabling us to discover and benefit from causes of results. Thus, we see how *GAAP Structure* is derived from and verified by *Securities and Exchange Commission (SEC)* data.

---

† Edward R. Tufte—*The Visual Display of Quantitative Information, Second Edition*

GAAP Alphabet

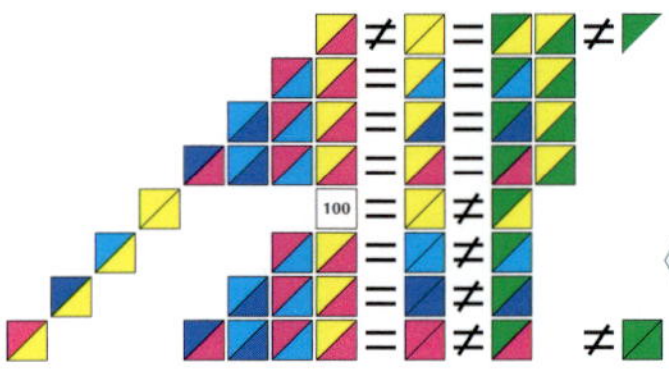

9 Solved Riddles

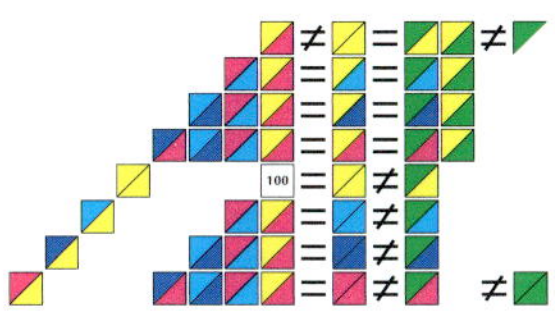

GAAP Structure

And from all over the world people came to Göttingen to join in .... The people who met here, the people who meet in laboratories still, only end their work with a mathematical formulation. They begin it by trying to solve conceptual riddles. The riddles of the sub-atomic particles—of the electrons and the rest—are mental riddles.

Jacob Bronowski—*The Ascent of Man*

GAAP Alphabet Riddle .... *GAAP Alphabet*—not random measures—builds *GAAP Structure*.

Monopoly Riddle .... Monopolies—not average companies—illustrate concepts fully.

Best Numbers Riddle .... *S&P* price growth—not other measures—is best numbers' criterion.

Annual Report Every Quarter Riddle .... Rolling four quarters—not yearly—displays data most frequently.

Revenue and Income Riddle .... Sum four quarters—not quarters—is the annual report convention.

Assets and Equity Riddle .... Average four quarters—not end-of-period—gives time to earn.

Growth Hierarchy Riddle .... Growth in a hierarchy—not random—maximizes company growth.

Ratios Riddle .... Four fundamentals form six ratios—not fewer—completing the set.

Leverage Riddle .... Assets to equity—not debt to equity—fits higher in *GAAP Structure*.

Per-Share Growth Riddle .... Per-share growth—not size—measures company progress.

Split-Adjusted Close Price Riddle .... Quarter-end price—not most-recent—aligns with company updates.

Mathematics Riddle .... Add, subtract, multiply, divide—not complex—compute measures.

Computable Riddle .... All measures—no exceptions—use absolute-values, zero-conditions.

Definitions Riddle .... Alternate definitions—not only traditional—flex in *GAAP Structure*.

Color Codes Riddle .... Colors—not only numbers—discriminate and identify measures.

Get Data Riddle .... *EDGAR*—not popular sources—shows all free quarterly *SEC* data.

The GAAP Alphabet Riddle

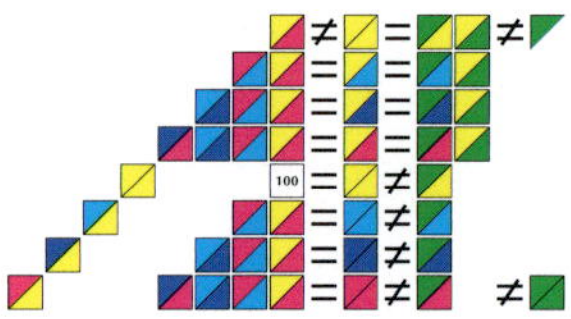

GAAP Structure

DATASTREAMS *MICROSOFT*

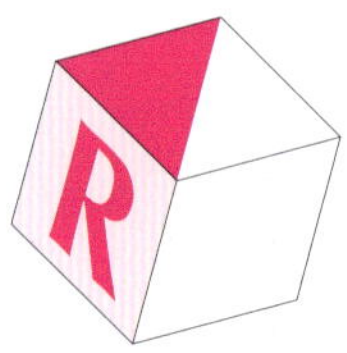

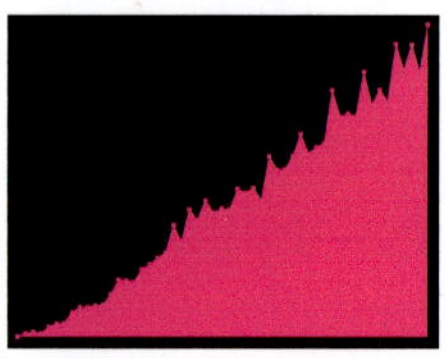

Revenue Quarterly

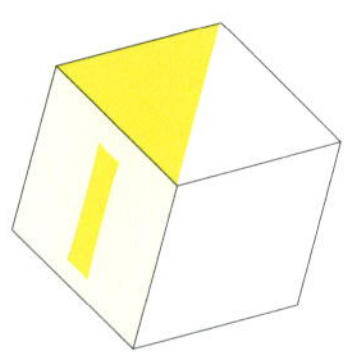

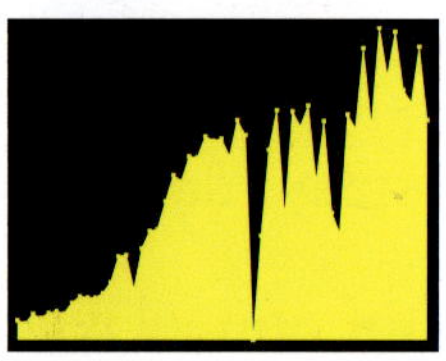

Income Quarterly

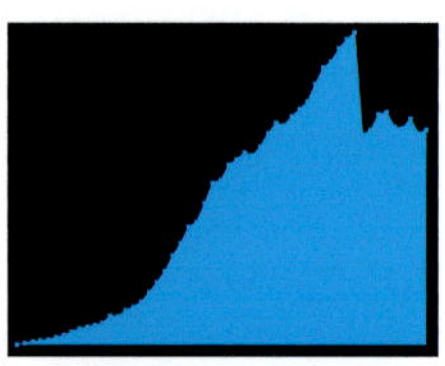

Assets Quarterly

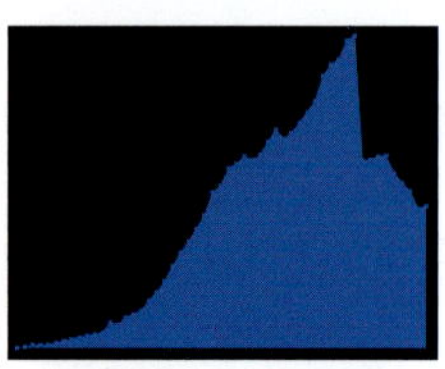

Equity Quarterly

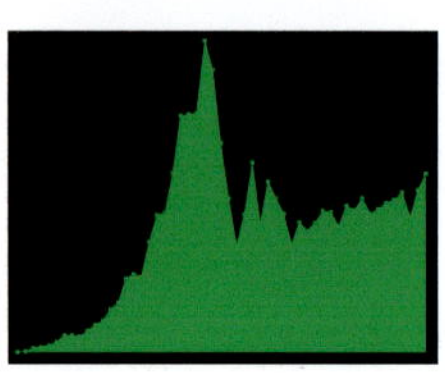

Price Quarterly

> Who today reads hieroglyphics? The upstart notion of the *Amu* has triumphed. Their picture letters were destined for billions of people. Like the wheel or the telephone, the alphabet was an invention to change the world.
>
> David Sacks—*Language Visible*

The *GAAP* † alphabet riddle asks: How does the *GAAP Alphabet* translate financial hieroglyphics into our common language?

Build *GAAP Structure*—letter by letter—with Revenue (magenta), Income (yellow), Assets (cyan), Equity (blue), and for public companies Price (green). Each letter represents some form of the raw data from our *inside front cover Quarterly Data Summary*. Forms include revenue and income sum four quarters, assets and equity average four quarters, and new-four minus old-four show the change.

We build *GAAP Structure* by stepping down rows on its diagonal, using *GAAP Alphabet* blocks facing *Solved Riddles* on page 97.

Row 1 begins, *I* over *R* is net profit margin (top row of the diagonal).

Row 2 begins, *R* over *A* is efficiency. Efficiency times net profit margin (cross-cancel *R* with *R*) equals *I* over *A* (return on assets), which equals *P* over *A* (price to assets) times *I* over *P* (income to price).

Row 3 begins, *A* over *E* is leverage. Leverage times efficiency times net profit margin equals *I* over *E* (return on equity), which equals *P* over *E* (price to equity) times *I* over *P* (income to price).

Row 4 begins, *E* over *R* is equity to revenue. Equity to revenue times leverage times efficiency times net profit margin equals *I* over *R* (return on revenue, interestingly known as net profit margin), which equals *P* over *R* (price to revenue) times *I* over *P* (income to price).

Rows 5–8 begin, change in *I*, *A*, *E*, *R*—each over Old Income—are change to income ratios. Multiply respectively by 100, return on assets, return on equity, and return on revenue to equal growth of income, assets, equity, and revenue. The *GAAP Alphabet* aggregates mathematically in *GAAP Structure* to aid astute investment decisions.

† United States *Generally Accepted Accounting Principles* (US GAAP)
Financial Accounting Standards Board (FASB) at **http://www.fasb.org/st/**

The Monopoly Riddle

> Companies such as Microsoft, Pfizer, and First Data all have very high ROEs (return on equity). People write books about how to manage a business as well as these companies do, and it's easy to see why—they're all money machines. Investors pour money into them, and large amounts of extra money get spit out. Their managements are very, very good at earning a high return on shareholders' money.
>
> Pat Dorsey—*The Five Rules for Successful Stock Investing*

The monopoly riddle asks: How does a consumer monopoly company (sheltered from competition) illustrate concepts fully?

A monopoly has an unusual—not illegal—competitive advantage. It illustrates concepts fully because you see company evolution—all the way to monopoly. Microsoft exhibits excellent growth characteristics during the period since 1993. Their success causes trend charts to look at first classic and then very unusual. As a conservative and well run company (from the view of financial management), they illustrate the research and experience of scholars and investors.

Microsoft's return on equity (ROE) illustrates one example of building a monopoly. As Microsoft built its equity base toward an astounding $76 ***billion***, their ROE trend classically increased, but then began a long decline. However, most of that equity base was $64 billion in ***cash***. By the end of 2004, Microsoft had reduced legal and associated business risks prerequisite to returning to shareholders a ***dividend payout*** of over $30 billion—roughly $3 per share—making it one of the largest dividends in corporate history. The sheer size of the dividend causes perturbations in Microsoft's financial numbers.

What's so excellent about very high return on equity decreasing? The long decline in return on equity is caused primarily by the long increase in equity, while income is increasing less quickly than equity. If you subtracted the huge pile of cash from equity, the equity involved in production of products that generate revenue would be much smaller, resulting in a much higher ratio of income to equity.

You see from the chart that just after the December 2004 one-time dividend, return on equity surges. The major contributor to this jump is, of course, the $30 billion drop in equity, not improved operating performance. *Equity Growth Events* on page 17 again shows increasing growth—even though *The Per Share Growth Riddle* on page 107 shows stock buyback, and Microsoft is funding record innovation.

MICROSOFT

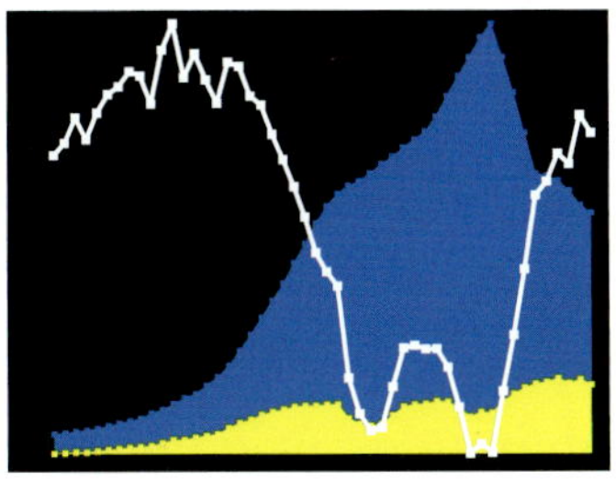

Return On Equity (white)

Trend charts require lots of data from lots of reports. Microsoft became the first company to submit its annual *Form 10-K* (for the year ending June 30, 2005) to the new *SEC eXtensible Business Reporting Language* (*XBRL*) *Voluntary Filing Program*. Next, the *SEC* will make *XBRL* filings available at http://www.sec.gov/cgi-bin/srch-edgar

Someday Microsoft's glimpse of the future will come true: "Making the Microsoft financial statement information available in XBRL enables any user, anywhere in the world, on any device, to perform reviews and analyses of the data via the Internet."

This is great news going forward, but past trend charts are built on data that is not in the new *XBRL* format.

Leaders like Microsoft could easily and appropriately side-step going back and publishing all their prior quarterly and annual reports in the *XBRL* format. One quick approach would use the *XBRL* format to include a table of all the quarters since 1993, like our *inside front cover Quarterly Data Summary*. Each company would update its table in quarterly (*10-Q*) and annual (*10-K*) reports—just add a nine-item top row, and replace all prices. This would indeed create a cheap and easy revolution in useful data for companies and investors.

The Best Numbers Riddle

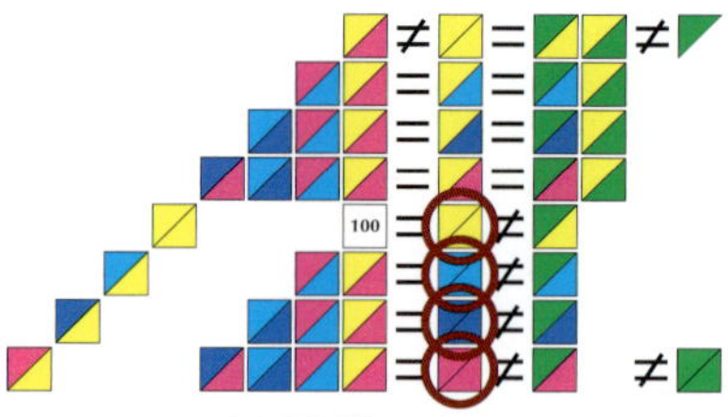

GAAP Structure

MICROSOFT

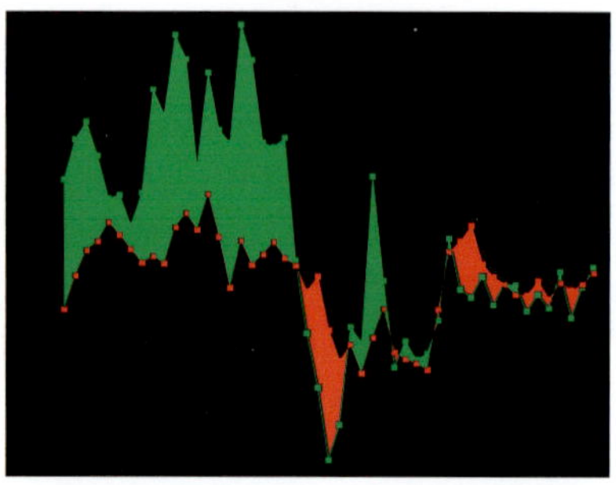

Share Price Growth—S&P Price Gro

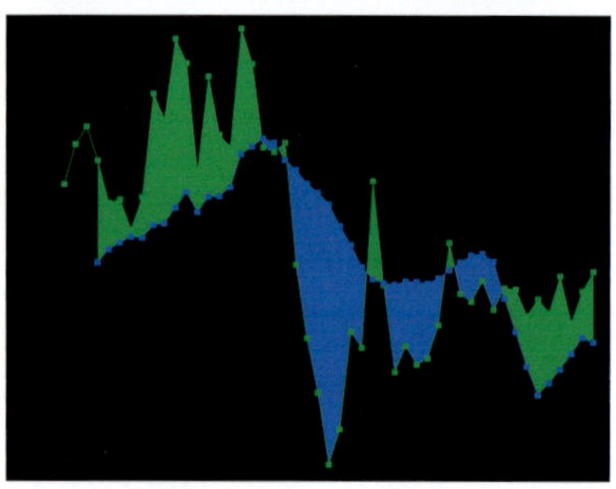

Share Price Growth—Equity Growth

In the top chart, green shows how much the company's share price growth beats the *S&P* price growth—not the average.

In the bottom chart, green shows you when, and how much, the company's share price growth beats its equity growth. For some companies (not all), share price growth may be close to equity growth—assuming popularity or unpopularity cause any differences. Microsoft average growth (1993–2006) ran 29% price and 23% equity.

> Our shareholders can buy the *S&P* through an index fund at very low cost. Unless we achieve gains in per-share intrinsic value (fair price growth) in the future that outdo the *S&P* (price growth), Charlie and I will be adding nothing to what you can accomplish on your own.
>
> Warren E. Buffett—*Letter to Berkshire Shareholders, 2004*

The best numbers riddle asks: What are the best numbers for each measure in the *GAAP Structure* matrix?

In the *GAAP Structure* matrix, some ***combinations of numbers*** beat cash growth, bonds growth, and *Standard & Poor's 500 Index (S&P)* price growth (since 1993 averaging 11%).

In his *Berkshire Owner's Manual, Intrinsic Value,* Buffett suggests that equity growth is often a shortcut to estimating fair price growth, but not a substitute. His *Letter to Berkshire Shareholders, 2005* reports average equity growth at 21.5%—but nothing on share price growth.

We think in terms of *GAAP Structure*, top left, knowing its details begin on page 87. The quotation above implies you want company fair price growth (and thus share price growth) to beat *S&P* price growth. The best numbers for other measures are, in short—Growth (four circles, top left) significantly beats the growth of cash, bonds, and the *S&P*; Growth factors multiply to equal growth; Duplicate measures are fill-ins; Remaining measures are calculated.

In other words, follow the ideal in *The Growth Hierarchy Riddle* on page 104 by setting growth (circles) equal—for example at 20% for income, equity, revenue, and assets. Then, any numbers to the left of each work—so long as they multiply to equal the example 20%. The rest of the numbers are duplicates of the growth factors, or calculated using them. The four growth measures are seldom equal—often temporarily out of the order prescribed by the growth hierarchy.

Buffett reports in his *Letter to Berkshire Shareholders, 2005*, that his 1965–2005 average equity growth of 21.5% outdoes *S&P* average price growth of 10.3%—causing overall growth of 305,134% versus 5,583%. Microsoft, in the table facing *Share and Fair Price Trends* on page 77, shows that average 1993–2006 share price growth of 29% and equity growth of 23% outdo *S&P* price growth of 11%—causing overall growth of 1270%, 791%, and 204% respectively. Investors set aside criteria, costs, and benefits for switching to the *S&P*, bonds, or cash when Microsoft roars home with 29% to beat the *S&P* 11%.

The Annual Report Every Quarter Riddle

MICROSOFT

Revenue

The *SEC* may require that each quarterly and annual report show a *Quarterly Data Summary* since 1993 like our *inside front cover*. Then, you need only the most recent report to calculate ***all*** trailing sets of four-quarters data.

Our charting tools essentially do this for you. The technique is known as ***rolling quarterly updates***. (Annual reports include sum four quarters of revenue and income, so companies obviously know the procedure.) Each quarter we obtain the latest quarterly data, and use it plus the prior three quarters to sum four quarters of data. We repeat this process, stepping backwards one quarter at a time, until we run out of data. Trend charts for revenue and income sum four quarters; while assets, equity, and shares average four quarters. Charts of quarterly data don't use sums.

The picture here shows the process of rolling the sum-of-four-quarters back in time, using all the data to show an annual report every quarter. In this revenue example, twenty-two quarters are rolled over one quarter at a time to show nineteen annualized data points. Why wait a year when you can calculate an annual report every quarter?

Realistically, we work off a rolling quarterly....

Bruce Chizen, Adobe CEO—*Interview, The Motley Fool, March 27, 2001*

The annual report every quarter riddle asks: Since companies file an annual report once a year, can they file the summary numbers for an annual report all four quarters, so investors can stay current?

Public companies file four reports each fiscal year—a ***first*** quarter report, a ***second*** quarter report, a ***third*** quarter report, and a final ***annual*** report. A subtle omission is a ***fourth*** quarter report.†

This strange reporting style creates difficulties, because you really would like four quarters of data with every quarterly update, so you can do all the calculations implied in the *SEC* data, as described in *The Revenue and Income Riddle* on page 102. In other words, you would like an annual report every quarter. But to obtain an annual report every quarter, you have to do arithmetic using the numbers from the three quarterly reports and from the annual report.

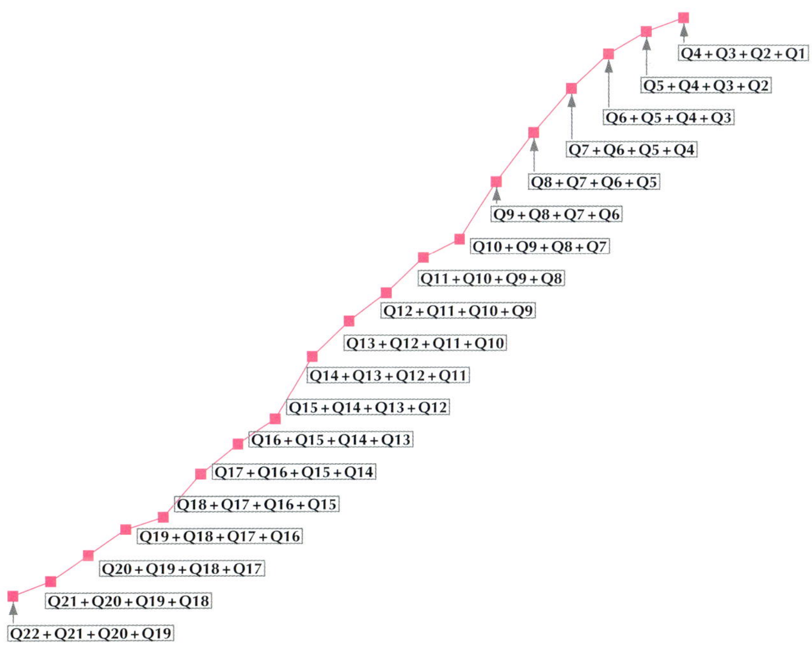

† In addition to the strange reporting style, the three quarterly reports are *not audited*.

The Revenue and Income Riddle

MICROSOFT

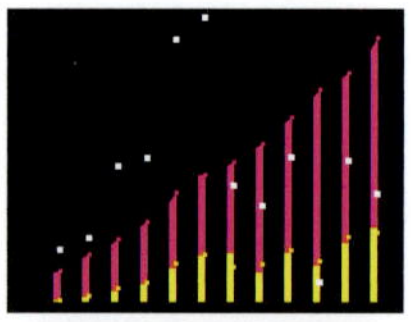

I / R 10-K Slices

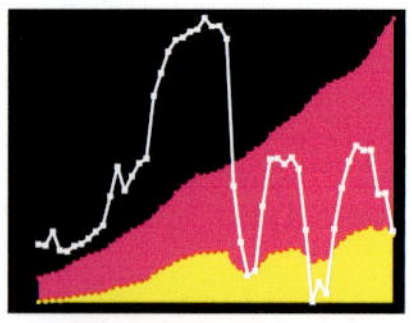

Income / Revenue

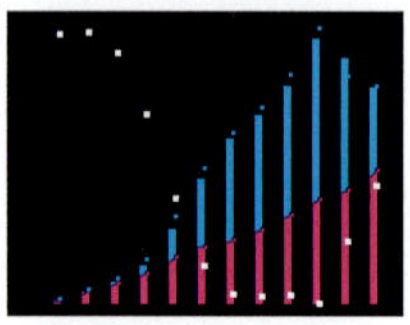

R / A 10-K Slices

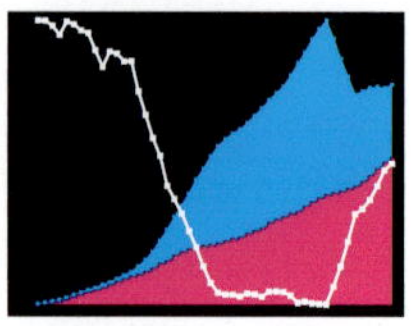

Revenue / Assets

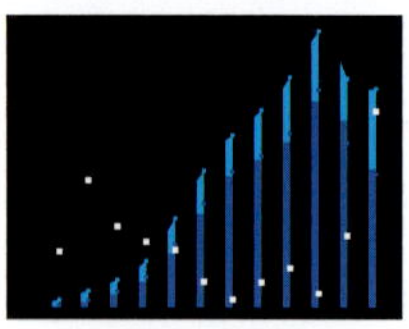

A / E 10-K Slices

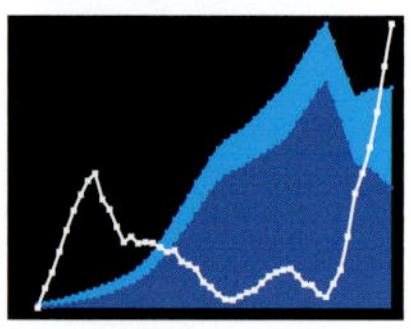

Assets / Equity

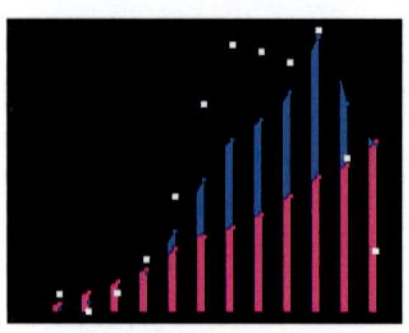

E / R 10-K Slices

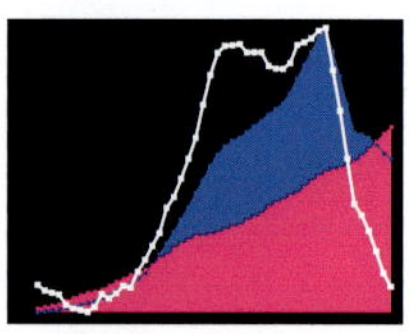

Equity / Revenue

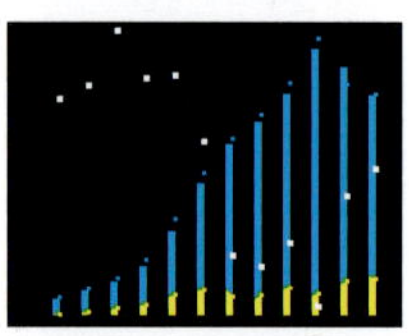

I / A 10-K Slices

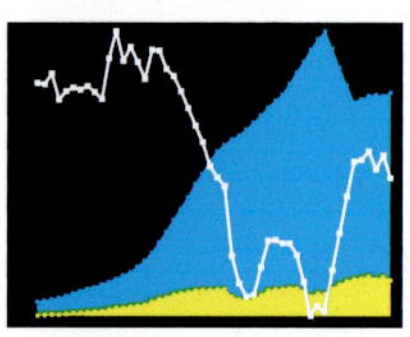

Income / Assets

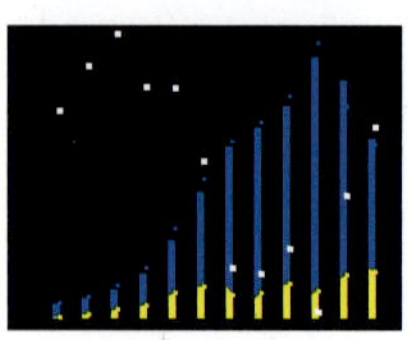

I / E 10-K Slices

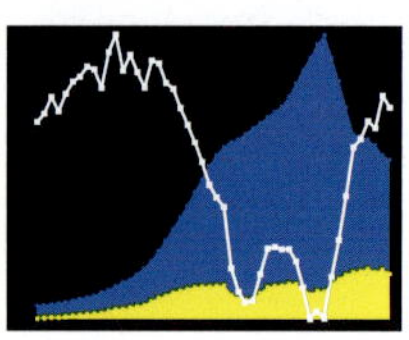

Income / Equity

> Only through the steady flow of timely, comprehensive, and accurate information can people make sound investment decisions.
>
> ——United States *Securities and Exchange Commission*, **www.sec.gov**

The revenue and income riddle asks: Which revenue and income should we use—quarterly, or the rolling sum of four quarters?

United States *Securities and Exchange Commission (SEC) Annual Reports (10-K)* require the sum 4 quarters revenue and income. You'll recognize this sum 4 quarters in 4 of 6 ratios in the *GAAP Structure Molecule* facing page 89—*R / A*, *I / A*, *I / E*, *E / R* (efficiency, return on assets, return on equity, equity to revenue).

The *GAAP Structure Molecule* on page 89 implies sum 4 quarters for revenue and income in the fifth of 6 ratios from *Ratio Trends* on page 21, *I / R* (net profit margin), because *GAAP* cross-cancelling implies that all *Rs* and *Is* must use the same dimensions—sum of 4 quarters.

GAAP CROSS-CANCELLING	*GAAP* RATIOS USING R OR I	
$\frac{R}{A} \times \frac{I}{R} = \frac{I}{A}$	$\frac{R}{A}$	$\frac{I}{A}$
$\frac{A}{E} \times \frac{R}{A} \times \frac{I}{R} = \frac{I}{E}$		$\frac{I}{E}$
$\frac{E}{R} \times \frac{A}{E} \times \frac{R}{A} \times \frac{I}{R} = \frac{I}{R}$	$\frac{E}{R}$	$\frac{I}{R}$

Inside *GAAP Structure*, the *SEC* implies the sum of 4 quarters rolling quarterly updates—fancy language for update by summing the most recent four, roll back one and sum four, repeat to the beginning.

Outside *GAAP Structure*, quarterly revenue and income are used in net profit margin and growth of revenue and income, when comparing quarter to quarter, or with less than 8 quarters of data available.

Quarterly updates—right-column charts—use all *SEC* data implied in "the steady flow of timely information", and are four times more frequent than annual slices to their left. The *SEC* requires revenue and income to be sum 4 quarters in every *Annual Report (10-K)*. The *SEC* can revolutionize useful timely data for investors by requiring that all *Quarterly Reports (10-Q)* and *Annual Reports (10-K)* include one downloadable table—our *inside front cover Quarterly Data Summary*.

The Assets and Equity Riddle

MICROSOFT

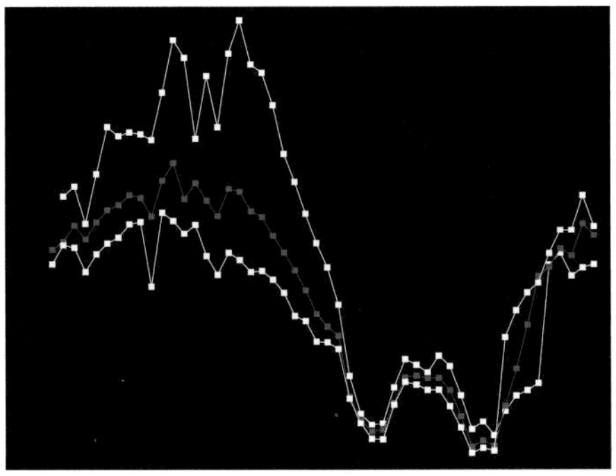

Return on Beginning 4 Quarters Equity
Return on Average 4 Quarters Equity
Return on Ending 4 Quarters Equity

> Return on beginning equity.... We believe... to be the most appropriate measure of single-year managerial economic performance.
>
> Warren E. Buffett—*Letter to Berkshire Shareholders, 1980*

The assets and equity riddle asks: Which assets and equity should we use—beginning, average, or ending 4 quarters?

Three forms of assets and equity can be used in *GAAP Structure Verified by SEC Data* on page 93. We'll use return on equity (income/equity) to rationalize our choice:

- ***beginning*** 4 quarters, written as *return on equity*$_{b\,4q}$;
- ***average*** 4 quarters, written as *return on equity*$_{a\,4q}$;
- ***ending*** 4 quarters, written as *return on equity*$_{e\,4q}$.

The return on equity is the income earned on equity. This income is earned in a sum 4 quarters period defined in *The Revenue and Income Riddle* on page 102. The problem is, do you pick equity as beginning, average, or ending a 4 quarter income period?

If equity during a 4 quarter period remains the same, then beginning, average, and ending are the same. However, if equity changes—as in the trend chart on the left—then answers may differ.

Return on equity$_{e\,4q}$—the current popular form—is nonsense because ending equity, by definition, has zero time to earn the 4 quarters of income. In contrast, average 4 quarters equity and beginning 4 quarters equity do have time to earn the income in the ratio.

In the case where equity is increasing, the equity in return on equity will be smaller for beginning and larger for average—causing *return on equity*$_{b\,4q}$ to climb and drop more steeply than *return on equity*$_{a\,4q}$, as you see in the trend chart on the left.

We prefer to follow Warren Buffett and Professor Robert Higgins in using return on beginning equity because it makes sense and is the most sensitive form of equity in return on equity.

However, instead we have chosen return on average 4 quarters equity—trading an acceptable decrease in sensitivity for increased simplicity. Average 4 quarters assets and equity make sense, and use the same 4 quarter period as revenue and income—enabling us to explain them simply in *GAAP Structure*.

The Growth Hierarchy Riddle

MICROSOFT

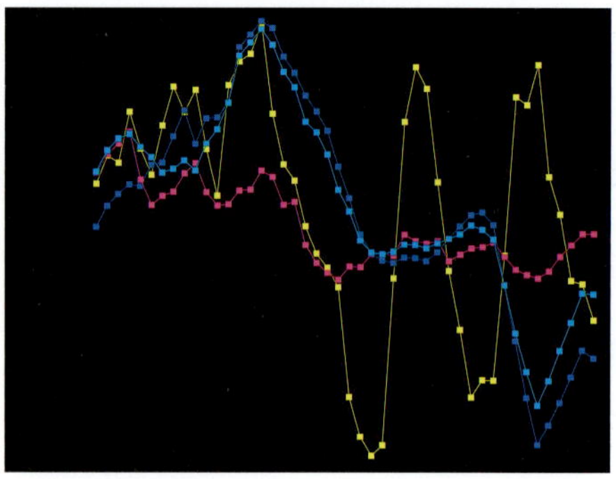

- *Income Growth*
- *Equity Growth*
- *Revenue Growth*
- *Assets Growth*

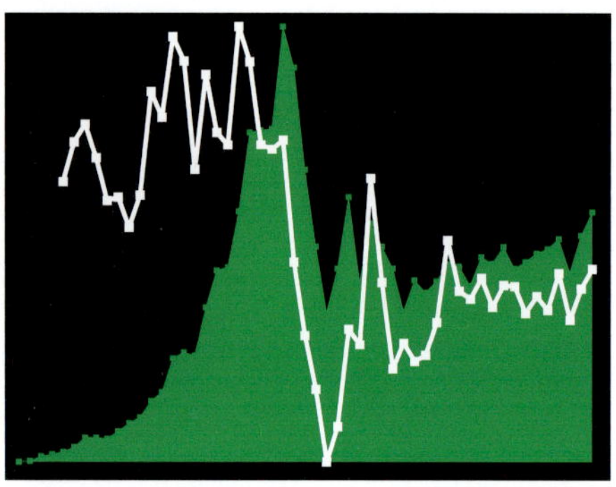

Share Price Growth (white)—Share Price

The four-growth hierarchy is the top chart. This chart compares the four *Growth Trends* on page 11 that summarize company performance. It has three purposes: Display relative growth of the dataplots; Display in the caption the theoretical order; Provide a sanity check for price growth.

The bottom chart shows share price growth (white) overlaid on share price (green). When investors pay a fair price, share price growth may approximate the dominant shape of dataplots in the top chart, adjusted by "business thinking"—last paragraph on the right.

> Over the last 41 years...(equity per share) has grown from \$19 to \$59,377, a rate of 21.5% compounded annually.
>
> Warren E. Buffett—*Letter to Berkshire Shareholders, 2005*

The growth hierarchy riddle asks: Can we infer a four-growth hierarchy that optimizes equity growth—with a dominant shape that forecasts share price growth when investors pay a fair price?

In the top chart, the trends of growth plots for equity, revenue, and assets approximately forecast the bottom chart trend in price growth, except when popularity or unpopularity increase or decrease share price. Some companies may show this forecasting, but not all.

Income growth is at the top of the theoretical hierarchy. Income growth is the popular growth factor in the formula for *Fair Price Estimate—Intrinsic Value* on page 85. Though it's too volatile to inspire confidence, its average would look more like the other three.

The theoretical hierarchy is the top chart caption. Considering facts below, growth of income must be equal to or above equity. You arrange the others. Ratios can increase (or decrease as with leverage) "only to their limits" in *Ratio Trends* on page 21. Ideally, growth of fundamentals will be equal, and as fast as possible.

You want to place the four fundamental growths in a hierarchy that causes five of the ratio measures to increase—and leverage to decrease. Facts about the six ratios dictate the order of the hierarchy:

- *Income / equity* increases as *income* grows faster than *equity*;
- *Equity / revenue* increases as *equity* grows faster than *revenue*;
- *Revenue / assets* increases as *revenue* grows faster than *assets*;
- *Income / revenue* increases as *income* grows faster than *revenue*;
- *Income / assets* increases as *income* grows faster than *assets*;
- *Assets / equity* **decreases** as *assets* grows slower than *equity*.

A company may strive toward the theoretical hierarchy, but one or more of the four growth trends may be temporarily out of order. To make sense of the four, imagine income growth is averaged; assume growth of equity and assets temporarily lowered by the December 2004 dividend; and assume pre-dividend growth of equity, revenue, and assets profile rational estimates of short-term fair price growth.

The Ratios Riddle

MICROSOFT

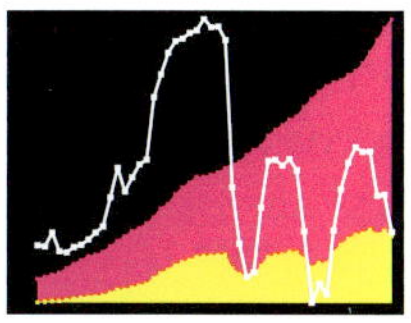

Income / Revenue

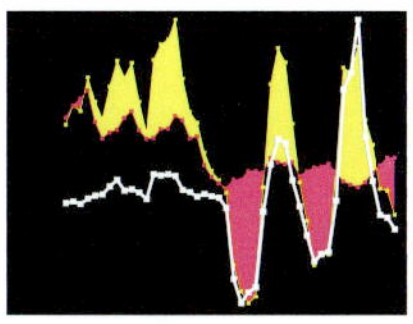

Inc Gro / Rev Gro

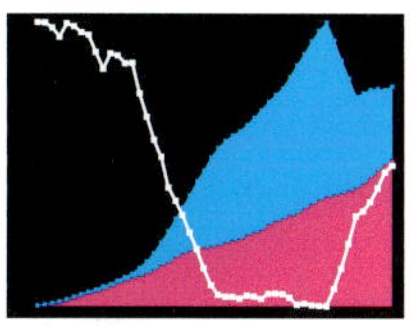

Revenue / Assets

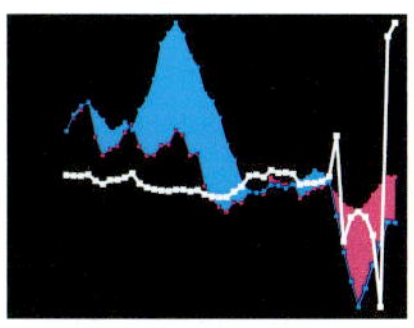

Rev Gro / Ass Gro

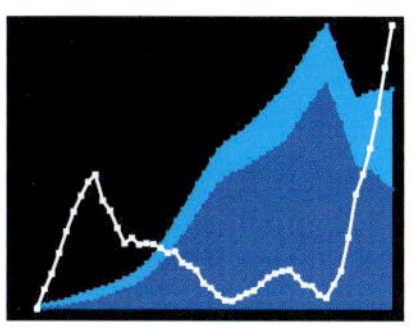

Assets / Equity

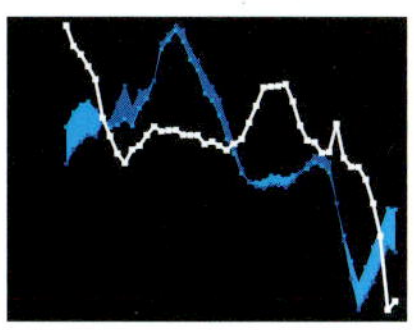

Ass Gro / Eqt Gro

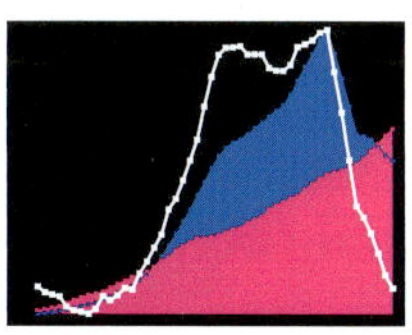

Equity / Revenue

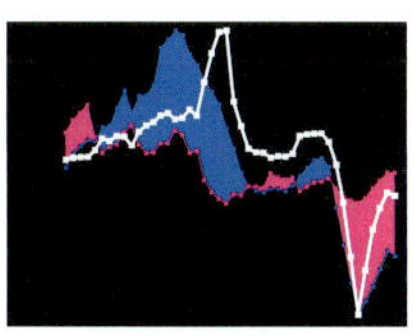

Eqt Gro / Rev Gro

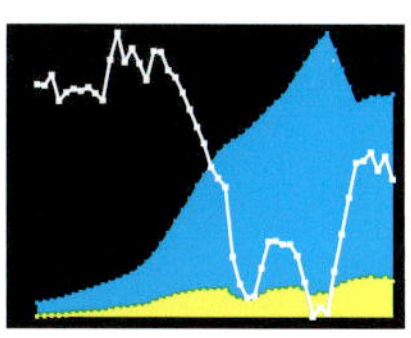

Income / Assets

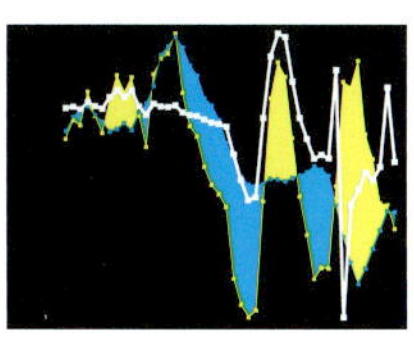

Inc Gro / Ass Gro

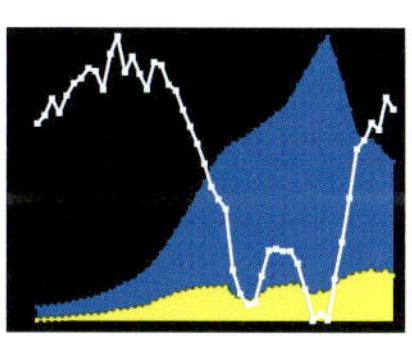

Income / Equity

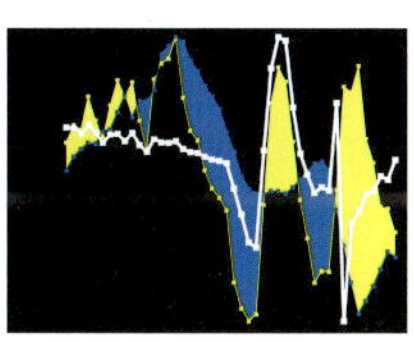

Inc Gro / Eqt Gro

> We chose to determine mathematically the best that a system's performance could be. Only then did we embark on a search for how to do it.
>
> Amar G. Bose—*The Maestro of Acoustics, Discover, October 2004*

The ratios riddle asks: Why are the *Ratio Trends* from page 21 (left column), and the corresponding *Sustainable Trends* from page 45 (right column), the only 6 unique pairs you can form using the 4 *Fundamental Trends* on page 1—Income, Assets, Equity, Revenue?

A binomial formula below proves that the 4 combine in only 6 unique reciprocal pairs—no identities. ***m*** is the 4 fundamentals. ***m!*** is (4 × 3 × 2 × 1). ***n*** is 2 fundamentals in a ratio. ***n!*** is (2 × 1).

$$\frac{m}{n} = \frac{m\,!}{(m-n)\,!\,n\,!} = \frac{4\,!}{(4-2)\,!\,2\,!} = \frac{4\,!}{2\,!\,2\,!} = \frac{4\times3\times2\times1}{2\times1\times2\times1} = \frac{24}{4} = 6$$

A systematic table below proves there are only 16 possible ratios: 4 identities (A/A, E/E, R/R, I/I); and 6 unique reciprocal pairs (R/A, A/R; I/A, A/I; A/E, E/A; I/E, E/I; E/R, R/E; I/R, R/I).

16 POSSIBLE RATIOS

$$\frac{E}{A}\quad \frac{A}{A}\quad \frac{R}{A}\quad \frac{I}{A}$$

$$\frac{E}{E}\quad \frac{A}{E}\quad \frac{R}{E}\quad \frac{I}{E}$$

$$\frac{E}{R}\quad \frac{A}{R}\quad \frac{R}{R}\quad \frac{I}{R}$$

$$\frac{E}{I}\quad \frac{A}{I}\quad \frac{R}{I}\quad \frac{I}{I}$$

GAAP Structure on page 87 proves which 6 to pick from 6 pairs.

GAAP STRUCTURE RATIOS	*GAAP STRUCTURE* 6 UNIQUE RATIOS
$\frac{R}{A} \times \frac{I}{R} = \frac{I}{A}$	$\frac{R}{A}$ $\frac{I}{A}$
$\frac{A}{E} \times \frac{R}{A} \times \frac{I}{R} = \frac{I}{E}$	$\frac{A}{E}$ $\frac{I}{E}$
$\frac{E}{R} \times \frac{A}{E} \times \frac{R}{A} \times \frac{I}{R} = \frac{I}{R}$	$\frac{E}{R}$ $\frac{I}{R}$

The Leverage Riddle

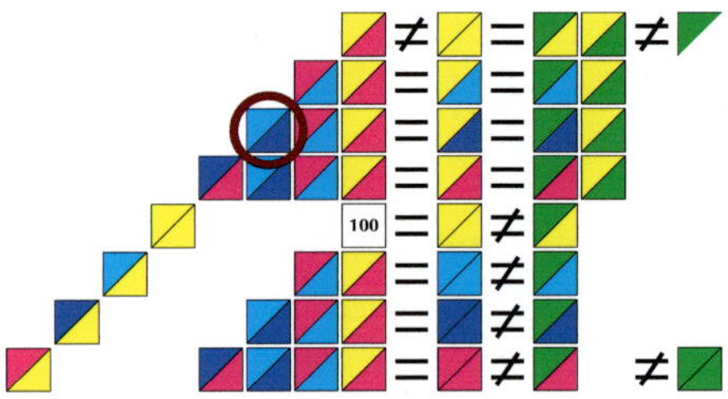

GAAP Structure

DATASTREAMS *MICROSOFT*

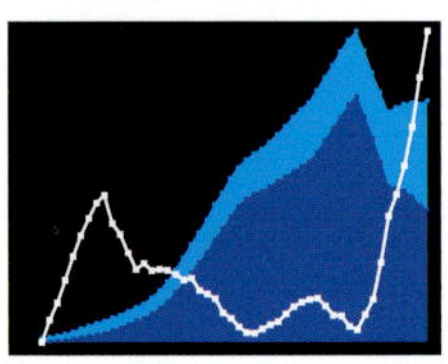

Leverage (white)

> The assets to equity ratio, is simply the (liabilities) to equity ratio plus 1.
>
> Robert C. Higgins—*Analysis for Financial Management*

The leverage riddle asks: How can leverage (assets to equity) cause return on equity greater than or equal to return on assets?

In *GAAP Structure* at the top left, assets to equity (cyan divided by blue) is circled at the head of its column. In the return on equity equation below, assets to equity provides assets you cross-cancel with assets, revealing that factors on the left equal income to equity.

$$\frac{assets}{equity} \times \frac{revenue}{assets} \times \frac{income}{revenue} = \frac{income}{equity}$$

Liabilities to equity (also known as debt to equity) is a complement of assets to equity, but not a substitute. Liabilities to equity makes nonsense of *GAAP Structure* on page 87—leaving investors stumbling. Professor Higgins recommends: "Instead of calculating ratios at random, hoping to stumble across one that might be meaningful, take advantage of the structure implicit in the levers (factors)."

For example, in *GAAP Structure*, compare rows three and two. If you use liabilities to equity in row three, and if liabilities equal zero, return on equity will equal zero—nonsense. Instead, as liabilities approach zero assets to equity approaches one—causing return on equity to approach return on assets. If liabilities equal zero, equity will equal assets—then return on equity will equal return on assets.

Here's how assets to equity and liabilities to equity are related.

$$\frac{assets}{equity} = \frac{liabilities + equity}{equity} = \frac{liabilities}{equity} + \frac{equity}{equity} = \frac{liabilities}{equity} + 1$$

In the leverage chart on the left, the assets datastream is cyan and equity is blue. Liabilities is the portion of cyan visible above the blue. Even if liabilities increase, if liabilities to equity decreases, then return on equity will approach return on assets.

The *GAAP Structure Molecule* on page 89 enables you to systematically evaluate a company, beginning with a result such as return on equity, then exploring its factors such as leverage.

The Per Share Growth Riddle

MICROSOFT

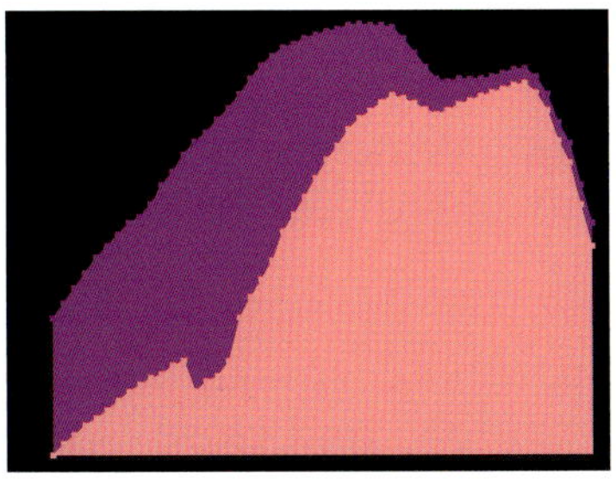

Shares

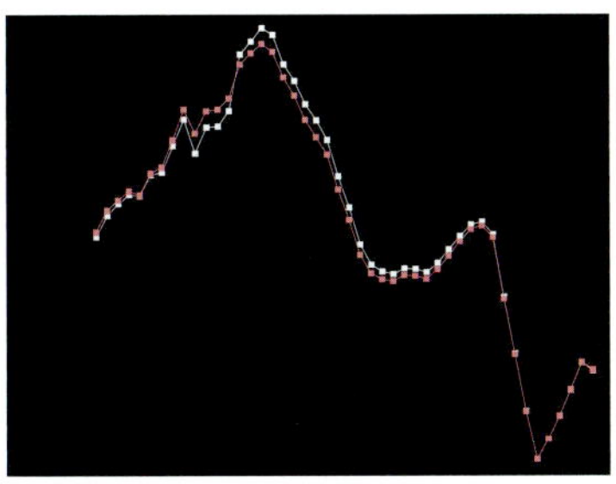

Equity Gro—Diluted versus Basic

The *inside front cover Quarterly Data Summary* shows *Shares Diluted* only slightly larger than *Shares Basic*. *Shares* above are scaled to begin at the number of shares—not at zero. This scaling magnifies the difference between diluted (purple) and basic (pink). The magnified difference may look large, but for this company the difference is small.

Equity Gro—Diluted versus Basic above shows *Equity Growth* per diluted shares on page 16 as the white data marker. (We substitute white for purple because white is easier to see on the black background.) Equity growth per basic shares is the pink data marker. You see in this case there is little or no difference in growth when dividing equity by diluted versus basic shares. Why? For this company, diluted shares are only slightly larger than basic shares.

> We do not measure the economic significance or performance of Berkshire by its size; we measure by per-share progress.
> Warren E. Buffett—Berkshire Owner's Manual, Principle 3

The per share growth riddle asks: How should we measure progress—by growth per share, or by size? If by growth per share, should we measure per diluted shares or per basic shares?

Measure by growth because when investors pay a fair price we expect the shape of share price growth to approximate the shape of our four-growth chart—adjusted for "business thinking"—as in *The Growth Hierarchy Riddle* on page 104. *Growth Trends* on page 11 measure the rate of change in the size of the four fundamentals. Measure growth per diluted shares because basic shares may be smaller, inflate growth, and contribute to misappraising a company.

The *Shares* chart shows diluted shares (purple) and basic (pink). Diluted shares are the sum of dilutive instruments and basic shares, discussed in *The Split-Adjusted Close Price Riddle* on page 108. As purple gets smaller, the company is diluting less. If dilution is zero, the chart shows no purple because all shares are pink (basic). When a dataplot decreases, the company may be buying back shares.

Shares may reveal characteristics of a great investment opportunity:

- Share value increases as shares decrease. For example, decreasing shares increases income per share and growth per share.
- Share value is expected to increase from the early years, so the company issues employees lots of options (part of the purple).
- Share value long-term trends may be more accurately reported in the popular press when diluted shares are closer to basic because dividing by basic shares—if they are lower—inflates values. The purveyors of numbers may argue that they use diluted shares in current calculations. But, since historical basic shares are currently not offered by data warehouses, diluted are often used for current calculations, while basic are used for historical.

Growth is (*new value* – *old value*) / *old value* . If average shares remain the same during the new and old 4 quarter periods, then per share and not per share growth are the same. However, if shares change—as in *Shares* on the left—then averages may differ, causing growth to differ. Thus, average per share growth is closest to the "truth", because it changes growth when shares change.

The Split-Adjusted Close Price Riddle

DATASTREAMS

MICROSOFT

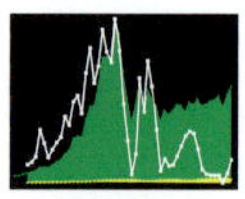

P/Income

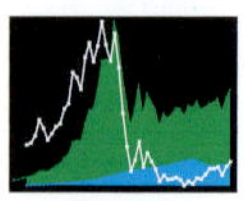

P/Assets

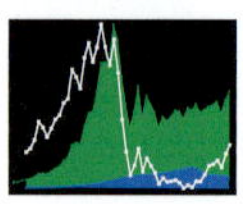

P/Equity

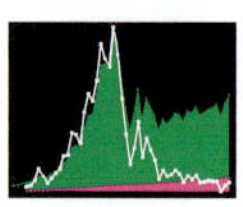

P/Revenue

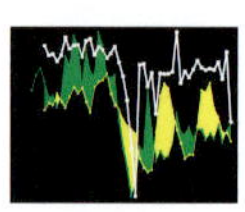

PG/IG

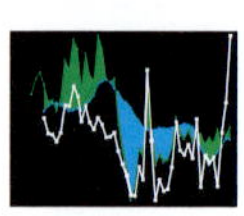

PG/AG

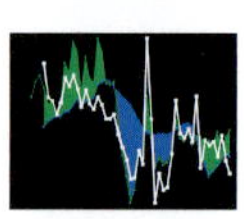

PG/EG

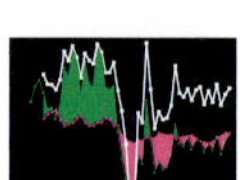

PG/RG

In June 1988, the price of Coca-Cola was approximately $10 per share (split-adjusted).

Robert G. Hagstrom, Jr.—*The Warren Buffett Way*

The split-adjusted close price riddle asks: Which price should we use for trend charts that adjusts for splits and dividends and aligns with all the other quarter-end numbers?

Only split-adjusted close price is appropriate for trend charts, because all other share prices—open, high, low, and close—are not adjusted. Follow instructions in *The Get Data Riddle* on page 113.

InvestorWords.com defines "split-adjusted price":

> The price per share of a stock after it splits—for historical price data, when the stock price in the past is adjusted to reflect subsequent splits, allowing the data to be compared with recent prices.

Quarter-end, split-adjusted close price aligns with all other quarter-end data required by *GAAP Structure* on page 87. When a quarter ends on a trading day, split-adjusted close price is available for that date—enabling you to compare apples to apples. When a quarter ends on a non-trading day—in the absence of a standard—we choose the date within that quarter, closest to the end.

Split-adjusted close price adjusts also for dividends—a three dollar per share dividend automatically decreases the price per share by exactly three dollars. You see an approximate decrease in *GAAP Original Data* on page 91 for 2004-12-31 to 2005-03-31, because there was a dividend payout for a share price before—not at—quarter end.

Split-adjusted prices may change—even without splits—as described by James Morton in his *Global Guide to Investing, Glossary*:

> The average number of shares outstanding should include not only the (basic) shares but also make some provision for any convertible preference shares or loan stock, outstanding warrants, or share option schemes. If shares under option exceed 5 percent of the total (basic) shares, a company will be required to report both (basic income) and fully diluted (income) per share. The fully diluted calculation assumes all options have been exercised and warrants converted.

Since price is adjusted using diluted shares, consistency requires that we use diluted shares in *GAAP Original Data* on page 91. Update all adjusted prices every quarter to be sure they are current.

The Mathematics Riddle

MICROSOFT

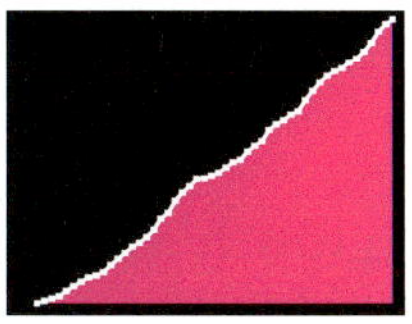

Revenue

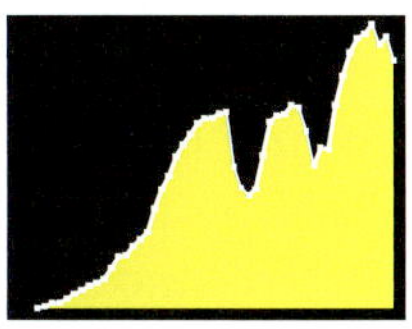

Income

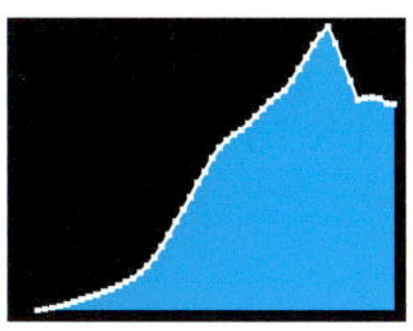

Assets

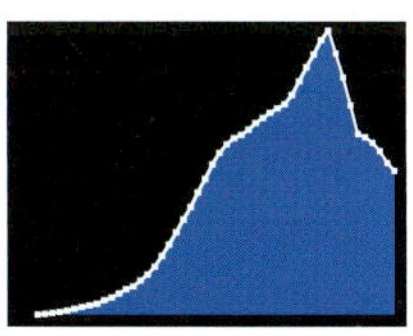

Equity

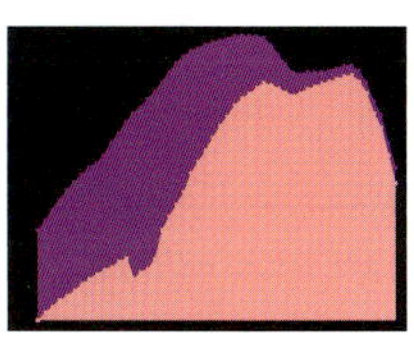

Shares

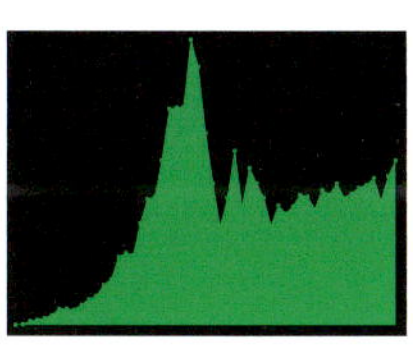

Price

> There are three kinds of people in the world: those who can count, and those who can't . . . .
>
> ——Anonymous

The mathematics riddle asks: Do you believe this evaluation of the company is done with only add, subtract, multiply, and divide?

Fundamental Trends on page 1 add four quarters for revenue and income; and add and divide for assets and equity.

Growth Trends on page 11 and *Change Trends* on page 35 start with the new and subtract the old, then divide by old.

Ratio Trends on page 21, *Sustainable Trends* on page 45, and *Popularity Trends* on page 59 all divide.

Share and Fair Price Trends on page 77, when calculating growth, start with the new price and subtract the old price, then divide by the old. The fair price estimate calculation uses a busy-looking formula to add, subtract, multiply, and divide.

GAAP Structure on page 87 and *Solved Riddles* on page 97 add, subtract, multiply, and divide.

The Ratios Riddle on page 105 uses factorials (!) in a binomial formula for its proof of six unique reciprocal pairs. But—when the dust settles—subtract, multiply, and divide are the only mathematics.

The Computable Riddle on page 110 uses only add, subtract, multiply, and divide to explore absolute values and conditions for zeros—which you build into your *GAAP Original Data* facing page 91, as we have in our table, to handle negative numbers and zeros.

You have seen all the electronically free *SEC* data, in one table, related in *GAAP Structure*, organized into results and their factors, trend-charted in colors, explained by investors and scholars, distilled down to the systematic tools on the *front cover* of this book! *GAAP Original Data* on page 91 and the review above should persuade you that add, subtract, multiply, and divide are the only mathematics required by this evaluation of a company to picture basic characteristics of great investment opportunities.

The Computable Riddle

DATASTREAMS *MICROSOFT*

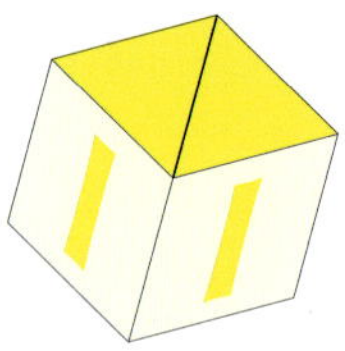

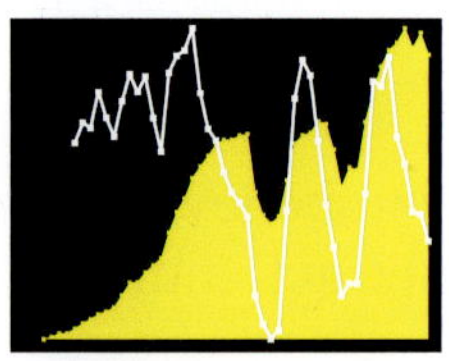

Income Growth

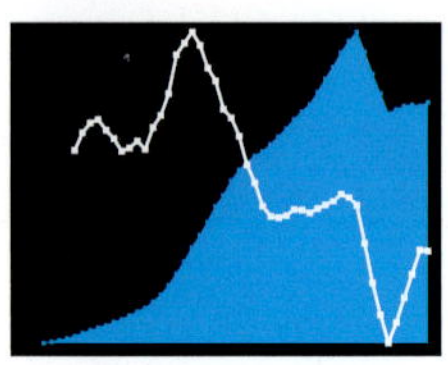

Assets Growth

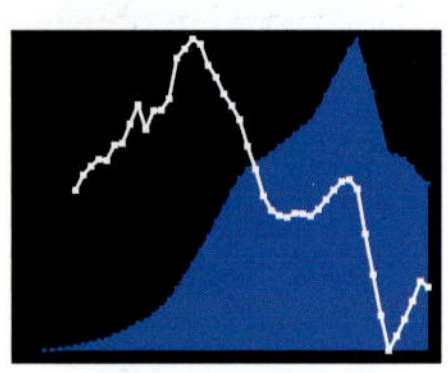

Equity Growth

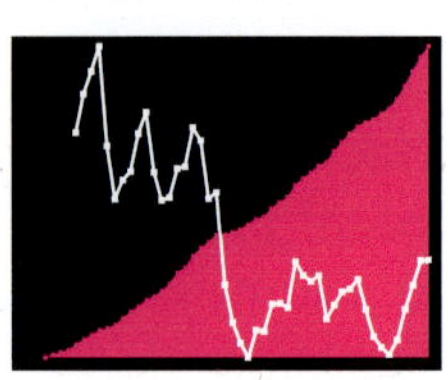

Revenue Growth

> It is a story replete with obscurantism and prejudice, of sound judgment often eclipsed by loyalty to tradition, and of reason long held subservient to custom. In short, it is a human story.
>
> Tobias Dantzig—*Number, The Language of Science*

The computable riddle asks: Can we see growth when the new value and old value are zero, or on different sides of zero?

Our *inside front cover Quarterly Data Summary* shows you all data required by the *GAAP Structure Molecule* facing page 89. In contradiction, financial websites and stories of "reason long held subservient to custom" may show some data not available (N/A) or not computable (N/C). If you are correct, then the contradictor made an error, is incompetent, or lied. Napoleon reminds us, "Never ascribe to malice that which is adequately explained by incompetence."

You solve the riddle by reasoning about zero, and calculating according to the rules of mathematics using the absolute value of positive and negative numbers to subtract and divide † in the *Growth Trends* formula on page 11: [(*new value* – *old value*) / *old value*] × 100.

As you become familiar with the growth formula, you'll realize growth is zero when the new value and old value are the same number with the same sign. In the special case when the new value is zero and the old value is zero, reason says growth is still zero. However, because reason says you can't divide by zero, you should bypass the formula and include zero as a valid growth datapoint. You should expect what we show—no gaps, with one exception.

The only case in which you should see a not computable (N/C) is when the new value is not zero and the old value is zero—because this produces a non-number, not useful to you as an investor. You can imagine that divisors close to zero produce very large quotients.

If the *SEC* becomes a stronger "shareholder advocate" of evaluation, will it require the popular analysts' view that growth must use positive numbers, or the mathematicians' view of absolute value that enables middle school students and us to show, with special conditions for zeros, that all growth can be computed and trends charted?

† *Math League, Positive and negative numbers*
http://www.mathleague.com/help/posandneg/posandneg.htm

The Definitions Riddle

MICROSOFT

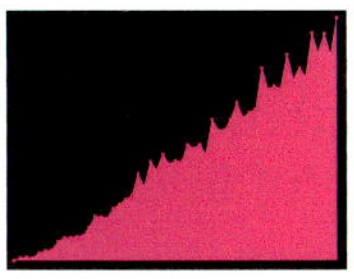

Revenue

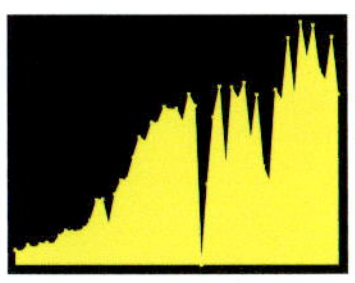

Income

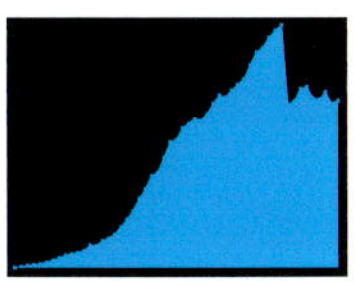

Assets

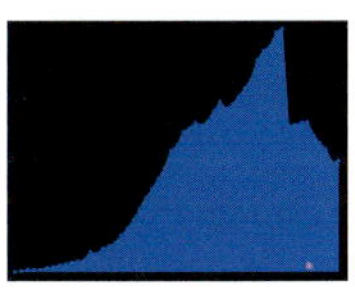

Equity

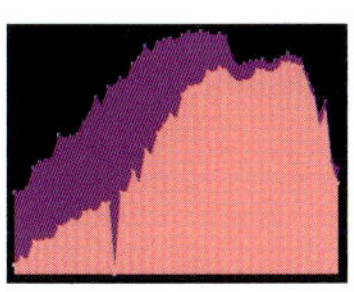

Shares

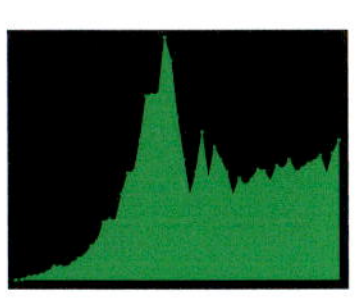

Price

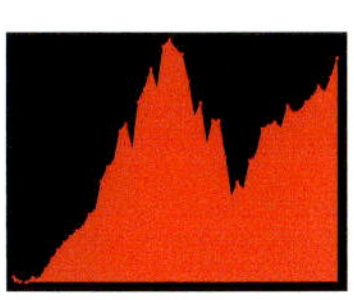

S&P Price

> Questioning *GAAP* figures may seem impious to some. After all, what are we paying the accountants for if it is not to deliver us the "truth" about our business. But the accountants' job is to record, not to evaluate. The evaluation job falls to investors and managers.
>
> Warren E. Buffett—*Letter to Berkshire Shareholders, 1986*

The definitions riddle asks: Can we use alternate definitions in the *GAAP Structure Molecule* facing page 89?

Quarter Ended Date, alternate *Fiscal Year Ended Date*
Bob Goodenough, Henry McGilton, *Invest In Company Evolution*
Quarter ended is 4 times more frequent than fiscal year ended.

Revenue (magenta), alternate *Sales*
Robert C. Higgins, *Analysis for Financial Management*
"I have never found a meaningful distinction between these terms."

Income (yellow), alternate *Owner Earnings*
Warren E. Buffett, *Letter to Berkshire Shareholders, Appendix, 1986*
(*owner earnings = income + depreciation − net change in property, plant, equipment − net change in working capital*)
"If we think through these questions, we can gain some insights about what may be called `owner earnings´."

Assets Market Values (cyan), alternate *Assets Historical Costs*
Robert C. Higgins, *Analysis for Financial Management*
"require . . . market values instead of at their historical costs . . . . greeted with howls of protest by commercial bankers, among others"

Equity (blue), alternate *Invested Capital*
Robert C. Higgins, *Analysis for Financial Management*
(*invested capital = equity + interest bearing debt*)
"To circumvent the distorting effects of leverage on ROE . . . . "

Shares Diluted (purple), alternate *Shares Basic* (pink)
James Morton, *Global Guide to Investing, Glossary*
(*shares basic = shares diluted − dilutive instruments like warrants*)
See *The Split-Adjusted Close Price Riddle* on page 108.

Split-Adjusted Close Share Price (green), alternate No Alternate
Split-Adjusted Close S&P Price (red), alternate No Alternate
See *The Split-Adjusted Close Price Riddle* on page 108.

The Color Codes Riddle

MICROSOFT

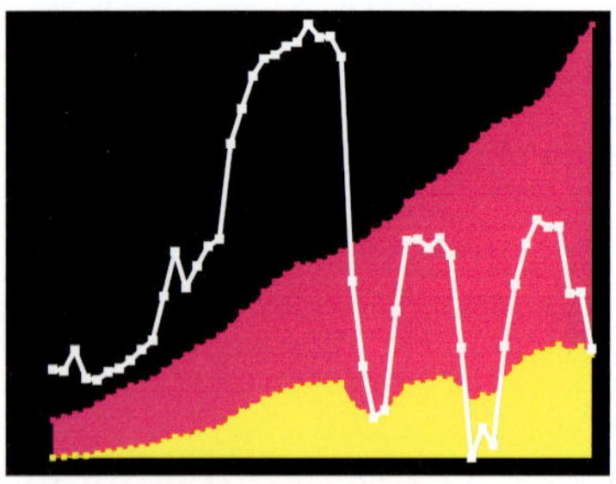

Net Profit Margin

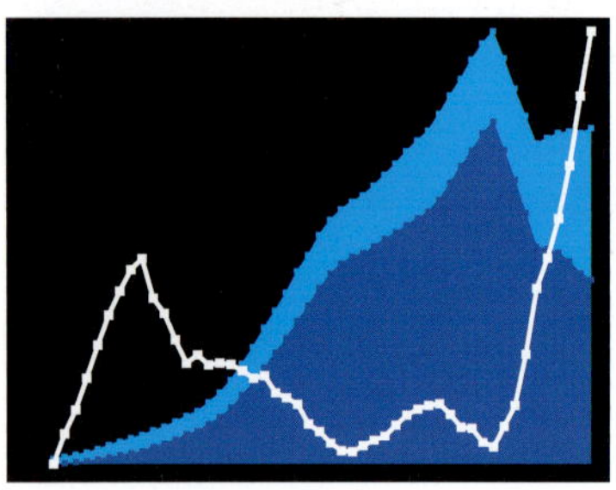

Leverage

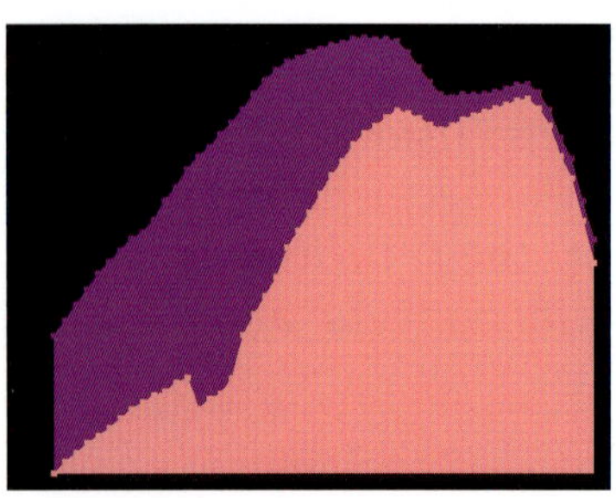

Shares

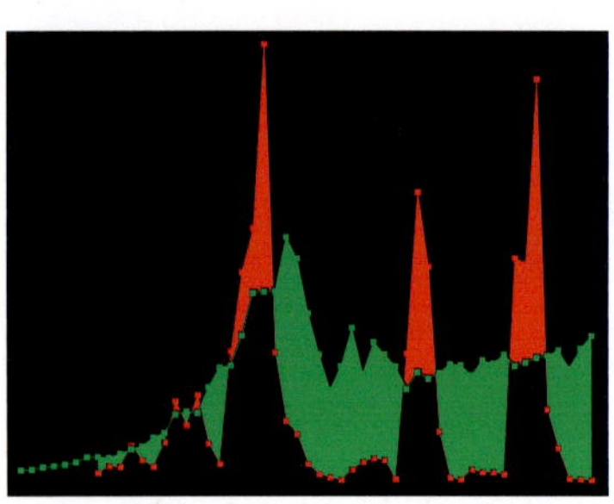

Fair Price—Share Price
Margin of Safety—Margin of Risk

> Color is all. When color is right, form is right.
>
> Marc Chagall—*Park West Gallery*

The color codes riddle asks: Do colors identify measures and discriminate patterns to make them more useful and memorable? †

MEASURE	COLOR	COLOR NAME
Revenue		Magenta
Income		Yellow
Assets		Cyan
Equity		Blue
Diluted Shares		Purple
Basic Shares		Pink
Share Price, Margin of Risk		Green
Fair Price, Margin of Safety, *S&P*		Red
Dataplot		White
Background		Black

Net profit margin (white) reveals the *dot-com bubble* in the only one of six *Ratio Trends* on page 21 using income (yellow) and revenue (magenta). Leverage (white) shows changes caused by the dividend payout of December 2004 using assets (cyan) and equity (blue). This company is diluting shares less and buying back shares—both visible in diluted shares (purple) and basic shares (pink). Margin of safety (red fill) pictures when share price (green markers) are below estimated fair price (red markers). Green fill estimates margin of risk when share price is above fair price. You want to buy at a discount (red fill), and sell at a premium (green fill)—higher than you bought.

† *Guidelines for Color Discrimination and Identification*
http://colorusage.arc.nasa.gov/guidelines_discrim_id.php

The Get Data Riddle

MICROSOFT

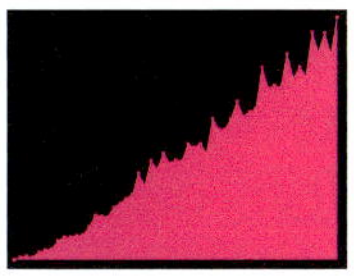

Revenue

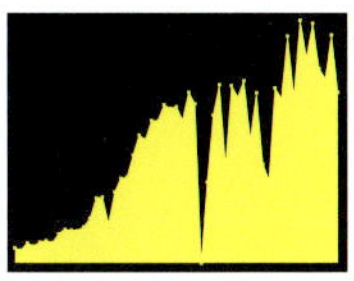

Income

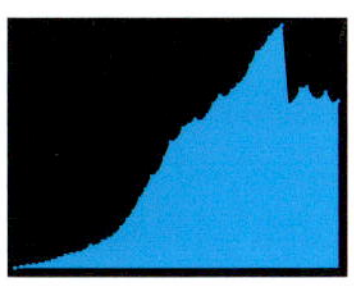

Assets

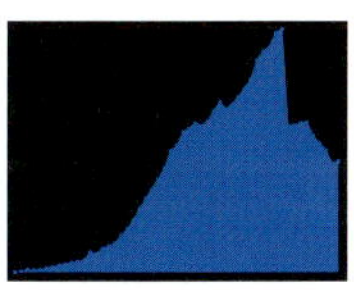

Equity

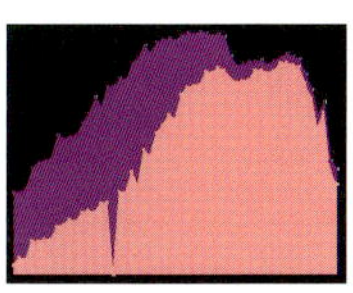

Shares

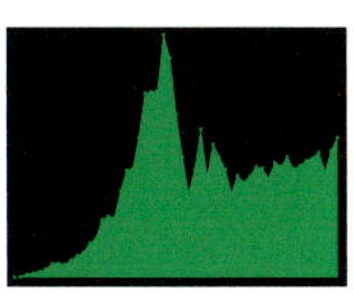

Price

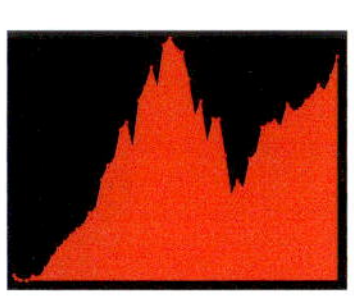

S&P Price

Get your facts first, and then you can distort 'em as much as you please.
——Mark Twain

The get data riddle asks: Can we get the *inside front cover Quarterly Data Summary* required by *GAAP Structure* facing page 87?

Access all quarterly and annual reports free on *SEC EDGAR Archives*: **http://www.sec.gov/cgi-bin/srch-edgar** *Caution*: Websites do remodel. To get the shortest list of reports for ***all*** years, enter "Search String"
`company-name="microsoft" AND form-type=(10-q* OR 10-k*)`
A shorthand works in some cases: **`microsoft (10-q* OR 10-k*)`**

Get recent data first. Why? Current shares are your reference for old shares not "adjusted" for stock splits. If old look small, multiply by an integer to make sense. Convert *EDGAR* numbers to billions (B). Find an *EDGAR FORM* for an *Ended Date* using its later *Filing Date*.

Practice building two rows of the *Quarterly Data Summary*.
EDGAR windows on the following pages illustrate how to get 6 items:
ANNUAL REPORT (10-K) 2004–06–30 (Filing Date 2004–09–01)

QUARTERLY INFORMATION
Revenue 9.292B, Income 2.690B

INCOME STATEMENTS
Shares Diluted 10.894B, Shares Basic 10.803B

BALANCE SHEETS
Assets 92.389B, Equity 74.825B.

Procedures for getting *Quarterly* data are different from *Annual*.
EDGAR windows on the following pages illustrate how to get 6 items:
QUARTERLY REPORT (10-Q) 2005–03–31 (Filing Date 2005–04–28)

INCOME STATEMENTS
Revenue 9.620B, Income 2.563B
Shares Diluted 10.931B, Shares Basic 10.856B

BALANCE SHEETS
Assets 66.275B, Equity 47.373B.

Yahoo is the last window on the following pages. It illustrates how to get 2 prices—as in *The Split-Adjusted Close Price Riddle* on page 108:
http://finance.yahoo.com/q/hp?s=MSFT Microsoft or another company,
http://finance.yahoo.com/q/hp?s=^GSPC *Standard & Poor's Index* (*S&P*).
Select—*Download To Spreadsheet*. Get *Adj Close* (split-adjusted close price) within a quarter, nearest the end. Update all prices.

MICROSOFT

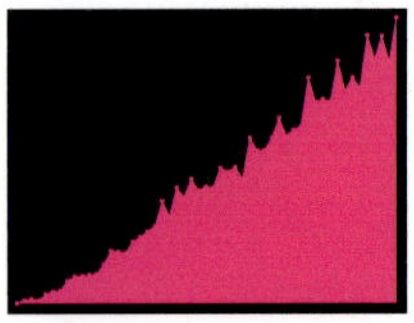

Revenue Quarterly

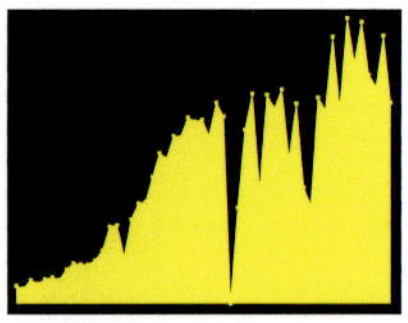

Income Quarterly

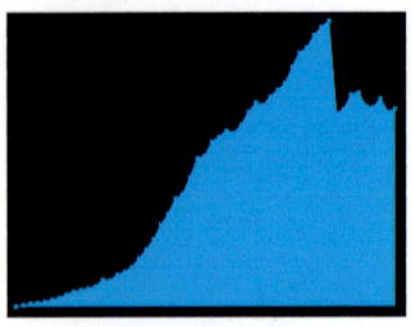

Assets Quarterly

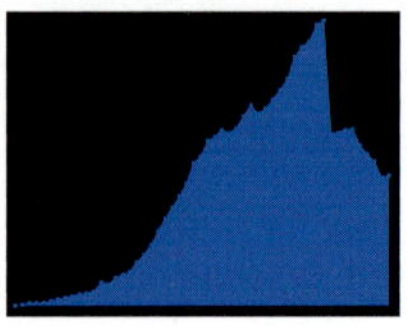

Equity Quarterly

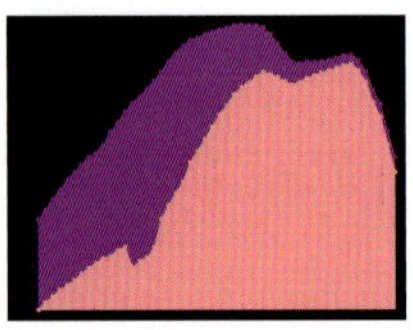

Shares Quarterly

Arthur Levitt, Chairman of the United States *Securities and Exchange Commission* 1993–2001, created the paradigm shift to "free and easy access to corporate filings". Arthur made it possible to hand-build in 5 hours a *Quarterly Data Summary* back to 1993.

Christopher Cox, Chairman 2005–, can create the next paradigm shift to "a revolution in informed investment decisions". He can ask Microsoft and other leaders to begin every new *Quarterly* and *Annual Report* with a downloadable *Quarterly Data Summary* in *XBRL* format.

In this book, you'll learn characteristics of excellence and opportunity without retrieving one item of data. Happily, we've already built software that instantly retrieves and charts expensive data for any company reporting to the *SEC* since 1993. Someday, the *SEC* will make free data useful enough to drive Internet versions of such software for all of us. Until then, we all settle for incomplete data, pay a data-provider lots of money, or hand-pick free data for 5 hours.

Procedures for hand-picking free data are summarized on the prior page, and are illustrated in the following windows. Data you get should match illustration-data from our *Quarterly Data Summary*.

The *EDGAR* window below is at **http://www.sec.gov/cgi-bin/srch-edgar** in your browser. Enter a "Search String". A shorthand works for some cases. Enter all exactly: `microsoft (10-q* OR 10-k*)` Otherwise, to find the "Search String" for all cases, select "header information" and scroll to the example that refers to `(10-q* OR 10-k*)` Select the "Start" date as 1994. Select the latest "End" date. Press "Search".

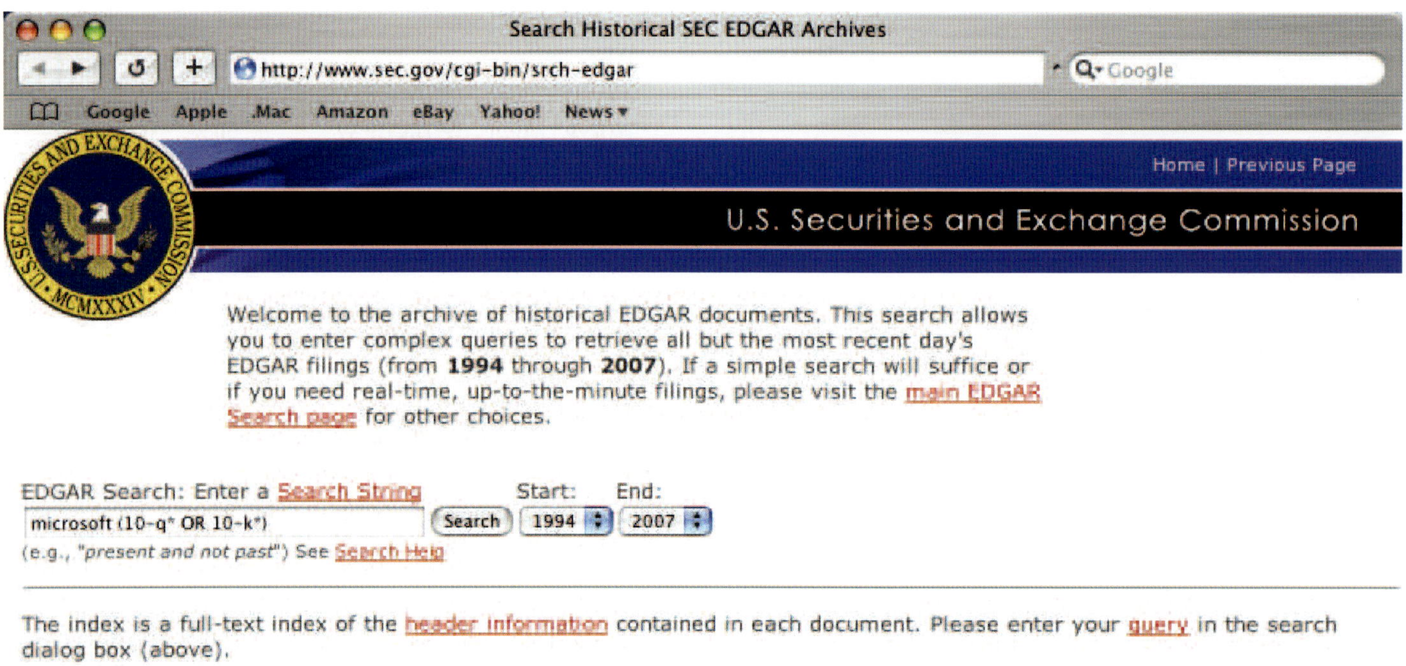

This *EDGAR* window gives you the shortest list that includes the *Quarterly* and *Annual Reports* and *Amendments (A)* you want. Find *ANNUAL REPORT (10-K) 2004–06–30 (Filing Date 2004–09–01)*. Get "Filing Documents" by pressing "Format, html".

Search Historical SEC EDGAR Archives

http://www.sec.gov/cgi-bin/srch-edgar?text=microsoft+%2810-q*+OR+10-k*

Google Apple .Mac Amazon eBay Yahoo! News

Home | Previous Page

U.S. Securities and Exchange Commission

Welcome to the archive of historical EDGAR documents. This search allows you to enter complex queries to retrieve all but the most recent day's EDGAR filings (from **1994** through **2007**). If a simple search will suffice or if you need real-time, up-to-the-minute filings, please visit the main EDGAR Search page for other choices.

EDGAR Search: Enter a Search String — microsoft (10-q* OR 10-k*) — Search — Start: 1994 — End: 2007

(e.g., "*cik = 0000222222*") See Search Help

SEC Home | EDGAR Search Home

Your search matched **58** documents.
58 are presented.

No.	Company	Format	Form Type	Filing Date	Size
1000	MICROSOFT CORP	[text] [html]	10-Q	01/25/2007	592390
1000	MICROSOFT CORP	[text] [html]	10-Q	10/26/2006	469162
1000	MICROSOFT CORP	[text] [html]	10-K	08/25/2006	1307904
1000	MICROSOFT CORP	[text] [html]	10-Q	04/27/2006	722554
1000	MICROSOFT CORP	[text] [html]	10-Q/A	03/03/2006	48513
1000	MICROSOFT CORP	[text] [html]	10-Q	01/26/2006	706375
1000	MICROSOFT CORP	[text] [html]	10-Q	10/27/2005	505735
1000	MICROSOFT CORP	[text] [html]	10-K	08/26/2005	1180419
1000	MICROSOFT CORP	[text] [html]	10-Q	04/28/2005	611112
1000	MICROSOFT CORP	[text] [html]	10-Q	01/27/2005	619877
1000	MICROSOFT CORP	[text] [html]	10-Q	11/09/2004	421207
1000	MICROSOFT CORP	[text] [html]	10-K	09/01/2004	1479205
1000	MICROSOFT CORP	[text] [html]	10-Q	05/03/2004	606269
1000	MICROSOFT CORP	[text] [html]	10-Q	02/06/2004	721303
1000	MICROSOFT CORP	[text] [html]	10-Q	11/13/2003	374581

This *EDGAR* window displays "Filing Documents" you want. Some companies make you hunt through the list. Microsoft makes it easy. To get their "FORM 10-K", press on the "Document, d10k.htm".

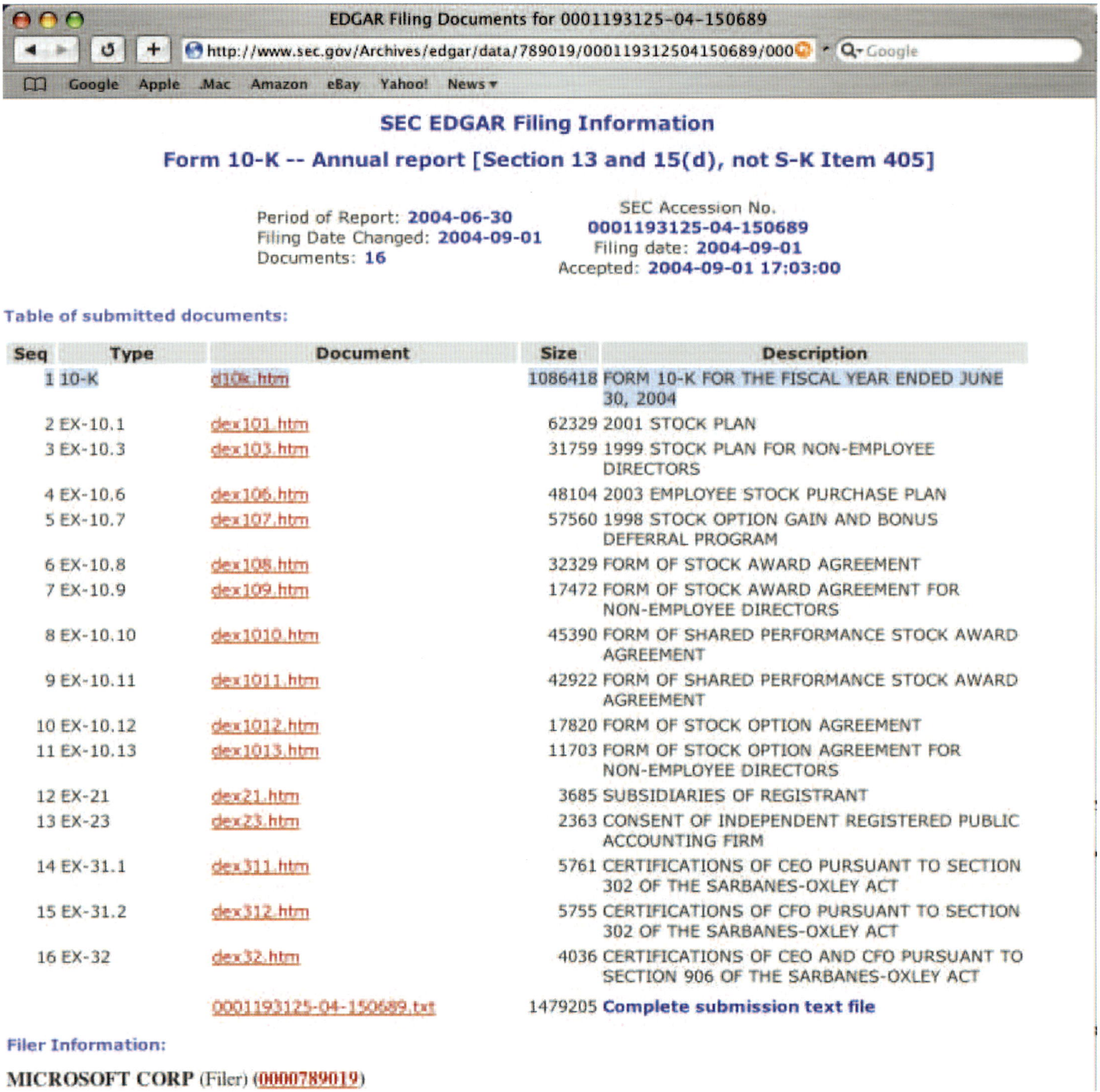

EDGAR Filing Documents for 0001193125-04-150689

http://www.sec.gov/Archives/edgar/data/789019/000119312504150689/000

Google Apple .Mac Amazon eBay Yahoo! News

SEC EDGAR Filing Information

Form 10-K -- Annual report [Section 13 and 15(d), not S-K Item 405]

Period of Report: **2004-06-30**
Filing Date Changed: **2004-09-01**
Documents: **16**

SEC Accession No.
0001193125-04-150689
Filing date: **2004-09-01**
Accepted: **2004-09-01 17:03:00**

Table of submitted documents:

Seq	Type	Document	Size	Description
1	10-K	d10k.htm	1086418	FORM 10-K FOR THE FISCAL YEAR ENDED JUNE 30, 2004
2	EX-10.1	dex101.htm	62329	2001 STOCK PLAN
3	EX-10.3	dex103.htm	31759	1999 STOCK PLAN FOR NON-EMPLOYEE DIRECTORS
4	EX-10.6	dex106.htm	48104	2003 EMPLOYEE STOCK PURCHASE PLAN
5	EX-10.7	dex107.htm	57560	1998 STOCK OPTION GAIN AND BONUS DEFERRAL PROGRAM
6	EX-10.8	dex108.htm	32329	FORM OF STOCK AWARD AGREEMENT
7	EX-10.9	dex109.htm	17472	FORM OF STOCK AWARD AGREEMENT FOR NON-EMPLOYEE DIRECTORS
8	EX-10.10	dex1010.htm	45390	FORM OF SHARED PERFORMANCE STOCK AWARD AGREEMENT
9	EX-10.11	dex1011.htm	42922	FORM OF SHARED PERFORMANCE STOCK AWARD AGREEMENT
10	EX-10.12	dex1012.htm	17820	FORM OF STOCK OPTION AGREEMENT
11	EX-10.13	dex1013.htm	11703	FORM OF STOCK OPTION AGREEMENT FOR NON-EMPLOYEE DIRECTORS
12	EX-21	dex21.htm	3685	SUBSIDIARIES OF REGISTRANT
13	EX-23	dex23.htm	2363	CONSENT OF INDEPENDENT REGISTERED PUBLIC ACCOUNTING FIRM
14	EX-31.1	dex311.htm	5761	CERTIFICATIONS OF CEO PURSUANT TO SECTION 302 OF THE SARBANES-OXLEY ACT
15	EX-31.2	dex312.htm	5755	CERTIFICATIONS OF CFO PURSUANT TO SECTION 302 OF THE SARBANES-OXLEY ACT
16	EX-32	dex32.htm	4036	CERTIFICATIONS OF CEO AND CFO PURSUANT TO SECTION 906 OF THE SARBANES-OXLEY ACT
		0001193125-04-150689.txt	1479205	**Complete submission text file**

Filer Information:

MICROSOFT CORP (Filer) (0000789019)

This *EDGAR* window displays the "FORM 10-K" you want. Now you want to find "quarterly information". Use your "Find" tool. If your operating system or browser is different from ours, your "Find" tool will look different from our sample pop up. The table may be headed "QUARTERLY INFORMATION". "Quarter" might work for other companies. Some companies don't label their quarterly data, so you have to scroll through the "FORM 10-K" until you find it.

Microsoft makes your search easy. In your "Find" tool, enter "quarterly information". Go to "quarterly information" by pressing "Next".

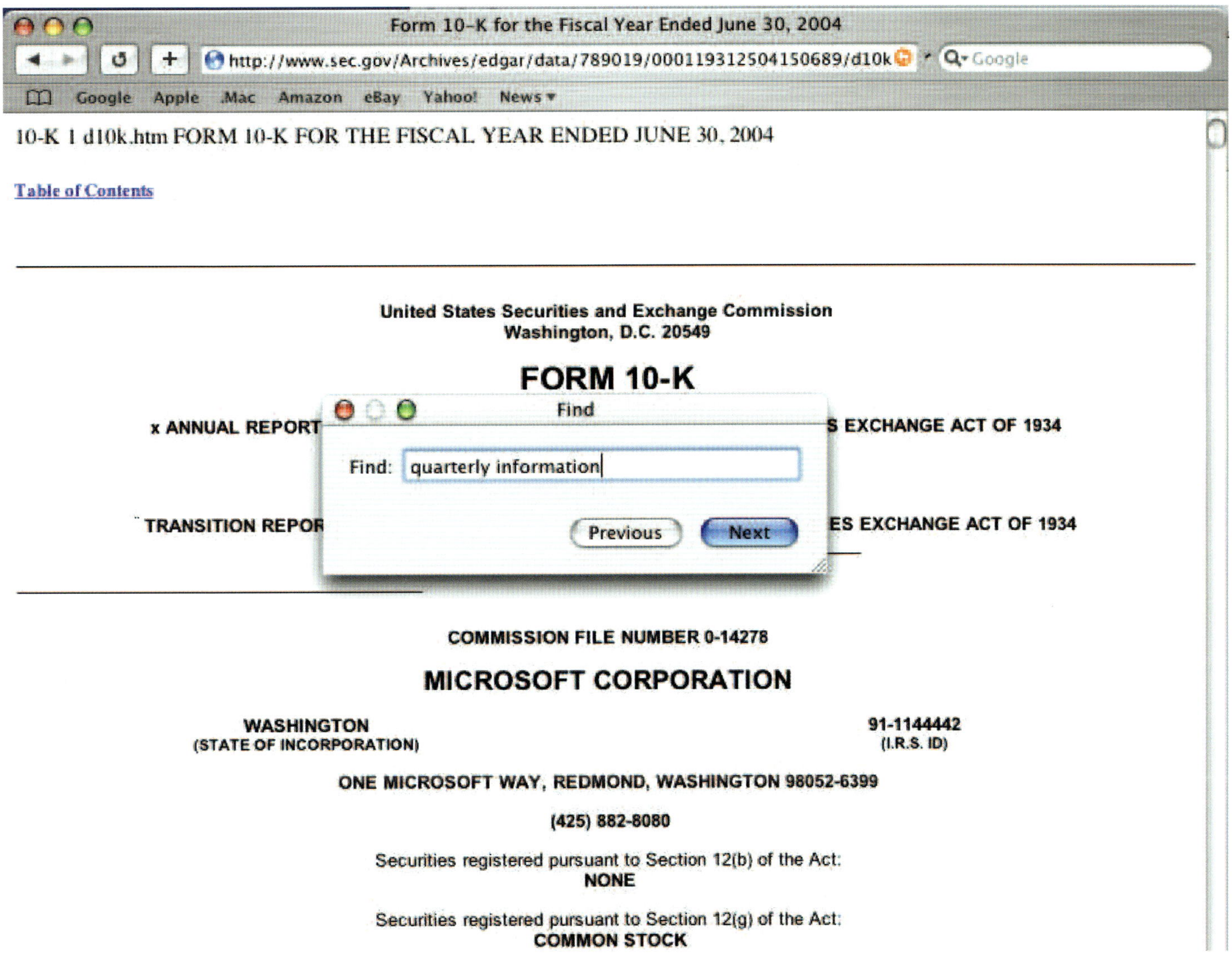

MICROSOFT

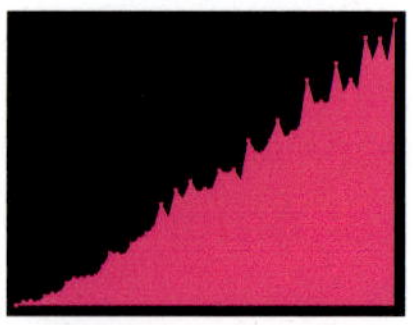

Revenue Quarterly

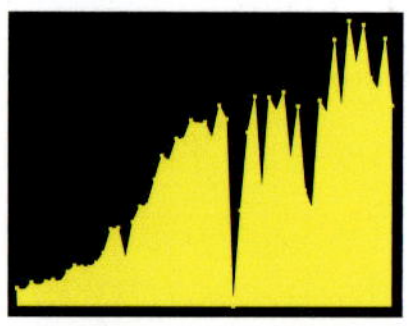

Income Quarterly

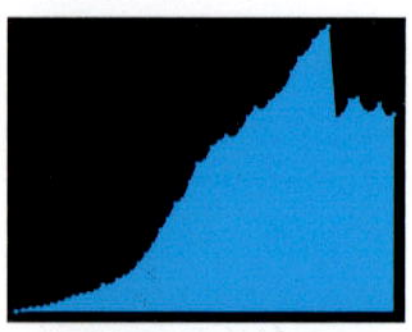

Assets Quarterly

Equity Quarterly

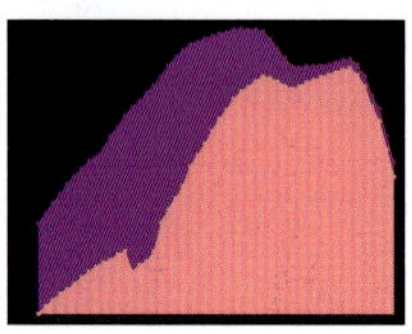

Shares Quarterly

This *EDGAR* window shows some *information* you want for your *Quarterly Data Summary* *ANNUAL REPORT (10-K) 2004-06-30 (Filing Date 2004-09-01)*: Revenue 9.292B and Income 2.690B.

In your "Find" tool, enter "balance sheets" and go to the table that displays Assets 92.389B and Equity 74.825B. (B is billions.)

In your "Find" tool, enter "income statements" and go to the table that displays Shares Diluted 10.894B and Shares Basic 10.803B.

"QUARTERLY INFORMATION" below displays three of nine items in our *Quarterly Data Summary*—date, revenue, income. It takes only one table for a company to update its *Quarterly Data Summary* back to 1993 in every new *Quarterly* and *Annual Report*. Someday on the Internet you'll enter a symbol like *MSFT*, select *Net Profit Margin*, and view its chart. Beyond that day, you'll give a cell phone voice command, "MSFT, Net Profit Margin", and instantly see its chart.

We are grateful to Arthur Levitt and his team for their vision to bring us the data we need to see company evolution. Now, Christopher Cox and Microsoft can boldly and quickly make the next paradigm shift. They can begin every *Quarterly* and *Annual Report* with a downloadable *Quarterly Data Summary* back to 1993, including share price and *S&P* price, in *eXtensible Business Reporting Language* (*XBRL*) format—so we can all make informed investment decisions.

Form 10-K for the Fiscal Year Ended June 30, 2004

http://www.sec.gov/Archives/edgar/data/789019/000119312504150689/d10k.htm

Google Apple .Mac Amazon eBay Yahoo! News

Part II
Item 8

QUARTERLY INFORMATION

(In millions, except per share amounts) (Unaudited)

Quarter Ended	**Sep. 30**	**Dec. 31**	**Mar. 31**	**June 30**	**Total**
Fiscal 2003					
Revenue	$ 7,746	$ 8,541	$ 7,835	$ 8,065	$ 32,187
Gross profit	6,402	6,404	6,561	6,761	26,128
Net income	2,041	1,865	2,142	1,483(1)	7,531
Basic earnings per share	0.19	0.17	0.20	0.14	0.70
Diluted earnings per share	0.19	0.17	0.20	0.14	0.69
Fiscal 2004					
Revenue	**$ 8,215**	**$ 10,153**	**$ 9,175**	**$ 9,292**	**$ 36,835**
Gross profit	**6,735**	**7,809**	**7,764**	**7,811**	**30,119**
Net income	**2,614**	**1,549(2)**	**1,315(3)**	**2,690**	**8,168**
Basic earnings per share	**0.24**	**0.14**	**0.12**	**0.25**	**0.76**
Diluted earnings per share	**0.24**	**0.14**	**0.12**	**0.25**	**0.75**

(1) Includes charges of $750 million (pre-tax) related to the Time Warner settlement and $1.15 billion in impairments of investments.
(2) Includes stock-based compensation charges of $2.2 billion for the employee stock option transfer program.
(3) Includes charges of $2.53 billion (pre-tax) related to the Sun Microsystems Inc. settlement and a fine imposed by the European Commission.

PAGE 63

MICROSOFT

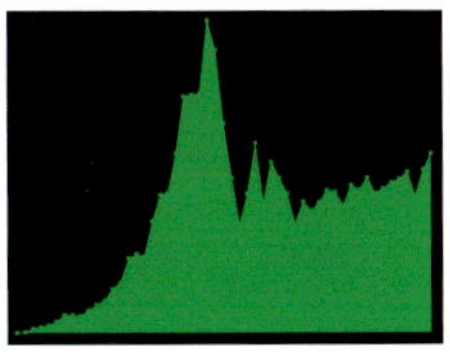

Price Quarterly

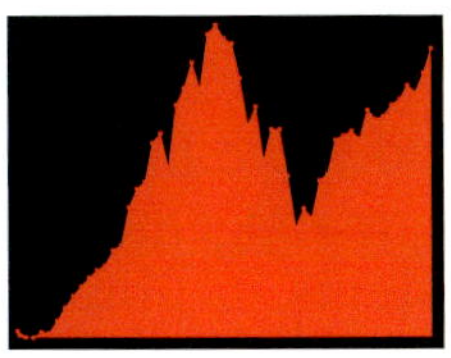

S&P Price Quarterly

This *Yahoo* window shows *Historical Prices*. In your browser, enter **http://finance.yahoo.com/q/hp?s=MSFT** To see all dates and prices in one table, scroll to and select "Download To Spreadsheet".

You want quarter-end, split-adjusted close price—within the quarter, nearest its end. In the downloaded spreadsheet, scroll to our date, *ANNUAL REPORT (10-K) 2004–06–30 (Not the Filing Date 2004–09–01)*—or the date within the quarter, nearest to our date. From the column headed "Adj Close", get the price for that date.

The last data-item you need is *Standard & Poor's Index* split-adjusted close price. Repeat the procedure above. In your browser, enter **http://finance.yahoo.com/q/hp?s=^GSPC** The circumflex (^) symbol, usually found on the numeric row of the keyboard, must precede *GSPC*.

You may believe you can get all the data for our *inside front cover Quarterly Data Summary* from financial websites, publications, or advisors. Our book can help make that a reality. Now, thanks to the efforts of many people, you're ready to use the tools we've shown you to build the *Quarterly Data Summary* for your company, and to evaluate if and when you will invest in that company's evolution.

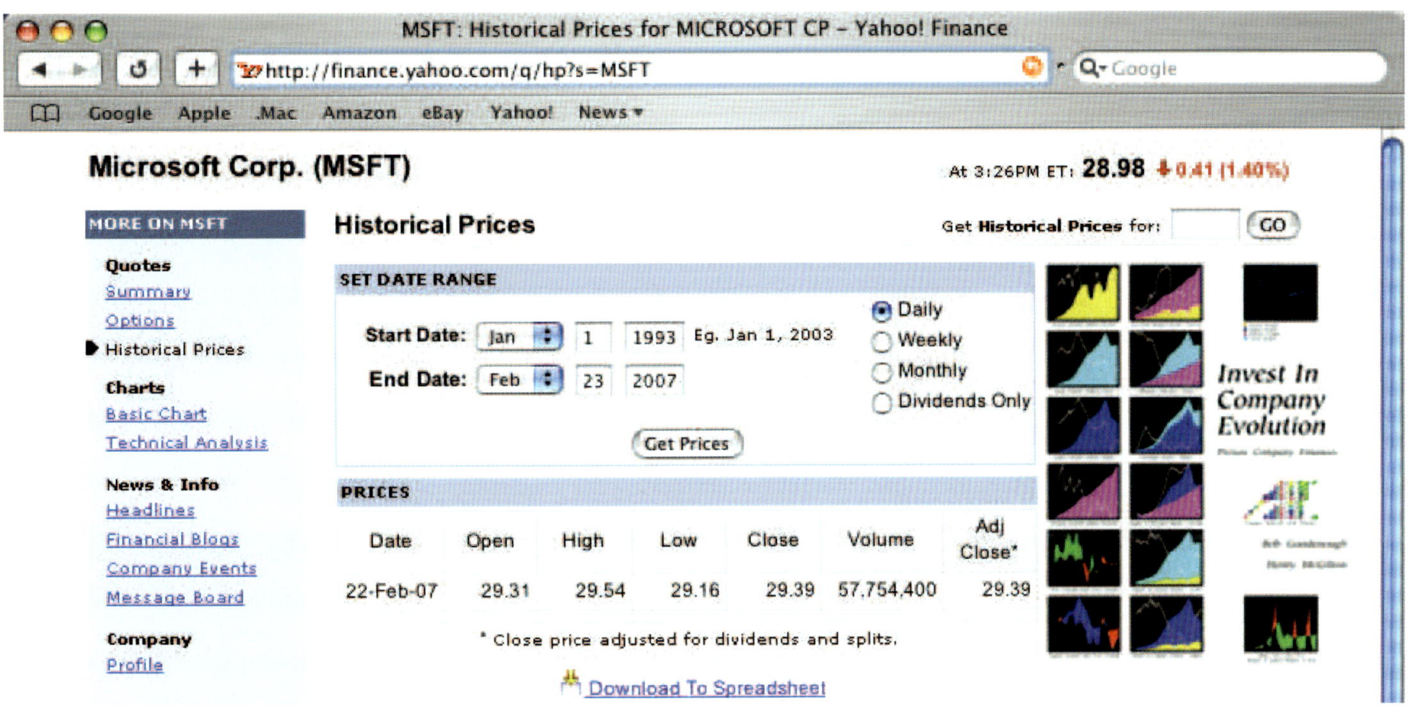

A Further Reading

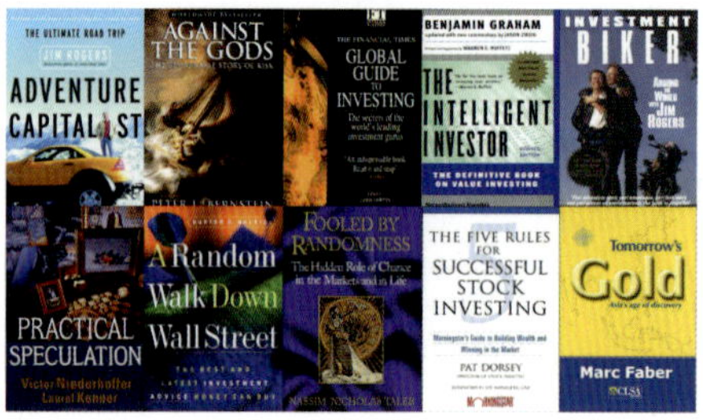

I've got a little list.
    I've got a little list.

Gilbert and Sullivan—*The Mikado*

Between us, we reckon we have read around three hundred books on finance, investing, trading, risk management, money management, inquiring systems, decision systems, truthful and persuasive visual displays, and the psychology of making money.

Additionally, we have read thousands of magazine and newspaper articles on all aspects of finance, investing, commodities, futures, options, derivatives, fundamental and technical analyses, and so on.

We believe that in the process of constructing our bibliography we have identified a few of those writers whose concepts make sense to us. Because our list is extensive, we suggest that you scan our reflections and start with the work that interests you most.

Investing

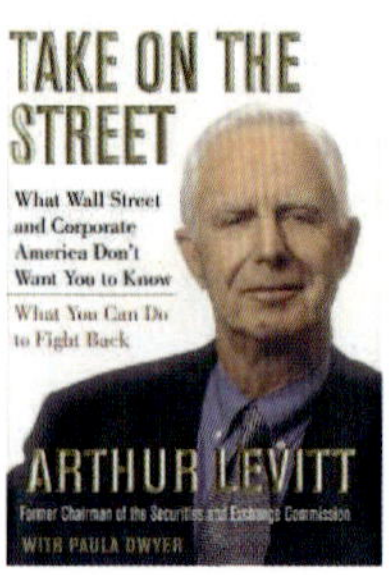

Take On The Street

How to Fight for Your Financial Future

Arthur Levitt—Former Chairman of the *Securities and Exchange Commission*—brought us free and easy Internet access to the data that is the starting point for making astute investment decisions. He reformed the regulations to better level the playing field on which honest small investors think. He reveals the high-view of dynamics that shape investing. He prepares us to make responsible decisions.

Arthur Levitt's vision, leadership, data, and reforms affect us all. His human story is of people who have prevailed in the face of opposition. Arthur Levitt worked with President Clinton, Congress, the Securities and Exchange Commission, company leaders, and investors to shape the context of investment today. He describes the truth behind investing, and achievements that created a more honest investment environment. He prepares us to act courageously. Once you have read Arthur Levitt's story, all your investment reading and investing will have a deeper, more useful, personal meaning.

Testimony of Ray Kurzweil on the Societal Implications of Nanotechnology

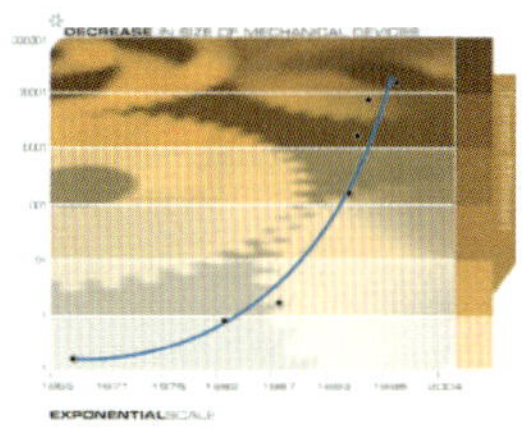

Decrease in Size of Mechanical Devices

Ray Kurzweil, in "Testimony presented April 9, 2003 at the Committee on Science, U.S. House of Representatives Hearing" addresses issues of nanotechnology that directly impact investing—inevitable miniaturization enabling investors to gain instant access to evaluations using Arthur Levitt's data for informed investment decisions:

> Despite calls to relinquish research in nanotechnology, we will have no choice but to confront the challenge of guiding nanotechnology in a constructive direction. Advances in nanotechnology and related advanced technologies are inevitable. Any broad attempt to relinquish nanotechnology will only push it underground, which would interfere with the benefits while actually making the dangers worse.

MICROSOFT (MSFT)

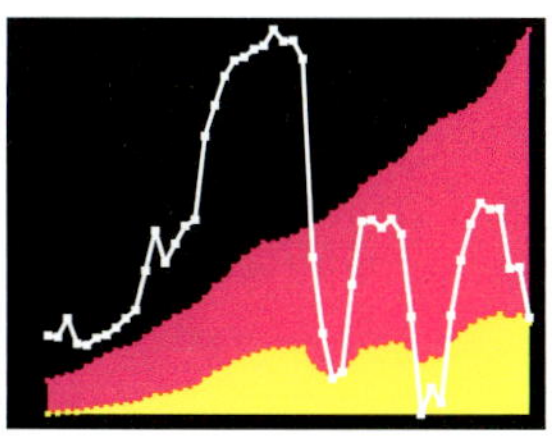

Net Profit Margin

Look at our small charts *versus* the size of your mobile telephone screen. In the foreseeable future, an investor could say: "MSFT Net Profit Margin", and see a trend chart on the screen. Then, investors will have a lot of questions. Guiding investors and their companies toward mutually constructive use of full information could strengthen our economy with less volatile, healthier markets. Before doubting, look seriously at Kurzweil's overwhelming long-term experience in many related fields. Then, look at your own experience, to realize what he says is true.

Triumph of the Optimists

101 Years of Global Investment Returns

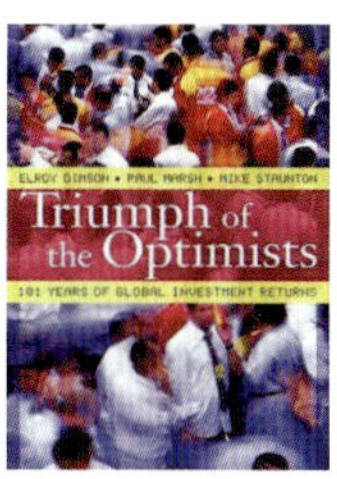

Optimism is more likely to triumph when reasoning is built on facts. The United States market has in fact grown to be the largest globally, and exhibits unique characteristics.

Elroy Dimson, *Paul Marsh*, and *Mike Staunton* provide a 1900–2000 perspective on global market returns. Their specific history of different economic regions offers persuasive evidence that these markets are unique—not just clones of the United States market, which the authors identify as an exception. The authors drive home the point that assuming all markets are similar is like extrapolating the future from the past. Profitable diversification of your portfolio into these markets is earned through careful study of unique characteristics, not unfounded assumptions.

In *Take On The Street*, Arthur Levitt shows us investing through the exceptional dynamics of the United States market—and his remarkable influence to make it fair. In *The Societal Implications of Nanotechnology*, Ray Kurzweil shows us different futures through the evolution of technologies that drive accelerating growth, rather than through specific companies and markets. In *Triumph of the Optimists*, London Business School's Dimson, Marsh, and Staunton show us investing in unique global markets through the historical facts that shape these opportunities.

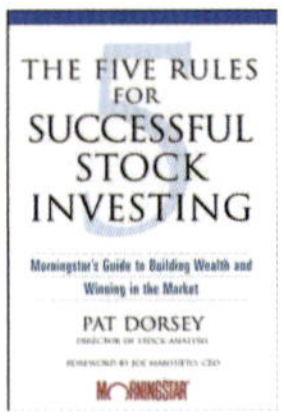

The Five Rules for Successful Stock Investing

By *Pat Dorsey*—former Director of Stock Analysis at Morningstar, the Chicago-based fund-rating company—this is arguably one of the best books on investing principles that we have read to date.

The first twelve chapters of this book give you a set of simple rules, plus specific applications of those rules, by examining various aspects of companies. Most of the rest of the book is devoted to examinations of unique characteristics of specific industries, discussing investment factors you should look for in a given industry.

The Four Pillars of Investing

Lessons for Building a Winning Portfolio

By *William Bernstein*, *The Four Pillars of Investing* offers a comprehensive, incisive, and pithy treatment of the issues. In a relaxed, nonthreatening style, Dr. Bernstein provides a distinctive blend of market history, investing theory, and behavioral finance, one designed to help every investor become more self-sufficient and make better informed investment decisions. *The Four Pillars of Investing* explains how any investor can build a solid foundation for investing by focusing on four essential lessons, each building upon the other.

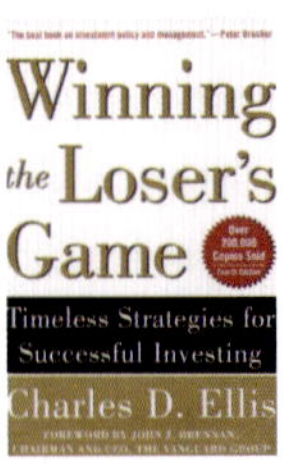

Winning the Loser's Game

Timeless Strategies for Successful Investing

Charles Ellis's Winning the Loser's Game tells you that the huge rise in institutional investment firms such as mutual funds has changed the investment process from a winner's game to a loser's game.

The "game" played by "professional" money managers is the game of "Beat the Market". But, the fund industry has grown so big that it *is* the market, and therefore, by definition, they are trying to beat themselves. You as an individual cannot hope to play "their" game and win. To win, you have to ignore "them" and play your own game. Charles Ellis shows you how.

More Than You Know

Finding Financial Wisdom in Unconventional Places

Michael J. Mauboussin gathered his collection of unusual essays in a newsletter titled *The Consilient Observer* while he was at Credit Suisse. Mauboussin believes (and we concur) that investing needs to be approached as a multi-disciplinary field of study, covering widely disparate fields of endeavour. The major areas of *More Than You Know* cover *Investment Philosophy*, *Psychology Of Investing*, *Innovation and Competitive Strategy*, *Science and Complexity Theory*.

Decades ago, science fiction author A. E. Van Vogt (writing in *The Space Beagle*) defined a science of *Nexialism*, as "the science of joining together in an orderly fashion the knowledge of one field of learning with that of other fields". Michael Mauboussin has brought science fiction to real life with his notions of consilience.

Our Brave New World

Is a thought-provoking book by *GaveKal Research* of Hong Kong: *Charles Gave, Anatole Kaletsky,* and *Louis-Vincent Gave*. They argue that new paradigms of design and manufacturing are creating what they denote "Platform Companies"—United States companies that perform high-value design and marketing, while manufacturing is done by out-sourcing. In the more pithy words of Andy Kessler in *Running Money*, "We Think, They Sweat". More optimistically, as has happened in Japan and India and is happening in Russia, people who take the opportunity to do sweat work may create the opportunities in their homelands to do thinking work. *Our Brave New World* is another must-read book, as it challenges many of the current doom and gloom scenarios espoused by economists and analysts who are analyzing the last economic cycle.

The Only Three Questions That Count

Investing by Knowing What Others Don't

The Only Three Questions That Count is the provocative latest book by money manager *Ken Fisher*. We say "provocative" because Fisher spends much time shooting down large areas of "conventional wisdom". A constant theme throughout is the notion that United States investors can no longer consider the United States in isolation from the increasingly global economy—what's happening overseas simply *must* be taken into account along with what's happening in the United States. We were pleasantly surprised to find many insightful ideas and "points to ponder" throughout the book. Any serious investor should read *The Only Three Questions That Count* and be ready for some intellectually challenging eye-openers.

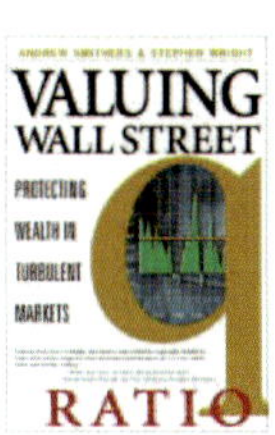

Valuing Wall Street

Protecting Wealth In Turbulent Markets

By Andrew Smithers and Stephen Wright, presents a way to value Wall Street as an objective stardard within which we can value individual stocks and even technology. Without this reality check, euphoria and anxiety can run wild.

With sane practicality, Smithers and Wright lay out "the need for an objective standard" to value Wall Street, and four tests for choosing an indicator: "an indicator of value must be measurable", "the ratio of price to fundamental value must mean-revert", "an indicator of value must make economic sense", "an indicator of value must tell you something (but not too much) about future stock returns".

Once you have a way to grasp the historical value of Wall Street, you have one context within which to consider the value of a company's stock. More importantly, you have a context within which to curb the human tendency to extrapolate the future from the past.

The Education of a Speculator
and
Practical Speculation

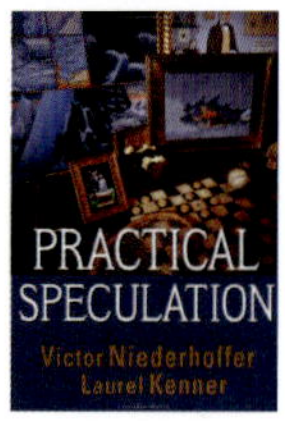

In these two books by *Victor Niederhoffer*, you gain a multi-spectral view of just about every field of thought that involves chance, speculation, statistical analyses, strategic thinking in fields such as chess and chequers, and more.

Practical Speculation, co-authored with *Laurel Kenner*, teaches scatter plots, back-of-the-envelope estimation, propaganda techniques for pulling the wool over the eyes of individual investors, spurious correlations, and many more topics.

The Financial Times Global Guide to Investing

Secrets of the World's Leading Investment Gurus

Editor *James Morton* put together a great book of essays and articles from some of the best brains in the investment business. The book is organised into seven sections, with topics ranging from *Surveying the Investment Spectrum* through *Building Blocks* for successful investing to *Learning from Living Legends*.

Contrarian Investment Strategies

The Next Generation

By *David Dreman, Beat the Market by Going Against the Crowd*, examines "Value Investing" through rational arguments for profiting from irrational share prices. He formulates strategies for contrarian investment, buying and selling stocks by going against prevailing investor opinion. He works through forty-one factors such as stock performance, volatility, and analyst opinions.

Unconventional Success

A Fundamental Approach To Personal Investment

Unconventional Success builds on a saying from John Maynard Keynes: "Worldly wisdom teaches that it is better for reputation to fail conventionally than to succeed unconventionally". In this book, author *David Swensen* takes a hard, critical look at the mutual fund "industry". Swensen contends that the majority of mutual fund companies concentrate on growing their asset base, when they should be focussing instead on growing the wealth of their shareholders.

Investing In Small Cap Stocks

Small Capitalization Stocks are a market segment all to themselves, with their own sets of behavior and difficulties. In this compact book, packed with useful advice, *Christopher Graja and Elizabeth Ungar*—editors for *Bloomberg* magazines—acknowledge the greater intrinsic volatility of small-cap stocks but maintain that sound investment strategies of small company equities can be more lucrative than investment in large-cap stocks.

Investment Intelligence from Insider Trading

By *H. Nejat Seyhun*, the "Insider Trading" in the title of the book is emphatically *not* the type of "Insider Trading" that sent various luminaries to jail. Rather, it is a rigorous academic study of your expected returns if you invest alongside publicly disclosed trades of corporate officers and directors.

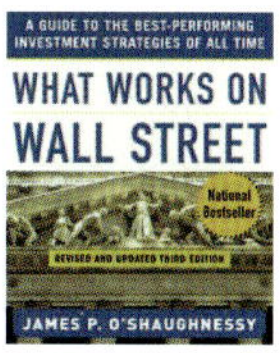

What Works on Wall Street

By *James P. O'Shaughnessy*, and sub-titled *A Guide to the Best-Performing Investment Strategies of All Time*, this book leads you through an analysis of a variety of financial measures you can use to determine potential future returns in the stock market.

After you've read O'Shaughnessy, you'll recognize a strategy when you see one. You'll see immediately which strategies are quantifiable. Most importantly, you'll see the components of a strategy and think more clearly about their contribution to your evaluation.

The Art of Short Selling

Kathryn Staley, leads you through the thickets and hedges of the fine art of "Buy High, Sell Low". Selling short is more difficult in many ways than being "long"—the notion of "Buy Cheap, Sell Dear". Quite apart from the long-term ten percent per annum upward drift of the stock market, would-be short sellers are confronted by a variety of regulatory barriers: problems such as margin requirements and sudden call-ins beset the short seller. In her book, Kathryn Staley does a great job of explaining how to go about finding flaws, over-valuations, or downright fraud in a business when its share prices are high and prior to a collapse.

General Interest

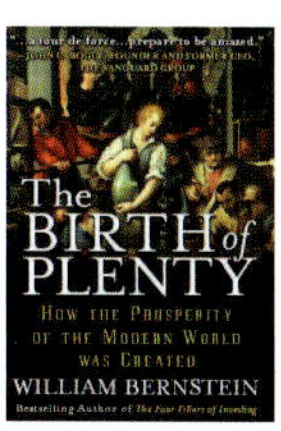

The Birth of Plenty

How the Prosperity of the Modern World was Created

By *William Bernstein*, this book leads us to conclude we are extremely fortunate to live in the age of plenty of today. Mr. Bernstein, reading from a huge variety of sources, starts with the somewhat startling notion that prior to about 1820, economic growth in the world had been essentially flat for all of the millennia of human existence. He goes on from there to examine why the situation altered so radically after that time, bringing more progress in two hundred years than in the past forty centuries.

Against The Gods

The Remarkable Story of Risk

Any investment—whether it be time or money—carries with it some notion of *risk*. In this superb book, *Peter Bernstein* takes us from the ancient Greeks, through renaissance painters and early examinations of gambling, chronicling luminaries such as Fibonacci, Cardano, Blaise Pascal, Edmund Halley, Francis Galton and into modern times of John von Neumann, and Harry Markowitz. This book is a fascinating journey from an era where neither probability theory nor risk were understood, to our present-day financial system.

Engines of Tomorrow

How the World's Best Companies Are Using Their Research Labs to Win the Future

By *Robert Buderi*, *Engines of Tomorrow* is a wonderful narrative, very much in the style of James Burke in *Connections*. Buderi makes a good case—reinforced by the work of Nobel Prize winner Robert Solow—that Research and Development activities are what actually drive the increase in capital wealth over long periods. Robert Buderi is a Vannevar Bush Fellow at MIT, former Editor in Chief of MIT's *Technology Review* magazine, former *BusinessWeek* technology editor, and the author of *The Invention That Changed the World*.

A Random Walk Down Wall Street

By *Burton Malkiel*, the first edition of *Random Walk* appeared in 1973. In the original edition, Malkiel debunked both fundamental analysis *and* technical analysis. The author has seen no reason to change his views in the intervening thirty years.

Fooled By Randomness
The Hidden Role of Chance In the Markets and in Life

Nassim Nicholas Taleb argues that we grossly under-estimate the role that chance plays in our lives. He constructs a table of opposites, in which people confuse luck with skill, anecdote with causality, the lucky idiot believes he is a skilled investor, noise (and news) is confused with real data, and in general points out how people are ill-equipped to deal with the vagaries of the *Goddess Fortuna*.

Riding the Millennial Storm

By *Nury Vittachi*, columnist for the *South China Morning Post* of Hong Kong, this book is a biography and commentary of *Marc Faber*—better known as "Doctor Doom". Faber is a well known international investment advisor—now based in Chiengmai, Thailand, with offices in Hong Kong—whose commentaries on markets and economies appear monthly in the *Gloom, Boom, and Doom Report*.

Tomorrow's Gold
Asia's Age of Discovery

By *Marc Faber*, guides you through analysis of where *tomorrow's gold*—the high-performing asset classes of the future—may be found. Faber argues that Asia's mass of three billion people will have profound affects on the world, and thus that present-day areas of the richest cities and nations are less than likely to retain their positions in the future.

Market Wizards *and* **New Market Wizards**

Created by *Jack Schwager*, these books focus primarily on commodities, futures, and currencies, with a few references to stock markets.

The books consist of interviews with a wide variety of traders acknowledged to be among the best in the world. You could read these books many times, and gain new insights on each fresh reading. Given the highly quantitative nature of the financial markets, the biggest surprise you get from these books is the strong focus on psychology and human behavior traits.

Stock Market Wizards

Jack Schwager returns with a relatively recent (2001) *Stock Market Wizards* book, this time concentrated primarily on a collection of investors who have made their names in the stock markets. What is truly remarkable about the interviews is the wide range of methodologies employed by the various investors, even when they arrive at similar results.

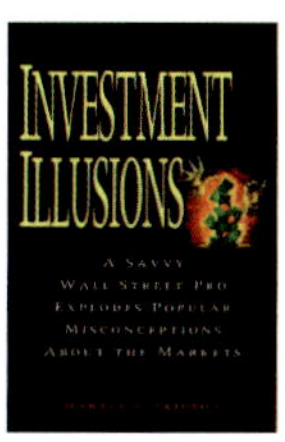

Investment Illusions

By *Martin Fridson*, author of *Financial Statement Analysis*, this humorous book leads you through a series of skeptical looks at various investment cliches. Starting with the first part of the book titled *Why Bad Things Happen to Good Investment Strategies*, you read through chapters with eye-catching titles such as *How to Run a Boiler Room*, *Pass the Trash*, *Buzzwords and BOMFOG*, *Incentive-Debased Pay*, and *The Deficient Market Hypothesis*.

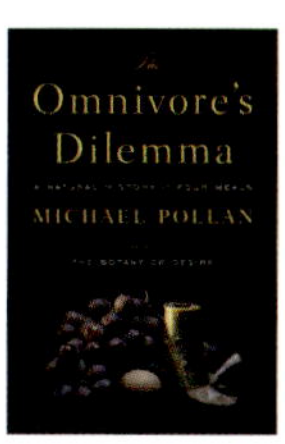

The Omnivore's Dilemma

Michael Pollan asks about identifying mushrooms what investors ask about any investment strategy—How can we develop our abilities to identify what we want? For example, one of Buffett's recommendations is to identify companies that are excellent, monopolies, and misappraised. In a few brief passages, Pollan elicits our memories of related experiences with which we can all identify. He encourages us along our journey from seeing nothing, through wonder, tools for identification, and accumulated wisdom, to the excitement of discovery, casting away fear, and arriving at our own confidence:

> I stared, but still saw nothing but a chaotic field of tan leaves and tangled branches. Angelo got down on his knees and brushed the leaves and soil away to reveal a bright and squash-colored trumpet the size of his fist.
>
> Either they had just popped up or visual perception is a lot more variable, and psychological, than we think.
>
> My ability to see mushrooms seemed to function less like a window than a tool, a constructed and wielded thing.

> As the case of mushrooms suggests the omnivore's dilemma often comes down to a question of identification—to knowing exactly what it is you are preparing to eat.
>
> The field guides contain our culture's accumulated wisdom on the subject of mushrooms.

Finally, in one eloquently sweeping passage, Michael Pollan gathers the wisdom mushroom hunters offer investors:

> Our ability to identify plants and fungi with confidence, which after all is one of the most crucial tools of our survival, involves far more sensory information than can ever be printed on a page; it is, truly, a form of `body knowledge´ not easily reduced or conveyed over a distance. But now that I have held a freshly picked chanterelle in my hands, smelled its apricoty scent, registered its specific heft and the precise quality of its cool dampness (and absorbed who knows how many other qualities beneath the threshold of conscious notice), I'll recognize the next one without a moment's hesitation. At least in the case of this one species, my mycophobic instinct has been stilled, allowing me to enjoy. It's not every day you acquire such a sturdy piece of knowledge.

An Inconvenient Truth

The Planetary Emergency Of Global Warming And What We Can Do About It

You might wonder why we are including former vice-president Al Gore's award-winning book (and documentary) in a book on finance. Well, it's not just your future financial success that's in doubt—it's your future existence.

The United States had two opportunities to get off the road to global warming after 1973 and 1979, and let those opportunities slip by both times. Now we have one more—perhaps last—chance to do something useful about the problems looming in front of our faces.

On the potential upside of all these problems is the "green tech" movements led by Silicon Valley venture capitalists such as John Doerr and Vinod Khosla, among others. New, "green" technologies for energy generation will undoubtedly lead to massive investment opportunities in decades to come.

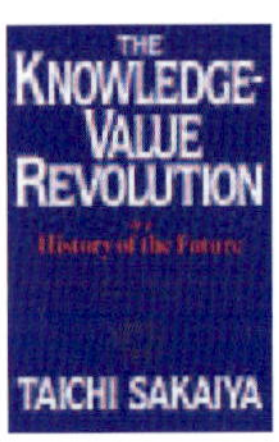

The Knowledge-Value Revolution

Or A History Of The Future

By *Taichi Sakaiya, The Knowledge-Value Revolution* "describes a society driven to consume those resources that will be most abundant in the future—knowledge and time—on a huge scale", as we read in a review by *The Asahi Shimbun*.

Sakaiya calls this "drive" an "empathic impulse". At one period in a person's life, the impulse may be to drive "gas-guzzling" vehicles. At a different period, that very same person may have an impulse to drive "fuel-efficient" vehicles.

Sakaiya hopes we will develop beyond a "herd-impulse"—to think smart and do good while doing well.

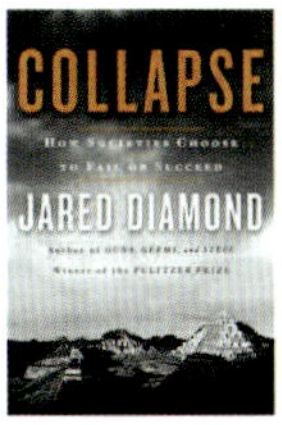

Collapse

How Societies Choose To Fail Or Succeed

By *Jared Diamond, Collapse* delivers a persuasive message of insight and personal discipline—much of our fate is in our own hands.

In his inspiring book, in his very personal style, Jared Diamond describes the vivid details of societies that have chosen and are currently choosing to fail or succeed.

Some societies apparently never saw the failing path they were creating. Some apparently saw but could imagine no way out. And some saw, imagined, and took the bold and drastic steps to success. Diamond summarizes for us what he has learned:

> For our society as a whole, the past societies that we have examined in this book suggest broader lessons. Two types of choices seem to me to have been crucial in tipping their outcomes towards success or failure: long-term planning, and willingness to reconsider core values. On reflection, we can also recognize the crucial role of these same two choices for the outcomes of our individual lives.

Jared Diamond concludes with this chilling and hopeful passage of choices and consequences:

> Our television documentaries and books show us in graphic detail why the Easter Islanders, Classic Maya, and other past societies collapsed. Thus, we have the opportunity to learn from the mistakes of distant peoples and past peoples. That's an opportunity that no past society enjoyed to such a degree. My hope in writing this book has been that enough people will choose to profit from that opportunity to make a difference.

Investment Inspirational

The Long Boom

A Vision for the Coming Age of Prosperity

By *Peter Schwartz, Peter Leyden,* and *Joel Garret, The Long Boom* appeared originally as an article in the July 1997 edition of *Wired* Magazine. Peter Schwartz and Peter Leyden (and Joel Hyatt in the book) argue that the economic boom of the late 1990s has at least another thirty years to run (albeit with corrections along the way).

Peter Schwartz founded the *Global Business Network*, and wrote *The Art of the Long View*—a well acclaimed book on Scenario Planning.

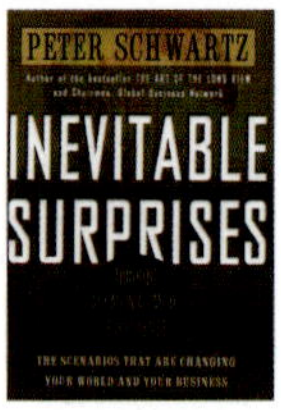

Inevitable Surprises

Thinking Ahead in a Time of Turbulence

By *Peter Schwartz, Inevitable Surprises* is the follow-on to *The Long Boom*. In this book, Schwartz debunks the notion that the near future is completely unknowable. He takes the view that there are trends unfolding around us right now, and that if we pay attention to these trends, we can find changes already underway that will shape the current century. According to Schwartz, these trends are *Inevitable Surprises*.

Investment Biker

Around the World With Jim Rogers

Author *Jim Rogers* does more than invest in *companies*—he invests in entire *countries*. In *Investment Biker*, Jim Rogers and companion spend two years and one hundred and ten thousand kilometres riding their motor bikes around the world. Reading this, you are educated in national histories, principles of economics (such as the basic laws of supply and demand), and commentaries on political systems. Written in the 1980s prior to the fall of the Soviet Union, Rogers made the prescient comment, "This place is a Third World Country with an Army and a Space Program."

Jim Rogers—along with Hungarian high finance master *George Soros*—founded the *Quantum Fund*, which was and still is an internationally renowned hedge fund that invests globally.

Real Money *and* **Mad Money**

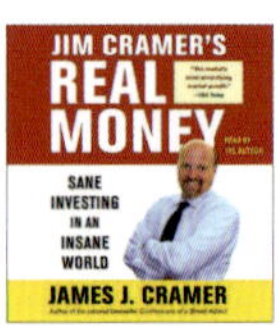

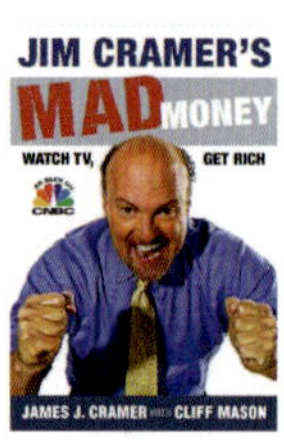

Jim Cramer is viewed by more people than any investment educator in the world. He uses his passion for the market, companies, and individuals to reveal the passions of many people. He attracts people with the quality of his advice, his understandable explanations, his flamboyant style, the recognizable leaders he challenges. His memorable words and stories present a unique view of investment, one human being's passion that stirs the passions of many.

Financial Analysis

The Visual Display of Quantitative Information

Professor Emeritus at Yale University, *Edward R. Tufte's* classic book is so important to us that it remains on our desk through years of design. Tufte defines and illustrates approaches to our obvious goals with ideas and images that are immediately applicable. Our *inside front cover Quarterly Data Summary* epitomizes our challenge:

> Only a picture can carry such a volume of data in such a small space. Furthermore, all that data, thanks to the graphic, can be thought about in many different ways at many different levels of analysis—ranging from the contemplation of general overall patterns to the detection of very fine . . . detail.

In one brief passage he dispenses with boring numbers:

> If the statistics are boring, then you've got the wrong numbers. Finding the right numbers requires as much specialized skill—statistical skill—and hard work as creating a beautiful design or covering a complex news story.

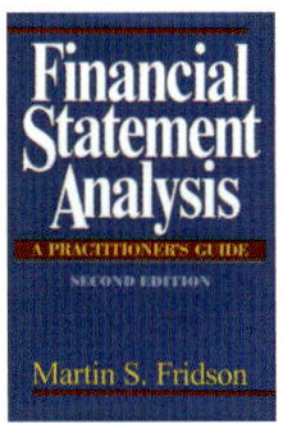

Financial Statement Analysis
A Practitioner's Guide

Martin Fridson, Fixed Income Analysts Society Hall of Fame Inductee, shows you how to read company financial statements. With real-world examples, he shows you the kinds of complications that come up when analysts apply text-book analysis to real-life number juggling on income statements, balance sheets, and other financial statements. This book demonstrates how to evaluate the facts behind the blizzard of numbers in most corporate financial reports.

We are grateful to Martin Fridson for our lengthy phone call regarding the equity growth equation. He helped us understand that net profit margin, efficiency, and leverage have limits, in contrast to income which can add continually to equity. Martin is one of those rare people whose insights actually unlock pivotal concepts.

Analysis for
Financial Management

By Professor *Robert Higgins*, this text presents standard techniques and modern developments in a practical and intuitive manner. It is intended for non-financial managers and business students interested in the practice of financial management. Emphasis is on making sense in managerial applications of financial analysis.

We are grateful to Robert Higgins for our communications on the equity growth equation. He explained that "equity change to income" presents all equity changes, not "retained income (earnings)" from a company's balance sheet. Data then worked in the equation.

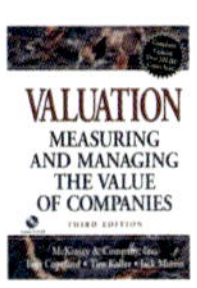

Valuation
Measuring and Managing
the Value of Companies

Tom Copeland, Tim Koller, and Jack Murrin walk you through the techniques for estimating company value, also known as fair price or fair value or intrinsic value or intrinsic business value or the present value of future cash flow. At the end of our research, we turned to *Valuation* for the fair price formula we entered into our charting tools.

These authors answered many of our questions on the topic in understandable language and gave us formulas that use electronically available data. They condense *Valuation* into one passage:

> Investors, portfolio managers, and securities analysts—These professionals should find this volume a useful guide to applying cash flow valuation approaches. This is the purest form of fundamental securities analysis since it links the value of the company directly to the economic returns it can generate from its businesses and assets.

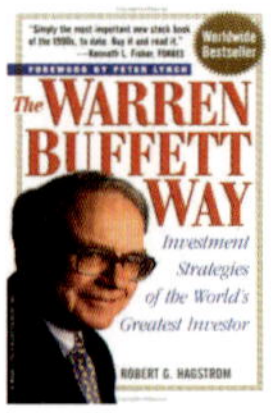

The Warren Buffett Way

Investment Strategies of the World's Greatest Investor

Robert G. Hagstrom introduces us to Warren Buffett's broad strategic framework and tenets that Buffett tests with data. Then, Robert shows how Warren applies his framework and tenets to the specific data of different companies at unique stages of their evolution.

You learn to identify different kinds of unusual circumstances using appropriate tenets. Then, you learn to apply the tenets to track that company's evolution. Hagstrom's approach to Buffett's strategy takes us far beyond simplistic, rigid routines of "right" answers and launches us into the data that supports what Buffett calls "business thinking". Hagstrom teaches not to copy but to think for yourself.

Robert Hagstrom never lets us merely settle into Warren Buffett's business thinking—but instead encourages us to continuously develop and value our own insights. Hagstrom's writing is so full of useful information that we found ourselves filling his margins with notes and eventually buying more copies to make room for more notes referenced to his ideas. Reading Robert Hagstrom inspired us to picture company finances so we could see with our own eyes.

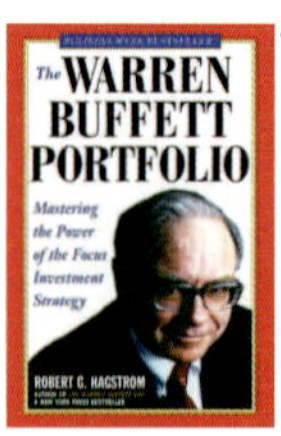

The Warren Buffett Portfolio

Mastering the Power of the Focus Investment Strategy

Robert G. Hagstrom drags us forcefully away from superstition—luck and diversification are the best bet because, when it comes to investing, people don't really know what they're doing. Instead, Hagstrom develops a powerful case for actually becoming capable of making astute investment decisions. Hagstrom essentially says, find companies worth your focus—companies you're passionate enough about to study—then, focus your learning on a handful of those outstanding companies that offer great investment opportunities.

Letters to Berkshire Shareholders
http://berkshirehathaway.com/

Warren Buffett continues to freely give his *Letters to Berkshire Shareholders*—every year since 1977. This is the largest, electronically available, annual gift of written wisdom and lessons in the global history of investing, available to the general public, managers, students, and investors.

You may wonder why we quote Buffett so often. We have several inescapable reasons. Warren's ideas are quantifiable using publicly available data from the United States *Securities and Exchange Commission (SEC)*, complying with United States *Generally Accepted Accounting Principles (GAAP)*. This data is available free using *The Get Data Riddle* on page 113. It is the only complete set of public company data presenting audited annual reports—starting in 1993—that enables Buffett to bring us closer to leveling the playing field for institutional and individual investors.

Measures Warren uses—like "owner earnings"—reflect the findings of scholars. When Warren expands a measure—like *GAAP* "income" to become "owner earnings"—he combines already existing *GAAP* measures. For example, Warren defines and applies "owner earnings" near the end of his *Letter to Berkshire Shareholders, 1986.*

Some skeptics say that Warren Buffett's concepts and principles don't apply to the individual investor because Buffett has gotten so big that he buys whole companies.

In response, we ask, "Which concepts and principles? Would it be owner earnings adding back depreciation to net income so income is closer to the income the company actually earned? Would it be per-share progress, or conservatism about acquiring debt? Would it be share price close to intrinsic value, or not taking advantage of your business partners? Or, would it be Warren Buffett's commitment of fiduciary responsibility to his shareholders?"

Most importantly, Warren Buffett's writings and investing make sense to us and represent an attempt to cooperatively benefit both the individual investor and our global society.

Owner's Manual
http://berkshirehathaway.com/

Warren Buffett begins: "At the time of the Blue Chip merger in 1983, I set down 13 owner-related business principles that I thought would help new shareholders understand our managerial approach. As is appropriate for "principles", all 13 remain alive and well today. . . . "

Investors, when they are reasonable, know that principles are more useful than rules—yet rules seem to attract people, like the proverbial moth to the flame. Buffett lays out his own principles—and leaves investors to get the point or not. He is wisely satisfied with the investor's personal answer to an ancient question: "Will you read the label, or must you drink the poison?"

"Principle 7" lays out Buffett's views on his use of debt. Never does he give a limiting number or percentage or criterion line. Yet when we grasp Buffett's explanation of his principle we have a broad and deep sense of what to do. We know to prefer a "long-term, fixed rate". We know to regularly check on our company and ourselves to see that the debt structure leaves us with a "good night's sleep".

B Words Of Wisdom

Present-Day Carthage

Some studies show that stocks always go up in the long term. If this theory were correct, any investment in the ancient centres of wealth such as Tyrus, Sidon, or Carthage—thanks to a comfortable head start of more than 2,000 years—would be worth substantially more than any investment in the United States or Japan.

At three percent compounded, one dollar invested in each of these cities would now be worth over $142,000,000,000,000,000,000,000,000. That is, one hundred and forty two trillion trillion dollars.

But in point of fact, can any of you even show me on a map where Tyrus, Sidon, and Carthage are today?

Marc Faber—*The Rise And The Fall Of Great Cities*

As in every field of human endeavour, investing and finance have accumulated a vast field of memorable (and otherwise) sayings by a variety of luminaries and would-be-luminaries.

Government

No man's life, liberty, or property are safe while the legislature is in session. *Samuel Clemens*, writing as *Mark Twain*.

Governments play their own unique roles relative to financial markets. Government policies have powerful effects on a country's economy at macro and micro levels. High interest rates, for instance, raise cost of capital for companies borrowing money, cutting into their profits. Taxation changes investors' behavior in sometimes unexpected directions. Subsidies cause price distortions (usually as higher prices to consumers). Price controls on goods eventually result in shortages of those goods, leading to higher prices.

Along with Mark Twain's implicit message above, telling Congress to continue playing golf, other commentators have caustic words for governmental bodies.

> ...People in national capitols think differently. I now believe they may be retarded in comparison to other humans.
>
> ——G. Harry Stine—*Starsea Invaders—Second Contact*

> Washington (D. C.)—300 square miles surrounded by reality. He wondered if the laws of physics even applied inside the Beltway. He had long since given up on the laws of logic.
>
> ——Tom Clancy—*The Sum of All Fears*

Even a former United States President had little regard for government:

If the Government made beer, it would cost fifty dollars for a six-pack, and it would taste bad....

——Gerald Ford, 14th July 1913–26th December 2006

In May 1945, British Labour Party fire-brand Aneurin Bevan said privation would be in the past as essentials would soon be abundant:

This island is made mainly of coal and surrounded by fish. Only an organising genius could produce a shortage of coal and fish at the same time.

——Aneurin Bevan—*British Labour Party Leader*, May 1945, reported in the *Daily Herald*.

George Will wrote, "...socialism rose to the challenge. Two years later, with the coal industry nationalised and food still rationed, coal and fish were scarce. There are indeed some things only government can do".

Value Investing

A funny thing about the stock market is that every time one man buys, another sells, and both think they are astute....

——William Feather (1889–1981)—American Author and Publisher

It is extraordinary to me that the idea of buying dollar bills for forty cents takes immediately with a person, or it doesn't take at all. It's like an inoculation. If it doesn't grab a person right away, I find that you can talk to him for years, and show him records, and it doesn't make a difference. He just doesn't seem to be able to grasp the concept simple as it is.

——Warren Buffett—the *Superinvestors of Graham-and-Doddsville*, 1984

First-class investment performance cannot be measured on a quarterly or annual basis. Outstanding investors don't work that way.

——Charles Ellis, Greenwich Associates 1987.

Accurate Data

If you torture data sufficiently, it will confess to almost anything.

——Fred Menger

Because of their unique financial structure, you could quote Berkshire's book value to the nearest hundred dollars without giving up much precision.

Obtaining accurate data is important, but at the same time, you need to view presented data with a skeptical eye.

For example, a well-known financial web site reported the ***book value*** (equity per share) of Berkshire Hathaway (Warren Buffett's enterprise) as $55,779.222656 per share. Carrying the amount to six decimal places might appear impressive, except when you realize that 22.2656 cents is 0.0004 of $55,000.†

† Okay, okay, if you ***absolutely insist***, it's really 0.000404829.

Attention to too-precise reporting is addressed in ***Media and Investing*** on page 137, and summed up by one of the foremost mathematicians of all time:

There's no sense being exact about something if you don't even know what you're talking about.
——John von Neumann

And then, Samuel Clemens—better known by his *nom de plume* Mark Twain, had these comments:

Most people use statistics the way a drunkard uses a lamp post, more for support than illumination.
——Mark Twain

Get your facts first, and then you can distort 'em as much as you please.
——Samuel Clemens, writing as Mark Twain

Forecasting

The clairvoyant Society of London will not meet Tuesday because of unforeseen circumstances.
——Advertisement in The Financial Times

Hundreds of billions (of any currency you wish to name) are spent every year in mostly doomed efforts to predict the future. In ***The Fortune Sellers: The Big Business of Buying and Selling Predictions***, William A. Sherden goes chapter by chapter through the dismal results of just about every form of forecasting.

Why did God create Economists?
To make Weather Forecasters look good.

Hard to believe, but ***Weather Forecasters*** top the list with the best track records. Other practitioners of prognostication go downhill from there, leading us to the joke in the sidebar.

John Maynard Keynes is always good for his views on economists.

Americans are apt to be unduly interested in discovering what average opinion believes average opinion to be...
——John Maynard Keynes

If economists could manage to get themselves thought of as humble, competent people on a level with dentists, that would be splendid.
——John Maynard Keynes

Psychology of Investing

If you don't know who you are, the market is an expensive place to find out
——George Goodman

Psychology (most of all, your own) is a dominant component of investing and an investor's ability to make (or lose) money.

The crowd always loses, wrote Mr. Fred C. Kelly in a noted work on the stock market in 1930, because the crowd is always wrong because it behaves normally.

Media and Investing

Trying to determine what is going on in the world by reading newspapers is like trying to tell the time by watching the second hand of a clock.
——*Ben Hecht* (1894–1964)—*American Author and Playwright*

The Media—television, newspapers, financial web sites—constitute an enormous industry with the purported aim of keeping people "informed". The reality is that the vast majority of what is touted as "news" is simply random blather, with no informational content to speak of.

This comment by Nassim Nicholas Taleb sums up perfectly the state of "news" reporting:

> . . . I see the following on my Bloomberg:
>
> ⇒ *Dow is up 1.03 on lower interest rates . . .*
>
> If I translate it well, the journalist claims to provide an explanation for something that amounts to ***perfect noise***. A move of 1.03 with the Dow at 11,000 constitutes less than a 0.01 percent move. Such a move does not warrant an explanation.
> ——Nassim Nicholas Taleb—*Fooled By Randomness*

Indeed. Were the so-called "news" to read "the market is up today", or, "the market is down today", or better yet, "the market traded sideways all day", one would see this for the silliness it is: on any given day, the market goes up, down, or sideways—those are the only three options.

Our ***bête noire*** is television—a medium that confuses motion with progress. Here are two quotes from people with the right viewpoint of television:

> I find television very educating. Every time somebody turns on the set, I go into the other room and read a book.
> ——Groucho Marx

> No matter what they tell you on TV, Information is not knowledge.
> ——Bill Fleckenstein

And comments on "news" reporting . . .

> Journalists: people who have nothing to say and know how to say that
> ——Carl Kraus 1874–1936, Austrian Satirist

> We need above all to know about changes; no one wants or needs to be reminded sixteen hours a day that his shoes are on.
> ——David Hubel

Market Manias

I have a general rule—whenever something becomes worth more than the whole state of California, sell it.
Alan Stuart Blinder, Professor of Economics, Princeton University, and Vice Chairman, Board of Governors of the Federal Reserve System, 1994–1996

Anyone who was awake during the late 1990s and into 2000 is no doubt aware that the United States stock market went through a financial bubble of gigantic proportions.

Professor Blinder's quote here refers to a prior financial bubble, namely, the Japanese stock (and real estate) markets in the late 1980s. The roughly 400-hectare area of Tokyo comprising the grounds of the Imperial Palace (皇 居) reached a "value" (at least on paper) such that had the "value" actually been realized, the Japanese could have purchased the entire state of California, at that time the world's fifth largest economy. Alternatively, the realized "value" could have purchased all of Canada.

Jim Rogers makes a similar assessment when explaining in January 1990 ***Barron's*** why the Japanese stock market would decline at least fifty percent:

> A day or so before I had noticed that the front page of a local newspaper printed an index of the average price of membership in Tokyo golf clubs.... It had hit a million dollars....

Well, that was Japan. Following the Japanese bubble, we went through the South East Asian bubble of the late 1990s, until it came to a crashing halt in 1997.

> When you see a value as out of whack as this, stand back and ask yourself if something is wrong.... In the real world, golf memberships can't be worth a million dollars....
>
> ——Jim Rogers—*Investment Biker*

And at the end of the 1990s and into 2000, we had the United States stock market bubble, largely revolving around potential uses of the Internet.

> In the Internet Business profitability is for wimps—it means your business plan wasn't aggressive enough
> ——*Mike Doonesbury* (Jerry Trudeau)

Financial Advisory Newsletters

This isn't right! It isn't even wrong!
——*Wolfgang Pauli*

A sub-class (if not an under-class) of the general print media is the large (and profitable—if only for the publishers) business of publishing ***Investment Newsletters***.

This memorable statement should make you re-consider subscribing to Investment Newsletters:

> My Grandfather told me you make more selling information than you do following it.
> ——Malcolm "Steve" Forbes, Jr

You are likely familiar with these instruments. We get dozens every week. They all follow familiar paths to induce you to subscribe.

They all give you a "no risk" guarantee to the effect that you can cancel your subscription for a refund at any time. The risk is not in subscribing, however: the real risk is in following their advice, for which, unfortunately, no refunds are offered.

We have read thousands of Investment Newsletters. There are four or five good ones that could genuinely help you make money. Here is a quote that sums up the situation in a nutshell:

> Of 108 market-timing newsletters studied from 1989–1994, only one beat the market.
>
> ——Mark Hulbert—*Hulbert Financial Digest*

When you get an "Investment Newsletter" promoting some obscure company, ask why the companies invariably trade on the OTC Bulletin Board or Pink Sheets. Ask why you rarely get recommendations for NYSE, NASDAQ, or AMEX-traded companies. Ask why touted companies rarely have information other than the stock price—no record of revenue, income, cash flow...

The vast majority of Investment Newsletters, however—about ninety-nine percent of them—consist of self-serving, money-losing drivel. They are good for comic relief and a demonstration that there is no such thing as unprintable nonsense.

Almost all Investment Newsletters we receive are "advertorials" for specific companies, and the Newsletters in question have been paid for directly or indirectly by the companies themselves.

Here is a typical example of the drivel ladled out daily:

This bloke must think he's the reincarnation of Rudyard Kipling.† Sure, just jump on a flight to Rio, no sweat.

> Things are heating up in Brazil. So brush up on your Spanish, convert your dollars into Pesos, and get on down there to Brazil.
>
> ——Financial Newsletter, *circa* 1986

Of course, the "advice" contains two egregious mistakes:

- ❏ The principal language of Brazil is Portuguese, not Spanish
- ❏ Never in history has Brazil used Pesos as a currency

† See Rudyard Kipling—*Rolling Down To Rio, in The Beginning of the Armadilloes.*

Index

. . . the professionals have introduced a new concept called ***indexing***, with which they promise faithfully to try and do ***at least as good*** as blindfolded baboons in future . . .

Don Lancaster—*The Incredible Secret Money Machine, 1978*

B

C

D

H

I

J

K

L

O

P

T

U

Acknowledgments

> It is only with the heart that one can see rightly;
> what is essential is invisible to the eye.
>
> Antoine de Saint-Exupéry—*The Little Prince, 1900–1944*

All over the world, people give their talents to bring you this book.

Victoria Slama, Partner *Passionate Advocate*	Turned us right side up—"Readers know what they believe is true. They'll see if your book is true. Then they'll consider new insights."
Yoshie Nakao (中尾 ヨシエ), Partner	For coming into our lives at the right time.
Lee Appelbaum, MS Mathematics *Rensselaer Polytechnic Institute*	Retrieval technology pioneer *(NASDAQ: VRTY)*, former *EDGAR* Online Knowledge Management Director, wrote our *SEC Search String*.
Bob Rand, WebMaster@SEC.GOV *Securities and Exchange Commission*	Generalized and installed on the *SEC* website our *Search String* for the shortest list of reports displaying all quarterly and annual data.
Arthur Carpenter, Jr. *Director of Business Development*	Gave 25 quarters of Media General *(NYSE: MEG)* research data on 400 public companies, and 3 years of invaluable technical support.
Amanda Sorensen 16, Our Editor *Scotts Valley High School, California*	From age 10 to 16 persistently edited our mathematics and text, ensuring she and friends could explain most of our book to adults.
Michael Goldeen, AB Physics *University of California at Berkeley*	Profoundly tuned details so they "snap into place" with concepts, encouraging you to get data you want and play with your own charts.
Tom Masino, PhD Neurobiology *University of Chicago*	Worked with us from the early days to develop server architecture, think through thorny problems, and write a product description.
Michael Ruddick, MBA Finance and *Accounting, University of Chicago*	Set up, guided, and maintained our legal and financial framework, and offered pivotal accounting insights.
Professor Nirvikar Singh, Economics *University of California at Santa Cruz*	Wrote a future offer to require his students to subscribe to an Internet full-version of the tool we developed to produce this book.
Aniruddha Joshi, MBA U of Auckland *Executive Vice President, Hirco Group*	Graciously made several high-level financial world introductions to leaders who offered invaluable perspectives on our work.

Joy Hoffmann, Vice President
Federal Reserve Bank of San Francisco

Expressed an "interest" in an Internet demonstration version of our tools for the Federal Reserve System's education website.

Joel Shaps and *Eric Lewis, Principals*
Bedrock Capital Management

Provided much-needed guidance through the tangled thickets of practical calculation and application of Intrinsic Value.

Ken Ruddock, MS Physics
Massachusetts Institute of Technology

Shared his cheerful mind that co-founded Spectra-Physics to sift the book for useful concepts, consistency, and technical excellence.

Chris Goodenough, Founder
Goodenough Construction

Inspired us, and shared his remarkable ability to listen, invent ideas that consistently drove the book forward, and kept us smiling.

John Goodenough, Artist
Goodenough Woodcrafting

Gave us the pivotal funding insight, and introduced us to a patent and trade secret wizard who defined our unique claims simply.

Jim Goodenough, Principal
Grove Elementary School, Oregon

Children, even with difficult lives, could play games with the relationships you describe to gain comfort with the concepts at an older age.

David Goodenough, Founder
The Goodenough Company

Intuitively and steadfastly refocused us on the project, and championed our work with his many colleagues.

Don Goodenough, Founder
Don Goodenough Architecture

You'll have to persuade Wall Street that better informed investors are immediately more profitable clients.

Martin Forster, Blacksmith
Clarinetist and Pilot

Patiently read the manuscript with the eyes of a craftsman, tuned to his art, and made insightful introductions in the financial world.

Rachel Schwab and Susan Hansen
Kennedy Middle School, California

Graciously taught their students to retrieve *EDGAR* data, build spreadsheets, chart performance, evaluate, and present companies.

Microsoft
Microsoft Corporation (MSFT)

SEC Quarterly and *Annual Reports* provide all data, except prices, for our *inside front cover Quarterly Data Summary* that powers our book.

Marti Starnes, MS Education
University of Illinois

Helped fund the book, arranged essential high-level introductions, and encouraged us with deep loyalty and friendship.

Mike Starnes, PhD Electrical Engineering, Texas A&M

Cypress Semiconductor co-founder, helped fund the book—as a tool to evaluate global powerbrokers of energy, agriculture, and software.

Anonymous Patrons

Your happiness to put your money to a worthwhile use completes our dream and makes it possible for us to get this book to the public.

Colophon

> Colophon was a city in Lydia and the titular see of Asia Minor. Its name comes from the word "summit", which is the origin of the bibliographic term "colophon", in the metaphorical sense of a "crowning touch".
>
> —— *Wikipedia*

Book Design by Julia D'Arcy, Teri Fujimoto (藤本), and Henry McGilton.

Body copy is set in eleven point ***Hiroshige*** on thirteen point leading. Chapter and section headings are set in **Optima Bold**.

Creation

Source Text for this manuscript was prepared using software tools available on ***Apple Macintosh*** computers running *Mac OS X*. Source text was typed and edited using *VI*—one of the primary visual editors available for *UNIX* systems, and **TextEdit**—the basic editor available on *Mac OS X*.

Composition

Formatting used *PSFIG* by Ned Batchelder and Trevor Darrell and the *GNU* suite of *TROFF*-related tools by James Clark. Tom Kiffe provided *MacGhost-View* 4.3 on *Mac OS X* used to test and refine ***PostScript pictures and charts***, and technical consulting on producing *PDF* graphics and text. ***Tables of contents***, ***cross references***, and ***index*** were generated using home-grown software and macro packages. The entire document was composed from source through formatting to printer with no manual intervention.

Henry McGilton of *Trilithon Software*, **www.trilithon.com** provided technical consulting on the documentation tools and color space used to produce the print-ready ***PostScript*** code; created the Java tools to generate the charts; provided ***PostScript*** programming expertise; and consulted on issues of book design, layout, mathematical typesetting, and typography.

Built On Macintosh

Graphics

Charts are vector graphics generated by ***awk scripts*** and a specialized ***Java*** program to generate files of ***PostScript*** code that were included using *PSFIG*.

Credits

S&P 500 (SPX) Adjusted Close Price data, courtesy Rudolph Cabral, Commodity Systems Inc. (CSI). ***Cessna***, *inside back cover*, photo by Paul Bowen, courtesy Cessna Aircraft. ***Earth at Night***, *back cover*, courtesy United States *National Aeronautics and Space Administration (NASA)*, via the *Defense Meteorological Satellites Program*. **http://visibleearth.nasa.gov/**

www.seroia.com

PDF Electronic Book distribution from **www.seroia.com** was implemented by Todd Sterling of **http://www.onetreeDesign.com/** who alerted us to issues in *e-commerce*, *taxation*, *pagination*, and *encryption* for editing and printing.

Authors

> Our Earth is degenerate in these latter days;
> bribery and corruption are common;
> children no longer obey their parents;
> ***every man wants to write a book***,
> and the end of the world is evidently approaching.
>
> *Assyrian Tablet, approximately 2,700 BC*

Oxford University Press wants "information about yourself on why you are qualified to write this book." We believe with these thinkers.

Grigori Perelman solved the Poincaré Conjecture (*The New Yorker, August 2006*), "Everybody understood that if the proof is correct then no other recognition is needed"; E. B. White (William Strunk, Jr., and E. B. White, *The Elements of Style*), "No one can write decently who is distrustful of the reader's intelligence, or whose attitude is patronizing"; and the *Harvard Business Review*, inviting "experts whose authority comes from careful analysis, study, and experience."

Bob Goodenough

Bob started his minimum-data decision systems career in 1967 as a USAF Mach-II fighter pilot—relying on cockpit instruments to make life and death decisions. He earned his PhD in Organizational Development in 1976 from the Union Institute. (The Institute was funded by Carnegie Mellon and the U. S. Department of Education.) Bob was Inventor's Consultant for Apple's HyperCard—shipped with every Mac for 10 years. His 1993–1997 consultation with Cypress Semiconductor convinced him and colleagues they had sufficient command of technology and *Securities and Exchange Commission* data to jump-start global investing literacy for students and adults.

Henry McGilton

Henry started his computer programming career in 1963. He founded Technical Publications at *Sun Microsystems*, and co-authored *Introducing the UNIX System* and *Introducing UNIX System V*—McGraw-Hill books that sold more than three-hundred thousand copies in five languages worldwide. Henry also co-authored *Typesetting Tables on the UNIX System* and *PostScript by Example*—an Addison-Wesley book. Forty years of programming including ten years of ***Java*** now bring Henry to use the ***Objective-C*** language to develop desktop applications for ***Mac OS X***. Henry is usually found on a squash court when he's not pursuing the life of a boulevardier.

Copyright

Trilithon—Stonehenge

You cannot name 20 persons in the whole United States who in the last 100 years have produced books which have outlived the copyright limit.

Mark Twain—*Congressional Hearing, December 7, 1906*

Trilithon Press, Santa Cruz, California 95060
 Hardback and Electronic edition published 2007
First edition published 2007.
Printed in Canada / Imprimé au Canada

16 15 14 13 12 11 10 09 08 07   1 2 3 4 5 6 7 8 9 10

ISBN-13: 978-0-9626289-5-5 (HARDBACK)

Library of Congress Control Number: 2006908270

Invest in company evolution, picture company finances. — 1st ed.

Includes bibliographical references, color illustrations, cross references, and index.

Cover Design	Bob Goodenough and Henry McGilton
Production	Typeset in Hiroshige and Optima at Trilithon Software
Indexing	Trilithon Software
Editor	Amanda S. Sorensen
Editor	Lee A. Appelbaum
Editor	Michael Goldeen

(∞) The paper used in the hardback book meets the minimum requirements of the American National Standard for Information Sciences—Permanence of Paper for Printed Library Materials, ANSI Z.39.48-1992.

Mixed Sources Product group from well-managed forests, controlled sources, and recycled wood or fiber.

FSC **www.fsc.org** Cert no **SW-COC-2080** © **1996 Forest Stewardship Council**

The Publisher's policy is to use paper manufactured from sustainable forests.

www.seroia.com